The Handmaid's Tale

Teaching Dystopia, Feminism, and Resistance Across Disciplines and Borders

The Handmaid's Tale

Teaching Dystopia, Feminism, and Resistance Across Disciplines and Borders

Edited by Karen A. Ritzenhoff
and Janis L. Goldie

LEXINGTON BOOKS
Lanham • Boulder • New York • London

Published by Lexington Books
An imprint of The Rowman & Littlefield Publishing Group, Inc.
4501 Forbes Boulevard, Suite 200, Lanham, Maryland 20706
www.rowman.com

6 Tinworth Street, London SE11 5AL, United Kingdom

British Library Cataloguing in Publication Information Available

Library of Congress Cataloging-in-Publication Data

ISBN 978-1-4985-8914-7 (cloth)
ISBN 978-1-4985-8915-4 (electronic)

For my daughter, Lea-Karoline
Nolite te Bastardes Carborundorum

(Karen A. Ritzenhoff)

For the women who've led the way,
and all those yet to come.

(Janis L. Goldie)

Contents

Introduction

Karen A. Ritzenhoff and Janis L. Goldie

Sex, the president, and the wall. These topics are hot-button issues in everyday American life in 2018. All three topics also feature prominently in the Hulu TV adaptation of Margaret Atwood's *The Handmaid's Tale* as dystopic themes. Firstly, the Handmaids' ritualized sexual assault during the monthly "Ceremonies;" secondly, the role of the Commanders in the Republic of Gilead, especially the double standard of morality, practiced by Fred Waterford (Joseph Fiennes).[1] Thirdly, Gilead is surrounded by a wall with armed guards who fire on escapees heading to Canada.

These are topics in the United States that, like other current events, are often difficult to discuss in the American college (or any school) classroom without raising conflict. Students can take sides, and feel overwhelmed, confused, or even attacked. Discussing *The Handmaid's Tale* and the controversial issues it raises allows instructors to address these topics in the classroom and helps direct discussions, point out resources, demonstrate analytical strategies that can aid critical thinking, foster close reading techniques, and evoke engaged debates. In the fall 2017, for example, Cindy L. White from the Department of Communication and Karen A. Ritzenhoff, the coeditor of this volume, offered a co-taught interdisciplinary honors class,[2] entitled "Dystopia in Film and Television." The seminar environment became a playground of new perspectives, exchanges, and discoveries, based on popular culture. This is what we want to evoke with this volume: we hope that these chapters, gathered from many different disciplinary points of view, will provoke discussion.

Initially, the university held a one-day symposium in the fall 2017 on the adaptation of *The Handmaid's Tale* in different disciplines and schools at Central Connecticut State University (CCSU). It brought together students from the honors class and our regular classes who shared their research projects, in addition to faculty who presented short position papers about the literary and media analysis of Atwood's work and their use in specific classroom environments. The symposium was organized by our small program for Women, Gender and Sexuality Studies (WGSS) where many of our authors are affiliated members and teaching faculty, and it was funded by a faculty development grant for teaching excellence. The day ended with an open forum to discuss sexual assault, guided by the director and staff of the university Ruth Boyea Women's Center, Jacqueline Cobbina-Boivin, and an evening screening of the 1990 film adaptation of *The Handmaid's Tale* by Volker Schlöndorff that nobody had seen before. The symposium created a sense of community that we had not seen on campus for a while. It opened the dialogue between different university organizations that help victims of sexual assault. Sarah Dodd, one of our authors, is the facilitator of the Office of Victim Advocacy and Violence Prevention on campus, part of the Office of Diversity and Equity.[3] It created spaces to discuss our scholarship with students, inspiring them to think across disciplines. It allowed us to learn from each other and cherish the many awe-evoking questions that were raised.

The next step was to present a panel about *The Handmaid's Tale* at the leading cinema studies conference, the international Society for Cinema and Media Studies (SCMS). Janis L. Goldie, the coeditor of this volume, presented on that panel in March 2018 in Toronto as did Clémentine Tholas from the Sorbonne in France. Since the three of us are also coeditors of a volume on *New Perspectives on the War Film*, we decided to collaborate again. Janis L. Goldie teaches at a comparable school, Huntington University, in Canada, and we discussed at length how an edited collection that focused on *The Handmaid's Tale* as a pedagogical tool across disciplines would be an exciting and relevant addition to the scholarship. When we were approached during the SCMS conference by acquisition editor Nicolette Amstutz from Rowman and Littlefield who asked whether we could pull a collection on *The Handmaid's Tale* together, we enthusiastically embraced this opportunity and settled on an early submission date. This meant that we drummed together colleagues at the conference, including Ellen Grabiner from Simmons College who presented her research at SCMS, as well as Eileen Rositzka from Germany, after approaching different caucuses to ask whether anybody might be interested to write for us. Then the topic also got around by word of mouth and before we knew it, our list of authors blossomed with a combination of international scholars from Canada, France, and Germany, as well as the core group from CCSU.

Many of the authors of this book teach at CCSU, which is nestled on the fringes of New Britain, a working class town south of Hartford, on highway I-84 between Boston and New York. CCSU is one of four embattled, underfunded state universities that have been merged with the community colleges. Many of our students are local. They all have different reasons to be at CCSU: the tuition is cheaper than private universities, they are able to live with parents and relatives and commute to school, many of our students work full-time jobs in low-paying employment, some have children to take care of, many are survivors of some kind of abuse. The student body is diverse. Managing a discussion in the classroom is a challenge—rewarding but tough. However, teaching about *The Handmaid's Tale* allows us to find common ground and approach this subject matter in a broad and multifaceted, interdisciplinary manner. Teaching Atwood demonstrates what liberal arts education combined with Science, Technology, Engineering and Math (STEM), not to mention Education or Health, among other areas, can be all about—discourse.

TAKING *THE HANDMAID'S TALE* ON THE ROAD

In the fall 2018, Karen A. Ritzenhoff was invited to present a talk about *The Handmaid's Tale* at two different universities in the United Kingdom. The talk focused on fashion, costumes, and politics in the current political climate in the United States. When she started the conversation with several cynical cartoons about the recent Brett Kavanaugh Senate Hearings, the audience did not laugh and appeared to have a hard time relating to the topic.[4] Kavanaugh was President Donald Trump's nominee for one of the critical seats on the U.S. Supreme Court. Shortly before the confirmation, he was accused by Dr. Christine Blasey Ford, a professor from California,[5] to have sexually assaulted her while both of them were high school students at a preparatory school in Maryland. Ford alleged that Kavanaugh was drunk and held her down on a bed by the wrists while trying to keep her quiet: he put his hand over her mouth, Ford described in painful detail. Her plea to reconsider the nomination of Kavanaugh to the highest Court in the country was not heard. Kavanaugh defended himself during senate hearings, tearful and aggressive, while his wife stoically looked on from behind him, and he was voted into office shortly after the hearings, in time to be seated before the Midterm Elections in November 2018 where the Republicans lost control over Congress.

Even though several people in the UK college audience had followed the hearings with a similar sense of turmoil, disgust, and horror that many Americans did, the topic was still seemingly removed. But there were also many points in the presentation where everybody was able to connect: the *#MeToo* Movement and the fact that women activists around the world have started to wear the red frocks and white bonnets of the Hulu TV adaptation to protest and raise awareness for women's reproductive rights: in Argentina,

Ireland, United Kingdom, in front of the American Capitol, the Texas legislative building; actually in the staircases during the Kavanaugh Hearings, protestors, dressed as Handmaids, looked on.[6] In Sarah Banet-Weiser's recent book publication, *Empowered: Popular Feminism and Popular Misogyny* (2018),[7] she discusses the parallel between the rise of feminist activism and the backlash it evokes from those in power. Her astute analysis can serve as a theoretical framework for our book as well. Connecting to her previous work on girl studies, neoliberalism, make-over TV, beauty pageants, and brand culture, Banet-Weiser, since the fall 2018 the Chair and Professor of Media and Communications at the London School of Economics, writes about the "economy" not as a "mere metaphor":

> Rather, I adopt a more nuanced account of the logistics and moralities of both economics and culture as a way to understand how identities are constructed within the economy of visibility, and to ask what is at stake in this kind of construction. For girls and women, adopting the logistics and moralities of an economy of visibility means that despite the fact that popular feminism claims to be about empowerment, this kind of empowerment is often achieved through a focus on the visible body—precisely one of the aspects of patriarchy feminism has been fighting against for centuries. The visible body is also the commodifiable body.[8]

Popular misogyny and popular feminism go hand in hand. The Kavanaugh hearings, played out on national U.S. television live, were a real-life example for what Banet-Weiser positions: "The lack of self-confidence for men is often understood as an explicit reaction to self-confident women; the injury to men in terms of self-confidence is apparently caused explicitly by women."[9] Kavanaugh reacted to Blasey Ford's calm composure and her detailed retelling of her memories of assault with outrage. Many lawyers distanced themselves from his impulsive and emotional performance for the TV cameras, claiming that he seemed unfit for office where impartial and rational law needs to be practiced. Of course, Kavanaugh's confirmation amplified the power balance in the Supreme Court toward Republican-held beliefs about women's reproductive rights, another theme that is central to *The Handmaid's Tale*. On social media sites, images went viral where the senators, all white men, were compared to the fake trial with "gender traitor" Emily (Alexis Bledel), also a former college professor in the Hulu TV adaptation, whose female partner is subsequently executed. The pictures of the television show were chillingly similar to the real-life photographs of the almost exclusively male, white, old senators.[10]

In November 2018, Margaret Atwood announced that she was going to write a sequel to *The Handmaid's Tale*, not based on the content of Season 2 of the Hulu adaptation, or Season 3 to be released in June 2019. Her sequel is to be published in September 2019. Although we worried briefly that our volume might be outdated before it even has a chance to hit the classrooms, we are confident that our collection will indeed facilitate course content and offer different tools to embrace Atwood's tale of empowerment, popular feminism, and popular misogyny however it moves forward. As *New York Times* reporter Alexander Alter writes in the "Arts" section, "Atwood said the novel's recent resurgence reflected our cultural preoccupation with imagining disastrous futures as a way of digesting current anxieties about political extremism and the fate of the planet."[11]

In this sense, we are hoping that Atwood's *The Handmaid's Tale* in all its forms will stimulate discussion in the classroom and that our authors provide the "flesh" to facilitate further research and debates. In what follows, we introduce the various sections of the edited collection and briefly outline the topics of the chapters embedded within.

SECTION ONE: *THE HANDMAID'S TALE* AS A PEDAGOGICAL TOOL

In the first section of the collection, our authors use *The Handmaid's Tale* (*THT*) as a multifaceted lens with which to further investigate a variety of interdisciplinary concepts and concerns, and manage to amass a wide and impressive display of perspective and approaches as a result, helpful to teachers in any discipline. They display how a complex artifact like *THT* in its multiple forms can offer numerous entry points for teachers to discuss relevant issues in their fields. In so doing, they also teach the reader about the interesting historical, theological, criminal justice, sexual assault prevention education, and translation issues that are central to any study of *THT*.

In the first chapter, Kelly Marino illustrates that using Hulu's TV series can be an engaging "hook" for students to learn about Puritanism and American society in the seventeenth century, a topic that she notes can often be seen as dry by students. In accessible detail, she outlines how *THT* can be used to discuss the Puritan religion and its views on gender norms, sexuality, and crime among other issues. She argues that using *THT* as a cultural artifact to engage students in this discussion is invaluable as a way to tie their popular culture knowledge to their historical knowledge.

In chapter 2, Aven McMaster tackles a current controversial issue in Classics—that of translation and the power and cultural ramifications that come from these choices by translators. Particularly, McMaster connects Atwood's novel *THT,* Homer's *Odyssey,* and Atwood's *Penelopiad* in order to unpack how each presents the status of women, their control (or lack thereof) over their bodies, and how translation choices—such as to referring to a female as a Handmaid or slave in this instance—has important effects on our understanding of the past, and naturally, the future.

Taking the study of the history of religion into account, Kate McGrath, in chapter 3, asks the reader to consider the Biblical and theological construction of Gilead. In particular, McGrath focuses on Jezebel's—the brothel for high-status men in Gilead—and argues that Jezebel's can be more easily understood when we look further into Christian theology's historical position on prostitution, where it functions as a necessary evil for male sexual desire and is directed away from "respectable" women. This is also in line with Atwood's presentation of Jezebel's, says McGrath, and helps us to understand authorial choices in this regard.

In chapter 4, Katherine Sugg uses *THT* to teach and examine the mechanics of literary fiction. Sugg writes about the complicated role of Offred as narrator in the novel, and compares this to the narrator June in the Hulu TV adaptation in comparison. Noting that students will become familiar with terms such as limited first person narrative, focalization, and plot via a close reading of the text, Sugg also argues that approaching *THT* in this way allows students to consider how language use reveals our own complicity and weakness in modern day.

Returning to historical concerns in chapter 5, Heather Munro Prescott shows the importance of considering the historical context of a published work. As Atwood's *THT* was written and released in the mid-1980s, Munro Prescott discusses the importance of the political and cultural climate of the 1980s, where perceived backlash against feminism and other social causes from the 1960s and 1970s was occurring at the time. Taking a close examination of the role of Offred's mother—as a feminist activist—and their relationship in the novel helps to better understand Atwood's complicated relationship to feminism and put the important cultural artifact into further historical perspective.

Susan Gilmore reflects on her experience of teaching *THT* over a span of eighteen years and across two generations in chapter 6, intertwining intergenerational contexts and connections that students and teachers alike can engage in. Gilmore discusses the context of the novel, addresses new issues via the Hulu TV adaptation, and illustrates the role of the uncanny—both in the popular and in the Freudian sense in this chapter. In this way, Gilmore importantly notes that one's own uncanny is often different than others', in both an intersectional and cross-generational approach, and she expertly discusses the pedagogical strategies needed to approach this and other elements in *THT*.

Criminal Justice scholar, Michelle Cubellis, tackles the important issues of consent, power, and sexual assault as approached by an analysis of *THT* in chapter 7. Specifically, Cubellis looks at the Hulu TV series and sees it as an important artifact to start discussions around the construction of rape myths, victim blaming, and sexual slavery with students and colleagues alike. By examining these issues more closely, and by using *THT* as a tool to do so, Cubellis argues that we may be better able respond to and help prevent future victimization.

Sarah Dodd, in chapter 8, continues with the timely discussion of sexual assault in the era of *#MeToo*, but draws on her role as a sexual assault prevention educator on a college campus to do so. Dodd provides practical tools in order to show readers how the Hulu TV series can be a useful pedagogical tool to enter into conversations and ask questions—about victims, about consent, and about myths surrounding sexual assault. Further, she argues that this approach can be used to inform and further campus prevention initiatives.

SECTION TWO: USING *THE HANDMAID'S TALE* AS A KALEIDOSCOPE TO UNDERSTAND PAST AND PRESENT SOCIAL CONCERNS

In the second section of the book, our authors use the various forms of *THT* as a way to consider crucial issues of concern in society today, such as reproductive technology, the role of journalism, increasing limits on women's health issues, as well as broader social concerns around racism and age. In these chapters, the frightening similarities in our current world to the dystopian world of Gilead are often highlighted and are used as a dire warning to readers, as well as a call to action.

In this section, we begin with chapter 9 from astronomy professor Kristine Larsen, who covers issues of science and religion in relation to *THT*. Specifically, Larsen examines infertility and explores how technology may be able to both cause and cure infertility at the same time that religion and culture can limit it. She argues that *THT* can be read as a cautionary tale, as well as an excellent jumping-off point to discuss a variety of issues where science and religion can collide, such as medical experimentation, use of genetic information without consent, and assisted reproductive technologies (ART).

Theodora Ruhs, in chapter 10, turns to examining the way that *THT* can help us to consider and discuss social and political oppression and the role of journalism (or lack of journalism) within. She argues that we need to remind ourselves that a truly free press is fundamental to a functioning democracy, and she uses Gilead in *THT* as a contrasting example to this, pointing in her conclusion to the importance of citizens themselves utilizing what journalists have to offer before their political power is lost as well.

In chapter 11, Rati Kumar makes an explicit call to readers to return to a focus on women's rights and women's healthcare priorities in an intersectional and international approach. She points to the divergences of women's health encounters within the United States as well as across the globe, and draws on *THT* as a frame of reference in this regard. She illustrates both the local and international concerns around women's health and policies, citing frightening statistics and policies that remind the reader that these are crucial issues to all of society today.

The call to "prevent and resist" is furthered by Charisse Levchak, who in chapter 12 discusses the socially constructed nature of racism and sexism. She draws on *THT* as an artifact with illustrations on ways that we can work to prevent and resist oppression so that Gilead does not become our reality. Working toward social justice in our daily lives is necessary, according to Levchak, and she encourages both students and readers to resist oppressive conditions before they take root permanently.

Paul Moffett, in chapter 13, also discusses race and highlights the problematic way that race is erased in Hulu's TV series. Moffett highlights the variations of race in both the novel and the television series, and argues that despite the attempt to include a more racially diverse cast in the television production, ignoring how race intersects with the characters' experiences and stories is an unfortunate injustice. As a kind of racial utopia—where race doesn't matter—the television adaptation of *THT* is based on an assumption that racial differences and prejudices can be irrelevant and displays an unexamined attitude about race more generally.

In chapter 14, Jessica Greenebaum and Beth Merenstein use a sociological and feminist perspective to compare religious, political, and cultural ideologies and policies that allow for forced motherhood, rape culture, and compulsory heterosexuality in our current society and in Hulu's TV series *THT*. The authors outline important discussions about patriarchal power and complicity and remind readers that this dystopian setting could be closer to reality than one thinks.

The final chapter in this section, chapter 15, comes from Christina Barmon, who uses a feminist gerontological perspective to examine the representations of age in both the novel and Hulu TV series of *THT*. She looks at the intersection of age with gender and notes that both the novel and the television adaption of the *THT* draw on ageist and sexist stereotypes of women, where youth and reproductive ability are privileged and where older women are characterized as disposable or evil hags.

SECTION THREE: PRODUCTION, CINEMATIC TECHNIQUES, AND FILM ADAPTATIONS

The third section of our collection focuses on production and cinematic techniques as well as film adaptations. These articulate and detailed chapters illuminate the crucial importance of cinematography and film production selections to the success or popularity of *THT.*

In chapter 16, Eileen Rositzka examines the aesthetics of both the Hulu TV series and Volker Schlöndorff's film in order to compare the two for their realism. Discussing colors, textures, lighting, as well as these artifacts' connection to art of the Victorian age, Rositzka's focus on cinematic realism in a comparative perspective is a way to begin to better understand what makes television and film productions more "realistic," or graspable, for viewers on a broader scale.

Dennis Tredy presents work from the relatively new field of adaptation studies in chapter 17 in order to make sense of the adaptation of the novel *THT* to first the film, and later, the television series. Notably, the film was much less successful than the current popular culture phenomenon, Hulu's TV series, and thus, Tredy compares the adaptation techniques used in the 1990 film to the 2017/2018 television series, and argues that both texts allow one to examine difficult choices that need to be made when doing adaptations, such as what to keep and what to cut or how to deal with time shifts, among many other issues.

Issues of adaptation are also relevant for Ellen Grabiner, who in chapter 18, discusses the cinematography of Colin Watkinson in Hulu's TV series *THT.* Here, Grabiner argues that Watkinson's aesthetic treatment is performative via the use of framing, lighting, color, jarring juxtapositions, and temporal shifts and manages to expertly illuminate the dystopic reality that Atwood outlines in her novel.

SECTION FOUR: INTERDISCIPLINARY LESSONS FROM *THE HANDMAID'S TALE*

The concluding essays offer important contextual perspectives within which to consider *THT.* Drawing on disciplines of theater, media studies, Canadian and border studies, as well as comparative film and literary studies, these chapters ask readers to go beyond traditional understandings of *THT* and apply the novel, the television series, and the film in new contexts and in new ways.

We begin with Sheila Siragusa, who in chapter 19, investigates the use of first person narration and explores its emotional effect. By utilizing first person performed narrative in other productions as in *THT*, Siragusa argues, we can allow audiences to be truly "with" the character and experience their oppression, silence, and violence in a more direct and powerful way. Further, turning more frequently to this approach in the performative arts may be a path to ease the frequent difficulties around political discourse about violence against women that we see.

Next, Jacqueline Maxwell considers the relationship between the artist and art in chapter 20. She compares Elisabeth Moss's roles as June in *THT* and Peggy in *Mad Men* and questions what it means to be a feminist, as well as a feminist who considers herself to be an artist. Maxwell challenges students and readers alike to be more critical of their popular cultural consumption in this chapter.

We take a slight detour in chapter 21, where Janis L. Goldie tackles the transnational media production of Hulu's TV series *THT* alongside its construction of Canada as the utopia to Gilead's (former United States) dystopia. By examining the multiple references to Canada and the Canadian border as a central plot motivator, Goldie argues that Canada is presented as the stark and explicit national idealization in contrast to the totalitarian regime of Gilead. This is considered in light of anti-Americanism in Canadian history, as well as Canadian cultural nationalism; however, the transnational media production of this television production makes the representation of Canada as safe haven quite unique.

Clémentine Tholas compares the film *Metropolis* and the film version of *THT* to examine important power struggles around issues of maternity in chapter 22. She questions the commodification of women and children in these films, as well as parenthood, and female sexuality presented on screen. In the end, Tholas argues that class issues matter in both of these artifacts— between the haves and have-nots—with powerful exploitation conducted by a small minority onto a large majority, while *Metropolis* presents a male-oriented perspective to *THT's* more female-oriented one.

Our final essay, chapter 23 by Cecilia Gigliotti, is focused on the epilogue to Atwood's *THT*, "Topia." Employing a literary perspective, Gigliotti analyzes the purpose and meaning of the inclusion of this at the end of the dystopic novel, providing strategies to consider the approaches, and the difficulties of teaching and studying literature.

MAKING OF THE COVER IMAGE

The cover image of our collection is original. Karen A. Ritzenhoff began art lessons in oil and water color in the fall 2018 to be able to produce an image for our title page. In the process of taking art lessons, she discovered so many facets of our argument. The fact that women's bodies are the platform on which the abuse in *The Handmaid's Tale* happens. They bear the burden of the assault, sometimes written in their faces (with the blue and yellow markings of assault), sometimes invisible, covered by dresses. In *The Handmaid's Tale*, the women go about their everyday business after the monthly "ceremonies," after the rape. They have to continue to go shopping for fruits and vegetables, eat their soup under the watchful eye of the Commander's Wives and their Marthas, continue to pretend that they do not carry the smell of the Commanders with them. Even their dowdy, white linen underwear is checked for traces of blood.

Rather than show gruesome torture or execution scenes from *The Handmaid's Tale*, criticized by some as "violence porn," Ritzenhoff decided to focus on the face of a token Handmaid. Under her bonnet, the shadow is cast on her bruised face.

Rather than show gruesome torture or execution scenes from The Handmaid's Tale, *criticized by some as "violence porn," Ritzenhoff decided to focus on the face of a token Handmaid. Under her bonnet, the shadow is cast on her bruised face. Image provided by Karen A. Ritzenhoff.*

If we achieve one goal with our volume, then it is to pay attention—to the markers of abuse and to the invisible signs of abuse that happen all around us to the women we work and live with. Even if they do not show bruised eyes, they will show signs of mistreatment. Our job as academics and leaders is to stand up to each other's plight, not to be silenced, and to build communities of support. *The Handmaid's Tale* can also teach that lesson to all of us.

ACKNOWLEDGMENTS

We would like to thank Sabrina Cofer, our fantastic student assistant, senior in the Department of Communication at Central Connecticut State University, who helped us put the manuscript together but also completed the index. Her passion for the project inspired us to go on. We would also like to thank our colleagues, students, and administrators who granted us travel money and financial support to organize the initial symposium at Central Connecticut State University that set us on the journey to complete this volume. We would like to express our gratitude to Nicolette Amstutz who entrusted us

A shot of editor Karen A. Ritzenhoff's studio setup.
Image provided by Karen A. Ritzenhoff.

with the task of assembling a theme-based volume on *The Handmaid's Tale* and whose support for this unique project has been steadfast. Also thanks to Jessica Tepper, her assistant editor, who navigated us through the final stages of production. We cherish the old networks and many new allies we have made in the process of our own discovery.

Karen A. Ritzenhoff is grateful that she found such a lovely companion and co-warrior in Janis L. Goldie who volunteered to coedit before she knew how short our timeline for the book would be. While I have been on sabbatical, she juggled being chair of her department and having numerous other responsibilities but always kept us on task. I also want to thank my art teachers Betty Ann Medeiros and Elizabeth Hill Seewald for their encouragement, guidance and support, and Jayson Roberts, director of the Village Center for the Arts, a nonprofit organization and safe haven for creativity in New Milford, Connecticut, for all his enthusiasm. I also want to thank the team at Marty's Café in Washington, Connecticut (especially Cheryl Pierce, Barbara Jackson, Danika Bennett, and Birma Ramirez, Marylinda Allen, and Blane Withers), who have tolerated me sitting in the same corner at the café from morning to afternoon closing time, editing away. Without their good humor, meals, and hugs, this manuscript would not have been completed in time.

Many thanks to my extraordinary Central colleagues, friends, and allies: the incredibly inspiring Aimee Pozorski and trusted ally Cindy L. White who co-taught the honors classes on "Post-9/11 Culture in Literature and Film" as well as "Dystopia in Television and Film"; Kathy Hermes, Fiona Pearson, and Heather Prescott who have all been co-coordinators of Women, Gender and Sexuality Studies (WGSS); Fumilayo Showers, Candace Barrington, Rati Kumar, Julie Kim, Adelaida Sarisley, MJ Moriarty, and Joan Walden. Thanks to Kelly Marino and Susan Gilmore for helping to organize the symposium of *The Handmaid's Tale;* also thanks to Anna S. Kelly and Talia Rose who keep fighting and talking about abuse, as well as the fierce Dahlia Schweitzer who came to CCSU in the spring 2018 to provide a workshop on dystopian film, "Going Viral," and contributed to our *#MeToo* panel. Thanks also to Debra White-Stanley and my cochair of the SCMS women's caucus, the fabulous and undeterred Cynthia Baron. I want to thank our international friends who keep me going: brilliant Karen Randell, Alexis Weedon, Mark Margaretten, and Wendy Leeks. Thanks for listening to *The Handmaid's Tale* lectures and giving so much needed feedback. Clémentine Tholas is always a fantastic colleague, scholar, and friend. She managed to help us connect to Dennis Tredy who submitted his analysis of the film adaptation to our book. Thanks to my friends at home: lovely Chez Liley who alerted me to rereading *The Handmaid's Tale* several summers ago; Bonnie Baldwin and Irmi Dumschott, my trusted friends; as well as Doris Honig Guenter and Ray Guenter, Bob Kagan, and Marcy Cain. Thanks also to Semra Efendic, Doreen Hampton, Tina Reardon, Melora Mennesson, Lu Nijdam, Donna Galluzzo, Liz Eden, and Raquel Pega. Most importantly, thanks to my sons Jan-Philipp and Dominik and to my beloved husband Michael who endured another series of neglectful evenings. The book is dedicated to my youngest child, my fifteen-year-old daughter Lea-Karoline. May she follow the theme of June's secret motto: Don't Let the Bastards Grind You Down!

Janis L. Goldie would like to thank her coeditor Karen A. Ritzenhoff for her patience, leadership, and wonderful sense of humor throughout the book editing process. This project was a pleasure to work on and develop, and is evidence of the truly great things that can be produced when working collaboratively with wonderful colleagues. I would also like to thank my friends and colleagues at Huntington University and Laurentian University in Sudbury, Ontario, for their unwavering support in my attempts to pursue important research projects while balancing my other roles on campus and life. My students also deserve great thanks, as their openness for knowledge and willingness to tackle difficult topics gives me hope for a brighter future. I would also like to thank the audience and members of the SCMS in 2018, whose enthusiastic response to our panel on *The Handmaid's Tale* encouraged us to pursue this project. Clémentine Tholas also deserves great thanks for her consistent support, patience, and expert advice, along all our academic journeys. Finally, my family deserves my eternal gratitude for their support and constant encouragement along this—and every—path.

NOTES

1. Commander Fred Waterford (Joseph Fiennes) penetrates his Handmaid Offred (Elisabeth Moss) on his wife's bed during the ritualized rape, and then clandestinely takes her to an exclusive, forbidden brothel, Jezebel's, cloaked in Serena Joy Waterford's (Yvonne Strahovski) green coat.

2. In the fall 2015 as well as fall 2016, Aimee Pozorski (English), a published scholar on post-9/11 literature and art, and I co-taught a similar course in the CCSU honors program but called it "Post 9/11 Culture in Literature and Film." When we assigned *The Reluctant Fundamentalist*, a 2007 novel by Pakistani author Mohsin Hamid and screened the 2012 film adaptation by woman director Mira Nair in class, students told us that they were uncomfortable discussing the politics of terrorism and Islam. We asked them to identify with the protagonist of the novel, a Pakistani graduate from Princeton University who works in corporate America until the attack on the Twin Towers. Students are far more willing to talk about current political issues if the discussion focuses on popular culture and a dystopic society than real-life events.

3. In the spring 2018, Central Connecticut State University experienced a traumatic event surrounding several sexual assault cases in the theater department. After a carefully investigated article in *The Central Recorder*, the CCSU Student newspaper, about sexual assault allegations raised by several students regarding a faculty member in the Theater Department, the university created forums, open meetings, and hearings. The local press coverage was extensive. The *Women, Gender and Sexuality Studies Program* organized a panel discussion in the spring 2018 preceded by a speak-out to let students voice their concerns, share stories, get moral support. A separate Title IX investigation concluded without further actions being taken. The male faculty member was put on paid administrative leave and may not return to teaching (after fifteen years of allegations had been filed). A special committee has been formed by the president, Dr. Zulma Toro, to investigate past and future policies. For more information, see Kathleen Megan from the *Hartford Courant* who reported on the situation repeatedly and with great care. "For More Than a Decade CCSU Administrators Took Little Action Despite Reports of Harassment by Professor," June 12, 2018, accessed on November 30, 2018, https://www.courant.com/education/hc-ccsu-sexual-assault-victims-speak-up-20180517-story.html.

4. One example could be the cartoon that was designed in response to the hearings with Supreme Court nominee Brett Kavanaugh in September 2018. The article, featuring the cartoon, was written by Alex Cooke, "Halifax artist's cartoon in response to Kavanaugh hearing grips internet" for the *Toronto CityNews*. Lady Liberty is seen in the cartoon, lying on her back while two male arms in suits (and with the icons of the GOP) hold her wrists down and cover her mouth with a hand. Lady Liberty is prevented from protesting; the balance, allegory for justice, has slipped out of her hands. See https://toronto.citynews.ca/2018/09/30/halifax-artists-cartoon-in-response-to-kavanaugh-hearing-grips-internet/ (accessed November 30, 2018). Another similar example can be seen from *The Washington Post* on September 29, 2018, in an article by Michael Cavna, entitled "Viral Kavanaugh cartoon powerfully depicts the assault of Lady Justice." Lady Liberty is standing on a pedestal with her eyes blind-folded, holding up a sign for the *#MeToo* movement. Next to her, President Donald Trump is leading the GOP elephant away and claims "When You're A Star, They Let You Do It." This quote is reminiscent of the president's earlier remarks that star status allows sexual predators to get away with their actions. See https://www.washingtonpost.com/news/comic-riffs/wp/2018/09/29/viral-kavanaugh-cartoon-powerfully-depicts-the-assault-of-lady-justice/?utm_term=.57997f2b6240.(accessed November 30, 2018).

5. One of the ironies is that Commander Fred Waterford (Joseph Fiennes) describes the women who work as prostitutes in Jezebel's to his Handmaid Offred (Elisabeth Moss) as former academics, similar to Dr. Blasey Ford.

6. Handmaids have swept from the screen into real life. Popular culture informs political protest and awareness. This has directly to do with the Hulu TV adaptation. Volker Schlöndorff did not dress the Handmaids in his film adaptation in white bonnets, as they were wearing red veils. So, this costuming of protestors is directly linked to the Hulu TV series.

7. Sarah Banet-Weiser, *Empowered: Popular Feminism and Popular Misogyny* (Durham: Duke University Press, 2018).

8. Banet-Weiser, Introduction, 25.

9. Banet-Weiser, chapter on "Confidence," 93.

10. Twitter feeds compared the picture from the Kavanaugh hearings in front of the US Senate with a screen shot of an episode of *The Handmaid's Tale*. *People Magazine* published an article by Maura Hohman where she compares the shots: "These Side-by-Side Pictures from the Kavanaugh Hearing and *Handmaid's Tale* Send Internet into Overdrive." September 28, 2018. https://people.com/tv/twitter -compares-handmaids-tale-kavanaugh-hearing/. (accessed November 30, 2018).

11. Alexander Alter, "Atwood is Writing 'Handmaid's' Sequel," *The New York Times*, "Arts" section, November 29, 2018, C1–C2.

WORKS CITED

Alter, Alexander. "Atwood Is Writing 'Handmaid's' Sequel." *The New York Times*, "Arts" section, November 29, 2018, C1–C2.

Banet-Weiser, Sarah. *Empowered: Popular Feminism and Popular Misogyny.* Durham: Duke University Press, 2018.

Cavna, Michael. "Viral Kavanaugh cartoon powerfully depicts the assault of Lady Justice." *The Washington Post*. September 29, 2018. https://www.washingtonpost .com/news/comic-riffs/wp/2018/09/29/viral-kavanaugh-cartoon-powerfully-de picts-the-assault-of-lady-justice/?utm_term=.57997f2b6240. (accessed November 30, 2018).

Cooke, Alex. "Halifax artist's cartoon in response to Kavanaugh hearing grips internet" for the *Toronto CityNews*. September 30, 2018. https://toronto.citynews .ca/2018/09/30/halifax-artists-cartoon-in-response-to-kavanaugh-hearing-grips -internet/. (accessed November 30, 2018).

Hohman, Maura. "These Side-by-Side Pictures from the Kavanaugh Hearing and *Handmaid's Tale* Send Internet into Overdrive." *People Magazine*. September 28, 2018. https://people.com/tv/twitter-compares-handmaids-tale-kavanaugh-hearing/ (accessed November 30, 2018).

Megan, Kathleen, "For more than a decade CCSU administrators took little action despite reports of harassment by professor." *Hartford Courant,* June 12, 2018. Education section. Accessed November 30, 2018. https://www.courant.com/educa tion/hc-ccsu-sexual-assault-victims-speak-up-20180517-story.html.

Section I

THE HANDMAID'S TALE AS A PEDAGOGICAL TOOL

The Handmaid's Tale as a Teaching Tool for Engaging Students in Colonial American History and Puritanism

Kelly Marino

Effective history professors and teachers constantly generate new ideas to engage students. They cultivate an appreciation for studying the past by trying different strategies to show that learning about history is relevant and important. One successful technique for drawing students into class material involves using artifacts from popular culture to start lessons or presentations and spark discussions. In this chapter, I argue that instructors can use events and episodes in the original book of *The Handmaid's Tale (THT)* as an opening "hook," initiation, or vehicle to begin larger conversations about American society and culture in the seventeenth century, particularly as a medium to help discuss colonial Puritanism, a topic that too often generates "eye rolls" among students. Specifically, *THT* can aid teachers in presenting complex issues, such as the Puritan religion, values and traditions, gender norms, sex and sexuality, morality, crime and punishment, and challenges and dissent, among many topics, by associating this material with the familiar characters, stories, and theatrical and literary content that students know and love.

THT and the history of early American society share many parallels. *THT* author Margaret Atwood notes close connections between the production of *THT* and the story of the Puritans. She argues that her study of seventeenth-century Puritan New England served as an important inspiration for her book. Atwood comments that she found a personal connection with the topic and period because of her own colonial roots, which traced back to the family name "Webster" that was prominent among the religious sect during the period. Atwood's fascination centers on the life and experiences of a woman named Mary Reeve Webster, an accused witch mentioned in a text by the famous Puritan minister, Cotton Mather, who she argues was a distinctive relative because of her controversial past. She dedicated *THT* to Webster's

difficult experiences and story. Webster struggled as an outsider in a supersti-
tious and anxiety-prone society.[1]

Given these connections to Atwood, Webster's shocking and tragic story
acts as an interesting anecdote and beginning point for lessons linking Puritanism to *THT*. A resident of Hadley, Massachusetts, Webster is portrayed
in contemporary sketches as a wretched, elderly outcast, tormented and os-
tracized, scorned, and accused of witchcraft. Skeptical about her beliefs and
activities, her accusers captured her one night and hung her from a tree, aspir-
ing to put her to death. Her body was left dangling all night. However, what
makes Webster's story so surprising and engaging as a hook for students is its
unexpected outcome. Accounts state that by some stroke of luck, she did not
die. When community members returned to the tree, Webster remained alive
and was cut down. By bizarre happenstance, she lived for another fourteen
years; Atwood even wrote an early poem about the incident, evidence of its
impact on her, called "Half-Hanged Mary."[2]

Instructors could use this incident or another similarly striking example
from *THT*, based on the historic religious group, to capture students' attention
and draw them into a presentation or learning segment about the Puritans,
their society, culture, and why they might have treated Webster so terribly.
Important teaching questions for an introductory class in early American history or essential questions for further inquiry that could be sparked by Webster's story include the following: On a basic level, who were the Puritans,
and where were they from? Where did they immigrate to, and why? What did
they believe about religion and morality? How were Puritan men and women
supposed to behave? How did they look and dress? Why was being an alleged
witch or an outsider so controversial? What types of punishments were common or uncommon? On a more complex level: How are Webster and other
Puritans different from or similar to characters in *THT*? How does the society
in *THT* compare to colonial Massachusetts? What are our modern perceptions
of the Puritans, and how have historians challenged these notions? These are
just a few of the many possible questions instructors could use as guiding issues for their presentations and lessons.

ORIGINS OF THE PURITANS AND RELIGION

As educators, to foster comprehension among our students, we need to spend
a certain amount of time early in our lessons laying out the basics, or the contextual framework for the subjects that we will address. Similar to the way we
ask students to present material in a research paper with an early background
section, as teachers, a fair amount of "stage setting" is necessary to answer

the foundational "who," "what," "when," and "where" questions and ensure that our students have the necessary context to understand the more specific and complex issues we will tackle in later discussions. The students should know a little about the origins of the Puritans and their chief ideologies, which can later be bolstered by more specific details from other scholarly secondary or primary sources.

It is significant to note, for example, that the Puritans were a religious faction that was displeased with the Church of England by the early seventeenth century because they thought that Catholic teachings had overly influenced the institution. The Puritans wanted to practice a "purer" form of Protestantism and received their name because of their goal of "purifying" or reforming the Church. In Europe, however, as Catholicism gained popularity, not everyone viewed those who aimed to change the Church in a positive light. People perceived Puritans as a threat because of their political power, and Puritan leaders faced persecution. Over time, certain Puritan ministers could no longer preach, and King Charles I, who took the British throne in 1625, stifled the group's influence further when he dissolved Parliament, a governing body with many Puritan members.[3]

Discontented with their declining circumstances in England, the Puritans immigrated to other areas. Although students often only consider the Puritan migrations to Massachusetts, teachers should urge them to think in a more global context by noting that most secondary sources state they also traveled to different locations in Europe, the West Indies, and North America. The Puritans came to present-day Massachusetts in 1630 not all at once, but in multiple waves. The first major Puritan migration included eleven ships and seven hundred people and the next, six ships and five hundred people. The Puritan immigrants differed from the Pilgrims because they were not "separatists" who hoped to permanently break away from the English Church.[4] Instead, they wanted their new settlement, Massachusetts Bay Colony, to serve as a "city upon a hill" or an example for the rest of the world of moral living.[5] They planned to return to England after the British Church followed their lead. John Winthrop, the first governor, argued that everyone was watching Massachusetts Bay and that community members had to do right by God and the world by proving that a more righteous way of life was possible.

Teachers should emphasize to students, however, that entering a barren wilderness and starting a new life was not an easy task for any immigrant. The "new" world lacked the established conveniences, institutions, and structures that guided life in England. Puritan leaders dealt with these issues in several ways. First, rather than allow people to spread out and live where they wanted, they kept people together for as long as possible in a localized area by establishing towns, with the Boston/Cambridge area (used as the backdrop in *THT*) serving as a major early epicenter. Besides the governor of the colony, each town had other powerful officials, including a council of elders, a minister, and aides to watch over members. Puritan New England was a tense and suspicious environment, in which leaders asked neighbors to police and report the behavior of other neighbors to ensure that they followed the rules.[6] This close-knit and vigilant culture is replicated in *THT*, where people are always "under the eye" and watch what others say and do; this is also an interesting topic to discuss with students, given current and past controversies over government and institutional surveillance.

Central to understanding Puritanism is comprehending the importance and centrality of religion to the community and how it shaped people's actions and behavior. The Puritans were primarily guided by God's will as communicated through the Bible. Worship was central to daily life, and Sunday was sacred. Teachers should emphasize that community leaders responded harshly to people frolicking, loitering, socializing, and drinking on Sundays. Not attending services and behaving inappropriately was against the law. Criminals faced fines and public humiliation, such as whippings, for failing to fall in line. Leaders locked the town gates on Sunday to discourage travel, limit movement, and promote the rules. They believed that it was necessary for all community members to hear the sermon because the religious message not only reinforced their faith but also addressed town problems and spread the news. To ensure that people in Puritan churches paid attention to the critical message, a patrol carried a long pole to wake up children or adults sleeping or joking in church.[7]

Teaching students about the Puritan belief in "predestination," a common topic discussed among churches and congregations, is imperative because of the concept's significance to the religious group. The Puritans believed that God had already chosen who would receive salvation, and no one had a way of knowing or shaping if they would be among the saved or the damned. A person's fate could not be influenced by "good works" or moral behavior, as Catholics typically believed. Puritans constantly worried about their spiritual status, sometimes even to the point of mental illness and insanity.[8] Given that doing good works did not necessarily guarantee a place among the saved, people needed other motivators to behave. Aside from fearing punishment, most Puritans followed the rules because they believed that they were in a "covenant" or a contract or agreement with God and with one another to be good religious subjects to ensure the community's success in its mission to serve as an example for the rest of the world. People living in the colony, therefore, tried to avoid temptations and appear saintly and godly in their interactions, just like in *THT*. The Puritans banned anything that might encourage rowdy, promiscuous, or illegal actions. The list of pleasures prohibited included music, dancing, and gambling. Leaders were especially concerned about dancing because they viewed the touching of bodies as too enticing, particularly for young people.[9] Conformity to these rules and values was as important in Puritan America as it was in Gilead, the fictional society created in *THT*.

PARALLELS TO GILEAD

The Puritans did, however, promote some activities still valued today, such as reading, and initiatives to create opportunities for education. Puritan leaders believed in the positive value of educating male and female children. Many Puritan towns offered free schooling because they argued everyone, including women, needed reading skills to study the Bible. In the Massachusetts Bay Colony, leaders required every town of at least fifty to hire a teacher, and if a town had at least one hundred families, it had to have a grammar school.[10] Instructors should stress to students that these trends were unique and contributed to higher literacy rates in New England than other areas of the Americas, particularly among women.

Women and men in Puritan culture, however, were not equal but fulfilled distinct gender roles. Society was very patriarchal, and men were the primary leaders, as in *THT*'s Gilead. Only men could serve as the community leaders governing town meetings and ministers overseeing the church. In marriage, men were the head of the home, they had full say over their wives, and they technically owned their children. Puritan wives took care of domestic duties and raised their children according to religious principles and community laws. Parents were supposed to be strict because children who behaved poorly could be publicly punished by local officials and, as a result, reflect badly on the entire family. Couples often named their children after biblical figures who could serve as role models or moral qualities, such as "patience," that they hoped to instill.[11]

Students might be shocked to learn that unlike most modern weddings, Puritan marriages were not overly celebratory or explicitly romantic. Unlike Catholics, who saw marriage as a sacrament, Puritans viewed marriage as a legal contract. A minister did not perform marriages, but instead, couples used a magistrate or other government official. Most men married at around age twenty-six, and most women married at around age twenty-three. The community promoted marriage as vital for stability and expansion. Leaders viewed marriage as essential to keeping women in line, as they viewed the female sex as more vulnerable to sin and temptation, and, correspondingly, all women, especially married women, had to dress in modest clothing. They could even be punished for breaking the dress code. Married women had few legal rights, except they could divorce in extreme circumstances, such as if they could prove adultery, impotence, physical abuse, or intentional desertion. Widowed women, in contrast, had the most rights because they could sue and own land and did not have the same male oversight.[12] However, although married Puritan women faced restrictions, teachers should note they were not completely oppressed and found loopholes to exercise agency both within their families and larger communities. At moments throughout history, they successfully manipulated both men and the legal system and used their roles as wives, women, and mothers skillfully to influence society to their benefit.

Just as in *THT,* the Puritans promoted sex between married partners for procreation and condemned sexual immorality. Most women had many children compared to contemporary standards, sometimes over ten, viewing them as important workhands, and did little to control or prevent pregnancy. Yet, pregnancy often was dangerous and infant mortality high, and instructors might find this an interesting opportunity to begin larger conversations about the histories of innovations in reproductive technologies and related health care services.[13] Instructors also should discuss with students when, why, and how attitudes about sex and gender changed, particularly in connection with the rise of Victorianism and the Industrial Revolution.

Despite the society's restrictive beliefs and standards, Puritan leaders found policing illicit romance, sex, and sexuality a challenge. Modern generations of scholars have revised earlier interpretations of the Puritans that made them seem like prudes and point to evidence in court records of numerous cases of unsanctioned behavior, including premarital and extramarital sex, bestiality, and sodomy.[14] Although same-sex relations between men were condemned, students should learn that punishment varied according to social class, and sex between women was rarely taken seriously.[15] "Seemingly" nonpenetrative liaisons between women were not viewed as sinful on the same scale as heterosexual intercourse outside of marriage or sexual penetration between men. Punishments for sexual immorality in colonial America might have been embarrassing, but often, leaders took these crimes more seriously in more established settings, such as Europe and England, than in the colonies, where every life mattered to the community's survival, especially early on.[16]

Young people and outsiders often were the prime culprits who challenged sexual mores, just as they are today, and as a history educator, including this discussion, particularly of the younger generation's role in testing these boundaries, can interest students in the class material by making it more relatable. In early America, over time, teachers should emphasize that the youth became more secular and experimental, which worried elders and community leaders. Not all people who lived in or near the colony were Puritans, either, which generated differences in sexual practices. Native Americans, for example, did not believe in monogamous relationships or a patriarchal society, nor did other immigrants who lived on the outskirts of the community and in rural areas with less oversight and more freedom. As more diverse people came to present-day Massachusetts, they brought different beliefs about sex and love.[17]

When leaders knew about crimes and were able to act, punishment centered on public humiliation and peer pressure to coerce people into behaving correctly, rather than modern conventions such as institutional detention. No prisons, jails, or police force existed. Those innovations were much more recent. Puritans would commonly be branded, whipped, or disfigured to mark their crime in a distinct manner that would serve as a reminder to themselves and others. When maiming did not occur, other forms of public torture included being placed in the pillory or stockade in the town center. Leaders relied heavily on community shaming and ruining one's reputation to keep people following the rules. In the most severe cases, convicted criminals could be put to death or banished from the community, but again, such harsh actions would mean a loss for everyone, as the town would have one less member. Anne Hutchinson, a Puritan woman from Massachusetts who held weekly religious meetings at her house, argued that God spoke directly to her and criticized the New England group for straying toward Catholic principles, and was one of the most notorious Puritan dissenters who flagrantly challenged the laws and faced excommunication. She was infamous for being a woman who stepped out of line in a very public and well-publicized way and defied male leadership in her community, which ultimately led her to be pushed out of the colony. She died in present-day New York, the victim of a Native American attack. Because it is so well-documented and her actions so unusual, Hutchinson's case is essential to highlight to students when covering crime, punishment, and challenges to Puritanism.[18]

IMPLEMENTING PURITAN IDEALS

Besides considering how crime spurred the dissolution of Puritan society, educators should stress how political and other types of social and cultural change also contributed to a diminishing Puritan influence in colonial New England leading into the eighteenth century. In England, the tides started to turn for the religious group by 1642, when a civil war known as the Puritan Revolution erupted because of the divisions between religious and government leaders. Charles I was eventually executed, and Puritans regained lost power. Subsequent British rulers did not challenge or stifle Puritanism in the same way, and Puritan leaders recovered their posts and influence in the British government. As Puritans became better satisfied again in England, their motivations to leave decreased.

In New England, Puritan power diminished not only because fewer new members of their group elected to come to the Americas, but also because population expansion in the colonies, while beneficial in some respects, made it even more difficult to control people's behavior. Policing a small settlement in Massachusetts might have been easy, but keeping track of growing and complex towns and cities was much more difficult. Over time, fewer people followed the rules and subscribed to Puritan beliefs, and their behaviors were more difficult to police. Church attendance dropped rapidly, especially among men more interested in economic and political affairs, and churches increasingly became feminized spaces.[19] These changes made Winthrop's city-upon-a-hill ideal for Massachusetts Bay increasingly difficult to uphold; just as challenges sprang up in Gilead, challenges similarly mounted in early America, forcing society to evolve.

Although most students are reluctant to learn about many aspects of early American society, such as Puritanism, because of preexisting ideas about how the associated course content can be dry or boring, one way to challenge these notions is to introduce the historical material beginning with an important contemporary connection or pop cultural medium, such as *THT*. Examples and episodes from *THT* serve as an effective opening hook and cultural artifact through which to engage students in discussions of seventeenth-century America because of the book's natural connections with the topic and Atwood's discussions of how history influenced her story. In *THT*, members of Gilead seem like a modern, and more extreme, sect of Puritans, serving as a vivid example for students of the realities and complexities of such a restrictive society, an example that can help to bring the history taught in survey courses and introduced in textbooks to life.

NOTES

1. Adam Wernick, "A 17th-Century Alleged Witch Inspired Margaret Atwood's 'The Handmaid's Tale,'" *Public Radio International*, May 13, 2017, https://www.pri.org/stories/2017-05-13/17th-century-alleged-witch-inspired-margaret-atwoods-handmaids-tale.

2. "Mary Webster, the Witch of Hadley, Survives a Hanging," *New England Historical Society*, accessed August 20, 2018, http://www.newenglandhistoricalsociety.com/mary-webster-witch-hadley-survives-hanging/.

3. John Mack Faragher, Mari Jo Buhle, Daniel H. Czitrom, and Susan H. Armitage, *Out of Many: A History of the American People,* Volume I, 8th ed. (New York: Pearson, 2015); James L. Roark, Michael P. Johnson, Patricia Cline Cohen, Sarah

Stage, Alan Lawson, and Susan M. Hartmann, *The American Promise: A Concise History, Volume 1: To 1877*, 6th ed. (New York: Bedford/St. Martin's, 2016).

4. Faragher et al., *Out of Many*; Roark et al., *The American Promise*.

5. John Winthrop, "A Model of Christian Charity," in *A Library of American Literature: Early Colonial Literature, 1607–1675*, eds. Edmund Clarence Stedman and Ellen Mackay Hutchinson (New York: Charles L. Webster & Company, 1892), 304–7.

6. Nancy Finlay, "The Importance of Being Puritan: Church and State in Colonial Connecticut," *Connecticut History.org*, accessed August 20, 2018, https://connect icuthistory.org/the-importance-of-being-puritan-church-and-state-in-colonial-con necticut/; "Puritan Women's Rights," *Women's History Blog*, last modified October 2007, http://www.womenhistoryblog.com/2007/10/puritan-women.html.

7. "Thirteen Colonies: New England Colonies," Sample Lessons (PDF), *Flexbook, CK-12 Foundation*, accessed August 20, 2018, www.ck12.org.

8. "Puritan Women's Rights."

9. Faragher et al., *Out of Many*; Roark et al., *The American Promise*.

10. "Massachusetts Education Laws of 1642 and 1647," accessed August 20, 2018, https://www3.nd.edu/~rbarger/www7/masslaws.html.

11. "Puritan Women's Rights."

12. "Puritan Women's Rights."

13. Miss Cellania, "The Historical Horror of Childbirth," *Mental Floss*, last modified May 9, 2013, http://mentalfloss.com/article/50513/historical-horror-childbirth.

14. John D'Emilio and Estelle B. Freedman, *Intimate Matters: A History of Sexuality in America* (Chicago: University of Chicago Press, 2012).

15. D'Emlio and Freedman, *Intimate Matters*; Jonathan Alexander, Deborah T. Meem, Michelle Gibson, *Finding Out: An Introduction to LGBTQ Studies* (Los Angeles, SAGE, 2018).

16. Alexander, Meem, Gibson, *Finding Out*.

17. Faragher et al., *Out of Many*; Roark et al., *The American Promise*.

18. Ibid.

19. Ibid.

WORKS CITED

D'Emilio, John, and Estelle B. Freedman. *Intimate Matters: A History of Sexuality in America*. Chicago: University of Chicago Press, 2012.

Faragher, John Mack, Mari Jo Buhle, Daniel H. Czitrom, and Susan H. Armitage. *Out of Many: A History of the American People*, Volume I, 8th ed. New York: Pearson, 2015.

Finlay, Nancy. "The Importance of Being Puritan: Church and State in Colonial Connecticut." *Connecticut History.org*. Accessed August 20, 2018. https://con

necticuthistory.org/the-importance-of-being-puritan-church-and-state-in-colonial -connecticut/.

"Mary Webster, the Witch of Hadley, Survives a Hanging." *New England Historical Society*. Accessed August 20, 2018. http://www.newenglandhistoricalsociety.com /mary-webster-witch-hadley-survives-hanging/.

"Massachusetts Education Laws of 1642 and 1647." *University of Notre Dame*. Accessed August 20, 2018. https://www3.nd.edu/~rbarger/www7/masslaws.html.

Meem, Deborah Townsend, Jonathon Alexander, and Michelle Gibson. *Finding Out: An Introduction to LGBT Studies*. Los Angeles: SAGE Publications, Inc., 2014.

Miss Cellania. "The Historical Horror of Childbirth." *Mental Floss*, May 9, 2013. http://mentalfloss.com/article/50513/historical-horror-childbirth.

"Puritan's Women's Rights." *Women's History Blog*, last modified October 2007. http://www.womenhistoryblog.com/2007/10/puritan-women.html.

Roark, James L., Michael P. Johnson, Patricia Cline Cohen, Sarah Stage, Alan Lawson, and Susan M. Hartmann. *The American Promise: A History of the United States Volume 1: To 1877*, 6th ed. New York: Bedford/St. Martin's, 2016.

"Thirteen Colonies: New England Colonies." *Flexbook, CK-12 Foundation*. Accessed August 20, 2018. www.ck12.org.

Wernick, Adam. "A 17th-Century Alleged Witch Inspired Margaret Atwood's 'The Handmaid's Tale.'" *Public Radio International*, May 13, 2017. https://www.pri .org/stories/2017-05-13/17th-century-alleged-witch-inspired-margaret-atwoods -handmaids-tale.

Winthrop, John. "A Model of Christian Charity." In *A Library of American Literature: Early Colonial Literature, 1607–1675*, edited by Edmund Clarence Stedman and Ellen Mackay Hutchinson, 304–7. New York: Charles L. Webster & Company, 1892.

FILMS AND TELEVISION

The Handmaid's Tale. Directed by Volker Schlöndorff. United States, 1990.

The Handmaid's Tale. Created by Bruce Miller. Produced by Warren Littlefield, Margaret Atwood, Dorothy Fortenberry. Aired April 26, 2017, on Hulu.

Chapter Two

Translation and Adaptation Matters

About the Differences between a Story Called The Handmaid's Tale *or* The Slave-Girl's Tale?

Aven McMaster

In Genesis, Rachel and Leah give to their husband Jacob their "handmaids" or "maids" Bilhah and Zilpah, to bear children in their place, in the story that provides the model and title for Margaret Atwood's *The Handmaid's Tale* and the Hulu TV show of the same name. The original Hebrew word used to describe these women can mean "slave" or "bondservant," but the Greek and Latin words used in the Septuagint and Vulgate unambiguously mean "female chattel slave." So why don't the English translations of the Bible say "slavegirl"? Why doesn't the Republic of Gilead use that term? The answer may seem obvious, but the question is one that is relevant to the entire field of Classics today. This chapter will look at *The Handmaid's Tale* from my perspective as a scholar of Latin poetry and Roman history who is accustomed to examining the exact meanings and connotations of words, and the importance of historical context to the interpretation and translation of those words, to see how the discipline of Classics can contribute to an understanding of contemporary literature and culture, and how that understanding of the present can help make us better scholars of the ancient world.

To start with one important example: in the *Odyssey*, the epic poem by Homer from around the sixth century BCE, after the hero has returned home and taken his revenge on the men who were harassing his wife and depleting his resources, he tells his son to execute the twelve "handmaids" who had been sleeping with those men. His son hangs the women in the courtyard of the house. Again, the words used for these women in Greek mean "slave," but in English translations they are usually called "maids" or "servingwomen." This episode from the *Odyssey* and the Hulu show are connected by Margaret Atwood's 2005 book *Penelopiad*, a reimagining of the Greek epic from the hero's wife's point of view which focuses in particular on the execution of these "maids." It has also been the focus of recent discussion by Classicists in the wake of the first published translation by a woman of the *Odyssey* into English. The translator, Emily Wilson, has spoken repeatedly about how she translated the Greek term for these women as the more direct "slaves" rather than "handmaids," and how that explicit recognition of their enslaved status fundamentally affects the reading of the scene, and the epic as a whole.[1] This has also contributed to an ongoing conversation about the ways translation, adaptation, selective use, and even intentional misrepresentation of Classical texts has affected and shaped societal values and political movements.

These three works: *The Handmaid's Tale*, the *Odyssey*, and the *Penelopiad*, are linked by the question of the status of the women involved, their control (or lack of control) over their own bodies, and how our use of language and the choices made by translators affect our understanding of the past, the present, and the possible future. The purpose of this chapter is to explore what the differences are between a story called *The Handmaid's Tale* and *The Slave-Girl's Tale,* and to see how translation of ancient sources is affected by, and also profoundly affects, our understanding of the ancient world, the modern world, and the relationships between them.

The system of Handmaids in the Republic of Gilead is based on passages from Genesis in which women who are not able to have children give their husband another woman to have sex with, and then claim the babies thus produced as legitimate children. The main model is the story of Jacob and Rachel and Leah,[2] as can be seen by the name of the Red Centers: the Rachel and Leah Centers.[3] In the King James version of the Bible (the most well-known popular translation, and the one Atwood quotes from in the book), the women who are given to Jacob (Bilhah and Zilpah) are called "maids" or "handmaids," words which in English refer to servants or attendants. If we go back to the original Hebrew of the Torah, however, or to its early ancient translations (the Greek of the Septuagint and the Latin of the Vulgate), we find that the words used to describe these women all mean "female slave," and clearly refer to women who are owned as property by the wives of Jacob.[4] The status of these slaves is also evident in their complete lack of power or agency in the stories: they are given by Laban to his daughters as wedding gifts or dowries, neither of them is ever asked if she is willing to be used for sex and child-bearing, their reactions or emotions are never described, and they are not mentioned again except in genealogies.[5] Wilda C. Gafney addresses the persistent use of "maid" or "handmaid" as a translation for the Hebrew words in her book *Womanist Midrash*:

> I choose the translation "slave" rather than "servant" for "shiphchah" and "amah" . . . to emphasize that these persons were bought and sold, used for sex, impregnated, and completely subjugated to the power of those called their

mistresses and masters. "Servitude" suggests employment, which is not the case for slaves in the biblical corpus.[6]

To understand the importance of this distinction, it is necessary to understand the cultural context of the original Biblical passage, and to define a "chattel slave." Sometimes "slaves" and "servants" are considered to be distinguished solely by whether or not their labor is remunerated—that is, whether or not people are paid for their work. This is not, however, the essential difference; some servants work for room and board only, some slaves are paid for some of their work. There are more fundamental differences between the two conditions. Slavery was widespread in the ancient world; we do not know of any major cultures around the Mediterranean or in the Middle East before the first century CE that did not practice some form of slavery.[7] To be a chattel slave was to have a specific legal status in society, and at its most basic signaled a lack of personal and physical autonomy: enslaved people had little to no protection against physical abuse, sexual exploitation, or direct violence; they could not own property; they had no legal family ties to parents, partners or children; nor did they have any legal right to choose where they lived, where they went, or what they did.[8]

SLAVERY AS "SOCIAL DEATH"

The condition of slavery has been called "social death,"[9] because it entails a removal of all meaningful social ties, such as home, family, social structure, and often religion and language; even a person's name was usually changed when s/he was enslaved, and could be changed repeatedly if s/he was resold. People in the ancient world could be enslaved in many different ways, of which the following were the most common: prisoners of war, populations captured as a result of conquest, people kidnapped or captured by slave traders, children sold into slavery by parents without the means to support them, adults who sold themselves into slavery to pay off debts or support their family, and children born to an enslaved woman. This variety of sources meant that although slaves were often from "foreign" or outside groups, that was certainly not always the case. It also meant that there was no ethnic, religious, linguistic, or racial homogeneity to the class of "slaves" within Hebrew, Greek, or Roman societies.

What distinguished an enslaved person from a free person was his or her legal and social status and the way he or she was treated, not skin color or any other observable trait. This is, of course, one of the biggest differences between slavery in the ancient world and slavery in Europe and the Americas from the sixteenth century onward, where slavery was restricted to racialized people (usually Black or Indigenous). These distinctions between the ancient world and the modern in terms of how slavery worked, who enslaved people were, and the relationships between slave owners and enslaved people are obscured by the fact that we use the same vocabulary for both systems. So when we use the word "slave-girl" or "slave" today, it has the potential to evoke a wide range of different associations in the audience's minds. All of those associations, however, are different from those evoked by "servant" or "maid"—and so we return to the importance of the linguistic choices made when translating from languages and cultures where slave-holding is usual, to one in which it is not (any longer) considered normal.[10] This brings us to the second work under examination in this chapter.

THE *ODYSSEY* AND TRANSLATION PRACTICES

The *Odyssey*, the ancient Greek epic by Homer, generally thought to have been written down around the seventh or sixth century BCE, is one of the foundational texts of the discipline of Classics. It has been translated into English many times, and so provides a useful example of how translation practices have changed over the years, and how the choices made by a translator can affect the way the narrative, and the characters and culture it describes, are viewed and understood. For the purposes of this chapter, I want to focus on one episode in the *Odyssey*, just after the hero Odysseus has returned to his home after a twenty year absence and killed the men who were living in his palace and trying to persuade his wife to marry one of them. Once this slaughter of the 108 suitors has been accomplished, Odysseus instructs his son Telemachus to summon the "disloyal women-servants" and force them to dispose of the dead bodies and clean the hall of blood, and then Telemachus hangs the twelve women as punishment for their rudeness to him and his mother, and for "sleeping with" the suitors.[11]

The Greek words used to describe these women, in this passage and elsewhere, mean "female chattel slaves." However, as with the passage from Genesis, in many of the most well-known English translations of the *Odyssey*, the women are always or usually called "maid-servants," "maids," or "serving-woman."[12] But in a new translation published in 2017, Emily Wilson calls them "female slaves" (though she also calls them "girls" when the Greek is not as specific). She is not the first translator to do so, but her choice is in keeping with her stated policy throughout the work:

> To translate a domestic female slave, called in the original a *dmoe* ("female-house-slave"), as a "maid" or "domestic servant" would imply that she was free. I have often used "slave," although it is less specific than many of the terms for

types of slaves in the original. The need to acknowledge the fact and the horror of slavery, and to mark the fact that the idealized society depicted in the poem is one where slavery is shockingly taken for granted, seems to me to outweigh the need to specify, in every instance, the type of slave.[13]

As the first woman to have a translation of this work published in English, Wilson has been seen by many commentators as having a "political agenda" and as making "radical choices" in her translation.[14] As she has repeatedly pointed out, however, all previous translators have also made choices about their translations, but presumably because they were men, such choices have only been critiqued on intellectual and aesthetic grounds, and not considered "political."[15] By calling these women "maids," previous translators have implied that they had a choice about whom to have sex with, and might be expected to have an amicable or even friendly relationship with their employers. Why did previous translators avoid the word "slave"? Did they feel uncomfortable about the presence of slaves in such an important cultural text, which has been used as an example of moral and heroic behavior for millennia? To compare this to the Handmaids of Gilead, consider what the difference is between: "Odysseus ordered the disloyal slaves to be killed" and "Odysseus ordered the disloyal servants to be killed." What loyalty does an enslaved woman owe to her enslaver? What do we feel about men who execute their slaves because they were rude, or were used for sex by their enemies?

When we turn to Atwood's treatment of this scene and the women involved in *Penelopiad*, we see that she explores this very issue. Atwood usually calls the women "maids," following the language of the 1946 E. V. Rieu translation of the *Odyssey* that she quotes in the epigraph to the book. But she does make their slavery explicit in some passages in the story: "We too were born to the wrong parents. Poor parents, slave parents, peasant parents, and serf parents; parents who sold us, parents from whom we were stolen."[16] On pages 87–88 Penelope explains how she learned to manage and rule over the slaves of the household, who are explicitly named as male and female slaves. Even so, the repeated use of "maids" to describe the women elsewhere keeps their slave status out of focus and allows Penelope to build up her version of the events, in which the girls are by turns her friends and her children, objects of her affection, women she trusts—and who, in their own versions of the story, feel betrayed by her. These questions of how to translate the Greek, then, are not merely academic or aesthetic. They affect our understanding of Odysseus and his son Telemachus, the ostensible heroes of the poem, and of ancient Greek society as a whole, and may contribute to a debate about how our contemporary society uses the Classical texts and world as a model or example.

WHY NOT CALL THE HANDMAIDS "SLAVES"?

Having looked at the ancient works and Atwood's direct response to some of these issues, let us now examine how these elements are handled in *The Hand-maid's Tale*. First, as we have seen, the title replicates the standard euphemistic translation of the Biblical terms for "slave," using the King James Bible's word "handmaid." In fact, neither the book nor the show use the word "slave" even once. Why is this? To start with, let us consider the in-universe reason for the Republic of Gilead to avoid the term. This seems straightforward: calling the women slaves would look bad, because the American people don't think slav-ery is good. But at the same time, the new government is comfortable empha-sizing other types of retrograde inequality, such as the redefinition of women as subservient to men and the removal of a woman's right to own property, be employed, or read. A new and explicit class system is also created, with Com-manders and Wives, Marthas, Aunts, Guardians, drivers, and shopkeepers, and so forth. But outright use of the term "slavery" is still avoided.

This is because the new state relies on the ideology of individual sacrifice for communal good, and the underlying principle is that every member of the new community is *choosing* to fulfill the role that God has laid out for them—and that if they don't, they must be removed from that community. At the same time, the propaganda of the Republic of Gilead stresses "freedom," but a new kind of freedom. As Aunt Lydia tells the Handmaids: "There is more than one kind of freedom . . . Freedom to and freedom from. In the days of anarchy, it was freedom to. Now you are being given freedom from."[17] The language of slavery is incompatible with this emphasis on freedom.

That the Republic of Gilead itself chooses to use "Handmaid" instead of "Slave-girl" is not, then, surprising. But why does Offred in the book never use the term? Why does no one in the TV show use the word "slave"? This choice by Atwood, carried forward by the showrunners, requires some dis-cussion. To begin with, what indication do we have that the Handmaids are, in fact, in the position of slaves? The avoidance of the term is only notable if it would conceivably be applicable, so let us look at that issue first. We are given little to no indication of the exact legal status of the Handmaids, so we will look only at the evidence for how they are treated. If we return to the common elements of slavery described above, we can see how these women fit into this pattern: the Handmaids have no protection against physi-cal abuse, and we see many examples of harsh treatment and cruelty; nor are they protected from sexual abuse, though there are limits on who can abuse them, limits which are put in place to protect the Commanders, not the women; they have no ability to choose where they live, what they do, or where they go, and have no freedom of movement; they are removed from their families, and all family ties are dissolved—they are not entitled to husbands or wives, and they have no legal claim to their own children, who are incorporated instead into other families.[18] All of these elements taken together, then, make the Handmaids *de facto* slaves, even if they are never explicitly bought or sold.

The separation of families is integral to slave experiences throughout history and is central to my argument that the Handmaids are indeed slaves. The primary metaphor used in the show to describe the women is "prisoners," but while this is reasonable, it doesn't cover the element of deracination—the loss of all family and social ties—that is fundamental to the Handmaids', and enslaved peoples', experience. This can be seen particularly clearly in the renaming of the women, and the prohibition on using their previous names. Renaming a person when s/he are enslaved has always been common practice, and slaves in the ancient world were often renamed every time they were sold.[19] They generally also were not allowed to use the full form of names common among free persons of their community (such as family names), and naming conventions often included some element that showed who owned them. The Handmaids are all given new names every time they are assigned to a new household, and these names indicate the man whose possession they are—for example, "Offred" is the Handmaid of Fred Waterford (Of-Fred). This is something that does not generally happen to prisoners, who even when they are assigned numbers as a way to dehumanize them are not forbidden to use their original names.

In this context, we should also briefly look at the Marthas, and examine their status and how they are portrayed in the book and the show. Are they slaves or servants? Their function within the house is as menial labor, and they appear to have the role of servant, though we are never told if they are paid, or what choice (or lack thereof) they had about their job.[20] The name given to this category of women, however, is illuminating. They are called Marthas, which references a story in the Gospel of Luke, in which Jesus visits the home of two sisters, Martha and Mary.[21] Mary acts as a disciple of Jesus while Martha serves them, and when Martha complains about having to serve by herself, Jesus rebukes her. In the story, Martha is represented as a free woman with her own house, not a slave, and the word used to describe her activity means to serve or minister. While the Marthas might appear to more closely match the role of "slave" in a household, the Biblical model for this new class of women suggests they are seen as servants, in contrast to the models for the handmaids, who are chattel slaves. This is a good example of the careful use of language (and intertextuality) by the Republic of Gilead (or, more properly, Atwood) as a signal of the ideological structures at play in the world of the novel and the show.

So, the Handmaids are represented as equivalent to enslaved peoples in multiple ways, but no one within the book or TV show uses the term. I suggest that there are several connected possible reasons for this, and they all bring us back to the central topic of translation across languages and across cultures. First, the theme of choice and consent is central to the book and show, and the explicit naming of the Handmaids as slaves might preempt that discussion by presenting them as having no choices at all. Second, the word "slaves" has strong connections to race and the history of Black slavery in America, and these elements could introduce too many complications to the story being told, which focuses on gender relations and reproductive choice. Finally, the world of Gilead is presented as a possible, and possibly imminent, future for the audience, and suggesting that religious fundamentalists would reintroduce slavery might be too unrealistic for an audience who considers legalized slavery an aspect of the past that will never return. I cannot say that any of these is the actual motivation behind the omission of the word "slave" from the TV show, but I will give some background and explanation for the first two suggestions, and then by way of conclusion discuss how all three, and the problems with them, reveal important aspects of how translation affects our understanding of the past and the present.

CONSENT AND THE LACK OF AUTONOMY

Let's begin with the issue of consent: the story of *The Handmaid's Tale* centers around the forcible use of women's bodies for sex and reproduction. This has historically been a common role of female slaves (male slaves have often been used for sex as well, but the story does not reference this). In the Biblical story on which the Handmaids are based, Bilhah and Zilpah are not asked to consent to the use to which their bodies are put, nor do they have any say over what happens to their children. It is not that their consent is assumed, it is that they are not considered to have a choice, as their bodies are literally owned by Rachel and Leah or Jacob.[22] This key issue, their lack of autonomy and therefore their inability to choose to do otherwise than they do, is obscured by the avoidance of the word "slave" to describe them in translations of the Bible. Of course, in using this story as their model, the Republic of Gilead obscures the enforced nature of their childbearing; they instead present the relationship between the Wife and the Handmaid as a cooperative one, where the Handmaid gives the gift of a child as part of her duty to the state.

The element of choice, however, is treated differently in the book and the show. In the book Offred explicitly refuses to call the "Ceremony" rape: "Nor does rape cover it: nothing is going on here that I haven't signed up for. There wasn't a lot of choice but there was some, and this is what I chose."[23] The "choice" she refers to here appears to have been between resisting until she was killed or sent to the Colonies (an extended death sentence) or acquiescing to her role as Handmaid. Most people would not consider this an actual choice. In the TV show, by contrast, June explicitly calls the Ceremony "rape" when speaking to the Mexican Ambassador[24] and says, "I didn't choose this." After this scene, the word is used again and again to describe the Ceremony by multiple characters, and there are also several scenes of very explicit, violent rape that are not in the book. This probably reflects a change in both the legal and social perceptions of rape in the three decades between the publishing of the book and the release of the show; under Canadian law now, for instance, consent given under threat of violence would not constitute consent.[25] Here again, though, we see that the vocabulary of slavery is avoided. In the scene with the Mexican ambassador (Zabryna Guevara), June refers to herself and the Handmaids as "prisoners" and stresses the violence to which they are subjected, conspicuously failing to point out the clear parallels of their situation to slavery. An enslaved person cannot give free consent to sex with her owner, no matter the circumstances.

This is in fact the central problem in the episode of the *Odyssey* discussed above, in which the choice to translate the Greek as "slave" or "maid" highlights the question of whether a slave has the ability to consent to sex or not—and therefore, whether she can be blamed for it. The slave women are hanged because, in Telemachus's words (Wilson's translation): "They poured down shame on me / and Mother, when they lay beside the suitors."[26] Their sexual relations with the suitors (the men who took over Odysseus's house and ate his food while he was away and tried to pressure Penelope into marrying one of them) is treated as disloyalty by Telemachus and his father. When the translation of "serving woman" or "maid" is used, this seems like it could be a fair complaint on the men's part, even if the penalty is very harsh. But if the women are slaves, what choice do we imagine them having?

Slaves in the ancient world were habitually used by their owners for sexual purposes, which might often include allowing a guest to use a slave for sex. To expect a slave to refuse sex to a free elite man who is, at least technically, a guest in the household of her owner, is to expect an act of defiance that would almost certainly result in violence and quite probably cost her her life. Beyond that, under the principles of affirmative consent, which underlies sexual assault laws in Canada and a growing number of other jurisdictions, even if a slave were to agree (seemingly) willingly to sex, her situation would render such consent "coerced," which means it isn't consent at all. But the Homeric text never raises this question or shows any recognition that it is unfair to blame slaves for actions they had no choice about, and the slave-women are not allowed to speak in their own defense.

However, Atwood's *Penelopiad* explores this aspect of the slave's condition explicitly in the "Lament by the Maids": "If our owners or the sons of our owners or a visiting nobleman or the sons of a visiting nobleman wanted to sleep with us, we could not refuse. It did us no good to weep, it did us no good to say we were in pain."[27] In the shifting narrative perspective of the work, we also see the episode of the slavewomen's "treachery" from several viewpoints, that of Penelope, of a "Judge," and of an "Attorney for the Defence" in a trial of Odysseus for the murder of the slavewomen. In her version of events, Penelope says that she ordered the twelve women to spy on the suitors, and that as a result "several of the girls were unfortunately raped, others were seduced, or were hard pressed and decided that it was better to give in than to resist."[28] The Attorney for the Defence says that Odysseus had the women killed because "they'd had sex without permission . . . with [his] client's enemies."[29] The Judge sums up by saying "So, in effect, these maids were forced to sleep with the Suitors because if they'd resisted they would have been raped anyway, and much more unpleasantly?"[30]

Here we see Atwood grappling with the idea of consent to sex, and the role that a woman's status has in determining her options, and we can see that her views on the matter seem to have changed somewhat since she wrote *The Handmaid's Tale*, in a way that comes closer to the show's handling of the issue. But even so, we don't see the use of the word "slave" here—Odysseus is called the women's "master," which implies their slavery, but they are still called "maids," and at no point do they explicitly cite their enslaved status as a factor in their—or Odysseus's—guilt. This ambivalence about the use of the word "slave," even for characters who unambiguously have that legal and social status in the original text, is instructive for our understanding of Atwood's avoidance of the term in *The Handmaid's Tale*, and perhaps the choice of the showrunners to continue to avoid it in the TV show.

If Atwood made the enslaved status of the maids more obvious in *Penelopiad*, it would weaken the argument that they were to blame (and therefore that their murder was justified) so much that she would not have been able to explore the question of responsibility from as many different perspectives. Similarly, in *The Handmaid's Tale*, especially in the TV series, a central theme is June/Offred's alternation between feeling powerless and feeling that she can, in fact, make choices and take action and resist. In the same way, some of the guilt that June feels about the people who are killed, mutilated, or otherwise punished because they helped her might be lessened or removed if she regarded herself as a slave, and that guilt that she feels is a powerful element of her characterization and the emotional arc of the show.

A second reason for avoiding the word "slave" may be the assumption that a modern North American audience is almost certainly going to think of American slavery when they hear that word, and of all the history of race and racism that is connected to it. This complicates the Biblical allusion of the title, so that instead of thinking of the book of Genesis, a modern reader or viewer seeing *The Slave-Girl's Tale* would be much more likely to think of the antebellum southern United States. This highlights the difficulties of translating from one language, with its historical and cultural context, into another language with its own very different context. Though "slave" might be the most literally correct translation of the Biblical word, if it evokes a situation (such as race-based enslavement and a legacy of racism) that is irrelevant to the original text, that may make it a poor choice of translation.

CONNOTATION OF AMERICAN SLAVERY

What is particularly interesting about this reason for avoiding the word "slave" in *The Handmaid's Tale*, however, is that the issue of race, and the history of American slavery, are at the same time fundamental to and completely ignored by the story in both the book and the TV show, though in different ways in the two media. In the book, the Republic of Gilead appears to be a white supremacist state; there are no indications that any of the Commanders, Wives, or Handmaids are people of color, and the only reference to Black people is a passing mention on a TV news broadcast that the "Children of Ham" are being resettled to North Dakota, amid ongoing fighting in Detroit. Even recognizing this as a reference to Black people requires knowledge of certain racist interpretations of the story of Noah in Genesis. This has provoked critical discussion of how the story adopts and exploits elements of the experience of Black slaves in America without including Black people or acknowledging that all the issues depicted in the book have in fact happened to women in America before, just not to white women.[31] The show, however, portrays a multiracial Republic of Gilead, while never remarking on the race of any character, or demonstrating any racial prejudice among the characters.

The Waterford household is made up of a white Commander, Wife, and Handmaid, and a Latina Martha, but there are many nonwhite Handmaids, and some Commanders, Wives, Marthas, and Aunts are nonwhite as well. In another major change from the book, June's husband Luke Bankole (O-T Fagbenle) and best friend Moira (Samira Wiley) are Black. I will leave a full discussion of the portrayal of race in the TV show to other chapters, but for the purposes of this discussion, what is important is how this affects the potential meaning and connotations of the word "slave" in the show, and the implications of portraying the Handmaids as enslaved.

There is only one glancing reference to the history of American slavery, in the use of the term "Underground Femaleroad" by Moira in Hulu's Season One.[32] This is taken directly from the book,[33] and is where the book comes closest to the explicit parallel of the Handmaids to American slaves, even down to the detail that many of the people running this underground network are Quakers, well-known for their role in the original Underground Railroad. But in the book, Moira, who was being smuggled out this way, was white; in the show, she's Black. Even she, though, doesn't remark on the irony or the parallel with more than a slight laugh and the line (not in the book), "cute, right?" So, this careful avoidance of overt references to American slavery in general could be seen as one explanation of the avoidance of the word "slave" itself, for an audience that would not think primarily of ancient Hebrew or Greek culture when they heard that word. This shows the perils of translation from one culture to another, because the word in the bible that means "slave" refers to a very different cultural and societal context than the word "slave" in twenty-first-century America, but "servant" doesn't work either.

In suggesting these as possible explanations, I am not arguing that they are valid or good reasons to make the decision to omit the slavery element of the Biblical story and avoid its language in the modern story. In terms of the theme of choice and consent, it is true that in the book, where Offred says that she had a choice, portraying her as a slave would be inconsistent, though in fact the narrative of the book is full of deliberate internal inconsistencies. In the TV show, however, the thematic focus is on the "internal" choices June makes, and so there is no reason not to present her as a slave, and the reluctance to use the word seems almost to assume that actual historical slaves had no ability to internally or externally rebel, which is not at all true. Slaves in both the ancient world and the Americas were not passive recipients of abuse: they had interior lives, they resisted in many small ways and large ways, and they ran away and fought for their freedom.

Perhaps the showrunners do not think we would respect June or root for her the same way if she were a slave—and is this also perhaps why the enslaved status of the maids in *Penelopiad* is rarely emphasized, or conversely, why the slave-owning status of Odysseus and Penelope is often obscured in translations of the *Odyssey*. Even more, I would argue that historical choices by translators to obscure the importance of slaves in some of the foundational texts of English literature have actually made it harder for audiences (and writers) to conceive of enslaved people as fully rounded characters worthy of being the focus of a narrative.

The second possible explanation, that the terminology of slavery complicates the story by introducing the element of race and racial oppression, suggests a nonintersectional approach to the feminism of the show (and book), where only one type of oppression can be considered at a time, and where all members of the oppressed group are portrayed as suffering equally, with no impact from other factors such as race.[34] This flattening of women's experience is made particularly notable by the color-blind casting of the show, which leads to a diverse cast who are nonetheless presented as having a uniform experience.

Finally, if the showrunners fear that the audience might consider it too far-fetched to imagine that any government in the United States, even one that took power by military coup and imposed fundamentalist religious law, would reestablish slavery, this assumes a lack of historical understanding and also an audience who cannot identify with the fear of the government removing their basic rights other than those centering on sex and reproduction. Thus, while the TV show seems to be commenting on present issues (e.g., separation of children from mothers), by refusing to call enslavement by that name it elides the actual fears and experiences of those who truly have suffered that fate in America, both in the past under slavery and in the present. But there is another way to look at this problem. By leaving out the word "slave," but making so many clear parallels to slave experience and referencing so many aspects of historical slavery, are the showrunners perhaps commenting on the importance of language—and its manipulation—and how clever use of language can hide the reality of a situation? Regardless of the intentions of the writers and producers, I would argue that we can indeed take this lesson from the show: that words matter, and by naming something other than what it is, by not taking care with translations, and by removing text from its cultural context, we lose crucial information, and we greatly impede our ability to understand the world and why things happen. So, *The Handmaid's Tale* can show us the importance of studying the past, and also the need for always reconsidering and interrogating how we translate words and concepts from then to now.

NOTES

1. See Wilson's Translator's Note in: Homer, *The Odyssey,* translated by Emily Wilson (New York and London: W.W. Norton & Company, 2018), 88–89.

2. Genesis 30.

3. *The Handmaid's Tale*, "Women's Work," Season 2, Episode 8, directed by Kari Skogland, written by Nina Fiore and John Herrera, Hulu, June 6, 2018.

4. The two Hebrew words used to refer to Bilhah and Zilpah are "shiphchah" and "amah," which are defined as "female slave, maidservant and concubine" and "female slave, maid-servant" respectively (Holloday); see Wilda Gafney, *Womanist Midrash: A Reintroduction to the Women of the Torah and the Throne* (Louisville, KY: Westminster John Knox Press, 2017), 75–81, for an extensive discussion of the meaning of these two terms, and the status of women so described. The Greek word used to translate these terms in the Septuagint is *paidiske*, which means "young female slave, bondmaid" (LSJ). The Latin words used in the Vulgate translation are *ancilla, famula,* and *serva,* all of which mean "female slave," though *famula* can also mean "attendant" (OLD, L&S).

5. Bilhah is mentioned one other time, a few chapters later, in one verse in which Jacob's son Reuben "went and lay with Bilhah, his father's concubine" Genesis 35.22.

6. Gafney, *Womanist Midrash: A Reintroduction to the Women of the Torah and the Throne,* 58.

7. Peter Hunt, *Ancient Greek and Roman Slavery* (Hoboken, NJ: Wiley-Blackwell, 2018), 5.

8. Hunt, *Ancient Greek and Roman Slavery,* 17–19.

9. This argument is made extensively in the important work of Orlando Patterson, *Slavery and Social Death: A Comparative Study* (Boston: Harvard University Press, 1982).

10. The confusions between ancient and modern slavery, and the misconceptions that can arise from these confusions, are treated in Hunt, *Ancient Greek and Roman Slavery,* 26–28 and 31.

11. Homer, *The Odyssey,* translated by E. V. Rieu, 1961 ed. (Penguin Books, 1946) 22.417–474.

12. The two words used at various times to refer to these women are *dmoia* and *amphipolis.* The first is defined as "female slave, serving-woman" [Charlton T. Lewis, ed., *A Latin Dictionary* (Oxford: Clarendon Press, 1879)], the second as "a handmaid, a female attendant or servant, hardly to be distinguished from *dmoia*" [R. J. Cunliffe, *A Lexicon of the Homeric Dialect* (Oklahoma: University of Oklahoma Press, 1977)].

13. Homer, translated by Wilson, *The Odyssey,* 88–89.

14. For example: "Her translation is lyrical, radically readable, and as politically relevant as ever. . . . Of course, being the first woman to translate one of the foundational texts of Western literature carries with it an enormous amount of pressure. Wilson may not have intended to write the definitive feminist translation, but her reading of the poem was always going to explore gender on some level" (Charlotte Ahlin, "'The Odyssey' Has FINALLY Been Translated by a Woman. Here's Why That's So Important," *Bustle,* November 16, 2017, https://www.bustle.com/p/how-emily -wilson-the-first-woman-to-translate-the-odyssey-into-english-is-rethinking-gender -roles-in-the-greek-epic-3540304); and "The first version of Homer's groundbreaking work by a woman will change our understanding of it forever. . . . Armed with a sharp, scholarly rigour, she has produced a translation that exposes centuries of masculinist readings of the poem" (Charlotte Higgins, "The Odyssey Translated by Emily Wilson Review—a New Cultural Landmark," *The Guardian,* December 8, 2017).

15. Wilson expresses this idea in an interview: "It's been unsurprising that many people have asked me about how my gender identity (as a cis-gendered woman) affects my translation of the *Odyssey*. It's also unsurprising, but highly problematic, that hardly anyone (except me, so far!) seems to ask male classical translators how their gender affects their work" (Amy Brady, "How Emily Wilson Translated 'The Odyssey,'" *Chicago Review of Books*, [blog], January 16, 2018, https://chireviewof books.com/2018/01/16/how-emily-wilson-translated-the-odyssey/).

16. Margaret Atwood, *The Penelopiad* (Toronto: Vintage Canada, 2006), 13.

17. Margaret Atwood, *The Handmaid's Tale* (Toronto: McClelland & Stewart, 1985), 28. See also *The Handmaid's Tale*, "June," Season 2, Episode 1, directed by Mike Barker, written by Bruce Miller, Hulu, April 25, 2018.

18. There are other categories of people within Gilead who might also be considered to have the status of "enslaved"—most notably the women in Jezebel's and the workers in the colonies—but they are given no formal name by the state, so there is no mismatch between their label and their real status, and they are not the focus of the story in either the book or the show, so I will not be focusing on them here. I address the question of the Marthas below.

19. Hunt, *Ancient Greek and Roman Slavery*, 179; Patterson, *Slavery and Social Death*, 55–58.

20. In the book, there are two Marthas, named Cora and Rita, and we are told almost nothing about them. In the show, there is one Martha in the Commander's house, Rita (Amanda Brugel), and we learn a little about her backstory: she had a son who died in the fighting around the establishment of the Republic, and she appears to be genuinely religious, though all such judgments are difficult in the world of the show. At the same time she is kind to June (Elisabeth Moss) and does not seem happy with the situation or her position. At the end of the second season of the show (*The Handmaid's Tale*, "The Word," Season 2, Episode 13, directed by Mike Barker, written by Bruce Miller, Hulu, July 11, 2018), the Marthas are seen to have a secret communication network, and they help June escape with her baby in a way that is clearly reminiscent of the Underground Railroad of American slavery. It is unclear whether this network usually helps Marthas escape—in which case it strengthens the case that the Marthas are themselves also in the position of enslaved people—or is usually used to help Handmaids and people who are in immediate danger from the authorities—in which case the Marthas are more analogous to the free people who acted as stations on the Underground Railroad in historical times.

21. Luke 10.38–42. Martha reappears with her sister in the story of Lazarus in the Gospel of John, and there again she serves at table. The Greek verb used is *diakoneo*, and the Latin translation in the Vulgate is *ministrare*; neither word connotes servile status.

22. They are not even said to be obeying a divine command as is, for instance Mary, mother of Jesus, in Luke 1:41 when she calls herself the *doule* or "slavegirl" of God as she signals her willingness to bear God's son; here again the Greek word for female slave is usually translated as "maidservant." Mary's "slavery" is, however, metaphorical since her legal status is that of a free person, and so she is paradoxically choosing to act as a slave, a choice no actual slave has the freedom to make. Though

this whole passage is a direct allusion to the stories of Bilhah and Zilpah from Genesis, the theological implications of the Mary story are beyond the scope of this chapter. I will only point out that the Wives in Gilead wear blue, presumably because that is the color of Mary in Christian iconography, though this is never explicitly stated.

23. Atwood, *The Handmaid's Tale*, 107.

24. *The Handmaid's Tale*, "A Woman's Place," Season 1, Episode 6, directed by Floria Sigismondi, written by Wendy Straker Hauser, Hulu, May 17, 2017.

25. Some articulations of this principle can be seen in various definitions of Affirmative Consent: "Consent cannot be given when it is the result of any coercion, intimidation, force, or threat of harm" ("Definition of Affirmative Consent," *SUNY*, http://system.suny.edu/sexual-violence-prevention-workgroup/policies/affirmative -consent/). Consent is not considered to be present when "the consent is a result of someone abusing a position of trust, power or authority" ("The Law of Consent in Sexual Assault," *Leaf*, http://www.leaf.ca/the-law-of-consent-in-sexual-assault/).

26. Homer, translated by Wilson, *The Odyssey,* 22.463–64.

27. Atwood, *The Penelopiad,* 13–14.

28. Atwood, *The Penelopiad,* 115.

29. Atwood, *The Penelopiad,* 178.

30. Atwood, *The Penelopiad,* 182.

31. For discussion of elements of Black slavery drawn on for the depiction of the Handmaids, and extensive critiques of the book and show's depiction of race, see for instance Ana Cottle, "'The Handmaid's Tale': A White Feminist's Dystopia," *Medium*, May 17, 2017, https://medium.com/the-establishment/the-handmaids-tale -a-white-feminist-s-dystopia-80da75a40dc5; Noah Berlatsky, "Both Versions of *The Handmaid's Tale* Have a Problem with Racial Erasure," *The Verge*, June 15, 2017, https://www.theverge.com/2017/6/15/15808530/handmaids-tale-hulu-margaret -atwood-black-history-racial-erasure; and Max S. Gordon, "On Race and Hulu's *The Handmaid's Tale*," *Medium*, January 25, 2018, https://medium.com/@maxgordon19 /on-race-and-hulus-the-handmaid-s-tale-67bcd304a224.

32. *The Handmaid's Tale*, "Jezebel's," Season 1, Episode 8, directed by Kate Dennis, written by Kira Snyder, Hulu, May 31, 2017. As mentioned above, the end of the second TV season also shows an escape route, facilitated by a network of Marthas, that is very reminiscent of the Underground Railroad (*The Handmaid's Tale*, "The Word," Season 2, Episode 13, directed by Mike Barker).

33. Atwood, *The Handmaid's Tale,* 235.

34. There is one moment in the first season of the show in which the issue of class is briefly raised, when Offred's shopping partner tells her to stop making trouble because this life is better than the life on the streets that she used to endure. But this theme is not picked up again and was not present in the book.

WORKS CITED

Ahlin, Charlotte. "'The Odyssey' Has FINALLY Been Translated by a Woman. Here's Why That's So Important." *Bustle*, November 16, 2017. https://www.bustle.com/p/how-emily-wilson-the-first-woman-to-translate-the-odyssey-into-english-is-rethinking-gender-roles-in-the-greek-epic-3540304.

Atwood, Margaret. *The Handmaid's Tale*. Toronto: McClelland & Stewart, 1985.

———. *The Penelopiad*. Toronto: Vintage Canada, 2006.

Berlatsky, Noah. "Both Versions of *The Handmaid's Tale* Have a Problem with Racial Erasure." *The Verge*, June 15, 2017. https://www.theverge.com/2017/6/15/15808530/hand maids-tale-hulu-margaret-atwood-black-history-racial-erasure.

Brady, Amy. "How Emily Wilson Translated 'The Odyssey.'" *Chicago Review of Books* (blog), January 16, 2018. https://chireviewofbooks.com/2018/01/16/how-emily-wilson-translated-the-odyssey/.

Cottle, Ana. "'The Handmaid's Tale': A White Feminist's Dystopia." *The Establishment*, May 17, 2017. https://theestablishment.co/the-handmaids-tale-a-white-feminist-s-dystopia-80da75a40dc5.

Cunliffe, R. J. *A Lexicon of the Homeric Dialect*. Oklahoma: University of Oklahoma Press, 1977.

Gafney, Wilda C. *Womanist Midrash: A Reintroduction to the Women of the Torah and the Throne*. Louisville, KY: Westminster John Knox Press, 2017.

Glare, P. G. W. *Oxford Latin Dictionary*. 2nd ed. Oxford: Oxford University Press, 2012.

Gordon, Max S. "On Race and Hulu's *The Handmaid's Tale*." *Medium*, January 26, 2018. https://medium.com/@maxgordon19/on-race-and-hulus-the-handmaids-tale-67bcd304a224.

Higgins, Charlotte. "The Odyssey Translated by Emily Wilson Review—a New Cultural Landmark." *The Guardian*, December 8, 2017, https://www.theguardian.com/books/2017/dec/08/the-odyssey-translated-emily-wilson-review.

Holloday, William L. *A Concise Hebrew and Aramaic Lexicon of the Old Testament*. Grand Rapids, MI: William B. Eerdmans Publishing Company, 1971.

Homer. *The Odyssey*. Translated by E. V. Rieu. 1961 ed. Penguin Books, 1946.

———. *The Odyssey*. Translated by Emily Wilson. New York: W. W. Norton & Company, Inc., 2018.

Hunt, Peter. *Ancient Greek and Roman Slavery*. Hoboken, NJ: Wiley-Blackwell, 2018.

Lewis, Charlton T., ed. *A Latin Dictionary*. Oxford: Clarendon Press, 1879.

Liddell, Henry George, Robert Scott, and Sir Henry Stuart Jones. *A Greek-English Lexicon.* Clarendon Press, 1940.

Patterson, Orlando. *Slavery and Social Death: A Comparative Study*. Boston: Harvard University Press, 1982.

FILMS AND TELEVISION

The Handmaid's Tale. "A Woman's Place." Season 1, Episode 6. Directed by Floria Sigismondi. Written by Wendy Straker Hauser. Hulu, May 17, 2017.

The Handmaid's Tale. "Jezebel's." Season 1, Episode 8. Directed by Kate Dennis. Written by Kira Snyder. Hulu, May 31, 2017.

The Handmaid's Tale. "June." Season 2, Episode 1. Directed by Mike Barker. Written by Bruce Miller. Hulu, April 25, 2018.

The Handmaid's Tale. "The Word." Season 2, Episode 13. Directed by Mike Barker. Written by Bruce Miller. Hulu, July 11, 2018.

The Handmaid's Tale. "Women's Work." Season 2, Episode 8. Directed by Kari Skogland. Written by Nina Fiore and John Herrera. Hulu, June 6, 2018.

Chapter Three

Jezebel's

Sex and Marriage in Early Christian Theology

Kate McGrath

Toward the end of the book version of Margaret Atwood's *The Handmaid's Tale*, the Commander surprises Offred by taking her to Jezebel's, a brothel for high-status men.[1] The existence and operation of such a place in the strongly theocratic society of Gilead surely shocked most readers in the same way that it shocked Offred. In a society that held such absolute control over female chastity in particular, how can one explain the existence of quasi-official prostitution to facilitate sex for pleasure rather than procreation? How can a society that felt the need to construct such elaborate ceremonies to allow for the use of Handmaids as surrogates in the first place reconcile such wanton adultery?

   The answer to this paradox lies in early Christian theology on prostitution. Rather than categorically condemning prostitution, many early theologians begrudgingly argued that it served as a necessary evil for male lust. While certainly a sin, they stated that it was an outlet for male sexual desires that served to protect the sexual purity of innocent women, especially wives and virgins. As for the prostitute herself, these theologians rationalized that women were only prostitutes because of their own depravity, and such women would be otherwise condemned by God anyway. For them, then, it made sense to sacrifice an already sinful woman to male sexual desire rather than risk the corruption of a so-called reputable woman. Margaret Atwood has masterfully adapted this aspect of early Christian theology in creating her version of Jezebel's, and by understanding this dimension, it is possible to have a more complex and nuanced understanding of Gilead itself. As Atwood has said, she took a tremendous amount of inspiration from the "heavy-handed theocracy of seventeenth-century Puritan New England," with its strong emphasis on the Bible.[2] Understanding how early Christian theology interpreted passages on sex and prostitution then helps us to understand Atwood's vision more clearly.

The Commander (Joseph Fiennes) violates a number of taboos, and even laws, in taking Offred (Elisabeth Moss) to visit Jezebel's, depicted in the eighth episode of the first season of Hulu's TV adaptation. He first has her put on a sexy, sequined dress and high heels, completing the look with make-up. This is in stark contrast to the very modest red Handmaid's uniform and the bonnet that the sumptuary laws of Gilead strictly enforce. During the scene at the Women's Prayvagzas, the Commander who is preaching, emphasizes the importance of clothing as it relates to sin. Echoing Biblical passages, he says, "I will that women adorn themselves in modest apparels . . . with shamefacedness and sobriety; not with braided hair, or gold, or pearls, or costly array; But (which becometh women professing godliness) with good works."[3] When changing, Offred reflects on the experience of wearing such clothes. She thinks that "it carries with it the childish allure of dressing up. And it would be so flaunting, such a sneer at the Aunts, so sinful, so free. Freedom, like everything else, is relative."[4] The Commander then has Nick (Max Mighella) help sneak Offred out of the house, now dressed as a wife with Serena Joy Waterford's (Yvonne Strahovski) green coat, and past checkpoints, at one point even forcing Offred to duck down below the seat so that she cannot be spotted by the secret police who control the streets at night. This is a clear violation of curfew laws designed to regulate and enforce female movement and behavior. Once at Jezebel's, he further transgresses by offering Offred alcohol, something prohibited to the Handmaids given their role as potential mothers.

The biggest violation, however, is at the end of the evening when he has sexual intercourse with Offred in a secluded suite at Jezebel's. While he would not only have been well within his rights, and even obligated, to have sex with her the following evening, this sexual act, however, is prohibited, because it is outside the prescribed raping ritual elaborately enacted each month as a means of sanctifying the act. This sexual act is for the Commander's own sexual gratification as opposed to the virtue of reproduction. Each of these transgressions alone is dangerous to both the Commander and Offred; in fact, they could have caused the death of them both. Offred could have been sent to the colonies for her participation in this salacious evening with the Commander, while he could have been gravely persecuted for his sacrilegious act with a Handmaid. In order to understand how powerful these violations would have been to the society of Gilead, it is important to understand the basic Christian theology on marriage, sex, and reproduction that frame them.

CHRISTIAN THEOLOGY ON MARRIAGE AND SEX

From very early in the development of Christianity, there was a strong emphasis placed on the virtue of celibacy, especially on virginity. Early Christian theologians, starting with the apostle Paul, had called for Christians to follow the model of Jesus and reject sexual temptations. In 1 Corinthians, Paul advises virgins and widows: "It is good for them to stay unmarried, as I do. But if they cannot control themselves, they should marry, for it is better to marry than to burn with passion."[5] For Paul, marriage functioned as a remedy for sin, as a more acceptable outlet for sexual desire. It is why he articulates the concept of the conjugal debt. He says:

> The husband should fulfill his marital duty to his wife, and likewise the wife to her husband. The wife does not have authority over her own body but yields it to her husband. In the same way, the husband does not have authority over his own body but yields it to his wife. Do not deprive each other except perhaps by mutual consent and for a time, so that you may devote yourselves to prayer. Then come together again so that Satan will not tempt you because of your lack of self-control. I say this as a concession, not as a command. I wish that all of you were as I am.[6]

Because marriage is a remedy for sexual immorality, one has an obligation to be available for the sexual desires of one's spouse; otherwise, you risk having them satisfy those desires outside of the virtue of wedlock and thus mortally sinning. He is clear that celibacy is preferable, but marriage is allowed for those who cannot control their lust. This view certainly makes sense given Paul's real belief that the Apocalypse was imminent. If the end of the world was likely to come in his own lifetime, then what would be the point of reproduction? For Paul, marriage is a temporary fix for those who cannot wait for Christ's Second Coming.[7]

As the imminent nature of the Apocalypse receded, the focus on marriage as only a remedy for sexual immorality, nonetheless, persisted in Christian theology. Saint Jerome (d. 420), for example, was adamant that marriage did not fully remove the taint of sin from sexual intercourse, and as such, virginity was the preferred state for Christians. In fact, his only concession for a benefit of marriage was that it produced more virgins! He had no concerns about the ending of the human population, because he recognized that there would always be people who were unable to control their sexual appetites.[8] The view that even marriage did not completely guard against the sin of sex was grounded in early Christian understandings of what would become the doctrine of original sin.

Adam and Eve, the first humans, introduced sin into the world when first Eve and then Adam were tempted by a serpent to transgress God's commandment that they not eat from the Tree of Knowledge. After doing so, they recognized their own nudity, and they were punished by God. They were expelled from the Garden of Eden, and God said to Eve, "I will make your pains in childbearing very severe with painful labor you will give birth to children. Your desire will be for your husband and he will rule over you."[9] To Adam, God pronounces, "Cursed is the ground because of you; through painful toil you will eat food from it all the days of your life. It will produce thorns and thistles for you, and you will eat the plants of the field. By the sweat of your brow you will eat your food until you return to the ground, since from it you were taken; for dust you are and to dust you will return."[10]

This episode has profound importance for understanding theological interpretations of sex, marriage, and reproduction. First, many early Christian writers were quick to point out Eve's role in not only sinning but also leading Adam to sin. They theorized that the serpent, as the personification of Satan, chose to seduce Eve first, because he knew she would be an easier target. Moreover, these writers argued that he knew that because Adam and Eve were married and were "one flesh" that she could be an effective agent in also tempting Adam into sin. Tertullian (d. 220), for example, writes, "And do you not know that you are [each] an Eve? The sentence of God on this sex of yours lives in this age: the guilt must of necessity live too. You are the devil's gateway: you are the unsealer of that [forbidden] tree: you are the first deserter of the divine law: you are she who persuaded him whom the devil was not valiant enough to attack. You destroyed so easily God's image, man."[11] The implications for women in particular are profound. These early Christian writers argued that not only were women more morally corruptible and weaker in virtue, but this weakness was also very dangerous as they could harm male virtue as well. In their view, it is why God punished women with subordination to male authority and control. We can see similar ideas reflected in Gilead as well. In the scene of the Women's Prayvaganzas, the Commander preaching makes their sanctity as Handmaids directly tied to the redemption of Eve's sin. He says:

> "Let the women learn in silence with all subjection." Here he looks us over, "All," he repeats. "But I suffer not a woman to teach, nor to usurp authority over the man, but to be in silence. For Adam was first formed, then Eve. And Adam was not deceived, but the woman being deceived was in the transgression. Notwithstanding she shall be saved by childbearing, if they continue in faith and charity and holiness with sobriety."[12]

In addition, Eve's punishment was pain in childbirth, not childbirth itself. In other words, Adam and Eve would have presumably had sexual intercourse and reproduced before Eve's sin. This sparked numerous debates among early Christian writers about the nature of sexual reproduction before the introduction of sin. Saint Augustine of Hippo (d. 430), one of the principal Christian theologians, for example, argued that Adam and Eve would have had sex before sin, but it would have been without the experience of lust and completely controlled by their will.[13] It would have been more akin to a handshake rather than a passionate experience. It was the effect of sin that had transformed sex into one of lust and pleasure.[14] For Augustine this was particularly dangerous, as sexual climax briefly removes rational control from one's mind and body and thereby reducing humans to animals. It robs them of what makes humans alone created in the image of God. As a result, sex after the introduction of sin cannot wholly divorce itself from the taint of sin if done in lust. For Augustine, it is only blameless if solely for reproduction. Nonetheless, if done out of lust between married people, it is only a venial, not a mortal, sin.[15] The necessity of divorcing pleasure from sex is at the heart of the Handmaid Ceremony, as the ritual works to strip gratification from the act of intercourse. As Offred reflects:

> What's going on in this room, under Serena Joy's silvery canopy, is not exciting. It has nothing to do with passion or love or romance or any of those other notions we used to titillate ourselves with. It has nothing to do with sexual desire, at least for me, and certainly not for Serena. Arousal and orgasm are no longer thought necessary; they would be a symptom of frivolity merely, like jazz garters or beauty spots: superfluous distractions for the light-minded. Outdated . . . This is not recreation, even for the Commander. This is serious business. The Commander, too, is doing his duty.[16]

Sex solely for reproduction is a key component of Augustine's theological defense of the institution of marriage. In response to some of the harshest critics of marriage, Augustine worked out a larger justification for what he labeled the "goods" of marriage: reproduction, fidelity, and sacrament. He believed that marriage had been instituted by God as the first sacrament in Genesis; therefore, it was a sacred institution that was part of the divine plan. Since it was created by God for reproduction, then the desire for a married couple to reproduce was one of the goods of the institution. Moreover, he argued that marital fidelity was also a virtue, as husbands and wives practiced such loyalty to each other. He writes:

So when he says: "The woman who is unmarried thinks of the things of the Lord, that she may be holy in both body and spirit," this must not be interpreted to make us believe that a chaste Christian wife is not holy in body; for the following words were addressed to all the faithful: "Do you not know that your bodies are the temple within you of the holy Spirit, whom you have from God?" So the bodies of married couples who preserve fidelity to each other and to the Lord are also holy.[17]

Finally, he argued that it was a sacrament because it reflected the relationship between Christ and the Church, or a human reflection of the marriage of Christ to the Church. This also served what Augustine saw as the divine balance: just as Christ is head of the Church, so too is the husband head of his household. This too, then, could serve as justification for the patriarchal structuring of Gilead, which enforced women's submission to the authority of men. Just as Christ rules the Church, so too do men rule women.

PROSTITUTION IN CHRISTENDOM

All of this helps us to understand Augustine's position on prostitution in Christendom. St. Paul had condemned prostitution in 1 Corinthians. He says:

Do you not know that your bodies are members of Christ himself? Shall I then take the members of Christ and unite them with a prostitute? Never! Do you not know that he who unites himself with a prostitute is one with her in body? For it is said, "The two will become one flesh." But whoever is united with the Lord is one with him in spirit. Flee from sexual immorality. All other sins a person commits are outside the body, but whoever sins sexually, sins against their own body. Do you not know that your bodies are temples of the Holy Spirit, who is in you, whom you have received from God? You are not your own; you were bought at a price. Therefore honor God with your bodies.[18]

Augustine, like many Church theologians, however, viewed prostitution as an unfortunate, but necessary evil.[19] He writes, "Remove prostitutes from human affairs and you will destroy everything with lust."[20] For Augustine, some people would inevitably be tempted to commit sexual immorality. Having struggled with his own celibacy during his youth and having fathered at least one child with a concubine, Augustine understood firsthand the difficulties of controlling lust. Prostitution, then, served as an important sexual safety valve in that it at least gave men targets for their lust besides so-called respectable women, such as wives, widows, and virgins. He is able to rationalize it as most early Christian writers believed that prostitution was always a choice made by otherwise sinful women.[21] They did not give license for economic or other types of coercion. As Jerome defined, "A whore [prostitute] is one who is available for the lust of many men."[22] In other words, prostitutes are only prostitutes because of their own lustful desires, and therefore, they are already damned. Their damnation, however, might serve to protect the virtue of other women from male lust.[23]

Another feature of Augustine's reluctant advocacy for prostitution was that it could also preserve the chastity of married women. If reproduction is one of the goods of marriage, then having nonprocreative sex of any sort was a direct perversion of this good. He warned husbands not to debase their wives' virtues by having any sexual intercourse that could not result in offspring.[24] Instead, he argued that if a husband planned to compromise his own virtue that it was better for him to do so with a prostitute than with his wife. He writes, "But when a man seeks to exploit a woman's sexual parts beyond what is granted in this way, a wife behaves more basely if she allows herself rather than another to be used in this way."[25]

These ideas help us to understand the complicated relationship between prostitution and the Church. During the Middle Ages, secular rulers at certain times and in certain places tried to outlaw prostitution by shutting down brothels, because they saw them as places of intoxication and public disorder. Their authority, however, could not extend to ecclesiastical lands. For example, King Henry II tried to eliminate prostitution from medieval London, but the bishop of Winchester allowed brothels to be run across the Thames River in Southwark. While he established pretty restrictive regulations that were largely meant to protect male clients and the freedom of the prostitutes to quit, he did not ban it out right.[26] Rather he recognized that brothels served an unfortunate but necessary role in Christendom.

All of this brings us back to the scene in Jezebel's in Margaret Atwood's novel. Shortly after arriving in the club, Offred comments to her Commander that surely all that she sees should be forbidden. He replies that of course it is, but "everyone's human, after all."[27] When asked to elaborate, he says, "It means you can't cheat Nature. [. . .] Nature demands variety, for men. It stands to reason, it's part of the procreational strategy. It's Nature's plan. [. . .] Women know that instinctively. Why did they buy so many different clothes, in the old days? To trick the men into thinking they were several different women."[28] Like Augustine, the Commander believes that sexual immorality is inevitable, and there needs to be some outlet for male lust. Jezebel's serves this purpose, even if it officially violates all the norms and rules for Gileadean society. What makes it palatable for this theocratic society is that it functions like prostitution in early Christian theology. Male sexual lust will result in illegitimate sexual acts, and so the question is who should be the recipient of these desires. As for early Christian writers, the women working at Jezebel's are more suitable than the corruption of their wives and Handmaids. The Commander tells Offred that some of the women working in the club were previously prostitutes who "couldn't be assimilated," but that much of them were women, often from positions of academic or financial status, who could not accept their new subordinate reality.[29] Women, such as her friend Moira whom she discovers working there, who are seen as too dangerous to be assimilated, are given the choice of working at Jezebel's or being sent to the Colonies. Moira tells Offred:

> So after that [being captured while on the run], they said I was too dangerous to be allowed the privilege of returning to the Red Center. They said I would be a corrupting influence. I had my choice, they said, this or the Colonies. Well, shit, nobody but a nun would pick the Colonies. I mean, I'm not a martyr. If I'd had my tubes tied years ago, I wouldn't even have needed the operation. Nobody in here with viable ovaries, you can see the kind of problems it would cause. So here I am. They even give you face cream. You should figure out some way of getting in here. You'd have three or four good years before your snatch wears out and they send you to the boneyard. The food's not bad and there's drink and drugs if you want it, and we only work nights.[30]

Like prostitutes in early Christian writings, these women have no legitimate way of fitting into Gileadean society. They are too damned and corrupting to be suitable to be a wife or even a Handmaid or Martha. It is better that male sexual immortality be channeled in their direction rather than having a corrupting influence on otherwise so-called respectable women. Rather than seeing Jezebel's as a hypocritical aspect of Gileadean's theocratic society, it might be more insightful to see it functioning in much the same way and with the same justifications as prostitution in early Christian theology.

Early Christian theologians developed a complex understanding of the relationship between sex, marriage, and reproduction that emphasized the subordination of women to male authority. In their interpretation of Biblical passages, they see such subordination as part of the divine plan to remedy human sin. It was Eve's role in disobeying God and getting Adam to also disobey that was punished by the introduction of lust and pleasure into sexual intercourse. Because of their beliefs in the inherent dangers posed by women, these theologians argued that women should be subservient to their husbands and men in general. Such a model proved to be the guiding justification for the patriarchal structuring of Gilead. In addition, it was lust and pleasure that made sex always some form of sin. As a result, they preferred virginity as the highest state. At the same time, however, they recognized that marriage had been instituted as the first sacrament, and so it had to also have some legitimacy. Following Augustine, many theologians argued that reproduction was one of the principal goods of matrimony. Such ideas also surely influenced the creators of Gilead. The elaborate ceremony was scripted into a highly religious ritual that worked to both connect wife and Handmaid and remove sensual pleasure from the experience. After reading Scripture, the Handmaid would lay between the legs of the wife, reduced to a vessel to receive her commander's semen. All elements of sexual desire are intentionally removed from the experience. With such almost clinical sexual intercourse, there is very little to satisfy male lust and desire. As a result, they created Jezebel's, staffed with prostitutes who were deemed to be unfit for the roles of respectable women in Gilead. Much like early Christian theologians, Gilead authorities reasoned that it was better to have such an outlet for male lust rather than have the wives or Handmaids as its recipients. By understanding the theological justification for prostitution in early Christianity, it is easier to understand the appropriateness of the existence of Jezebel's in Gilead; it functioned as a necessary evil for male sexual desire.

NOTES

1. Margaret Atwood likely chose the name to reflect the Biblical figure of Jezebel from the Book of Kings. She was a Phoenician princess married to King Ahab, who got many of the Israelites to practice paganism. By the medieval period, she was also associated with sexually promiscuous and wantonly dressed women.

2. Margaret Atwood, "Haunted by *The Handmaid's Tale*," *The Guardian*, January 20, 2012. https://www.theguardian.com/books/2012/jan/20/handmaids-tale-margaret-atwood (accessed November 21, 2018).

3. Margaret Atwood, *The Handmaid's Tale* (New York: Penguin, 1986), 221. This is similar to 1 Timothy 2:9–10 ("I also want the women to dress modestly, with decency and propriety, adorning themselves, not with elaborate hairstyles or gold or pearls or expensive clothes, but with good deeds, appropriate for women who profess to worship God.") and 1 Peter 3:3–4 ("Your beauty should not come from outward adornment, such as elaborate hairstyles and the wearing of gold jewelry or fine clothes. Rather, it should be that of your inner self, the unfading beauty of a gentle and quiet spirit, which is of great worth in God's sight.")

4. Atwood, *The Handmaid's Tale*, 230–31.

5. 1 Cor 7:8–9. For more on Paul's views on sexual morality, see James A. Brundage, "'Allas! That Evere Love Was Synne': Sex and Medieval Canon Law," *The Catholic Historical Review* 72, no. 1 (1986): 1–13. See also Pat Cullum, "'Give Me Chastity': Masculinity and Attitudes to Chastity and Celibacy in the Middle Ages," *Gender & History* 25, no. 3 (2013): 621–36.

6. 1 Cor 7:3–7.

7. Kyle Harper, "Porneia: The Making of a Christian Sexual Norm," *Journal of Biblical Literature* 131, no. 2 (2012): 363–83.

8. Philip Schaff and Henry Wace, eds., "Jerome: The Principal Works of Saint Jerome," in *Nicene and Post-Nicene Fathers,* Series II, vol. 6 (Grand Rapids, MI: Wm. B. Eerdmans Publishing, 1892), 374.

9. Gen 3:16.

10. Gen 3:17–19.

11. Tertullian, *On the Dress of Women*, ch. 1 (http://www.tertullian.org/anf/anf04 /anf04-06.htm).

12. Atwood, *The Handmaid's Tale*, 221. It is also a reference to 1 Corinthians 14:34. "Women should remain silent in the churches. They are not allowed to speak, but must be in submission, as the law says."

13. This was, however, not universally accepted. Origen, for example, argued that sex and death were the punishments for sin. See discussion in Brundage, "Sex and Medieval Canon Law," 4. For more on Augustine see Miles Hollingworth, *Saint Augustine of Hippo: An Intellectual Biography* (Oxford: Oxford University Press, 2013); Henry Chadwick, *Augustine of Hippo: A Life* (Oxford: Oxford University Press, 2009); and Roland J. Teske, *Augustine of Hippo: Philosopher, Exegete, and Theologian: A Second Collection of Essays* (Milwaukee: Marquette University Press, 2009).

14. Vern L. Bullough, "Sex Education in Medieval Christianity," *The Journal of Sex Research* 13, no. 3 (1977): 185–86.

15. Brundage, "Sex and Medieval Canon Law," 6–8.

16. Atwood, *The Handmaid's Tale*, 94–95.

17. Augustine of Hippo, *De Bono Coniugali*, ed. and trans. P. G. Walsh (Oxford: Oxford University Press, 2001), 27.

18. 1 Cor 6:15–20.

19. It was, however, not universally accepted. John Chrysostom, for example, still condemned prostitution with anyone who was not one's spouse. See discussion in Harper, 382.

20. Augustine, *De Ordine* 2.4, Patrologiae Cursus Completus Series Latina, ed. J. P. Migne (Paris, 1845), 32:1000.

21. This is paralleled in Gilead. The women working at Jezebel's are given a choice: Jezebel's or the Colonies. It is, of course, no true choice in that the fate of those in the Colonies is grim and brutal. Moira also tells Offred that they are given great liberties, including sexual freedoms because "the Aunts figure we're all damned anyway, they've given up on us, so it doesn't matter what sort of vice we get up to, and the Commanders don't give a piss what we do in our off time." Atwood, *The Handmaid's Tale*, 249.

22. Jerome, Epist. 64.7 ad Fabiolem. Cited in James A. Brundage, "Prostitution in Medieval Canon Law," *Signs* 1, no. 4 (1976): 827.

23. Ruth Mazo Karras, "The Regulation of Brothels in Later Medieval England," *Signs* 14, no. 2, Working Together in the Middle Ages: Perspectives on Women's Communities (1989): 399–400. See also Marjorie O'Rourke Boyle, "Augustine in the Garden of Zeus: Lust, Love, and Language," *The Harvard Theological Review* 83, no. 2 (1990): 117–39.

24. For Augustine, reproduction remained a good of marriage even in the cases of infertility or old age. As long as the couple did not do anything that could have limited

conception, it still left the possibility for God's will, as the Bible provides examples, like Abraham and Sarah, of couples gifted by God with offspring after menopause.

25. Augustine, *De Bono Coniugali*, 27. Kyle Harper argues that it was the status of the woman that determined the nature of the sin. The more problematic her status, the more of an abomination it was ("Porneia," 363–83).

26. Ruth Mazo Karras includes these regulations in her appendix ("Regulation of Brothels," 427–33).

27. Atwood, *The Handmaid's Tale*, 237.

28. Atwood, *The Handmaid's Tale*, 237.

29. Atwood, *The Handmaid's Tale*, 238. Offred's Commander says that women, like the sociologist and business executive he points out to Offred, prefer this work to the alternative. He implies that their former positions make them incapable of submitting to the patriarchal authority of Gilead.

30. Atwood, *The Handmaid's Tale*, 249.

WORKS CITED

Atwood, Margaret. *The Handmaid's Tale*. New York: Penguin, 1986.

———. "Haunted by *The Handmaid's Tale*." *The Guardian*, January 20, 2012. Accessed November 21, 2018. https://www.theguardian.com/books/2012/jan/20/handmaids-tale-margaret-atwood.

Augustine of Hippo. *De Bono Coniugali*. Edited and translated by P. G. Walsh. Oxford: Oxford University Press, 2001.

———. *De Ordine*. Patrologiae Cursus Completus Series Latina. Edited by J. P. Migne. Paris, 1845.

Boyle, Marjorie O'Rourke. "Augustine in the Garden of Zeus: Lust, Love, and Language." *The Harvard Theological Review* 83, no. 2 (1990): 117–39.

Brundage, James A. "'Allas! That Evere Love Was Synne': Sex and Medieval Canon Law." *The Catholic Historical Review* 72, no. 1 (1986): 1–13.

———. "Prostitution in Medieval Canon Law." *Signs* 1, no. 4 (1976): 825–45.

Bullough, Vern L. "Sex Education in Medieval Christianity." *The Journal of Sex Research* 13, no. 3 (1977): 185–86.

Chadwick, Henry. *Augustine of Hippo: A Life*. Oxford: Oxford University Press, 2009.

Cullum, Pat. "'Give Me Chastity': Masculinity and Attitudes to Chastity and Celibacy in the Middle Ages." *Gender & History* 25, no. 3 (2013): 621–36.

Harper, Kyle. "Porneia: The Making of a Christian Sexual Norm," *Journal of Biblical Literature* 131, no. 2 (2012): 363–83.

Hollingworth, Miles. *Saint Augustine of Hippo: An Intellectual Biography*. Oxford: Oxford University Press, 2013.

Karras, Ruth Mazo. "The Regulation of Brothels in Later Medieval England," *Signs* 14, no. 2, Working Together in the Middle Ages: Perspectives on Women's Communities (1989): 399–433.

Schaff, Philip, and Henry Wace, eds. *Nicene and Post-Nicene Fathers,* Series II, Vol. 6. Grand Rapids, MI: Wm. B. Eerdmans Publishing, 1892.

Tertullian. *On the Dress of Women.* Accessed November 21, 2018. http://www.tertul lian.org/anf /anf04/anf04-06.htm.

Teske, Roland J. *Augustine of Hippo: Philosopher, Exegete, and Theologian: A Second Collection of Essays.* Milwaukee: Marquette University Press, 2009.

FILMS AND TELEVISION

The Handmaid's Tale. "Jezebel's." Season 1, Episode 8. Directed by Kate Dennis. Written by Kira Snyder. Hulu, May 31, 2017.

Chapter Four

Literary Narration, Complicity, and Political Dystopia in Margaret Atwood's *The Handmaid's Tale*

Katherine Sugg

From the opening lines of Margaret Atwood's 1985 novel, *The Handmaid's Tale,* we are put into the mind and immersed in the voice of the main character and narrator, the titular "Handmaid" known as Offred. But Offred starts off speaking as "we" not "I" ("We slept in what had once been the gymnasium"), and this collective identity and experience is the novel's first indication of its larger project, a project of revealing who "we" are through one character's voice and perspective, and her story (or tale). *The Handmaid's Tale* was also Atwood's first foray into speculative fiction—an area of literature in which she has since become extraordinarily successful and influential; Atwood has commented (somewhat controversially) on this move to the so-called ghetto of genre fiction from the relative literary heights that she had already attained as a well-regarded poet and novelist by the mid-1980s.[1] Atwood's recently published new preface to the novel, following the immense popularity of the Hulu television show, underlines her desire to make the story of *The Handmaid's Tale* not just plausible, but "real"— particularly through the strategies of literary representation and the facts of history: "No imaginary gizmos, no imaginary laws, no imaginary atrocities. God is in the details, they say. So is the devil."[2]

These "details" are clearly historical in nature for Atwood, but they are also the primary material of literary realism: the verisimilitude in description and psychological characterization that creates both a recognizable linguistic facsimile of setting and character and plausible sequences of cause and effect—using words alone. Yet, although Atwood also insists in this preface that she wanted to avoid "veering into allegory," the genre of dystopian speculative fiction is arguably always allegorical and always political (and historical), as renowned literary theorist Walter Benjamin (1928) insists.[3] Imagined dystopias, like apocalypses, reflect fears, or warnings, about the present, and the past, even though they are usually set in a possible, if not plausible, future. The wide-ranging and influential American literary scholar Frank Kermode (1967) argues that apocalypse narrative is, like all fiction, an exercise in temporal imagination, one that "concords" an imagined past and a projected future to align with investments and conceptions of the present moment. For Kermode, writing in the previous apocalypse-soaked era of the 1960s, the danger of apocalypse narratives is that when their fictionality is forgotten, "we sink quickly into myth, into stereotype."[4]

The Handmaid's Tale includes various literary signals that underline its fictionality, even as they also emphasize that the problematic situation in which Offred finds herself is not just a harrowing picture of how bad things could get: it's a satire of what women are and have been made to be (and have let themselves become) circa 1986, as well as now. The novel's form of narration, using the voice of Offred—whose earlier, original, and real name we never learn in the novel—is what subtly forces readers to see, and to examine, the operation of convenient fictions and biases within Offred's consciousness, and by implication, our own. Among these convenient fictions forged in the long history of misogyny and patriarchy is the assumption that begins the novel: that it's always that other woman who is most suspicious and just "does such things to look good" as Offred complains about Ofglen, another "Handmaid" who is her newly assigned companion for excursions outside the households of the Commanders. In the novel Offred continues, "I think of her as a woman for whom every act is done for show, is acting rather than a real act." Offred also admits that "but that is what I must look like to her, as well. How can it be otherwise?" which indicates the thread of self-awareness and intelligence that makes Offred's narration so compelling and persuasive—we believe her information and identify with her responses to the new and dangerous situation she finds herself in. Like Offred, the reader knows that even as we try to be good people, all of us are "out to make the best of it."[5]

Such revealing pronouncements are among the many "details" that keep *The Handmaid's Tale* both psychologically plausible and historically real, rather than mythical. Because literary narration makes tangible, and analyzable, the dynamics of consciousness and how our perceptions are shaped and colored by our assumptions about others as well as ourselves, it is a powerful vehicle for the exploration and critical understanding of how we all are shaped by histories and ideologies, even those that we might hate and resist—such as the religious patriarchal dictatorship of "Gilead" that has been recently installed in the novel's storyworld. *The Handmaid's Tale* thus provides an opportunity to teach and carefully examine the mechanics of literary fiction and what they allow us to "see" and to learn, connecting to key themes of both speculative fiction and cultural studies.

THE COMPLICITY OF LANGUAGE

Equally important, the novel invites the vocabulary of narratology and close reading, which encourages students to understand and analyze terms such as limited first person narration, focalization, plot, and discourse. In so doing, it also offers the opportunity to consider how language, especially Atwood's language, can reveal the dynamics of "our" internal complicity and, arguably, cowardice. As a pedagogical and theoretical tool, then, *The Handmaid's Tale* allows a double vision at both the societal and the individual levels, encouraging feminist theoretical and historical analyses along with an analysis of psychic dynamics and language. *The Handmaid's Tale* performs its revelation through the figure of Offred, using her own discourse and point of view, and it does this in ways that I suggest are often more searing and harrowing than even the acclaimed Hulu TV series can manage. In this chapter, I outline a few key elements and episodes that make possible this double vision and the novel's complex critique of patriarchal society and its profound impact on us all.

The dynamics and rigor of literary representation are particularly easy to track in *The Handmaid's Tale*, especially by comparing some of Atwood's choices and those of the recent television series adaptation of the novel: in particular, how the reader/viewer "sees" Offred and relates to her predicament.[6] I suggest that the novel follows other "spec fic" writers, notably Octavia Butler, in its relentless exposure of Offred's psychic maneuverings as well as the reader's seduction into an identification, a complicity, with her character's emotions and, therefore, her choices. The clarity with which the narrator, Offred—as in "Of Fred"—displays her cowardice and unconscious complicity with the forces that have brought the world to this point is what makes the novel most effective in its gradual "revelation" of what this imaginary gender dystopia shares with our own time. Offred is a smart, witty, and careful observer of herself and those around her, but she can't help being both self-interested and self-preserving.

A similar narrator, the protagonist Dana in Octavia Butler's landmark 1979 neoslavery novel, *Kindred,* notes with alarm, "Us, the children . . . I never realized how easily people could be trained to accept slavery."[7] Although this moment appears at first to be an epiphany, a realization, and coming to consciousness, some astute critics have noted that Butler shapes Dana's voice and perspective to reveal her character's persistently limited understanding of both her position and the role of her own choices and actions in perpetuating the horrors of 1850s antebellum slavery, which Dana experiences as a time traveler from 1976 Los Angeles. As contemporary critic Alys Eve Weinbaum (2013) writes, "Butler subtly portrays Dana as an unreliable narrator who appears blind to her complicity in the historical violence that she witnesses, and who thus possesses a blinkered view of her present, and a diminished capacity to accurately represent it."[8]

The Handmaid's Tale is framed by two moments, which are as much shifts in Offred's mood as they are specific events, that give the reader a similar window into her character and thus ourselves. The opening of the novel, as I mention, focuses on one of Offred's walks with Ofglen, who is her assigned partner in the Handmaids' collective daily excursion to do the household shopping and a bit of wandering through the streets of a near-future Cambridge, Massachusetts. Atwood takes advantage of the medium of literature to underline the two temporalities of narrative—the time and sequence of events that make up the plot—that is, the time of the story itself ("histoire" or plot) and the fictional or "reading" time of how that story is told, what narratologists call the "discourse-time."[9] In the novel, we accompany Offred out of the house and to the street to meet Ofglen, whom she has walked with for about two weeks. As they proceed to do the shopping, they take their "usual" meandering path through Cambridge: along the river, then over to see "the wall" where recent enemies of the Gilead regime are hung after being tortured and killed. When they set out, Offred notes, "The truth is that she is my spy, as I am hers."[10] Here and throughout the novel, Atwood deploys the standard modernist literary strategy of conveying information about the setting and characters' mind-sets through Offred's tone, word choices, and judgments as she engages in plot-time actions. By "musing" in her first person voice about the Handmaids being one another's spies, Offred underlines the corrupting impact of this totalitarian regime and its oppressive patriarchal power on personal interactions—particularly between women.

In addition to these informative judgments, the dialogue further tells us about other violence and distortions exposed by the rhetoric of Gilead, as in the Handmaids' ritual exchanges of information and the codes of the expected responses: "'The war is going well, I hear,' she says. 'Praise be,' I reply. 'We've been sent good weather.' 'Which I receive with joy.'"[11]

THE TELEVISION HULU ADAPTATION

The first season of the Hulu TV series adaptation of *The Handmaid's Tale* (2017) follows the novel closely and also highlights the omnipresence of this language of Christian and Puritan piety in ways that signal its "performative" purposes: displaying the codes of this dystopic society while also ironically signaling the gap between Offred's (Elisabeth Moss's) downcast eyes and rote utterances with her real feelings. On television, that gap is indicated through a heavy reliance on close-up shots of Offred's face plus extensive use of voice-over narration, much of which echoes Offred's narration in the novel. However, the long-seeming period of mutual suspicion and watchfulness that marks Offred and Ofglen's/Emily's (Alexis Bledel) eventual friendship in the novel (a period that lasts more than halfway through the novel, to chapter 27) is resolved by the end of the first episode of the television series, which has interesting effects that reverberate in how we understand Offred's character. The novel Offred is less resolute and more passive than TV Offred, and while Atwood's Offred can be cannily self-aware, she also reveals that she isn't quite as honest with herself, or the reader, as she claims. In an early chapter, she watches Nick, the Commander's driver and later her lover, as he smokes a cigarette: "Despite myself, I think of how he might smell. Not fish or decaying rat; tanned skin, moist in the sun, filmed with smoke. I sigh, inhaling."[12] When Nick catches her looking, he puts out his cigarette and winks at her. Offred is surprised, even shocked at the risk Nick has taken, "Perhaps he was merely being friendly. Perhaps he saw the look on my face and mistook it for something else. Really what I wanted was the cigarette."[13] Here, the alert reader pauses, wondering at the lie about "what I wanted."

Literary narration exposes these contradictions within consciousness and through "discourse" signals their complex roots in social and personal histories. *The Handmaid's Tale* tracks the etiology (origins and reasons) of Offred's contradictory urges toward desire, rebellion, and resignation through her mental digressions in her memories as well as through her internal negotiations and justifications.

The second important framing moment occurs in the last forty pages of the novel: her affair with Nick and its impact on her. By now, she and Ofglen have recognized one another—quite literally "seen" the other's face—and have had the conversation in which each admits she thought the other was "a true believer." It is Ofglen who comments, "'You were always so stinking pious.' 'So were you,' I reply. I want to laugh, shout, hug her.'"[14] Ofglen uses this opportunity to try to recruit Offred to an underground resistance group, imploring "You can join us." Offred initially responds internally with joy, then suspicion, "It occurs to me that she may be a spy, a plant, sent to trap me; such is the soil in which we grow."[15] Offred's hesitation to act, specifically to rebel, is something she understands about herself, though not with pride. A bit later she reunites briefly with her best friend Moira, a college friend and lesbian who is now a government prostitute; Offred is disappointed by Moira's resignation to a life of "drink and drugs" after nearly escaping to Canada the time she managed to get away from the Aunts at the training school for the Handmaids.[16] Offred comments to herself, "I don't want her to be like me. Give in, go along, save your skin."[17] A few pages later, Offred must talk herself into not recoiling in revulsion when her Commander wants to have "real," that is unofficial, sex with her in one of the brothel's rooms. Offred struggles to comply convincingly: "Fake it, I scream at myself inside my head. You must remember how . . . Bestir yourself. Move your flesh around, breathe audibly. It's the least you can do."[18]

DECEPTION AND TRANSGRESSION

These desperate, self-negating words mark the end of chapter 30, and the next chapter opens with Offred being helped by the Commander's wife, Serena Joy, to sneak into Nick's quarters. The three have arranged this tryst in order to get Offred pregnant. Here, the details that distinguish the novel from the television presentation of Offred and her actions, choices, and mind-set further reveal their significance. In the television show, Moira (Samira Wiley) and Offred plan the escape from the Aunts together, as seen in a flashback that has them equally eager to make it work; but in the novel, that escape is a "story"—one that Offred hears from other Handmaids and retells to the reader as a distraction from her own, about which she says repeatedly, "I don't want to be telling this story."[19] So TV Offred has made active and planned efforts to escape since losing her husband Luke (O-T. Fagbenle) and young daughter in their initial effort to get out of Gilead months or years earlier (another story that Offred returns to often in her mind but does not want to fully tell, or remember, as it is so painful). In the TV series when Offred and Nick (Max Minghella) have their arranged sex, Serena Joy (Yvonne Strahovski) stays in the room with them, looking away as the two copulate wordlessly, eyes open and without expression; then later they meet secretly and have intense, "sexy" sex. The novel, however, uses both Offred's consciousness and the tricks of narration to reveal this split more subtly and show Offred's complex and messy ambivalence—largely an ambivalence toward her feelings about "love," as well as Nick.

In the novel, Serena Joy does not take her to his room; Offred goes alone to his apartment and describes the scene in affecting terms: "Outside, like punctuation, there's a flash of lightening; almost no pause then the thunder. He's undoing my dress, a man made of darkness, I can't see his face, and I can hardly breathe, hardly stand, and I'm not standing. His mouth is on me, his hands, I can't wait and he's moving, already, love, it's been so long, I'm alive in my skin, again, arms around him, falling and water softly everywhere, never-ending. I knew it might only be once."[20] But the next paragraph starts with this sentence: "I made that up. It didn't happen that way. Here is what happened." The reader is pulled up, stopped in her own progress to the end of the novel by this admission, and the foray into falsehood and unreliability that Offred, the narrator, has exposed and risked. When she resumes this "story," Offred describes her encounter with Nick as more awkward and a little "brutal" but also suggests there were feelings between them: "I knew it might only be once. Good-by, I thought, even at the time, good-by. There wasn't any thunder though, I added that in. To cover up the sounds, which I am ashamed of making." But even now, the next sentence starts, "It didn't happen that way either. I'm not sure how it happened; not exactly."[21] In two pages, Offred has told the story effectively three times, each with a distinct detail that puts the whole event into question, as well as the veracity, and accuracy, of her presentation of that event. Which version of the story is true? This is a question both Offred and Atwood have forced the reader to ask herself. But Offred ends the chapter evasively, hinting at even other questions we have not thought to ask, "I would like to be without shame. I would like to be shameless. I would like to be ignorant. Then I would not know how ignorant I was."[22]

OFFRED'S ROLE AS NARRATOR

Offred's narration throughout *The Handmaid's Tale* is digressive and evasive, even when she is narrating what seems to be present-tense actions that move the story, the histoire, or plot, forward. After sex with Nick, Offred speaks directly to her reader, who is a "you" that "I will to exist" even though she has admitted again, "I wish this story were different."[23] Here, Atwood foregrounds Offred's discourse-time of both her telling and our reading, what we begin to realize is a highly constructed representation of her actions and thoughts during the events she describes. Giving the reader a different "Offred" (less heroic and resolute and more passive and complicit than TV Offred) means that we experience a different narrative, one whose purpose and goal are insistently literary, as well as political and historical. Once Offred resumes the "story-time" of Gilead and her affair with Nick, the novel moves quickly through its sequence of events, most of which occur in the television adaptation of the first season as well.

I am suggesting that the impact of Atwood's Offred is stranger, more difficult than even the harrowing television series, though this chapter cannot offer a detailed analysis of both. One key plot change is that the violent "salvaging" that punctuates the first episode of the first season in the Hulu TV series occurs almost at the end of the novel, after Offred confesses that "I went back to Nick. Time after time, on my own, without Serena knowing." She oscillates in these pages between sex with Nick and sex with the

Commander where "I close my eyes . . . I do not want to see him up close."[24] For Offred, these personal sexual experiences frame and organize her world and her thoughts, but it turns out that Ofglen has continued her efforts to get Offred's help and participation in the resistance. "The things she whispers seem to me unreal. What use are they, for me, now?" Offred isn't interested: "I can't, I say to Ofglen. I'm too afraid. Anyway I'd be no good at that. I'd get caught."[25]

Both not wanting to "see" the Commander and repeating—in a "murmur"— her "lazy" refusals to Ofglen, Offred shows herself to be a master of avoidance, as well as passivity. She even admits, "The fact is that I no longer want to leave, escape, cross the border to freedom. I want to be here, with Nick, where I can get to him."[26] Like the overdetermined suspicion between women fighting for individual survival in an oppressively literal "man's world," the word "love" weaves through *The Handmaid's Tale* as a tortured memory, dream, and perhaps illusion. Much of Offred's narration of love, especially for her husband Luke and lost daughter, is painful, melancholy, and grieving, but her latching onto Nick, or the idea of him, toward the novel's end offers another facet of her desire to "make the best of it" and implies that her "love" has become an excuse for solipsistic blindness and acquiescence to the status quo.

At the climactic "Salvaging," the Handmaids and the Commanders' Wives are gathered in an assembly to witness the hanging of enemies of the state, and the Handmaids are called on to beat to death a man accused of raping a Handmaid. Offred is horrified and "nauseated," especially when she sees Ofglen strike first, though it turns out that he was "one of us" and Ofglen had kicked him to knock him unconscious; a merciful act that she pays for with her life in the novel, whereas in the TV adaptation she becomes a leader of the resistance.[27]

The final two chapters that follow move quickly to the end of Offred's story. She begins the second-to-last chapter with "Things are back to normal" as another sign of her will to maintain this normalcy, and acceptance, in the face of events that are clearly and dangerously overtaking her. That same night, in the last chapter, a black van appears, for her it seems, and Nick tells her it's safe for her to go with them: "'Trust me,' he says."[28] As she steps into the van, not knowing whether it is taking her to prison and death or toward some chance at freedom, Offred muses in her final words, "I have given myself over into the hands of strangers, because it can't be helped."[29]

As Butler does in *Kindred*, Atwood slyly works on our identification with Offred, and our sympathy with her personal situation and history, in order to highlight the historical continuity—the plausible similarities—between Gilead and our own society, and thus between Offred and the reader. Her excuses and delays in acting reflect a complex of factors and historical currents that the novel traces in various details of its discourse. One key revelation of her wavering consciousness is that the fictional, but realistically rendered, context of the 1980s prepares Offred psychologically to survive and adapt to the insane escalation of patriarchal dominance and control in Gilead. She has been internally trained, and perhaps is inclined by temperament, to "go along." Offred's ironic awareness of both the old "rules" (about dating and managing masculine dominance, and threat) and the new, more extreme, ones in Gilead helps her cope, and, it seems, survive.

What Offred reveals in her love story with Nick, as well as many fascinating moments where she voices her inclinations to trust or believe in some personal connection with the Commander, is her stubborn internal compliance to patriarchy. Because the novel version of *The Handmaid's Tale* is as much a satire as it is a dystopic thriller, its purposes are distinct from the television series. The novel's coda, entitled "Historical Notes on *The Handmaid's Tale*" underlines this divergence in tone and purpose through its metafictional reflection on the story we have just read, but now from the perspective of an academic conference in 2195, introduced as the "proceedings of the Twelfth Symposium on Gileadean Studies"[30] (see chapter 22 by Cecilia Gigliotti in this volume). Oddly and rather horrifyingly, this snarky imagined academic discussion of the "document" of Offred's narrative reveals that just as our time of late twentieth and now early twenty-first century United States could produce the rules, the assumptions, and the hierarchies around gender and reproduction that are installed in Gilead, even almost two hundred years later, the conference's own "discourse" shows that gender (and governance, knowledge, and class) norms remain uncannily the same.

When the featured lecturer, a male professor, makes a rather obscene joke about "enjoying" both last night's dinner and the female professor who is presiding over the meeting ("now we are enjoying an equally charming Arctic Chair"), Atwood adds yet another detail from the language of sexism to warn what might stick around, the linguistic "devils" that reveal how nothing really changed that much to produce Gilead and nothing really changed once it was gone. Now that's dystopic.

NOTES

1. See Margaret Atwood, *The MaddAddam Trilogy: Oryx and Crake* (2003), *The Year of the Flood* (2009), *MaddAddam* (2013). Atwood and acclaimed science fiction author Ursula LeGuin (1929–2018) had an infamous ongoing debate about the terminology and literary implications of "science fiction," with Atwood resisting the label and eventually embracing "speculative fiction." For some overview, see "Margaret

Atwood on Science Fiction, Dystopias, and *Intestinal Parasites*," *WIRED,* September 21, 2013, https://www.wired.com/2013/09/geeks-guide-margaret-atwood/.

2. Margaret Atwood, *The Handmaid's Tale*, First Anchor Books Edition, 1998 ("Introduction," April 2017, xiv).

3. Walter Benjamin, *The Origin of German Tragic Drama*, translated by John Osborne (Verso Press, 2003; originally published in German in 1928).

4. Frank Kermode, *The Sense of an Ending: Studies in the Theory of Fiction* (Oxford University Press, 1967), 124.

5. Atwood, *The Handmaid's Tale*, 31.

6. *The Handmaid's Tale* (TV Series), created by Bruce Miller, produced by Warren Littlefield, Margaret Atwood, Dorothy Fortenberry, aired April 26, 2017, on Hulu.

7. Octavia Butler. *Kindred* (Beacon Press, 1979), 101.

8. Alys Eve Weinbaum, "The Afterlife of Slavery and the Problem of Reproductive Freedom," *Social Text 115* 31, no. 2 (Summer 2013): 53.

9. Seymour Chatman writes, "What is fundamental to narrative, regardless of medium, is that these two time orders are independent." "What Novels Can Do That Films Can't (And Vice Versa)," in *Critical Inquiry* 7, no. 1 (Autumn 1980): 111.

10. Atwood, *The Handmaid's Tale*, 19.

11. Ibid.

12. Atwood *The Handmaid's Tale*, 18

13. Ibid.

14. Atwood, *The Handmaid's Tale,* 168.

15. Atwood, *The Handmaid's Tale,* 168–69.

16. Offred's narration includes many flashbacks to her time at the secret training school, where fertile women were indoctrinated by the "Aunts" who work for the new regime to become surrogate mothers for powerful Commanders whose wives, like much of the population of the United States, cannot produce healthy babies. In both the novel and the television show, these flashbacks also include much information about the ideology, practices, and evolution of Gilead's society and state practices of patriarchal control and domination; and in both, characters reveal that the infertility in question is often actually the men's.

17. Atwood, *The Handmaid's Tale,* 249.

18. Atwood, *The Handmaid's Tale*, 255.

19. Atwood, *The Handmaid's Tale*, 273.

20. Atwood, *The Handmaid's Tale*, 261.

21. Atwood, *The Handmaid's Tale,* 263.

22. Ibid.

23. Atwood, *The Handmaid's Tale*, 268, 267.

24. Atwood, *The Handmaid's Tale*, 268, 269.

25. Atwood, *The Handmaid's Tale,* 271.

26. Ibid.

27. Atwood, *The Handmaid's Tale,* 280. The Salvaging occurs in episode 1 of the TV series, and Ofglen (Alexis Bledel) remains a recurring character throughout

season 1. She is taken by the "black van" for her lesbianism in a later episode, but neither event is portrayed as implicating Offred in any way.

28. In Atwood's novel, the possibility that Nick is an "Eye" and thus spy for the government of Gilead is not confirmed through Offred's narration, but it underlines the paranoiac and adversarial nature of relations between men and women that the novel highlights throughout—which reach a crisis in its opaque ending. In the television series, Nick himself tells Offred he's an Eye, and further affirms his trustworthiness by continuing to help Offred, taking on an explicitly, and highly traditional, masculine protector role, as her lover and father of the child she is carrying by the end of season 1.

29. Atwood, *The Handmaid's Tale,* 295.

30. Atwood, *The Handmaid's Tale,* 299.

WORKS CITED

Atwood, Margaret. *The MaddAddam Trilogy.* New York: Penguin Random House. Anchor Books Reprint. *Oryx and Crake* (2003), *The Year of the Flood* (2009), *MaddAddam* (2013).

———. *The Handmaid's Tale.* New York: Penguin Random House. First Anchor Books Edition, 1998 [1986].

———. Introduction to *The Handmaid's Tale.* New York: Penguin Random House. First Anchor Books Edition, 1998 [1986].

Benjamin, Walter. *The Origin of German Tragic Drama.* Translated by John Osborne. New York: Verso Books, 2003 [1928].

Butler, Octavia. *Kindred.* Boston: Beacon Press, 1979.

Chatman, Seymour. "What Novels Can Do That Films Can't (And Vice Versa)." *Critical Inquiry* Vol. 7. No. 1 (Autumn 1980): 121–40.

Kermode, Frank. *The Sense of an Ending: Studies in the Theory of Fiction.* London: Oxford University Press, 1967.

"Margaret Atwood on Science Fiction, Dystopias, and *Intestinal Parasites.*" *WIRED,* September 21, 2013. https://www.wired.com/2013/09/geeks-guide-margaret-atwood/.

Weinbaum, Alys Eve. "The Afterlife of Slavery and the Problem of Reproductive Freedom." Special Issue on Genres of Neoliberalism, edited by Gillian Harkins and Jane Elliot. *Social Text 115* 31, no. 2 (Summer 2013): 49–68.

FILM AND TELEVISION

The Handmaid's Tale. Created by Bruce Miller. Produced by Warren Littlefield, Margaret Atwood, Dorothy Fortenberry. Aired April 26, 2017, on Hulu.

Chapter Five

"You don't know what we had to go through"

Feminist Generations in The Handmaid's Tale

Heather Munro Prescott

This chapter will explore how the book version of *The Handmaid's Tale* can be used in the history classroom. An essential component of historical research and writing is understanding how a particular work, whether it be fiction or nonfiction, reflects the ideas and concerns of a specific time and place. *The Handmaid's Tale* was written and released during the 1980s, an era of perceived "backlash" against feminism and other progressive social causes in the United States.[1] In a recent profile in *The New Yorker*, Atwood recalls she kept a clipping file of current events while she was writing the novel. Stories included extreme pronatalist policies in Romania that encouraged women to have as many children as possible and outlawed contraception and abortion; reports of declining birth rates in Western nations; and efforts by the Reagan administration to defund clinics that provided abortion.[2]

The term "backlash" appears in the novel during Offred's recollection of an argument with her mother:

> As for you, she'd say to me, you're just a backlash. Flash in the pan. History will absolve me. . . . You young people don't appreciate things, she'd say. You don't know what we had to go through, just to get you where you are. . . . Don't you know how many women's lives, how many women's *bodies*, the tanks had to roll over just to get that far?"[3]

Although Offred admires her mother, she also feels "she expected too much of me. . . . She expected me to vindicate her life for her, and choices she'd made." Yet Offred thinks: "I didn't want to live my life on her terms. I didn't want to be the model offspring, the incarnation of her ideas. . . . I am not your justification for existence, I said to her once."[4]

The exchange between Offred and her mother can be viewed as a microcosm of intergenerational conflicts among women in the 1980s. Like Offred's mother, Second Wave feminists of the 1960s and 1970s criticized the younger cohort of women for rejecting the term "feminist" and taking the accomplishments of Second Wave activists for granted. This perspective is based on what historian Sara Evans calls a declension model of recent U.S. history that charts the rise of feminist radicalism in the 1960s and 1970s and its fall during the reactionary period of the 1980s.[5]

It is important to place *The Handmaid's Tale* within a longer tradition of feminist utopian and dystopian fiction. One way to do this is to compare Atwood's novel with American author Charlotte Perkins Gilman's novel *Herland*, a book that has recently been described as an "antidote" to Atwood's dystopian world.[6] The novel was originally published in serial form in Gilman's magazine *The Forerunner* in 1915, amidst the battle for women's suffrage and early twentieth-century debates about women's proper place in society. During the 1970s, historian Ann J. Lane rediscovered *Herland* while researching a biography of Gilman. Pantheon Press republished the book in 1979. The book cover described *Herland* as "A Lost Feminist Utopian Novel" that was "as on target today as when it was written sixty-five years ago."[7]

The reissue of *Herland* represented a larger effort by feminist activists who entered academia during the late 1960s and 1970s to retrieve the "lost" or "neglected" works of women writers from the past. For these feminist professors, the recovery of Gilman and other women writers was not only a scholarly endeavor but a form of feminist activism. In her introduction to the 1979 edition of *Herland*, Lane described the novel as a "call to action" for Second Wave feminists by offering a model of liberated, self-governing womanhood that was still beyond the reach of readers in the 1970s. The book and other works by Gilman, especially her short story "The Yellow Wallpaper," soon became incorporated into women's studies programs that emerged as the scholarly and pedagogical arm of the women's movement.[8]

Herland is told from the perspective of Van Dyck "Van" Jennings who sets out in a biplane with his friends Terry O. Nicholson and Jeff Margrave to search for a mythical "strange and terrible Woman Land" in an unspecified remote corner of the world.[9] Van describes the view of this country from the air: "It looked—well, it looked like any other country—a civilized one, I mean." He surmises that men must be present, since no women could be capable of creating such an advanced society.[10] When he first spots the residents of *Herland*, he sees they have short hair and wear loose fitting tunics and trousers. Despite this "sexless" costume, Van is sure they are female because "no boys could ever have shown such sparkling beauty."[11]

Although the "mannish" style of *Herland* did not catch on during Gilman's lifetime, it became increasingly fashionable by the 1970s, especially among those committed to women's liberation from oppressive gender norms. This trend is described in *The Handmaid's Tale* as Offred recalls a clip of her mother at a pro-choice march from a documentary shown at the so-called Red Center, where Handmaids are indoctrinated:

> She's wearing the kind of outfit Aunt Lydia told us was typical of Unwomen in those days, overall jeans with a green and mauve plaid shirt underneath and sneakers on her feet . . . the sort of thing I can remember wearing, long ago, myself. Her hair is tucked into a mauve kerchief tied behind her head. Her face is very young, very serious, even pretty. I've forgotten my mother was once as pretty and as earnest as that.[12]

In *Herland*, Van finds that not only is this society created solely by women, but the inhabitants have also evolved the ability to have children parthenogenically, that is, without sexual intercourse. The country had once had both men and women, but warfare and natural disasters wiped out most of the male population, and a volcanic eruption made the country inaccessible by land. The surviving men had attempted to kill or subdue the women, but these women resisted and "slew their brutal conquerors."[13] After a few years, one woman was miraculously able to conceive a daughter simply through intense longing for a child. This woman went on to have five daughters, from whom the current residents of *Herland* were descended.[14]

Some radical feminists during the 1960s and 1970s attempted to create similar all-female communities free from male oppression. Many of these women felt alienated by male-dominated leftist organizations, such as *Students for a Democratic Society*, that mocked women's concerns and relegated women to secondary positions within the movement. Convinced of the futility of working in mixed-sex groups, these feminists created women's collectives where they could free themselves from male chauvinism, find mutual aid and support, and mobilize for far-reaching social change. At the most extreme end of this position were the Manhattan group *Radicalesbians*, and the Washington, DC, collective the *Furies*, who argued that the only way to completely dismantle male supremacy was for all women to become "woman identified," for example, lesbians.[15]

In *The Handmaid's Tale*, Atwood critiques lesbian separatism through the characters of Offred's mother and Offred's lesbian friend Moira. Offred's mother says, "I don't want a man around, what use are they except for ten seconds' worth of half babies. A man is just a woman's strategy for making other women," she says. By having a sexual relationship with a man and choosing to keep the child, however, Offred's mother lets down the sisterhood.

She continually reminds Offred she was a "wanted child all right, and did I get shit from some quarters! My oldest buddy Tricia Foreman accused me of being pronatalist, the bitch."[16] Later in the novel Offred recalls a similar argument with Moira. "If Moira thought she could create Utopia by shutting herself up in a women-only enclave she was sadly mistaken. Men were not just going to go way, I said. You couldn't just ignore them."[17]

In Gilead, the community of Handmaids, Wives, and Servants is a perverse version of the all-female utopia envisioned in *Herland*. At the so-called Rachel and Leah Re-education Center, aka the Red Center, where Handmaids receive their indoctrination, Aunt Lydia gushes enthusiastically, "For the women who come after . . . it will be so much better. The women will live in harmony together. . . . Women united for a common end! Helping one another with their daily chores as they walk the path of life together."[18] Moira escapes from the Red Center but winds up in another all-female enclave: Jezebel's, the state-run brothel, created by the leaders of Gilead as a sexual outlet for the Commanders. When Offred discovers Moira working at Jezebel's, Moira tells her: "Look at it this way: it's not so bad, there's lots of women around. Butch paradise you might say." When Offred asks Moira if the Aunts who run Jezebel's allow women to have sex with each other, Moira says, "let, hell they encourage it. . . . The Aunts figure we're all damned anyway . . . and the Commanders don't give a piss what we do in our off time. Anyway, women on women sort of turns them on."[19]

There are dystopian elements in *Herland* too, which reflect Gilman's support of eugenics or the science of human breeding. Van says that the residents of *Herland* were undoubtedly "of Aryan stock and were once in contact with the best civilization of the old world."[20] Although Motherhood was considered the highest social duty, in order to keep the population in check and breed out the "lowest types" of humans, women who were deemed "unfit" were convinced to forgo motherhood for the good of the country. Only women with the best physical and mental characteristics, a royal class referred to as "Over Mothers," were allowed to have more than one child. When Van asks them if they limited population by killing the unborn, the women of *Herland* expressed ghastly horror at the very idea.[21] Eventually, the leaders of *Herland* decide that bisexual parentage will improve the population and allow the men to marry and father children. The sole purpose of these unions is reproduction. In fact, the women express horror and revulsion at "the male creature whose desires quite ignore parentage" and seek only sexual pleasure.[22]

Despite widespread infertility, Gilead also practices eugenics. The use of Handmaids clearly prioritizes reproduction by what the society deems the most "fit" individuals—the Commanders. In the novel (but not the television series), all nonwhite persons have been deported to the Colonies where they clean up toxic waste and radiation spills. This is also the fate of "Unwomen" like Offred's mother. Lower class men are allowed to marry "econowives," but these women are often infertile or give birth to dead or deformed babies. With the exception of Jezebel's, nonprocreative sex is forbidden. Rape, especially if committed on a Handmaid, is punishable by death. Homosexuals are executed or exiled to the Colonies. Needless to say, abortion and birth control of any kind are outlawed. At the Red Center, Aunt Lydia proclaims how this has liberated women from the fear of sexual violence: "There is more than one kind of freedom, said Aunt Lydia. Freedom to and freedom from. In the days of anarchy, it was freedom to. Now you are being given freedom from. Don't underrate it."[23]

These restrictions on sexual behavior are a twisted cooptation of Offred's mother's protest against sexual violence and pornography. Offred recollects a pornography burning her mother tricked her into attending as a child:

> There were some men, too, among the women, and the books were magazines. They must have poured gasoline, because the flames shot high, and they began dumping magazines, from boxes, not too many at a time. Some of them were chanting; onlookers gathered.
>   Their faces were happy, ecstatic almost. Fire can do that. Even my mother's face, usually pale, thinnish, looked ruddy and cheerful, like a Christmas card.[24]

Atwood's depiction of the pornography bonfire, also represented prominently in the third episode of the second Hulu TV adaptation season, draws on the feminist antipornography movement that emerged out of women's liberation groups in the 1970s. During consciousness-raising sessions, some radical feminists came to view violence against women as a common experience of oppression. They argued that pornography was at the root of discrimination against women, since it conditioned men to see women as sex objects ripe for male domination. In 1979, the group *Women Against Pornography* (WAP) held the first mass demonstration against pornography in the United States, which drew over five thousand demonstrators to Times Square in New York City.[25] Feminist opponents of pornography insisted that their position differed from that of conservative antipornography crusaders. In a classic essay entitled "Let's Put Pornography Back in the Closet," WAP founder Susan Brownmiller explained the group's feminist position on pornography:

> The feminist objection to pornography is not based on prurience. . . . We are not opposed to sex and desire . . . and we certainly believe that explicit sexual material has its place in literature, art, science and education. Here we part company rather swiftly with old-line conservatives who don't want sex education in the high schools, for example. No, the feminist objection to pornography is based

on our belief that pornography represents hatred of women, that pornography's intent is to humiliate, degrade and dehumanize the female body for the purpose of erotic stimulation and pleasure.[26]

After the election of President Ronald Reagan, the federal government also mobilized against pornography. In 1984, President Reagan signed the Child Protection Act, which toughened laws against child pornography and set up a commission headed by Attorney General Edwin Meese to study the impact of pornography on American society. The commission, popularly known as the Meese Commission, found that pornography had a negative effect on the body politic, and exposure to violent pornography in particular increased punitive behavior toward women.[27]

The feminist position on pornography was not monolithic: by the mid-1980s, growing numbers of feminists spoke out against the antipornography movement and criticized extremism on both the feminist left and the religious right. In her book *Defending Pornography: Free Speech, Sex, and the Fight for Women's Rights*, Nadine Strossen, president of the *American Civil Liberties Union* and founder of *Feminists for Free Expression*, called feminist antipornography activism "fatally flawed" because it would not only restrict the free speech rights of pornographers, but also inhibit free expression of women's rights, reproductive rights, and the rights of the LGBT community. She argued that the feminist antipornography movement was no different from nineteenth-century social purity campaigns that restricted women's sexual freedoms and outlawed birth control because it was deemed "obscene."[28]

In Atwood's fictional universe, this is precisely what happens. The Republic of Gilead confiscates and bans all obscene materials. At the Red Center, these developments are touted as a triumph for women. Offred recounts being shown old pornography films from the 1970s or 1980s at the Red Center depicting "women being raped, beaten up, killed. . . . Consider the alternatives, said Aunt Lydia. You see what things used to be like? That was what they thought of women, then."[29]

Atwood concludes her novel with "historical notes" from the Twelfth Symposium on Gileadean Studies held as part of the International Historical Association Convention at the University of Denay, Nunavit in 2195. The notes are a brilliant satire of a stuffy history conference that provides an object lesson in how *not* to do historical research and writing. The symposium includes not only academic papers but a fishing expedition, a nature walk, and an "Outdoor Period-Costume Sing-Song." In his keynote address, "Problems of Authentication in Reference to *The Handmaid's Tale*," Cambridge University history Professor James Darcy Pieixoto describes how Offred's recollections were discovered on thirty cassette tapes in a footlocker in Bangor, Maine, which was once a way station on "The Underground Femaleroad" that assisted escapees from Gilead. Pieixoto sprinkles his talk with sexist puns and devalues the account of an "ordinary" person, a woman at that: "What would we not give, now, for even twenty pages or so of print-out from Waterford's private computer! However, we must be grateful for any crumbs the Goddess of History has deigned to vouchsafe us."[30] It looks like even in the future, the stories of great men are the only ones worth remembering. Pieixoto cautions the audience against "passing moral judgment upon the Gileadeans," since "such judgments are of necessity culture-specific." He takes this cultural relativism to an absurd extreme, however, noting "Gileadean society was under a good deal of pressure, demographic and otherwise, and was subject to factors from which we ourselves are happily more free. Our job is not to censure but to understand."[31] Pieixoto is dead wrong, of course. One can understand the past on its own terms while also condemning atrocities like those committed in Gilead.

Atwood's characterization of Offred's mother as a man-hating harridan reflects the author's troubled relationship with Second Wave feminism. In various interviews, Atwood has been reluctant to label herself a feminist, saying she found the term "insufficiently inclusive" of her interests. Just before *The Handmaid's Tale* was published in 1985, Atwood told feminist theorist Elizabeth Reese that while she agreed with a definition of feminism as "a belief in the rights of women . . . [as] equal human beings," she was sharply critical of radical separatist feminist organizations. Atwood insisted "if practical, hardline, anti-male feminists took over and became the government, I would resist them."[32]

At the same time, the book is meant to serve as a wakeup call for those who, like Offred, were apathetic about the accomplishments of Second Wave feminism and ignored the attacks on women's freedoms until it was too late. "We lived, as usual, by ignoring," Offred recalls. "Ignoring isn't the same as ignorance, you have to work at it. Nothing changes instantaneously: in a gradually heating bathtub you'd be boiled to death before you knew it."[33] Yet, by emphasizing the conservative backlash of the 1980s, Atwood overlooks ongoing feminist activism during that decade and beyond. As historian Sara Evans argues, "despite regular pronouncements of its 'death,' feminism has not only weathered the right-wing backlash . . . but also continued to grow."[34] This feminist activity seldom made the headlines: to paraphrase Atwood, it was done by people who lived their lives "in the gaps between the stories." It is the historian's job to look beyond the big news stories and recover the forgotten voices of those who "lived in the blank white spaces at the edge of the print."[35]

NOTES

1. These trends are described in Susan Faludi, *Backlash: The Undeclared War Against Women* (New York: Crown, 1991).

2. Rebecca Mead, "Margaret Atwood: The Prophet of Dystopia," *New Yorker*, April 17, 2017, accessed June 12, 2018, https://www.newyorker.com/maga zine/2017/04/17/margaret-atwood-the-prophet-of-dystopia.

3. Margaret Atwood, *The Handmaid's Tale* (New York: Anchor Books, 1998), 121. This argument between Offred and her mother is dramatized in season 2, episode 3 of the Hulu series.

4. Atwood, *The Handmaid's Tale*, 121–22.

5. Sara M. Evans, "Beyond Declension: Feminist Radicalism in the 1970s and 1980s," in *The World the Sixties Made: Politics and Culture in Recent America*, eds. Van Gosse and Richard Moser (Philadelphia: Temple University Press, 2003), 52.

6. Denise Balkissoon, "Seeking an Antidote to *The Handmaid's Tale*," *Globe and Mail*, May 26, 2017, accessed June 12, 2018, https://www.theglobeandmail.com /opinion/seeking-an-antidote-to-the-handmaids-tale/article35116900/.

7. Charlotte Perkins Gilman, *Herland* (New York: Pantheon Books, 1979).

8. Jennifer S. Tuttle, "Recovering the Work of Charlotte Perkins Gilman; or, Reading Gilman in Rome," in *Charlotte Perkins Gilman and Woman's Place in America*, ed. Jill Bergman (Tuscaloosa: University of Alabama Press, 2017), 191.

9. Gilman, *Herland*, 2.

10. Gilman, *Herland*, 10.

11. Gilman, *Herland*, 15.

12. Atwood, *The Handmaid's Tale*, 119.

13. Gilman, *Herland*, 55.

14. Gilman, *Herland*, 56-57.

15. Anne Valk, *Radical Sisters: Second Wave Feminism and Black Liberation in Washington, DC* (Urbana and Chicago: University of Illinois Press, 2008), 135–57.

16. Atwood, *The Handmaid's Tale*, 120–21.

17. Atwood, *The Handmaid's Tale*, 172.

18. Atwood, *The Handmaid's Tale*, 162.

19. Atwood, *The Handmaid's Tale*, 249.

20. Gilman, *Herland*, 54.

21. Gilman, *Herland*, 69.

22. Gilman, *Herland*, 139.

23. Atwood, *The Handmaid's Tale*, 24.

24. Atwood, *The Handmaid's Tale*, 38.

25. Susan Brownmiller, *In Our Time: Memoir of a Revolution* (New York: The Dial Press, 1999), 298–99.

26. Susan Brownmiller, "Let's Put Pornography Back in the Closet," accessed June 5, 2018, http://www.susanbrownmiller.com/susanbrownmiller/html/antiporno .html.

27. United States Attorney General's Commission on Pornography/The Meese Commission, *Final Report of the Attorney General's Commission on Pornography* (Washington, DC: Department of Justice, 1986).

28. Nadine Strossen, *Defending Pornography: Free Speech, Sex, and the Fight for Women's Rights* (New York and London: New York University Press, 1995).

29. Atwood, *The Handmaid's Tale*, 118.

30. Atwood, *The Handmaid's Tale*, 310.

31. Atwood, *The Handmaid's Tale*, 102.

32. Shirley Neuman, "'Just a Backlash': Margaret Atwood, Feminism, and *The Handmaid's Tale*," *University of Toronto Quarterly* 75, no. 3 (2006): 858.

33. Atwood, *The Handmaid's Tale*, 56.

34. Evans, "Beyond Declension," 52.

35. Atwood, *The Handmaid's Tale*, 57.

WORKS CITED

Atwood, Margaret. *The Handmaid's Tale.* New York: Anchor Books, 1998.

Balkissoon, Denise. "Seeking an Antidote to *The Handmaid's Tale.*" *Globe and Mail*, May 26, 2017. https://www.theglobeandmail.com/opinion/seeking-an-antidote-to-the-hand maidstale/article35116900/.

Brownmiller, Susan. *In Our Time: Memoir of a Revolution.* New York: The Dial Press, 1999.

———. "Let's Put Pornography Back in the Closet." Accessed June 5, 2018. http://www.susanbrownmiller.com/susanbrownmiller/html/antiporno.html.

Evans, Sara M. "Beyond Declension: Feminist Radicalism in the 1970s and 1980s." In *The World the Sixties Made: Politics and Culture in Recent America*, edited by Van Gosse and Richard Moser, 52–66. Philadelphia: Temple University Press, 2003.

Faludi, Susan. *Backlash: The Undeclared War against Women.* New York: Crown Publishing Group, 1991.

Gilman, Charlotte Perkins. *Herland.* New York: Pantheon Books, 1979.

Mead, Rebecca. "Margaret Atwood: The Prophet of Dystopia." *New Yorker*, April 17, 2017. https://www.newyorker.com/magazine/2017/04/17/margaret-atwood-the-prophet-of-dystopia.

Neuman, Shirley. "'Just a Backlash': Margaret Atwood, Feminism, and *The Handmaid's Tale.*" *University of Toronto Quarterly* 75, no. 3 (2006): 857–68.

Strossen, Nadine. *Defending Pornography: Free Speech, Sex, and the Fight for Women's Rights.* New York: New York University Press, 1995.

Tuttle, Jennifer S. "Recovering the Work of Charlotte Perkins Gilman; or Reading Gilman in Rome." In *Charlotte Perkins Gilman and Woman's Place in America*, edited by Jillian Bergman, 186–218. Tuscaloosa: University of Alabama Press, 2017.

United States Attorney General's Commission on Pornography. *Final Report of the Attorney General's Commission on Pornography*. Washington, DC: Department of Justice, 1986.

Valk, Anne. *Radical Sisters: Second Wave Feminism and Black Liberation in Washington, DC.* Chicago: University of Illinois Press, 2008.

TELEVISION

The Handmaid's Tale. "Baggage." Season 2, Episode 3. Directed by Kari Skogland. Written by Dorothy Fortenberry. Hulu, May 2, 2018.

Chapter Six

"Don't let the bastards grind you down" *again*

Returning to The Handmaid's Tale

Susan Gilmore

What does it mean to teach *The Handmaid's Tale* across generations? How do we as readers and teachers grow with this novel and shift allegiances within it over time, and how can these questions and their answers be part of the lessons *The Handmaid's Tale* moves us to learn? When I taught Margaret Atwood's novel most recently, I reached a milestone. Teaching *The Handmaid's Tale* across eighteen years now has meant introducing Atwood's novel to at least two generations. I will share here how I have necessarily combined English *and* Women's and Gender Studies approaches to Atwood's novel from day one in my classroom as well as how teaching *The Handmaid's Tale* now creates new intergenerational contexts and connections with which we as teachers and students can engage.

I must confess that I hadn't planned on returning to *The Handmaid's Tale*. Even after the upshot of the 2016 presidential election prompted me to schedule my course featuring women's dystopian literature for the fall 2017 semester, Atwood's novel wasn't the frontrunner for a place on my syllabus. I had included it when I debuted my course, "Women Writing Fantasy, Mystery, and Science Fiction" in 2000 and again in 2002 and 2005; however, in more recent years I had swapped it out for *Woman on the Edge of Time* (1976), hoping Marge Piercy's Latina heroine "Connie" and her battles with sexism, racism, and classism on many contemporary and futuristic fronts would speak to my state university students, many of whom are Latinx and other minorities as well as first generation college students.[1] This time around, I toyed with teaching Octavia Butler's 1998 novel *Parable of the Talents* for its prescient depiction of right-wing religious demagogue and president-elect Andrew Steele Jarret, who vows on the stump to "make America great again."[2] The renewed popularity of *The Handmaid's Tale* courtesy of the first season of the Hulu television adaptation gave me one reason to teach Atwood's novel again. The Trump-Pence victory gave me another. I hadn't planned to return to *The Handmaid's Tale*, but as many of us took to the streets, in the days and months following the inauguration, dressed as Handmaids and their pussy-hatted familiars, I realized we'd never really left it.[3]

Though its cultural moment has (and hasn't) changed, the course catalog parameters of my class have remained the same. My English department regularly offers my class as a 200-level, "Studies in Literature" course for nonmajors, and we've cross-listed it as an elective for minors in our *Women, Gender, and Sexuality Studies* (WGSS) program. It attracts a mix of female *and* male students, some avid fans of one or another featured writer or genre, others present chiefly to check a general education box on their curriculum sheets, though my hope, always, is to entice if not recruit these students to become English majors and/or WGSS minors. The only prerequisite for taking this course is satisfactory completion of Freshman Composition. Being a feminist has never been a requirement for taking my course, steeped in feminism as it is. I've never put my students on the spot and suspect few would openly declare themselves feminists, though perhaps a few more would nowadays than in my early years teaching as first a graduate teaching assistant and then an assistant professor in the 1990s, when my students routinely prefaced their most feminist arguments and insights with "I'm not a feminist but . . ." By then the backlash against feminism that American author and journalist Susan Faludi so aptly described in her 1991 book *Backlash: The Undeclared War against American Women* cowed my students and had a firm hold on American culture at large.[4] Many of my current students seem openly and wonderfully progressive, yet as American political scientist and activist Cathy Cohen, reporting the results of her *GenForward* survey of millennials, observes, "the majority of young people say they don't identify as what they consider to be a traditional feminist, but support women's rights and equality."[5] What explains this mix of advocacy and ambivalence? Cohen argues, "The media has narrated a pretty rigid understanding of feminism."[6] Revisiting *The Handmaid's Tale* gives us a timely opportunity to question rigid narratives and envision more supple stories of women's rights.

The Handmaid's Tale occupies the dark dystopian midpoint of my course. It is bracketed on one side by my unit on women's revisionist folk and fairy tales, featuring selections from American poet Anne Sexton's *Transformations* (1971) and British author Angela Carter's short story collection, *The Bloody Chamber* (1979). On the other, I follow it with my unit on women mystery writers and their detective-protagonists, featuring British mystery maven Agatha Christie's impeccable Miss Marple and American detective fiction author Sara Paretsky's hard-driving V. I. Warshawski. I immediately preface *The Handmaid's Tale* with a visit to American essayist and fiction writer Charlotte Perkins Gilman's utopian *Herland* (1915), and it occurs to me now that had Hillary Clinton succeeded in November 2016 to become the first female president of the United States, the government of *Herland*, an all-female and near perfect nation as Gilman envisioned it, might have served as a high bar against which to measure her new administration. Running through the course from the start we consider the provocative question American feminist critic and science fiction writer Joanna Russ poses in "What Can a Heroine Do? or Why Women Can't Write" (1971), her positive (despite the negative subtitle) appraisal of avenues for female agency in the genres of detective, supernatural, and science fiction.[7] In the works leading up to and following *The Handmaid's Tale*, we found a host of capable female protagonists instrumental in challenging what Russ calls "the old myths"[8] reinventing themselves, founding new nations, and solving and resolving conflicts and crimes—in Miss Marple's case without so much as dropping a knitting stitch. Agency in *The Handmaid's Tale* is far more covert. In the novel, it comes through Offred's choice to tell her story intimately, to herself, and ultimately, across the dystopian void to us: "You don't tell a story only to yourself. There's always someone else. Even when there is no one. A story is like a letter. *Dear You*, I'll say."[9] We can ask our students to compare the under-the-radar Mayday resistance work Offred and her fellow handmaids accomplish veiled and "shopping" on foot in Gilead with current demonstrations on behalf of women's reproductive rights by costumed brigades of the Handmaid Coalition, inspired by Atwood's novel and the Hulu television series, who "fight to keep fiction from becoming reality."[10]

UNPACKING *THE HANDMAID'S TALE*

I can't help feeling that the novel *The Handmaid's Tale* belongs first and foremost to me and my fellow English professors. Atwood's novel offers us a trove of literary tropes to identify and unpack, including generous helpings of Orwellian jargon delivered with Atwood's trademark satiric panache. There is macabre fun as well as revelation to be had in deconstructing Gilead's lingo. Remove just one letter from "Salvagings"[11] and you expose this public execution ritual's savage underpinnings. However, a literary analysis of the language of Gilead can't be divorced from a feminist analysis of how its propaganda is steeped in patriarchy. "Prayvaganzas" jokily conveys what mass marketing can do to worship but also signals the staged surrenders of nuns, whom Gilead coerces to give up their habits for the Handmaid's "red veil."[12] "Econowife"[13] likewise markets marriage and puts a price on women's heads, and it's worth asking, when we use terms like "trophy wife" (and perhaps other examples our classes can list), how far these really stand from the commodification of women in Gilead.

We can bring literary and feminist perspectives to bear on Atwood's description of the "Ceremony," the term the Commanders of Gilead use to give a religious gloss to monthly attempts to rape and forcibly impregnate the Handmaids.[14] Their use of "ceremony" here functions as what George Orwell has called political "euphemism" served up as "largely the defence [*sic*] of the indefensible."[15] What intrigues me here, in light of current discourse on sexual assault, is the way in which Offred describes the Ceremony, in the novel, in terms of what it is not: "I do not say making love, because this is not what he's doing. Copulating too would be inaccurate, because it would imply two people and only one is involved. Nor does rape cover it: nothing is going on here that I haven't signed up for. There wasn't a lot of choice but there was some, and this is what I chose."[16] When I taught Atwood's novel most recently, I was still playing catch-up with season 1 of the Hulu series and screened only the convincing and, thus, terrifying takeover sequence in episode 3 ("Late").[17] Next time around, I plan to ask my students what they make of Offred's tone in the quotation above, her qualified sense of "choice" and complicity, and whether June's testimony to the Mexican ambassador in season 1, episode 6 ("A Woman's Place"), offers a much needed #MeToo era update: "This is a brutal place. We're prisoners. . . . They rape me. . . . I didn't choose this. They caught me. I was trying to escape."[18]

Scenes like this one in the Hulu series and hindsight from the cultural moment we're in can enrich our understanding of Atwood's novel. If we read Offred's narration in the novel as testimony, in light of the #MeToo movement and everything we know about trauma, we can necessarily question the ways in which the literary concept of the "unreliable narrator" misreads and even revictimizes Offred's experiences and tactics. Offred has little in common with Edgar Allan Poe's titillating, protest-too-much, first-person madmen, the certifiably unreliable narrators of "The Tell-Tale Heart," "The Black Cat," and several other Poe stories. Instead, Offred's is a reliable voice in unreliable circumstances. In our classes we can explore the many reasons why she must keep her cards close to the chest, why information is not only withheld from her but also by her, as she navigates secretively with no trust in her captors and limited trust in her auditors.

UNCANNY RETURNS

Returning to *The Handmaid's Tale*, I'm struck by how Atwood's novel stages its own returns. Offred repeatedly checks Gilead's defamiliarized landscape against her gut sense that she or someone like her has been there before. Nothing says this more loudly and clearly than "Nolite te bastardes carborundorum"—"Don't let the bastards grind you down"—however furtively Offred's predecessor has carved it in her closet.[19] I take this missive—as I believe Offred does, judging how frequently she, like her Hulu series counterpart, "June" (Elisabeth Moss), takes to her closet floor to commune with it—as not a portent of doom but a sign of sisterly solidarity—as a morale booster and a call to action. The Handmaids' carvings and codes in Atwood's novel, as well as its television and film adaptations, can suggest staying power as much as dismay.[20] The Handmaid's motto, a re-appropriation of an already appropriated Latin schoolboy's joke, signals that perhaps sometimes (with apologies to Audre Lorde) the master's tools CAN dismantle the Commander's house.[21]

The Uncanny is pervasive in *The Handmaid's Tale*, and I call my students' attention to Atwood's *Uncanny* using the term in the popular as well as Freudian sense. Casually, we use it to describe what is like but unlike, familiar yet strange, that "haven't we been here before?" feeling that reaffirms and unsettles, that tests our memory as well as our fortitude in the face of "again." In his 1919 essay, Freud describes one expression of "The Uncanny" as "the sense of helplessness experienced in some dream-states":

> So, for instance, when, caught in a mist perhaps, one has lost one's way in a mountain forest, every attempt to find the marked or familiar path may bring one back again and again to one and the same spot, which one can identify by some particular landmark. Or one may wander about in a dark, strange room, looking for the door or the electric switch, and collide time after time with the same piece of furniture—though it is true that Mark Twain succeeded by wild exaggeration in turning this latter situation into something irresistibly comic.[22]

We can find, in this description of the Uncanny, an analog for Offred's gallows humor narration of her and fellow Handmaids' daily sojourns through Gilead as well as an allegory of our own frustrated wanderings through the current political wilderness, bumping up against the same dusty furniture of patriarchy again and again.

The caveat to teaching Atwood's Uncanny is that to do so from an intersectional and cross-generational perspective means reaching those who haven't "been here before" or whose "before" is different than one's own. This applies to discussions of Atwood's setting the heart of Gilead in Cambridge, Massachusetts, and even more locally, in Harvard Yard. I grew up just west of Cambridge, and Harvard Square was a cultural mecca to me from my restless teen years into my twenties. I first read Atwood's novel shortly after it was published and discovered its setting was my stomping grounds without spoilers and with delicious horror. It's worth helping students understand why Atwood chose this liberal, academic "hub" as her setting, but it's also worth asking this generation's students where they have felt most free and being prepared for them to point to other geographical places as well as unconventional spaces. The stakes go up when we are willing to imagine how readily our meccas and safe harbors—whether they are college towns, Provincetown, Comic Con, or a chat room—might become spheres of a regime.

Atwood's novel relies on geographical as well as historical returns by design. As Atwood notes in her new (2017) introduction, "One of my rules was that I would not put any events into the book that had not already happened in what James Joyce called the 'nightmare' of history."[23] Atwood laces her novel with reminders of the Salem witch trials, and requires us to reacquaint ourselves with "the seventeenth-century Puritan roots" which are Gilead's "foundation"[24] (see Kelly Marino's chapter in this volume for more on Gilead's Puritan roots).

Teaching *The Handmaid's Tale* more than thirty years after its debut, I've found it also helps to give students a crash course in the 1980s, the immediate present when Atwood published the novel but now the distant past to current cohorts of students who hadn't even been born when the novel debuted (see Heather Munro Prescott's chapter in this volume for more on the novel's historical tie to the 1980s). We revisited, or perhaps visited for the first time, President Ronald Reagan's "we begin bombing in five minutes" gaffe[25] and other Cold War scares and reviewed the careers of high-profile religious and conservative female figures such as Eagle Forum founder and Equal Rights Amendment opponent Phyllis Schlafly and televangelist Tammy Faye Bakker—sources for Atwood's "Serena Joy" that current students may not recognize.[26] A review of 1980s-era fraught antipornography alliances between Christian conservatives and some feminists, such as the American antiporn activist Andrea Dworkin, can help students understand the flashback scene in the novel in which Offred's mother and her cohorts burn pornographic magazines *and* Offred's ambivalence as she regards the women "pin ups" they are setting aflame.[27] The Hulu TV adaptation changes this scene in the novel to one in season 2, episode 3 ("Baggage"), in which June's mother, "Holly" (Cherry Jones), and her peers demonstrate against sexual assault by burning the names of their rapists, and we can ask what is lost and gained by this change.[28]

HEEDING OUR MOTHERS *AND* AUNTS

Offred's remembered clashes with her mother in Atwood's novel and its Hulu adaptation invite us to look more broadly at conflicts between feminist generations and to speak more candidly about our own evolving status and stakes in Atwood's tale and the story of women's activism writ large. Atwood first directed her novel as a cautionary tale at my peers and me, according to *Vox* cultural writer Constance Grady: "In some ways, the entire book can be read as a rebuke to the young women who came of age in the '80s and felt that they no longer needed feminism: 'You may think you've grown past the need for political campaigns,' the book seems to say, 'but look what they'll do the minute you let your guard down.'"[29]

In 1985, when Atwood published *The Handmaid's Tale*, I graduated college and headed to graduate school for a Ph.D. in English reaping the benefits of women's studies and revering second wave feminists who brought this discipline to the academy and the literary canon. Reading *The Handmaid's Tale* in my twenties, I sided with Offred against her mother's harshest remarks: "As for you, she'd say to me, you're just a backlash. Flash in the pan. History will absolve me."[30] In my fifties, like the "middle-aged witch" who narrates *Transformations*, Anne Sexton's 1971 feminist revision of Grimm's fairy tales,[31] I find myself siding with transgressive mothers and evil aunts. I find myself nodding when Holly laments to her daughter, June, in season 2, episode 3 ("Baggage"), "I sacrificed for you and it pisses me off that you're just settling."[32] Though some critics found "jarring"[33] Margaret Atwood's shadowy, split-second cameo in season 1, episode 1 ("Offred") of the Hulu series[34] as a "Red Center"[35] aunt slapping June/Offred into submission, I read this scene as a fun-house inversion of Atwood's original call to "get woke." I'm drawn to the Hulu series portrayal of "Aunt Lydia" (Ann Dowd), thanks not only to Dowd's charismatic performance, but perhaps also to the way she built Aunt Lydia's character by keeping in mind showrunner Bruce Miller's suggestion "that Aunt Lydia might have been a real teacher before the coup that created Gilead."[36] Forced to choose between joining my fellow "Unwomen"[37] in the Colonies and taking a teaching post in a Red Center classroom, I'm not certain my choice would be heroic.

We need to recognize that the "Aunts" are as much the objects as the agents of Gilead's oppression. As they appear in the Hulu series, they resemble not just a little bit the caricatures in 1910s political cartoons of mannish, postmenopausal, suffragette battle axes policing femininity out of sweet young things. When my classes read Gilman's 1915 utopian novel *Herland*, I share these cartoons from the same era[38] and note their affinities with the hostile view of women's authority Gilman represents by way of her "man's man"[39] explorer, "Terry," who refers to the officers who govern Herland disparagingly as "aunts."[40] Returning to *The Handmaid's Tale* gives us new opportunities to challenge the ways in which women's power continues to be twisted into grotesque shapes in the popular imagination as patriarchy keeps pitting successive generations of mothers and daughters, teachers and students against each another. When we assess our rank and power relative to Atwood's characters and each other, we can begin to move together toward more utopian common ground.

NOTES

1. Marge Piercy, *Woman on the Edge of Time* (New York: Fawcett-Random House, 1976).

2. Octavia E. Butler, *The Parable of the Talents* (New York: Seven Stories Press, 1998), 24.

3. I refer here to the Women's March on Washington and protests staged by the Handmaid Coalition. The first Women's March on Washington was held on January 21, 2017, the day following Donald J. Trump's presidential inauguration; many marchers donned pink knit, cat-eared "pussy hats" to protest Trump's infamous *Access Hollywood* "Grab 'em by the pussy" boasts. For a full transcript of Trump's *Access Hollywood* remarks, see "Transcript: Donald Trump's Taped Comments about Women," *New York Times*, October 8, 2016, https://www.nytimes.com/2016/10/08 /us/donald-trump-tape-transcript.html. According to its website, the Handmaid Coalition traces its formation to "Handmaid's Tale themed protests" by NARAL Texas in March and Action Together New Hampshire (ATNH) in April 2017, emerging as the Handmaid Coalition in a growing number of chapters and demonstrations by May 2017. "Our Story," Handmaid Coalition, accessed November 18, 2018, https:// handmaidcoalition.org /ourstory/.

4. In 1991, Susan Faludi observed "that the last decade has seen a powerful counterassault on women's rights, a backlash, an attempt to retract the handful of small and hard-won victories that the feminist movement did manage to win for women." We can see affinities between Faludi's description of how backlash operates and how the architects of Gilead preach women back into the patriarchy: "This counterassault is largely insidious: in a kind of pop-culture version of the Big Lie, it stands the truth boldly on its head and proclaims that the very steps that have elevated women's position have actually led to their downfall" (*Backlash: The Undeclared War against American Women* [1991; 15th Anniversary ed., New York: Three Rivers Press-Random House, 2006], 9–10).

5. David Brancaccio, Jonaki Mehta, and Sarah Menendez, "Most Millennials Believe in Gender Equity, but Avoid the 'Feminist' Label," *Marketplace*, National Public Radio, August 27, 2018, https://www.marketplace.org/2018/08/27/economy /most-millennials-believe-gender-equity-avoid-feminist-label.

6. Brancaccio, et al, "Most Millennials Believe in Gender Equity, but Avoid the 'Feminist' Label."

7. Joanna Russ, "What Can a Heroine Do? or Why Women Can't Write," in *To Write like a Woman: Essays in Feminism and Science Fiction* (Bloomington: Indiana University Press, 1995), 91.

8. Russ, 93.

9. Margaret Atwood, *The Handmaid's Tale* (1985; reprinted with a new author's introduction, New York: Anchor-Penguin Random House, 2017), 40.

10. Website header, Handmaid Coalition, accessed November 18, 2018, https://handmaidcoalition.org/.

11. Atwood, *The Handmaid's Tale*, 272.

12. Atwood, *The Handmaid's Tale*, 220.

13. Atwood, *The Handmaid's Tale*, 44.

14. Atwood, *The Handmaid's Tale*, 93.

15. George Orwell, "Politics and the English Language," in *The Collected Essays, Journalism, and Letters of George Orwell*, ed. Sonia Orwell and Ian Angos, 1st ed. (New York: Harcourt, Brace, Javanovich, 1968), 4:136.

16. Atwood, *The Handmaid's Tale*, 94.

17. *The Handmaid's Tale*, "Late," Season 1, Episode 3, directed by Reed Morano, Hulu, April 26, 2017, 53:09, https://www.hulu.com/watch/fbc9149e-7ad8-4826 - bb8e-7c27f342aa01.

18. *The Handmaid's Tale*, "A Woman's Place," Season 1, Episode 6, directed by Floria Sigismondi, Hulu, May 17, 2017, 54:53, https://www.hulu.com /watch/23dfc835-06d9-46c1-9111-18dd6620a6a4. Atwood, 52, 186–87.

19. Atwood, *The Handmaid's Tale*, 52, 186–87.

20. My students were somewhat underwhelmed by the 1990 film adaptation of *The Handmaid's Tale* the one time I screened it, so I don't address teaching it here, though I'm a fan of Natasha Richardson's smart and vulnerable "Offred" and of Faye Dunaway's steely "Serena Joy."

21. Audre Lorde, "The Master's Tools Will Never Dismantle the Master's House," in *Sister Outsider*: *Essays and Speeches* (Berkeley, CA: Crossing Press, 1984), 110–13.

22. Freud, "The 'Uncanny,'" in *The Standard Edition of the Complete Psychological Works of Sigmund Freud,* translated by James Strachey (London: Hogarth, 1955), 17:237.

23. Atwood, *The Handmaid's Tale*, xiv.

24. Atwood, *The Handmaid's Tale*, xiv.

25. Andrew Glass, "Reagan 'Jokes' about Bombing Soviet Union, Aug. 11, 1984," *Politico*, August 11, 2017, https://www.politico.com/story/2017/08/11/this-day-in -politics-aug-11-1984-241413.

26. Sarah Jones affirms that Atwood's "Serena Joy" is "an amalgam of Phyllis Schlafly and Tammy Faye Bakker with a dash of Aimee Semple McPherson" and sin-gles out Kellyanne Conway as one example of why "America is rich in Serena Joys" today. Sarah Jones, *"The Handmaid's Tale* Is a Warning to Conservative Women," *New Republic*, April 20, 2017, https://newrepublic.com/article/141674/handmaids -tale-hulu-warning-conservative-women. It's worth asking students to respond to Jones's argument and to nominate contemporary Serena Joys of their own.

27. Atwood, *The Handmaid's Tale*, 38–39. For a critical review of women's antipornography activism in the 1980s, see Wendy Kaminer, "Feminists against the First Amendment," *Atlantic,* November 1992, https://www.theatlantic.com/magazine

/archive/1992/11/feminists-against-the-first-amendment/305051/. Kaminer argues that "By the mid-1980s right-wing advocates of traditional family values had co-opted feminist anti-porn protests—or, at least, they'd co-opted feminist rhetoric."

28. *The Handmaid's Tale*, "Baggage," Season 2, Episode 3, directed by Kari Skogland, Hulu, May 2, 2018, 58:08, https://www.hulu.com/watch/67517156-6a63 -42ce-96d4-0d99b2ef4849.

29. Todd VanDerWerff, Caroline Framke, and Constance Grady, *"The Handmaid's Tale* Introduces One of the Book's Most Important Characters in 'Baggage,'" *Vox*, May 2, 2018, https://www.vox.com/culture/2018/5/2/17305814/the-handmaids-tale -season-2-episode-3-recap-baggage-june-escape-capture.

30. Atwood, *The Handmaid's Tale*, 121.

31. Anne Sexton, *Transformations* (Boston: Houghton Mifflin, 1971), 1.

32. *The Handmaid's Tale*, "Baggage," Season 2, Episode 3, directed by Kari Skogland, Hulu, May 2, 2018, 58:08, https://www.hulu.com/watch/67517156-6a63 -42ce-96d4-0d99b2ef4849.

33. "Margaret Atwood's *Handmaid's Tale* Cameo Is Literally a Slap in the Face," *CBC Radio*, April 26, 2017, https://www.cbc.ca/radio/q/blog/margaret-atwood-s -handmaid-s-tale-cameo-is-literally-a-slap-in-the-face-1.4086380.

34. *The Handmaid's Tale*, "Offred," Season 1, Episode 1, directed by Reed Morano, Hulu, April 26, 2017, 57:25, https://www.hulu.com/watch/671f8878 -bdba-40bd-ae6d-f85c55cecbb4.

35. Atwood, *The Handmaid's Tale*, 96.

36. Laura Bradley, *"The Handmaid's Tale*: How Ann Dowd Found Aunt Lydia's Twisted Soul," *Vanity Fair*, April 25, 2018, https://www.vanityfair.com/holly wood/2018/04/handmaids-tale-season-2-aunt-lydia-ann-dowd-interview.

37. Atwood, *The Handmaid's Tale*, 118.

38. For a treasure trove of suffrage-era cartoons, see Martha Banta, *Imaging American Women: Idea and Ideals in Cultural History* (New York: Columbia University Press, 1987).

39. Charlotte Perkins Gilman, *Herland*, (1915; New York: Pantheon, 1979), 9.

40. Gilman, 20, 59.

WORKS CITED

Atwood, Margaret. *The Handmaid's Tale*. 1985. Reprinted with a new introduction by the author. New York: Anchor-Penguin Random House, 2017.

Banta, Martha. *Imaging American Women: Idea and Ideals in Cultural History*. New York: Columbia University Press, 1987.

Bradley, Laura. *"The Handmaid's Tale*: How Ann Dowd Found Aunt Lydia's Twisted Soul." *Vanity Fair*. April 25, 2018. https://www.vanityfair.com/holly-wood/2018/04/hand maids-tale-season-2-aunt-lydia-ann-dowd-interview.

Brancaccio, David, Jonaki Mehta, and Sarah Menendez. "Most Millenials Believe in Gender Equity, but Avoid the 'Feminist' Label." *Marketplace*, National Public

Radio. August 27, 2018. https://www.marketplace.org/2018/08/27/economy/most-millennials-believe-gender-equity-avoid-feminist-label.

Butler, Octavia E. *The Parable of the Talents*. New York: Seven Stories Press, 1998.

Faludi, Susan. *Backlash: The Undeclared War against American Women*. 15th Anniversary ed. New York: Three Rivers Press-Random House, 2006 [1991].

Freud, Sigmund. "The Uncanny." 1919. In *The Standard Edition of the Complete Psychological Works of Sigmund Freud*. Translated by James Strachey. Vol. 17, *An Infantile Neurosis and Other Works, 1917–1919* 217–52. London: Hogarth, 1955.

Gilman, Charlotte Perkins. *Herland*. 1915. Reprinted with an introduction by Ann J. Lane. New York: Pantheon, 1979.

Glass, Andrew. "Reagan 'Jokes' about Bombing Soviet Union, Aug. 11, 1984." *Politico*. August 11, 2017. https://www.politico.com/story/2017/08/11/this-day-in-politics-aug-11-1984-241413.

"Handmaid Coalition." Accessed November 18, 2018. https://handmaidcoalition.org/.

Jones, Sarah. "*The Handmaid's Tale* Is a Warning to Conservative Women." *New Republic*. April 20, 2017. https://newrepublic.com/article/141674/handmaids-tale-hulu-warning-conservative-women.

Kaminer, Wendy. "Feminists against the First Amendment." *Atlantic*. November 1992. https://www.theatlantic.com/magazine/archive/1992/11/feminists-against-the-first-amendment/305051/.

Lorde, Audre. "The Master's Tools Will Never Dismantle the Master's House." In *Sister Outsider: Essays and Speeches*, 110–13. Berkeley, CA: Crossing Press, 1984.

"Margaret Atwood's *Handmaid's Tale* Cameo Is Literally a Slap in the Face." *CBC Radio*. April 26, 2017. https://www.cbc.ca/radio/q/blog/margaret-atwood-s-handmaid-s-tale-cameo-is-literally-a-slap-in-the-face-1.4086380.

Orwell, George. "Politics and the English Language." In *The Collected Essays, Journalism, and Letters of George Orwell*. Edited by Sonia Orwell and Ian Angos. 1st ed., vol. 4, 127–40. New York: Harcourt, Brace, Javanovich, 1968.

Piercy, Marge. *Woman on the Edge of Time*. New York: Fawcett-Random House, 1976.

Russ, Joanna. "What Can a Heroine Do? or Why Women Can't Write." In *To Write like a Woman: Essays in Feminism and Science Fiction*, 79–93. Bloomington: Indiana University Press, 1995.

Sexton, Anne. *Transformations*. Preface by Kurt Vonnegut, Jr. Illustrations by Barbara Swan. Boston: Houghton Mifflin, 1971.

"Transcript: Donald Trump's Taped Comments about Women." *New York Times*. October 8, 2016. https://www.nytimes.com/2016/10/08/us/donald-trump-tape-transcript.html.

VanDerWerff, Todd, Caroline Framke, and Constance Grady. "*The Handmaid's Tale* Introduces One of the Book's Most Important Characters in 'Baggage.'" *Vox*. May 2, 2018, https://www.vox.com/culture/2018/5/2/17305814/the-handmaids-tale-season-2-episode-3-recap-baggage-june-escape-capture.

FILM AND TELEVISION

The Handmaid's Tale. Directed by Volker Schlöndorff. USA / Germany: Cinecom, 1990.

The Handmaid's Tale. "Baggage." Season 2, Episode 3. Directed by Kari Skogland. Hulu. May 2, 2018. 58:08. https://www.hulu.com/watch/67517156-6a63-42ce -96d4-0d99b2ef4849.

The Handmaid's Tale. "A Woman's Place." Season 1, Episode 6. Directed by Floria Sigismondi. Hulu, May 17, 2017, 54:53, https://www.hulu.com/watch/23dfc835 -06d9-46c1-9111-18dd6620a6a4.

The Handmaid's Tale. "Late." Season 1, Episode 3. Directed by Reed Morano. Hulu. April 26, 2017. 53:09. https://www.hulu.com/watch/fbc9149e-7ad8-4826-bb8e -7c27f342aa01.

The Handmaid's Tale. "Offred." Season 1, Episode 1. Directed by Reed Morano. Hulu. April 26, 2017. 57:25. https://www.hulu.com/watch/671f8878-bdba-40bd ae6d-f85c55cecbb4.

Chapter Seven

Consent, Power, and Sexual Assault in *The Handmaid's Tale*

Handmaids, Sexual Slavery, and Victim Blaming

Michelle A. Cubellis

Margaret Atwood's *The Handmaid's Tale* presents a graphic and disturbing picture of the insidious nature of sexual assault and the misconceptions held about sexual assault and rape. While other narratives are more blatant in their depiction of sexual assault as a physically violent act, Atwood's discussion of it more accurately reflects the features of sexual assault that are likely to occur in real-life such as victimization, power, control, and coercion. The Hulu television series also provides a poignant depiction of victim precipitation theories and how criminology has attempted to explain the active role victims play in their own victimization. Criticized for blaming victims and placing the onus for preventing crime on victims instead of offenders, these theories have been repeatedly applied to sexual assault and are front and center throughout much of *The Handmaid's Tale*. For criminal justice scholars, the TV adaptation offers an opportunity to discuss rape myths and victim blaming, and how these concepts influence our understanding of sexual assault and ability to respond to and prevent this form of victimization.

In Margaret Atwood's *The Handmaid's Tale,* the social structure of the Republic of Gilead, an authoritarian regime based on the control and oppression of women, creates a unique environment in which viewers are forced to address criminology as well as criminal justice issues including sexual assault and rape, the use of power and control in sexual assault, and the pervasiveness of rape culture and myths in the imaginary world created by Atwood—and within our own. Women are viewed as second-class citizens and subject to complete obedience to all men in Gilead. Gilead successfully overthrew the United States government, firing all employed women and instituting a patriarchal society whereby women were banned from access to education or employment opportunities outside of traditional housework. While there exist different classes of women in Gilead, ranging from Wives (the wives of Commanders) who have some power, to Handmaids (those charged with bearing children) who have none, all women are oppressed by men. These views of Gilead conform to traditional gender roles and societal constructions of gender that view women as homemakers and mothers.[1]

Handmaids, especially, are viewed as only a uterus. Their usefulness and status in the Gilead are inherently linked to their ability to conceive and bear children. Handmaids have no autonomy over their bodies and are viewed as the property of their Commander. This point is further emphasized by the fact that Handmaids are given names based on who their Commander is. For example, Offred/June (Elisabeth Moss) is the Handmaid of Commander Fred Waterford (Joseph Fiennes), and thus given the name Offred to symbolize she is "of Fred." The removal of the given name of Handmaids and renaming based on their Commander further symbolizes that they are viewed as a possession, and nothing more. Their forced sexual activity and subsequent pregnancies are unequivocally a form of sexual slavery. Sexual slavery is defined as coercing or forcing someone to engage in sexual activities by assigning ownership of the person.[2] While common belief would suggest that sexual slavery results when unsuspecting individuals are kidnapped and sold into an underground sex market, sexual slavery does not have to occur in this way. The forced sexual activity of Handmaids, without the ability to say no or leave the Commander's house without dire consequences, represents a less obvious form of sexual slavery.

An even more apparent example of sexual slavery in *The Handmaid's Tale* is the example of forced prostitution depicted at Jezebel's.[3] Forced prostitution occurs when individuals are forced, through physical, verbal, or emotional methods, to engage in the selling of sex or work in brothels.[4] In Gilead, Jezebel's (a name associated with prostitutes in the Bible) functions as an underground brothel catering to diplomat and officials such as Commander Fred Waterford. Women in Gilead, usually those who rebel against the social order, are given the option of being sent to the Colonies (areas of North America contaminated by pollution and radioactive waste where prisoners engage in manual labor until death),[5] or working as a prostitute at Jezebel's. In the television series, Moira (Samira Wiley) escaped the Red Center during Handmaid training and was forced to choose between the Colonies and becoming a prostitute at Jezebel's due to her rebellious nature. After learning this, it is clear to the viewer that the decision to work as a prostitute at Jezebel's is not actually a freely made choice, but a decision to engage in forced prostitution over manual labor and eventual death.

POWER AND SEXUAL ASSAULT

When first examining the issue of sexual assault and rape, it is often surprising and sometimes confusing to learn that most instances of sexual assault are about power and control, not sexual gratification. Research has repeatedly found that sexual assault is not usually about the act of fulfilling sexual desire, but instead the power the perpetrators exert over their victim.[6] Throughout history, rape has been used as a form of social control. In areas such as postapartheid South Africa,[7] rape and the threat of rape is used as a tool to control women in the context of civil war, placing them in a state of constant anxiety and fear. In this compromised emotional state, women are more easily controlled and obedient.[8] In Gilead, the rape of Handmaids is not depicted as a means to obtain sexual gratification, but rather as a tool to ensure the impregnation of Handmaids and repopulation of Gilead. This sexual activity represents the power the Commanders and their wives have over the Handmaids, the power to rape under a guise of procreation to create families. While sexual gratification undoubtedly occurs for Commanders through these ceremonies, the stated public goal for all involved is pregnancy.

The ceremonies themselves further emphasize the importance of sexual assault to obtain power and control due to the sterile nature of many Commanders. While the Republic of Gilead makes it known that women are increasingly affected by sterility, the ability of men, especially commanders, to procreate is largely unaddressed. Through our observation of Offred's interaction with Commander Waterford, the audience comes to learn that he, along with many other Commanders, are sterile. Despite the inability of Commanders to impregnate Handmaids, they are still required to participate in the ceremonies and forced sexual activity. This occurrence emphasizes the importance of the sexual assault to maintain control over Handmaids and ensure their continued submission. Since it is impossible for Handmaids to become pregnant in these situations, the purported purpose of procreation no longer applies, and the rape of Handmaids occurs for no other reason than for Commanders and Wives to maintain power.

Victim precipitation theories,[9] also referred to as lifestyle theories, examine criminal behavior as an interaction between an offender, victim, and environment. They suggest that the action of an individual, whether personal lifestyle or daily routine, can impact an individual's likelihood of victimization.[10] These theories have been harshly criticized as they suggest victims engage in some sort of behavior that provokes or contributes to their victimization, entering the territory of victim blaming. Often applied to instances of sexual assault/rape, victim precipitation theories suggest that victims have acted in some way to cause their sexual assault.

This belief that victims, especially women, have done something to cause their victimization is especially apparent in the first episode of the 2017 version of *The Handmaid's Tale*. Upon being captured and determined to be fertile, Handmaids are taken to the Red Center, where they undergo indoctrination into their new role as Handmaid. It is at this center that Aunts, older women who have been tasked with ensuring Handmaids follow the rules, instruct the women that the rampant infertility overtaking the world is due in large part to the promiscuous nature of women of earlier times. They call these women "sluts" and "dirty," suggesting that infertility was a form of punishment because of the sexual nature of these women, which caused sexually transmitted diseases that decreased fertility.

An even clearer example of victim precipitation and victim blaming is exhibited by the shaming of Handmaid Ofwarren/Janine (Madeline Brewer) during her time at the Red Center. During a group lesson, Janine discloses that when she was fourteen she was gang-raped by six different boys that she went to high school with. She recounts that she was at a party and had been drinking, but believed the boys were her friends and was caught off-guard by the attack. As a result of her rape she became pregnant and later had an abortion. Upon sharing this incredibly personal and traumatic experience, Aunt Helena (the novel version; "Aunt Lydia" [Ann Dowd] in the TV series), began questioning the other Handmaids about Janine's experience: "But *whose* fault was it? . . . *Her* fault, *her* fault, *her* fault. . . . *Who* led them on? . . . *She* did. *She* did. *She* did. Why did God allow such a terrible thing to happen? Teach her a *lesson*. Teach her a *lesson*. Teach her a *lesson*."[11] It is after this repeated shaming that Janine breaks down, attributing blame for her rape to her own actions. During this exchange, it is apparent that Aunt Helena/Lydia suggests Janine brought her rape on herself due to her own behavior. In addition to Janine taking the blame upon herself by stating "I led them on," the other Handmaids are forced to point their fingers at her and exclaim in unison that the victim is guilty.[12]

Victim blaming associated with rape and sexual assault is often based on specific characteristics of the victim and situational aspects of the event itself.[13] Were the victims intoxicated? What were they wearing? Were they alone? Did they consent to some sexual acts? These are all questions that are frequently asked when attempting to understand cases of sexual assault and present the most common features of victim blaming. In the case of Janine, she was alone with six boys, engaged in drinking, and at a party, all characteristics that victim precipitation theories would argue put her at increased risk for sexual victimization. Had she not been intoxicated, not been alone, or not been at a party, the implied belief is that her rape would not have occurred, and thus, she is at least partially at fault for her rape. Aunt Helena/ Lydia uses strategically developed questions to further impress these beliefs upon the Handmaids, placing full responsibility for Janine's rape on herself, and denying the active role played by the six boys who raped her. Ultimately, victim blaming is inherently linked to rape culture and rape myth acceptance, another concept expressly depicted in the above-mentioned scene and throughout *The Handmaid's Tale*.

RAPE CULTURE AND RAPE MYTHS: RITUALIZED RAPE IN *THE HANDMAID'S TALE*

Rape is often underreported, leading to misperception of how rape occurs, what actually constitutes rape, and how experiences of rape impact victims.[14] Rape experiences are often underreported due to victims' feelings of powerlessness and shame, and fear of degradation or not being believed by others.[15] Rape myths are defined as "prejudicial, stereotyped, or false beliefs about rape, rape victims and rapists."[16] While inherently false, rape myths are persistently held beliefs that are used, either consciously or unconsciously, to justify or deny sexual aggression and violence by men against women.[17] Rape myths are incredibly important as they can be used by both the perpetrator, outside observers, and the victim themselves to justify sexual aggression, eliminate social prohibitions against sexual assault and rape, and minimize the seriousness of this type of offense.[18] Ultimately, rape myth acceptance perpetuates a social environment where rape not only occurs but is justified by the circumstance and the victim. In the world of Gilead, the rape of Handmaids is encouraged and justified as a biblical ritual, drawing upon the Old Testament story of Rachel and her handmaid, Bilhah.[19]

Rape myths usually fall under four categories: (1) blame the victim for their rape; (2) disbelieve claims of rape; (3) exonerate perpetrators of rape; or (4) suggest that only certain types of women are raped.[20] Rape myths often feature claims such as: "she liked it," "she asked for it," or "it wasn't really rape." Rape myth acceptance can be particularly damaging as it can lead to inaccurate perceptions of the likelihood of false rape allegations[21] or encourage a culture of victim blaming.[22] The United States is currently plagued by this culture of rape myth acceptance, with allegations of rape often being met with disbelief and doubt despite research suggesting that only roughly 3 percent of rape allegations are false.[23]

The concept that rape myths can be used to create an environment that justifies rape is evident in Gilead. Each month, Commanders engage in ritualized rape of their Handmaids with the help of their wives. These "ceremonies" are justified using passages from the Old Testament of the Bible in which Rachel and Jacob are unable to conceive, and as such they use her Handmaid, Bilhah, to conceive a child. This passage is incredibly important as it allows those in power in Gilead to justify the rape of Handmaids by Commanders by explaining that they are charged with bringing children into Gilead. Their fertility leads Handmaids to be both the most important, and most oppressed women, in Gilead. The Commanders and their Wives also seem to justify the rape of Handmaids by focusing on the protection afforded to those Handmaids who do become pregnant. In season 1, episode 1 of the series, the Handmaids are instructed to beat a man to death after being informed by Aunt Lydia that he raped a pregnant Handmaid, a crime punishable by death. While the monthly rape of Handmaids by Commanders is permitted, even encouraged, the forcible rape of a Handmaid (especially pregnant) by someone other than her Commander threatens the work of Gilead and is treated as a horrible affront to the Handmaid and the Republic. This dichotomy between sexual assault that is viewed as consenting behavior and sexual assault that is unacceptable presents a clear example of how rape myths, specifically the myth that rape involves physical force, can be used to deny that rape has occurred, and in some situations justify the act itself.

The pervasiveness of rape culture and rape myth acceptance is especially apparent when analyzing two different instances of rape that occur against Handmaid Offred/June. Each month, Offred/June is ritually raped by Commander Waterford (Joseph Fiennes) as part of the "ceremony" designed to ensure Handmaids become pregnant. These assaults occur numerous times throughout the television show depicting the rape of Offred/June and other Handmaids. However, it is not until the outwardly and explicitly violent "ceremony" rape of Offred/June in season 2, episode 10 that the show depicts violence as a part of rape. After going into false labor, Serena Waterford (Yvonne Strahovski), Commander Waterford's wife, is so humiliated and furious that she suggests sex can be used to induce labor. This leads to the violent rape of Offred/June by Commander Waterford where the Handmaid protests and tries to end the act of penetration, denying her consent. While the ceremonies usually depicted in the series do not feature violence, they still represent instances of rape. A common rape myth suggests that rape has to occur by force or violence, causing some to view these instances as less disturbing than the outwardly violent rape meant to induce labor. In reality, this is not true as rape can feature both manipulation and coercion. This also sheds light on the issue of force and consent when determining whether rape or sexual assault has occurred.

RAPE, CONSENT, AND FORCE

The depictions of rape in *The Handmaid's Tale* present a unique opportunity to address common misconceptions about rape, force, and consent, namely: physical force does not need to occur for an act to be considered rape; Handmaids are not consenting to sexual activity with Commanders due to their lack of physical attempts to refuse; the ceremony represents a form of coercion and manipulation through threat of bodily harm. While rape myths would suggest that violence or physical force is required for an event to be considered rape, this is not the case. Forcible rape can occur, featuring force, threat of force, or threat of injury, but force is not necessary for a sexual encounter to be considered rape. Rape can be defined as any unwanted sexual activity through lack of consent or inability to give consent.[24] This includes instances of husbands or wives raping their partner, as entrance into an intimate relationship at one point in time cannot be construed as blanket consent for all future sexual encounters. Although the instances of rape displayed in *The Handmaid's Tale* do not feature overt physical violence, they are still clear instances of rape. The lack of physical force that often occurs during ceremonies does not, in any way, suggest that Handmaids are consenting to the sexual assault, but instead emphasizes the importance of coercion in rape. These instances of rape can be easily compared to instances of rape in society where physical force is not present.

Those watching the series, the prior movie version of Atwood's work, or Schlöndorff's 1990 film, must also confront the question of whether the Handmaids are consenting to sexual activity. In very few instances do the Handmaids attempt to fight back against rape during the monthly ceremonies. Some may question why these women appear to passively accept their fate. While viewed as cooperative, these women are manipulated and coerced into compliance using power, control, and threat exerted by Commanders and Wives. When Handmaids do fight back against the ceremonies and their role as Handmaid, they are punished. This reality is presented to the viewer when Ofsteven (Alexis Bledel) steals a car at the marketplace, runs over a Guardian, and is sent to the Colonies because of her transgression.

The greatest threat used to ensure that Handmaids comply is the threat of bodily harm, a threat that viewers/readers quickly come to understand is not an empty one. Throughout the story of Offred/June, it becomes clear that those Handmaids who do not conform to Gilead's rules and norms will be subject to physical pain and torture. Offred/June explains in the television series that during her time at the Red Center, Janine/Ofwarren had her right eye removed after talking back to Aunt Lydia. Another example of violence being used to ensure compliance came when Ofglen/Emily (Alexis Bledel) was discovered to be having a sexual, lesbian relationship with a Martha (sterile women who serve as domestic servants to high-ranking officials), a severe violation of the rules of Gilead. Upon this discovery, she was subjected to a clitoridectomy, a form of female genital mutilation, eliminating any future sexual pleasure. In addition to the threat of bodily harm, the novel version outlines that Handmaids have three chances (placement in the houses of three different Commanders) to become pregnant. Failure to become pregnant after these three chances results in them being labeled "unwomen" (sterile women incapable of social integration) and sent to the Colonies. These outcomes of resisting the ceremony or failure to become pregnant serve as forms of coercion, manipulation, and threats to ensure that Handmaids submit to rape at the hands of Commanders and Wives.[25]

Atwood's development of Gilead and the nature of rape and sexual assault against Handmaids in this fictional world is not always the brutal and forced picture of rape often held by the general public. Instead, it presents a perfect example of the insidious nature of sexual assault, and the importance that concepts including power, coercion, and force play when understanding sexual assault. This story provides a unique example to apply knowledge about criminology/criminal justice issues such as sexual assault and rape to visual scenarios in an effort to more deeply understand the complex environment in which sexual violence occurs and is interpreted.[26]

NOTES

1. Amy Grubb and Emily Turner, "Attribution of Blame in Rape Cases: A Review of the Impact of Rape Myth Acceptance, Gender Role Conformity and Substance Use on Victim Blaming," in *Aggression and Violent Behavior* 17, no. 5 (2012): 443–52.

2. Jackie Jones, Anna Grear, Rachel Anne Fenton, and Kim Stevenson, eds., *Gender, Sexualities and Law* (New York: Routledge, 2011).

3. In *The Handmaid's Tale*, Jezebel's is a secret brothel where women who are rebellious against the Republic of Gilead are sent. They often have the choice of going to Jezebel's, or the Colonies where they face certain death. The clientele at Jezebel's includes foreign diplomats and often Commanders, although the brothel is not officially recognized and violates the laws of Gilead.

4. Nora V. Demleitner, "Forced Prostitution: Naming an International Offense," in *Fordham International Law Journal* 18 (1994): 163.

5. Margaret Atwood, *The Handmaid's Tale* (New York: Anchor Books, 1998).

6. Richard G. Wright, *Sex Offender Laws: Failed Policies, New Directions* (New York: Springer Publishing Company, 2014).

7. Helen Moffett, "'These Women, They Force Us to Rape Them': Rape as Narrative of Social Control in Post-Apartheid South Africa," *Journal of Southern African Studies* 32, no. 1 (June 2006): 129–44. doi: 10.1080/03057070500493845.

8. Moffett, "'These Women,'"

9. For more information on victim precipitation theories, see the following: Pat Gilmartin-Zena, "Attribution Theory and Rape Victim Responsibility," *Deviant Behavior* 4, no. 3–4 (1983): 357–74. doi: 10.1080/01639625.1983.9967622; T. D. Miethe, "The Myth or Reality of Victim Involvement in Crime: A Review and Comment on Victim-Precipitation Research," *Sociological Focus* (1985): 209–20. doi.org/10.1177/0093854897024002003; Robert F. Meier and Terance D. Miethe, "Understanding Theories of Criminal Victimization," *Crime and Justice* 17 (1993): 459–99. JSTOR (1147556).

10. Robert F. Meier and Terance D. Miethe, "Understanding Theories of Criminal Victimization," *Crime and Justice* 17 (1993): 466. JSTOR (1147556).

11. Atwood, *The Handmaid's Tale*, 72.

12. *The Handmaid's Tale*, "Offred," Season 1, Episode 1, directed by Reed Morano, written by Bruce Miller, Hulu, Arpil 26, 2017. When June/Offred (Elisabeth Moss) refuses to join in, she is hit until she follows suit. Moira, a lesbian African-American female in the TV series (Samira Wiley) encourages June to comply and participate in the blame game. At the end of season 1, June leads the resistance when the same Handmaid Ofwarren/Janine is supposed to be stoned for wanting to commit suicide. The Handmaids refuse and drop the stones, walking away from Aunt Lydia. The television adaptation asserts that Janine has been psychologically traumatized by the sexual politics and the isolation she has been subjected to, following her fate in the second season when she has been sent to the toxic Colonies.

13. Diane Horgan and Glenn Reeder, "Sexual Harassment: The Eye of the Beholder," *American Association of Occupational Health Nursing Journal* 34 (1986): 83–86.

14. Amy Grubb and Julie Harrower, "Attribution of Blame in Cases of Rape: An Analysis of Participant Gender, Type of Rape and Perceived Similarity to the Victim," *Aggression and Violent Behavior* 13, no. 5 (February 2008): 396–405.

15. Rita Gunn and Rick Linden, "The Impact of Law Reform on the Processing of Sexual Assault Cases," *Canadian Review of Sociology/Revue Canadienne de Sociologie* 34, no. 2 (1997): 155–74.

16. Martha R. Burt, "Cultural Myths and Supports for Rape," *Journal of Personality and Social Psychology* 38, no. 2 (1980): 217.

17. Kimberly A. Lonsway and Louise F. Fitzgerald, "Rape Myths: In Review," *Psychology of Women Quarterly* 18, no. 2 (1994): 133–64.

18. Burt, 217; Gerd Bohner, Frank Siebler, and Jürgen Schmelcher, "Social Norms and the Likelihood of Raping: Perceived Rape Myth Acceptance of Others Affects Men's Rape Proclivity," *Personality and Social Psychology Bulletin* 32, no. 3 (2006): 286–97.

19. Rachel, and her sister Leah, are both married to Jacob. While Leah can provide Jacob with son after son, Rachel is not as fortunate. After trying and failing to become pregnant multiple times, Rachel convinces her husband to impregnate her handmaid Bilhah, so that Rachel can raise those children as her own.

20. Gerd Bohner, Marc-André Reinhard, Stefanie Rutz, Sabine Sturm, Bernd Kerschbaum, and Dagmar Effler, "Rape Myths as Neutralizing Cognitions: Evidence

for a Causal Impact of Anti-Victim Attitudes on Men's Self-Reported Likelihood of Raping," *European Journal of Social Psychology* 28, no. 2 (May 1999): 257–68; Heike Gerger, Hanna Kley, Gerd Bohner, and Frank Siebler, "The Acceptance of Modern Myths about Sexual Aggression Scale: Development and Validation in German and English," *Aggressive Behavior: Official Journal of the International Society for Research on Aggression* 33, no. 5 (March 2007): 422–40.

21. Julie A. Allison and Lawrence S. Wrightsman, *Rape: The Misunderstood Crime* (Newbury Park: Sage Publications, Inc, 1993).

22. Antonia Abbey, Pam McAuslan, and Lisa T. Ross, "Sexual Assault Perpetration by College Men: The Role of Alcohol, Misperception of Sexual Intent, and Sexual Beliefs and Experiences," *Journal of Social and Clinical Psychology* 17, no. 2 (June 1998): 167–95.

23. Lesley Mcmillian, "Police Officers' Perceptions of False Allegations of Rape," *Journal of Gender Studies* 27, no. 1 (2018): 9–21.

24. Heidi M. Zinzow, S. Resnick, Jenna L. McCauley, Ananda B. Amstadter, Kenneth J. Ruggiero, and Dean G. Kilpatrick, "The Role of Rape Tactics in Risk for Posttraumatic Stress Disorder and Major Depression: Results from a National Sample of College Women," *Depression and Anxiety* 27, no. 8 (2010): 708–15.

25. During examinations by Gilead doctors, many Handmaids learn that their Commanders are sterile. Upon learning this, Handmaids are sometimes left with no choice but to sleep with these doctors in the hopes of becoming pregnant and avoiding being transferred to a new Commander or the Colonies.

26. For more discussion questions and supplemental materials the author and editorial team would like to refer you to our Facebook page on *"The Handmaid's Tale as a Pedagogical Tool."*

WORKS CITED

Abbey, Antonia, Pam McAuslan, and Lisa Thomson Ross. "Sexual Assault Perpetration by College Men: The Role of Alcohol, Misperception of Sexual Intent, and Sexual Beliefs and Experiences." *Journal of Social and Clinical Psychology* 17, no. 2 (1998): 167–95.

Allison, Julie A., and Lawrence S. Wrightsman. *Rape: The Misunderstood Crime.* Newbury Park: Sage, 1993.

Atwood, Margaret. *The Handmaid's Tale.* New York: Anchor Books, 1998.

Bohner, Gerd, Frank Siebler, and Jürgen Schmelcher. "Social Norms and the Likelihood of Raping: Perceived Rape Myth Acceptance of Others Affects Men's Rape Proclivity." *Personality and Social Psychology Bulletin* 32, no. 3 (2006): 286–97.

Bohner, Gerd, Marc-André Reinhard, Stefanie Rutz, Sabine Sturm, Bernd Kerschbaum, and Dagmar Effler. "Rape Myths as Neutralizing Cognitions: Evidence for a Causal Impact of Anti-Victim Attitudes on Men's Self-Reported Likelihood of Raping." *European Journal of Social Psychology* 28, no. 2 (1998): 257–68. doi: 10.1002.

Burt, Martha R. "Cultural Myths and Supports for Rape." *Journal of Personality and Social Psychology* 38, no. 2 (1980): 217.

Demleitner, Nora V. "Forced Prostitution: Naming an International Offense." *Fordham International Law Journal* 18 (1994): 163.

Gerger, Heike, Hanna Kley, Gerd Bohner, and Frank Siebler. "The Acceptance of Modern Myths about Sexual Aggression Scale: Development and Validation in German and English." *Aggressive Behavior: Official Journal of the International Society for Research on Aggression* 33, no. 5 (2007): 422–40.

Gilmartin-Zena, P. "Attribution Theory and Rape Victim Responsibility." *Deviant Behavior 4,* no. 3–4 (1983): 357–74. doi: 10.1080/01639625.1983.9967622.

Grubb, Amy, and Emily Turner. "Attribution of Blame in Rape Cases: A Review of the Impact of Rape Myth Acceptance, Gender Role Conformity and Substance Use on Victim Blaming." *Aggression and Violent Behavior* 17, no. 5 (2012): 443–52.

Grubb, Amy, and Julie Harrower. "Attribution of Blame in Cases of Rape: An Analysis of Participant Gender, Type of Rape and Perceived Similarity to the Victim." *Aggression and Violent Behavior* 13, no. 5 (2008): 396–405.

Gunn, Rita, and Rick Linden. "The Impact of Law Reform on the Processing of Sexual Assault Cases." *Canadian Review of Sociology/Revue Canadienne de Sociologie* 34, no. 2 (1997): 155–74.

Horgan, Diane, and Glenn Reeder. "Sexual Harassment: The Eye of the Beholder." *American Association of Occupational Health Nursing Journal* 34 (1986): 83–86.

Jones, Jackie, Anna Grear, Rachel Anne Fenton, and Kim Stevenson, eds. *Gender, Sexualities and Law*. Routledge, 2011.

Lonsway, Kimberly A., and Louise F. Fitzgerald. "Rape Myths: In Review." *Psychology of Women Quarterly* 18, no. 2 (1994): 133–64.

Miethe, T. D. "The Myth or Reality of Victim Involvement in Crime: A Review and Comment on Victim-Precipitation Research." *Sociological Focus* (1985): 209–20. doi.org/10.1177/0093854897024002003.

Meier, Robert F., and Terance D. Miethe. "Understanding Theories of Criminal Victimization." *Crime and Justice* 17 (1993): 459–99.

McMillan, Lesley. "Police Officers' Perceptions of False Allegations of Rape." *Journal of Gender Studies* 27, no. 1 (2018): 9–21.

Moffett, Helen. "'These Women, They Force Us to Rape Them': Rape as Narrative of Social Control in Post-Apartheid South Africa." *Journal of Southern African Studies* 32, no. 1 (2006): 129–44. doi: 10.1080/03057070500493845.

Wright, Richard, ed. *Sex Offender Laws: Failed Policies, New Directions*. New York: Springer Publishing Company, 2014.

Zinzow, Heidi M., S. Resnick, Jenna L. McCauley, Ananda B. Amstadter, Kenneth J. Ruggiero, and Dean G. Kilpatrick. "The Role of Rape Tactics in Risk for Post-traumatic Stress Disorder and Major Depression: Results from a National Sample of College Women." *Depression and Anxiety* 27, no. 8 (2010): 708–15.

FILMS AND TELEVISION

The Handmaid's Tale. "Offred." Season 1, Episode 1. Directed by Reed Morano. Written by Bruce Miller. Hulu, Arpil 26, 2017.

The Handmaid's Tale. "The Last Ceremony." Season 2, Episode 10. Directed by Jeremy Podeswa. Written by Yahlin Chang. Hulu, June 20, 2018.

Chapter Eight

Advancing Student Understanding of Rape Culture

The Handmaid's Tale *as a Tool in the Primary Prevention of Sexual Assault on College Campuses*

Sarah Dodd

Every year, for many years, I have sat across from college students who want the world to change. They are survivors who have experienced sexual violence, who know it close up. They are women who speak with a well-worn urgency of the fear of victimization, and the way that fear shapes their lives. They are allies, grappling with a world where sexual assault on college campuses continues to persist, despite decades of efforts by activists and administrators. These students contend with the ugliness of the problem. All of them, invariably, already know the statistics. One in five women, in college, have experienced assault.[1] One in thirty-three men have been subjected to sexual violence.[2] They have dismantled old mythologies about victims and perpetrators. They have sought an intersectional approach. This is to say, every year I meet a small group of college students who have an advanced knowledge of these issues and who are deeply invested in eradicating the problem. This chapter provides a framework, and practical tools, to utilize the questions surrounding victims of sexual assault and state-instituted violence in the Hulu television series *The Handmaid's Tale* to inform and strengthen campus prevention initiatives.

Since 2010 I have worked on college campuses in the United States providing direct advocacy services to survivors and coordinating prevention efforts. Roles like mine have been created in response to legislation at the federal level that has strengthened the obligations that colleges have to both prevent sexual assault from occurring, and to respond appropriately to survivors when it does. As a prevention educator and social worker, it is always a great joy to find individuals who are eager to look beyond what is mandated by law and toward significant change within their own campus community. These students are on every one of our state campuses, and they are looking for us, too. They often become an essential component in peer education programs, social media campaigns and the development of institutional primary prevention strategies. Throughout the years, I have conducted an advanced workshop intended for students just like this—those with a strong foundation of understanding about the nature of sexual assault already in place. The purpose is to help them make the leap from thinking about prevention as interrupting individual behavior, to primary prevention,[3] where the goal is to stop sexual assault from ever occurring in the first place. At the end of the workshop I typically provide space and art supplies and music and ask participants to create, however they choose, a visual representation of how their world would be different if sexual violence was at 0 percent prevalence in our community. I ask, what would a world without violence really look like? Despite the depth of their knowledge and the richness of their lived experiences, this question invariably gives even the most advanced students pause.

There is a valid reason why this is such a challenging exercise. Student activists, and prevention educators ourselves, are trying to create change in communities where sexual violence operates as the outcome of a culture of violence, sometimes referred to as rape culture.[4] That is to say, sexual assault in college communities continues to be a problem because there are deeply rooted social norms within our communities that normalize, facilitate, uphold, and reinforce sexually aggressive behavior. While it may be a natural step, for many, to intellectually understand the concept of social norms, it proves vastly more difficult to identify, in a tangible manner, the way these norms manifest in our own everyday lives, not just on the television screens. Social norms can be hard for students to pin down because they are as close to us as the air that we breathe. They are so present, all around us, that they become invisible.

It is here, in this place, that the Hulu TV adaptation of Margaret Atwood's novel, *The Handmaid's Tale*, serves as a powerful educational tool to help activists and educators make visible the invisible, so as to plan concrete strategies for change in the world of here and now. In the Hulu series, viewers enter an alternate reality that is both vastly different to and constantly reflective of the world that we know. In this dystopian world called Gilead, the United States government has been overthrown by a militarized group of Christian fanatics who are purportedly seeking to address population growth issues by restructuring society on the basis of literal interpretations of the Bible. Women in Gilead who still have the ability to procreate are enslaved as Handmaids in the households of the ultra-elite within Gilead's newly formed government. These women are captured from their former lives as educated leaders of society, as professors and editors and doctors, their assets are frozen, their access to even pencil and paper denied, and they are sent to a training center where they are primed for their new role as men's servants. Once ready, they are sent to a Commander's home and then, regularly and ceremonially, raped by the Commander, with his Wife present. If the Handmaid becomes pregnant, the newborn is the child of the Commander and the Wife.

In the world of Gilead, all women have been stripped of power, regardless of whether they are Handmaids or hold an alternate role. The law prohibits them from owning property, being employed, having a bank account, or reading and writing. As the rights of women were taken away, men in Gilead, regardless of their status, were bestowed additional powers. Men soon had full control over the autonomy of women. Black-booted soldiers mill the streets with oversized machine guns at the ready. The viewer is often given a visual perspective of Gilead from the eyes of the Handmaids, with the camera panning in different directions, catching the eyes of the soldiers ever watching, ever monitoring, and ensuring compliance.

The world of Gilead is *not* our world. Yet, the social norms that perpetuate a rape culture in our world are chillingly similar and present in Gilead too. Through the use of flashbacks to both before Gilead and during the transition of the overthrow of the government, viewers are able to trace these norms from our reality and into this alternate universe. In the context of a new societal structure, where rape is overtly central to the particular way the community functions, these social norms lose their very normality, and are brought into the light. It is this balance of familiarity and difference that makes it such a useful tool for educators dedicated to ending sexual violence.

FRAMEWORK TO CHALLENGE SOCIAL NORMS

The National Sexual Violence Resource Center (NSVRC) developed a framework for challenging social norms that contribute to violence in their 2006 publication, *Sexual Violence and the Spectrum of Prevention.*[5] Their framework, born out of the movement of activists to shift prevention of sexual assault to a public health primary prevention model, identifies key social norms that contribute to rape culture, including: limited roles for women, toxic masculinity, tolerance of violence, and entrenched silence around violence against women. *The Handmaid's Tale* can be used as a tool to illuminate these social norms, thereby activating a broader discussion of prevention strategies with college students and promoting innovative strategies for change.

SOCIAL NORM #1: THE ROLE OF WOMEN

Scholars have long sought to understand the connection between limited roles for women and sexual violence. Research confirms that beliefs and values that promulgate restrictive rights and gender roles for women are strongly associated with the acceptance of rape myths.[6] Rape myths have been defined as "attitudes and beliefs that are generally false but are widely and persistently held, and that serve to deny and justify male sexual aggression against women."[7] For example, the belief that most women lie about rape, while proven empirically to be false,[8] is still deeply rooted in the narrative of sexual violence in many communities. Rape myths are often focused on several key themes: the victim asked for it, the perpetrator did not mean it, the act was not "really" rape, and the accusers lie about rape.[9] Despite the advances in awareness around sexual assault in college communities, myths about rape still persist on our campuses.[10] Adherence to rape myth acceptance is strongly associated with sexual aggression,[11] which makes addressing these myths an essential component of primary prevention efforts.

In Gilead, everyone knows his or her place. The role of each individual in society is clearly defined and, for women, these roles are colorfully and visually marked. The Wives of Commanders are draped in dresses and cloaks of eggshell blue. Handmaids, white bonnets in place, shielding them from conversation in public, wear crimson. The household servants, the Marthas, complete their daily tasks in outfits of pale green. The Aunts go about the business of training Handmaids in olive green attire. In the poorer subsets of society, men are permitted to marry so-called Econowives, women who must fulfill the role of wife and Martha and, when possible, Handmaid. In the Hulu series these women go about their day swathed in grey. Wife. Servant. Aunt. Bearer of children. These are the options available to women in Gilead.

In the world of Gilead, the limited roles and rights for women is a lynchpin for a rape-supportive culture. Women have been stripped of all of their rights and given specific, extremely restrictive roles to fulfill, all of which are bound to stereotypical and traditional female gender roles. The beliefs and values inherent in this oppression have, essentially, been codified into the law. In season 2 of the series, Serena Joy (Yvonne Strahovski), the wife of Commander Fred (Joseph Fiennes), head of the primary household in the show, begins doing her husband's work when he is hospitalized after an attack on a new government facility. Serena, who was a public speaker, writer, and activist prior to the overthrow of the U.S government (and had helped facilitate the governmental change as one of the lead ideologues), begins to write orders and sign documents, forging her husband's name. She invites her Handmaid, June (Elisabeth Moss), a former book editor, to assist. Upon

Commander Fred's recovery he learns of this transgression and beats Serena severely, while June is forced to watch. This punishment is not just permitted, it is expected as a response to Serena stepping out of her assigned role.

In Gilead, the belief that women are intended for these particular roles permits a cultural acceptance of rape, executed by men who remain unpunished. In the first TV season, one of the Handmaids, Janine (Madeline Brewer), is moved to a new household.[12] On her first night she is expected to take part in the ceremony, in which the Commander Warren Putman (Steven Kunken) of the household rapes her while she lies between the legs of his Wife, Naomi Putman (Ever Carradine). In this instance, the Wife attempts to gently comfort Janine before the ceremony but also has no visible empathy for Janine's clear distress. When the Commander enters the room, he immediately comes to the edge of the bed and Janine says "No, I don't . . .," but before she can even finish that sentence he has begun to rape her, his eyes never looking down at her. His expression is never changing. To the Commander and his Wife, Janine is no longer a person, but a Handmaid, an object meant for men to violate, an object that cannot say "no." The values the founders of Gilead hold regarding the roles of women are essential for this culture of rape to persist.

SOCIAL NORM #2: MASCULINITY

The NSVRC framework highlights specific social norms centered on how hegemonic masculinity is constructed with an emphasis on "domination, control and risk taking."[13] When cultural norms teach boys and men to aspire towards these types of characteristics, rape culture is further cultivated. Social theorists have recently begun to grapple with the meaning of this connection.[14] Hegemonic masculinity in the Unites States sets an expectation for boys and men to be strong, emotionless, heterosexual, assertive, and in control at all times. While not all individual men strive to fulfill this expectation, all men do navigate a world where the pressure of these expectations looms and influences their daily life. Men's understanding of sexual assault is influenced by their perception of how other men understand this crime. In fact, college men often misperceive other men's actual beliefs, believing that other men are more sexist and rape affirming than they actually are.[15] Social norms that permit toxic masculinity normalize rape-supportive attitudes.

In the world of Gilead, to be a man is to have power—of the law, of the house, and of the women. To be a man is to reject all things perceived as nonmasculine within the context of the hegemony. Early in the first season of *The Handmaid's Tale*, June and another Handmaid walk back from the store, and in doing so, pass The Wall. Hanging from a high white wall, against the backdrop of a clear blue sky and under the watchful gaze of gun-wielding military men, are several bodies, their faces covered, flies buzzing nearby. The bag over each face has a symbol indicating why they were executed, one being a gay man, another a doctor, and, finally, a theologian. All were executed due to their beliefs rather than crimes they committed. In Gilead, members of the LGBTQ community are referred to as "gender traitors." Gay men have rejected one of the key tenets of masculinity in this world by not having sex with women. In order to sustain the hegemony, the consequences for not fulfilling masculine expectations are swift and severe. Men who challenge the standard, in any way, are removed. Those who fulfill it are rewarded. The construction of masculinity as a mantel of power and control both sustains and reinforces the culture of violence against women in Gilead.

SOCIAL NORM #3: TOLERANCE OF VIOLENCE

Within the NSVRC framework, the norms around how violence is under-stood, and constructed, in a society are critically important. When sexual aggression is normalized and victims are blamed for sexual violence, a cul-ture of violence will persist. Blame of victims, particularly when they are assaulted by an acquaintance and alcohol was involved, occurs not only in the general population but also amongst service providers such as nurses and police.[16] As a function of victim blame, sexually aggressive behaviors, such as coercive techniques to "obtain" sex, are minimized and offenders are never held accountable.

Commanders and Wives in Gilead do not consider the rape of Handmaids to be sexually violent. In the world they have constructed, this act of violence is a ceremony, a sacrifice, a necessary and important function of the new world order. The ceremony is structured, the Handmaid laying on her back, head laying the between the legs of the Wife who holds down her wrists, thereby helping her husband commit the rape on the marital bed. The Com-mander stands at the end of the bed and, without a word, inserts himself into the Handmaid. Throughout the first season of *The Handmaid's Tale*, scene after scene portrays the ceremony. It is silent except for the breath of the commander and the jostling of the Handmaid's body. Again and again, the viewer is privy to this act, which on its surface appears brief and sanitized. This changes in season two, episode 10, entitled "The Last Ceremony," when Commander Fred and his Wife, Serena, decide the best way to induce labor in their Handmaid, June, is for Commander Fred to have sex with her. Serena holds June down as she screams and struggles and cries out "no." The brutal violence of the ceremony, always present under the surface, is brought to the forefront in this scene. The viewer recognizes that it was there all along.

While the ceremony itself is so normalized that it is not considered sexual violence by the elites of Gilead, women *are* overtly blamed when acts that are considered rape, happen to them. Early in season one, Handmaid Janine is at the Red Center, a facility where the Aunts train and prepare women for their role as Handmaids. She sits in a circle of other women, describing a gang rape that she endured before Gilead. Aunt Lydia (Ann Dowd), the leader of the Aunts, demands of the room of women, "And who led them on? Whose fault was it?" With fingers pointed at Janine, the women respond in unison, "Her fault. Her fault." Women are both blamed for rape and yet their bodies must be protected from rape, at all costs. Later, in the same season, the Handmaids are asked to stone a man to death for allegedly raping a Handmaid. Women are expected to both take responsibility for ending rape and blamed when it does occur.

SOCIAL NORM #4: PRIVACY

Silence has been identified as a strikingly dangerous social norm. Sexual violence has long been relegated to the private sphere, considered a topic that is a personal problem that should be kept out of public discussions.[17] This silence is deeply entwined with shame and real individual risks—to reputation, to social networks, to employment. In Gilead, not remaining silent has the physical risk of death. When communities are silent about sexual assault, when barriers are created to survivors speaking out about their experience, the problem cannot be addressed, perpetrators fail to be held accountable, and survivors are forced to hold the shame of what was done to them.

From the very beginning of the adaptation of *The Handmaid's Tale* we, the viewers, are drawn into a secret. June, the Handmaid and narrator of the series, speaks to us in a soft whisper. To voice her own experience in Gilead is not permitted. To speak out is a radical act. So she speaks to us as one who is concerned that she will be overheard, worried that someone may be actively trying to listen. The voice-over reflects the origin of the adaptation as a "diary," a tale, written in the first person.

Silence permeates Gilead. It follows the Handmaids as they travel in pairs to the store, past the wall. They are shielded from the exterior world as well as each other with their white bonnets. Silence engulfs the households of the Commanders and their Wives, ever present in each scene. Of all that is taboo in this world, the most silenced experience is the rape of the Handmaids. In the first season, Gilead is visited by a delegation from Mexico to discuss possible trades. Commander Fred introduces June to the ambassador to Mexico, a woman, (Zabryna Guevara), so that she can learn of the Handmaid's experience. The ambassador asks June if she is happy and, with the Commander and his Wife staring intently at her, June responds that she "has found happiness." In order for the narrative of Gilead to be maintained, the rape of the Handmaids cannot come into the light. Offred is not silenced in the episode—she eventually tells her story to the ambassador in private. Unlike the book, the TV show displays multiple instances of voicing protest. In this example, Offred is initially silenced in a public setting—but goes on to speak in a more intimate interaction—which is still very high a risk. To speak the truth of one's lived experience, for the Handmaids, is to put oneself in great danger. However, by challenging the prevailing narrative, speaking out can also create a revolution.

Of all the social norms discussed in this chapter, it is the silence around sexual assault that has been most seriously challenged, both in Gilead and in the present day of our reality. In the wake of the #MeToo movement, where women across the globe began speaking out about their experiences with sexual harassment and sexual misconduct, powerful men are being held accountable through both formal and informal mechanisms. The voices of survivors are being highlighted in the mainstream media. Institutions are being questioned, and pressured to change. The silence around sexual violence is crumbling, and the true lived experience of survivors is taking its place.

Yet, dismantling rape culture does not end here. As discussed throughout this chapter, other social norms are operating to uphold a world where sexual violence is tolerated and permitted. Student activists on college campuses can use *The Handmaid's Tale* to help identify where these social norms are manifesting in their own community, so as to strategize for change. Through the exploration of a world so close, yet so vastly different from their own, they may be able to bring the social norms around them into a sharper relief and begin to construct a vision for a new world.

NOTES

1. Bonnie S. Fisher, Francis T. Cullen, and Michael G. Turner, *The Sexual Victimization of College Women* (Washington DC: United States Bureau of Justice Statistics, 2000), PDF file, accessed February 4, 2018, https://www.ncjrs.gov/pdf files1/nij/182369.pdf.

2. Christopher P. Krebs, Christine H. Lindquist, Tara D. Warner, Bonnie S. Fisher, and Sandra L. Martin, *The Campus Sexual Assault (CSA) Study* (Washington, DC: National Institute of Justice, 2007), PDF file, accessed June 5, 2018, https://www.ncjrs.gov/pdffiles1/nij/grants/221153.pdf.

3. Rachel Davis, Lisa Fujie Parks, and Larry Cohen, *Sexual Violence and the Spectrum of Prevention: Towards a Community Solution* (Enola, PA: National Sexual Violence Resource Center, Prevention Institute, 2006), PDF file, accessed July 1, 2018, https://www.nsvrc.org/sites/default/files/2012-04/Publications_NSVRC_Booklets_Sexual-Violence-and-the-Spectrum-of-Prevention_Towards-a-Community-Solution_0.pdf.

4. Diane F. Herman, "The Rape Culture," *Women: A Feminist Perspective,* edited by Jo Freeman (Palo Alto: McGraw Hill, 1988), 52.

5. Davis, Parks and Cohen, *Sexual Violence and the Spectrum of Prevention.*

6. James V. P. Check and Neil M. Malamuth, "Sex Role Stereotyping and Reactions to Depictions of Stranger versus Acquaintance Rape," *Journal of Personality and Social Psychology* 45, no. 2 (1983): 352; Frank Costin and Norbert Schwarz, "Beliefs about Rape and Women's Social Roles: A Four-Nation Study," *Journal of Interpersonal Violence* 2, no. 1 (1987): 50; Eleanor R. Hall, Judith A. Howard, and Sherrie L. Boezio, "Tolerance of Rape: A Sexist or Antisocial Attitude?" *Psychology of Women Quarterly* 10, no. 2 (1986): 101.

7. Kimberly A. Lonsway and Louise F. Fitzgerald, "Rape Myths: In Review," *Psychology of Women Quarterly* 18 (1994): 134.

8. David Lisak, Lori Gardinier, Sarah C. Nicksa, and Ashley M. Cote, "False Allegations of Sexual Assault: An Analysis of Ten Years of Reported Cases," *Violence against Women* 16, no. 12 (2010): 1329.

9. Diana A. Payne, Kimberly A. Lonsway, and Louise F. Fitzgerald, "Rape Myth Acceptance: Exploration of Its Structure and Its Measurement Using the Illinois Rape Myth Acceptance Scale," *Journal of Research in Personality* 33, no. 1 (1999): 27–68; Sarah McMahon and G. Lawrence Farmer, "An Updated Measure for Assessing Subtle Rape Myths," *Social Work Research* 35, no. 2 (2011): 71–81.

10. Sarah McMahon, "Rape Myth Beliefs and Bystander Attitudes among Incoming College Students," *Journal of American College Health* 59, no. 1 (2010): 9.

11. Emma Yapp and Ethel Quayle, "A Systematic Review of the Association between Rape Myth Acceptance and Male-on-Female Sexual Violence," *Aggression and Violent Behavior* 41 (2018): 9.

12. *The Handmaid's Tale,* "The Bridge," Season 1, Episode 9, directed by Kate Dennis, written by Eric Tuchman, Hulu, June 7, 2017.

13. Davis, Parks, and Cohen, *Sexual Violence and the Spectrum of Prevention.*

14. Jackson Katz, *The Macho Paradox: Why Some Men Hurt Women and How All Men Can Help* (Naperville: Sourcebooks, 2006).

15. Christina M. Dardis, Megan J. Murphy, Alexander C. Bill, and Christine A. Gidycz, "An Investigation of the Tenets of Social Norms Theory as They Relate to Sexually Aggressive Attitudes and Sexual Assault Perpetration: A Comparison of Men and Their Friends," *Psychology of Violence* 6, no. 1 (2016): 167.

16. Steve Loughnan, Afroditi Pina, Eduardo Vasquez, and Elisa Puvia, "Sexual Objectification Increases Rape Victim Blame and Decreases Perceived Suffering," *Psychology of Women Quarterly* 37, no. 4 (2013): 459; Sofia Persson, Katie Dhingra, and Sarah Grogan,"Attributions of Victim Blame in Stranger and Acquaintance Rape: A Quantitative Study," *Journal of Clinical Nursing* 27, no. 13–14 (2018):

2646; Madeleine Van Der Bruggen and Amy Grubb, "A Review of the Literature Relating to Rape Victim Blaming: An Analysis of the Impact of Observer and Victim Characteristics on Attribution of Blame in Rape Cases," *Aggression and Violent Behavior* 19, no. 5 (2014): 524–29.

    17. Judith Herman, *Trauma and Recovery* (New York: BasicBooks, 1992), 7–32.

WORKS CITED

Check, James V. P., and Neil M. Malamuth. "Sex Role Stereotyping and Reactions to Depictions of Stranger versus Acquaintance Rape." *Journal of Personality and Social Psychology* 45, no. 2 (1983): 344–56.

Costin, Frank, and Norbert Schwarz. "Beliefs about Rape and Women's Social Roles: A Four-Nation Study." *Journal of Interpersonal Violence* 2, no. 1 (1987): 46–56.

Dardis, Christina M., Megan J. Murphy, Alexander C. Bill, and Christine A. Gidycz. "An Investigation of the Tenets of Social Norms Theory as They Relate to Sexually Aggressive Attitudes and Sexual Assault Perpetration: A Comparison of Men and Their Friends." *Psychology of Violence* 6, no. 1 (2016): 163–71.

Davis, Rachel, Lisa Fujie Parks, and Larry Cohen. *Sexual Violence and the Spectrum of Prevention: Towards a Community Solution.* Enola, PA: National Sexual Violence Resource Center, Prevention Institute, 2006. PDF File. https://www.nsvrc .org /sites/default/files/2012-04/Publications_NSVRC_Booklets_Sexual-Violence -and-the-Spectrum-of-Prevention_Towards-a-Community-Solution_0.pdf.

Fisher, Bonnie S., Francis T. Cullen, and Michael G. Turner. *The Sexual Victimization of College Women.* Washington DC: United States Bureau of Justice Statistics, 2000. PDF File. https://www.ncjrs.gov/pdffiles1/nij/182369.pdf.

Hall, Eleanor R., Judith A. Howard, and Sherrie L. Boezio. "Tolerance of Rape: A Sexist or Antisocial Attitude?" *Psychology of Women Quarterly* 10, no. 2. (1986): 101–18. Herman, Diane F. "The Rape Culture." In *Women: A Feminist Perspective,* edited by Jo Freeman, 45–53. Palo Alto: McGraw Hill, 1988.

Herman, Judith. *Trauma and Recovery.* New York: Basic Books, 1992.

Katz, Jackson. *The Macho Paradox: Why Some Men Hurt Women and How All Men Can Help.* Naperville: Sourcebooks, 2006.

Krebs, Christopher P., Christine H. Lindquist, Tara D. Warner, Bonnie S. Fisher, and Sandra L. Martin. *The Campus Sexual Assault (CSA) Study.* Washington, DC: National Institute of Justice, 2007. PDF File. https://www.ncjrs.gov/pdffiles1/nij /grants/221153.pdf.

Lisak, David, Lori Gardinier, Sarah C. Nicksa, and Ashley M. Cote. "False Allegations of Sexual Assault: An Analysis of Ten Years of Reported Cases." *Violence against Women* 16, no. 12 (2010): 1318–34.

Lonsway, Kimberly A., and Louise F. Fitzgerald. "Rape Myths: In Review." *Psychology of Women Quarterly* 18 (1994): 133–64.

Loughnan, Steve, Afroditi Pina, Eduardo Vasquez, and Elisa Puvia. "Sexual Objectification Increases Rape Victim Blame and Decreases Perceived Suffering." *Psychology of Women Quarterly* 37, no. 4 (2013): 455–61.

Payne, Diana A., Kimberly A. Lonsway, and Louise F. Fitzgerald. "Rape Myth Acceptance: Exploration of Its Structure and Its Measurement Using the Illinois Rape Myth Acceptance Scale." *Journal of Research in Personality* 33, no. 1 (1999): 27–68.

McMahon, Sarah. "Rape Myth Beliefs and Bystander Attitudes among Incoming College Students." *Journal of American College Health* 59, no. 1 (2010): 3–11.

McMahon, Sarah, and G. Lawrence Farmer. "An Updated Measure for Assessing Subtle Rape Myths." *Social Work Research* 35, no. 2 (2011): 71–81.

Persson, Sofia, Katie Dhingra, and Sarah Grogan. "Attributions of Victim Blame in Stranger and Acquaintance Rape: A Quantitative Study." *Journal of Clinical Nursing* 27, no. 13–14 (2018): 2640–49.

Van Der Bruggen, Madeleine, and Amy Grubb. "A Review of the Literature Relating to Rape Victim Blaming: An Analysis of the Impact of Observer and Victim Characteristics on Attribution of Blame in Rape Cases." *Aggression and Violent Behavior* 19, no. 5 (2014): 523–31.

Yapp, Emma, and Ethel Quayle. "A Systematic Review of the Association between Rape Myth Acceptance and Male-on-Female Sexual Violence." *Aggression and Violent Behavior* 41 (2018): 1–19.

FILM AND TELEVISION

The Handmaid's Tale. "The Bridge." Season 1, Episode 9. Directed by Kate Dennis. Written by Eric Tuchman. Hulu, June 7, 2017.

Section II:

USING *THE HANDMAID'S TALE* AS A KALEIDOSCOPE TO UNDERSTAND PAST AND PRESENT SOCIAL CONCERNS

Chapter Nine

Fertility and Fetal Containers

Science, Religion, and The Handmaid's Tale

Kristine Larsen

INFERTILITY: THE CANARY IN THE COALMINE

Speaking of the wave of infertility that has gripped the world of Margaret Atwood's 1985 novel *The Handmaid's Tale*, Offred recalls "There was no one cause, says Aunt Lydia. . . . Pulled down in front of the blackboard, where once there would have been a map, is a graph, showing the birthrate per thousand, for years and years: a slippery slope, down past the zero line of replacement, and down and down."[1] According to the work's concluding faux academic talk "Historical Notes," the probable reasons for the precipitous drop in population were myriad. Among these were the pre-Gilead access to birth control and abortion, sexually transmitted diseases, pollution from toxic waste dumps, nuclear power plant accidents, agents developed for chemical and biological warfare (including a genetically engineered "sterility-causing virus"[2]) and "the uncontrolled use of chemical insecticides, herbicides, and other sprays."[3] The television series echoes these largely technological causes. In season 1, episode 6, "A Woman's Place," Gilead officials explain to the Mexican delegation that they are counteracting their infertility in part by significantly reducing carbon emissions, relying on organic crops, and relegating colony workers to the lethal job of cleaning up radioactive waste.[4]

Although the universe of *The Handmaid's Tale* is clearly fictional, in many respects it hits uncomfortably close to home in the second decade of the twenty-first century. While other essays in this volume tackle issues of politics, religion, and feminism more broadly, here we will consider the scientific issue of infertility and explore how *The Handmaid's Tale* provides a valuable thought experiment in not only how technology can both cause (through pollution) and cure infertility, but how the impinging of religion and culture on science and technology can also limit fertility. A contemplation of

how society deals with infertility simultaneously as a scientific and social issue leads to the conclusion that infertility is the proverbial canary in the coal
mine, indicative of the combative atmosphere between science and religion
in many respects in modern culture.

Chandra, Copen, and Stephen (2013) define infertility as "a lack of pregnancy in the twelve months prior to the survey . . . despite having had unpro-
tected sexual intercourse in each of those months with the same husband or
partner."[5] Closely related is "impaired fecundity," defined as the "physical
difficulty in either getting pregnant or carrying a pregnancy to live birth."[6]
Their study found that among American women aged 15–44, impaired fecundity increased from 8.4 percent in 1982 to 12 percent in 2002, remaining
stable at 11 percent between 2006 and 2010.[7] This same study found that
among married infertile women aged 15–44, primary infertility (difficulties in having their first child) "increased significantly, from 17% in 1965
to 41%–46% in 1982–2010, which is consistent with patterns and trends in
delayed childbearing over these years."[8]

While delaying childbearing explains part of the statistics, it is definitely
not the entire story. Female infertility is most often due to issues with ovula-
tion. Uterine fibroids and blocked fallopian tubes can also cause infertility,
but environmental and lifestyle factors—including use of tobacco and alcohol, body weight, and stress—can also play a role.[9] Another cause, mentioned
in *The Handmaid's Tale*, is sexually transmitted diseases (STDs). In particular, chlamydia and gonorrhea can lead to pelvic inflammatory disease (PID),
which can permanently damage a woman's reproductive system and lead to
infertility.[10] Environmental stressors can also increase infertility in women.
For example, as noted in the novel, there is increasing evidence that exposure
to air pollution can decrease fertility.[11] Regardless of the cause, American
women are currently only producing 1.8 children on average, less than the 2.1
replacement rate.[12] While some of this reflects varying amounts of personal
choice and economic or social pressures, the infertility industry is "expected
to be valued at more than $21 billion globally by 2020."[13] But while this mar-
ket almost exclusively focuses on women, "the male partner is either the sole
or contributing cause in about 40 percent of cases of infertility."[14]

Infertility in men is most often caused by a lack of healthy sperm caused
by a congenital issue, injury, or lifestyle. Similar to infertility in women,
lifestyle factors include age, stress, BMI, alcohol and tobacco use.[15] A 2017
meta-analysis of other studies found that between 1973 and 2011 both sperm
concentrations and total sperm counts in semen samples collected in North
America, Europe, Australia, and New Zealand significantly dropped (by 52.4
percent and 59.3 percent respectively).[16] Numerous studies suggest that the
increasing amounts of manufactured endocrine-disrupting chemicals released

into our environment (for example, bisphenol A [BPA] found in plastics) are at least partly to blame.[17] Climate change may also play a role, since sperm production is temperature sensitive. A 2015 study[18] found a correlation between high summer temperatures and low birthrates nine months later. This research suggests that climate change may lead to reductions in birthrates. Again, Atwood's novel appears eerily prophetic, and can play a central role in student discussions and speculative writing projects that reflect upon how the already complex interplay between environmental factors, lifestyle choices, and fertility could be further enhanced in a post–climate change world.

As technology and science journalist Bryan Walsh opines, ignoring "male infertility is, in its way, another form of male privilege. Pretending that pregnancy is almost entirely a female responsibility means that women are forced to carry the burden and the blame when it goes wrong, while men, who are just as vital to healthy conception, rarely worry about how their lifestyles impact their own fertility or their possible children." [19] This double standard is also reflected in Atwood's novel. Offred is given the option to be secretly impregnated by her physician, who notes "Most of those old guys can't make it anymore. . . . Or they're sterile."[20] But in Gilead "There is no such thing as a sterile man anymore, not officially. There are only women who are fruitful and women who are barren, that's the law."[21] Officially this might be true, but nonetheless, Serena Joy has Offred sleep with Nick, the Commander's Guardian, in the hopes that she will conceive. The novel's historical notes support the necessity of these desperate acts, as it is said that "many of the commanders" had been rendered sterile due to "secret pre-Gilead gene-splicing experiments with mumps" intended as a biological weapon against Russia.[22] Both the doctor and Serena Joy are effectively suggesting sperm donation as a treatment for male infertility, one of the many options open to real-world couples today.

ASSISTED REPRODUCTION TECHNOLOGIES: PLAYING GOD?

Assisted Reproductive Technologies (ART) that give women and men power over their reproduction include birth control, abortion, and sterilization by choice; prenatal testing; genetic screening; sperm donors and sperm sorting; paternity tests; delaying parenthood (freezing eggs and sperm); sperm and egg donation; *in vitro* fertilization (IVF); and gestational carriers. Some of these technologies are ancient, while others have only recently become technologically possible. Among the oldest is artificial insemination, which was first reported in the 1770s.[23] The first successful use of frozen sperm to impregnate a woman came nearly two centuries later, in 1953, but due to a social backlash against the ethics of using donated sperm, the first successful birth using this technique was to wait for nearly a decade.[24]

The most effective methodology[25] is *in vitro* fertilization (IVF), first accomplished with the birth of Louise Brown in 1978. Multiple eggs are removed from a woman and fertilized by sperm in the laboratory. Resulting embryos are then implanted in the woman's uterus between three to five days later. In intracytoplasmic sperm injection (ICSI) a single sperm is injected into an egg to produce the embryo. ART can also involve donor sperm and/ or eggs, or the implantation of embryos (either the couple's own or donated ones) that have been frozen and thawed. For a woman (whom we will call A) who cannot carry a pregnancy to term, additional ART methodologies include surrogacy and gestational carriers, in which another woman (B) carries the embryo for her. In the first, the embryo is the genetic child of the woman B and the male partner of woman A (or a sperm donor). In the second, the egg used to conceive the embryo is not woman B's (coming from either woman A or another donor).

Despite the fact that over three million babies were born using IVF and similar techniques in the three decades after Louise Brown's birth,[26] many people remain troubled by the ethical and religious issues raised by these technological wonders. The juxtaposition of the words "reproduction" and "technologies" draws attention to the boundary being transgressed here, between the natural and the artificial. It is therefore not surprising that these technologies are considered by some to be inherently unnatural, repulsive, and threatening, although opinions often change over time. For example, as Nicholas Wade describes, "Though in vitro fertilization is now widely accepted, the birth of the first test tube baby was greeted with intense concern that the moral order was being subverted by unnatural intervention in the mysterious process of creating a human being."[27]

I have found that this shift in society's perceptions of particular ARTs is of particular interest to students. Original newspaper and magazine articles describing Brown's conception and the controversies it birthed can be read in parallel with *The Handmaid's Tale*, as we see echoes of societal acceptance of technology played out in reverse in the book. In the novel's "Historical Notes," it is explained that "the need for what I may call birth services was already recognized in the pre-Gilead period, where it was being inadequately met by 'artificial insemination,' 'fertility clinics,' and the use of 'surrogate mothers,' who were hired for the purpose. Gilead outlawed the first two as irreligious but legitimized and enforced the third, which was considered to have Biblical precedents."[28] Indeed, all ART are forbidden in the theocracy of Gilead, with the exception of the Biblical concept of a surrogate mother, conceived the old-fashioned way and with the resulting child the unequivocal property of the biological father's wife. According to Atwood, "The biblical precedent is the story of Jacob and his two wives, Rachel and Leah, and their two handmaids. One man, four women, twelve sons — but the handmaids could not claim the sons. They belonged to the respective wives. And so the tale unfolds."[29]

Both in the real and fictional worlds, the societal boundaries defining what is acceptable and legal (as opposed to technologically possible) greatly reflect the dominant religious movements of that society. It should be noted that the doctrines of such belief systems are, as in the case of Gilead, largely determined by men.[30] Not only do the definitions of what is acceptable vary from religion to religion, but sect to sect, and even one congregation to another. For example, Sallam and Sallam[31] note that different Jewish traditions accept or reject varying forms of ART, not the least reason being prohibitions against "spilling of the seed" in the Old Testament. In addition, while surrogacy is not accepted by most rabbis, some will allow single Jewish women to act in this role, leading to a situation where infertile couples may "have to search for the 'right Rabbi' for advice."[32]

The Catholic Church largely condemns all ART, but as opposed to Gilead, also disallows the use of surrogates. In general it is believed that "children are a gift and a blessing from God" and that although science makes some things possible, it does not make them right.[33] In contrast, Hinduism and Buddhism generally have few issues with ART.[34] The Catholic Church's blanket condemnation of ART follows from the belief that it is dehumanizing: "The marital bed is replaced by the laboratory. The husband is replaced by the doctor manipulating the gametes, and the union of bodies is replaced by a purely technological act. Medically assisted procreation introduces, with full knowledge, a breach in the most private area, the most personal and perhaps the most rich part of the human person."[35] Any child produced via ART "is no longer a gift, but a right," leading infertile couples to "demand that society place at their disposal the necessary technique to satisfy such a desire, and then the right to demand that technicians 'produce' a child."[36] These Catholic condemnations find an exception that proves the rule in Gilead. While there is no technology used in a Handmaid's conception of their master's child, both the sanctity of the marital bed and the inviolability of the Handmaid's body are perverted in symbolic union of three bodies (including the master's wife) in the bedroom ritual. In addition, it is indeed the very belief that the upper class have the right to have children and not the lower class Handmaids and their husbands and partners that leads to human trafficking in Gilead.

INFORMED CONSENT WITHOUT COERCION AND OWNERSHIP OVER ONE'S BODY

As is evident in the ongoing debate over abortion in the United States, battles over reproductive rights often focus on defining the limits of a woman's ownership over her own body. While discussions over abortion may be too fraught with political, religious, racial, and classist overtones to comfortably discuss in classroom situations, there are other numerous examples that provide avenues for discussing both Atwood's novel and critical issues of informed consent and personal reproductive freedoms.

Arguably, the most interesting in recent memory is the case of Henrietta Lacks.[37] On October 4, 1951, this thirty-one-year-old African-American mother died from cervical cancer despite treatment received at Johns Hopkins Hospital in Baltimore, Maryland. Without her or her family's consent, some of her tumor cells were grown in culture and continue to be used in medical research to this day, leading to (among other breakthroughs) the development of the polio vaccine. In recent decades, the moral quandaries concerning these so-called HeLa cells has led to discussions in the scientific community over ownership of tissues and genetic information.[38] Meaningful classroom discussions and position papers can result from a comparison of the fates of Henrietta Lack and Offred. Issues of privacy, consent, and ownership of one's own body (or, more correctly, a lack thereof) are central to the lives of both women.

Ethical issues concerning the reproduction of the HeLa cell-line parallel those also considered in ART. For example, there is not only the issue of making sure that sperm and egg donations are done in keeping with both informed consent and respecting donor privacy, but the legal definition of the mother has not kept up with the technology. Is the mother the egg donor, the gestational carrier, or "the woman for whom the baby is intended."[39] This third woman has no legal designation as mother without an adoption. There are also other cases where another woman could be involved, so-called mitochondrial donation techniques in which the mitochondria from a female donor are used in IVF in order to prevent the genetic transmission of mitochondrial disease.[40] While the biological connection between the egg donor and the resulting child is without question, a biologically unrelated gestational carrier also puts an indelible mark on the child she carries. Not only does the lifestyle and health of the gestational carrier affect the fetus, but "the transfer of maternal hormones through the placenta can impact the behaviors of the fetus and contribute to the child's [development]."[41] In Gilead, the lifestyle of the Handmaids is rigorously controlled in large part to increase their fertility and encourage the healthy development of their fetus.

In our modern world "surrogate mothers" or "gestational carriers" (the difference between the two terms interesting in and of itself) enter into the legal relationship willingly (unlike in Gilead). What if a pregnant woman is unable to give her informed consent, such as in the case where the mother has been declared to be in a persistent vegetative state, or is legally brain dead? Such a "fetal container" can be kept "alive" by order of her parents or the fetus's biological father in order to try and bring the pregnancy to term. Similar cases occur in the real world in the case of mothers in vegetative states (irreversible comas) and those who have suffered brain death. In the latter case, they are technically dead, except that their bodies are sustained through artificial means (including ventilators) for the sole purpose of allowing their fetus to develop to the point where it can survive outside of the womb.

Dehumanizing terms such as "postmortem or perimortem pregnancy, cadaveric pregnancy, maternal organism, and posthumous motherhood" are commonly used to describe the status of brain-dead pregnant woman.[42] We see similar language in the euphemistic eponymous term "handmaid" of Atwood's novel. The legal and ethical ramifications of keeping a woman alive without her expressed consent for the purpose of being a womb are myriad, and have been discussed at length in the literature.[43] Such discussions are not merely academic, as several fetuses have been successfully delivered after over one hundred days in their dead mother's womb.[44] I have found students to be eager to discuss ethical issues raised by individual cases, with most arguing against the courts or relatives who rule that the incapacitated woman should be used as a fetal container without her informed consent. Comparing these cases to those of Gilead's Handmaids would be interesting indeed.

There are also examples where embryos that were conceived through IVF and frozen are implanted and brought to term after one or both of the biological parents have died. There are a number of ethical and legal issues surrounding these scenarios, and many countries have laws regulating these types of births.[45] There have also been cases where sperm has been harvested postmortem,[46] and in a case in Israel, the parents of a dead seventeen-year-old girl won the right to have her eggs harvested and frozen for future pregnancies using a surrogate and sperm donor.[47] Although these are admittedly extreme cases, the lack of informed consent without coercion on the part of one or more parties involved in reproduction certainly parallel themes of *The Handmaid's Tale*. There is also the subhuman position of deformed infants in Gilead (referred to as unbabies or shredders), but this important topic must, of necessity, fall beyond the scope of this brief chapter. I would encourage others to explore this topic in depth, not only in a scholarly treatment, but in classroom discussions as well.

Perhaps more obviously aligned with the fate of Gilead's Handmaids is human trafficking resulting from so-called procreative or reproductive tourism in which infertile couples travel to countries with more relaxed controls on IVF.[48] One of the most popular destinations has been Thailand, where new regulations on the incredible lucrative business of "commercial surrogacy" were put into place in 2015 following international scandals highlighting the exploitation of these women.[49] Once again, Atwood's crystal ball has proven to be uncannily clear: sufficient amounts of currency and high social class unfortunately have the potential to subvert the egalitarian intentions of science. Juxtaposing the legal and ethical issues surrounding commercial surrogacy in our real world with the fate of Atwood's Handmaids would be a valuable exercise for students, again eliciting deep reflection on the actual meaning of informed consent without duress.

WORLDS IN COLLISION: SCIENCE AND RELIGION

Political anthropologist Cris Shore reflects that the "lesson from anthropology is that every society has a vested interest in controlling reproduction, and in each we tend to find dominant institutions—the church, the state, the medical profession, or whatever—competing to monopolize the discourses through which legitimate reproduction is conceptualized."[50] Similarly, in her introduction to a 1998 edition of her novel, Margaret Atwood notes that the "control of women and babies has been a feature of every repressive regime on the planet."[51] She includes a real-world example in her novel's concluding "Historical Notes," namely "Rumania [*sic*]" which had "anticipated Gilead in the eighties by banning all forms of birth control, imposing compulsory pregnancy tests on the female population, and linking promotion and wage increases to fertility."[52] This is a reference to communist dictator Nicolae Ceausescu's banning of all contraception and abortion in 1966, leading to the deaths and maiming of women in illegal abortions and the abandoning of over one hundred thousand children in notoriously ill-equipped orphanages. Two decades after the overthrow of Ceausescu in 1989 and the reversal of his reproductive restrictions, Romania still suffered from the highest rate of infant mortality in the European Union as well as a documented lack of knowledge concerning (and trust in) contraceptives among reproductive age citizens, thanks to Ceausescu's disinformation campaign.[53] Romania demonstrates how the citizens of a totalitarian regime can be brainwashed into believing "truths" about reproduction that fly in the face of science, as happens in Atwood's novel.

The Handmaid's Tale can be read as a cautionary tale against the dangers of the systematized loss of agency over one's own body. In this way it can be an effective springboard for the discussion of virtually any aspect of this important issue, including scientific/technological applications such as medical experimentation, illegal harvesting of organs and tissues, use of genetic information without consent, and broader issues of ownership of genetic material and information. In particular, since reproduction is perhaps the most private, and in an evolutionary sense the most important, action our bodies perform, topics in infertility and ART easily lend themselves to inclusion in discussions of the novel.

As previously noted, there is a significant difference between what is scientifically possible and culturally permitted when it comes to ART, and the locus of the battle line between the two continually shifts as a function of time and place. Current debates in Western culture include "whether there should be stricter limits on how many embryos can be transferred to a woman's uterus during a single cycle . . . whether insurance coverage for fertility treatment ought to be mandated; whether access to ARTs can be ethically restricted based on age, health, sexual orientation."[54] As science continues to push the envelope of what is possible, and humanity continues to be faced with issues of infertility, scientists and cultural/religious leaders will continue to find themselves at odds with each other. In the middle are women and their doctors.

While the laws of nature (as manipulated by science) ultimately decide what is physically possible it is politicians who decide what is prosecutable as a crime. *The Handmaid's Tale* offers a viewpoint of a potential future in which individual rights are curtailed, reproductive science is criminalized, and politics are controlled by a patriarchal cult performing the role of a state religion. As such, Atwood's work is not only a dystopian novel, but as a scientist, I would argue both a work of hard science fiction and horror as well.

NOTES

1. Margaret Atwood. *The Handmaid's Tale* (New York: Anchor Books, 1998), 113.

2. Margaret Atwood. *The Handmaid's Tale*, 309.

3. Margaret Atwood. *The Handmaid's Tale*, 304.

4. Elena Nicolaou, "What Caused Infertility in The Handmaid's Tale, Anyway?" *Refinery 29*, April 24, 2018, https://www.refinery29.com/en-us/2018/04/197236/infertility-cause-handmaids-tale-pollution-virus.

5. Anjani Chandra, Casey E. Copen, and Elizabeth Hervey Stephen, "Infertility and Impaired Fecundity in the United States, 1982–2010: Data from the National Survey of Family Growth," *National Health Statistics Reports* 67 (2013): 1.

6. Chandra et al., "Infertility and Impaired Fecundity in the United States, 1982–2010 data from the National Survey of Family Growth" 1.

7. Chandra et al., "Infertility and Impaired Fecundity in the United States, 1982–2010," 5.

8. Chandra et al., "Infertility and Impaired Fecundity in the United States, 1982–2010," 6.

9. "STDs & Infertility," Centers for Disease Control, October 6, 2017, https://www.cdc.gov/std/in fertility/default.htm.

10. "STDs & Infertility," CDC.

11. Julie Carré, Nicolas Gatimel, Jessika Moreau, Jean Parinaud, and Roger Léandri, "Does Air Pollution Play a Role in Infertility?: A Systematic Review," *Environmental Health* 16 (2017): 82.

12. Bryan Walsh, "Male Infertility Crisis in U.S. Has Experts Baffled," *Newsweek,* September 12, 2017.

13. Walsh, "Male Infertility Crisis."

14. Walsh, "Male Infertility Crisis."

15. Hagai Levine, Niels Jørgensen, Anderson Martino-Andrade, Jaime Mendiola, Dan Weksler-Derri, Irina Mindlis, Rachel Pinotti, and Shanna H. Swan, "Temporal Trends in Sperm Count: A Systematic Review and Meta-Regression Analysis," *Human Reproduction Update* 23 (2017): 647.

16. Levine et. al., "Temporal Trends," 652.

17. Walsh, "Male Infertility Crisis."

18. Alan Barreca, Oliver Deschenes, Melanie Guldi, "Maybe Next Month? Temperature Shocks, Climate Change, and Dynamic Adjustments in Birth Rates," *National Bureau of Economic Research Working Paper* 21681 (October 2015).

19. Walsh, "Male Infertility Crisis."

20. Atwood, *The Handmaid's Tale*, 61.

21. Atwood, *The Handmaid's Tale*, 61.

22. Atwood, *The Handmaid's Tale*, 309.

23. W. Ombelet and J. Van Robays, "Artificial Insemination History: Hurdles and Milestones." *Facts, Views, & Visions in ObGyn* 7, no. 2 (2015): 139.

24. Ombelet and Van Robays, "Artificial Insemination History," 140.

25. Office on Women's Health. "Infertility." May 22, 2018.

26. Anne Drapkin Lyerly, "Marking the Fine Line: Ethics and the Regulation of Innovative Technologies in Human Reproduction," *Minnesota Journal of Law, Science and Technology* 11, no. 2 (2010): 686.

27. Nicholas Wade, "Pioneer of In Vitro Fertilization Wins Nobel Prize," *New York Times*, October 4, 2010.

28. Atwood, *The Handmaid's Tale*, 305.

29. Atwood, *The Handmaid's Tale*, xvi.

30. Gila Stopler, "'A Rank Usurpation of Power'—The Role of Patriarchal Religion and Culture in the Subordination of Women," *Duke Journal of Gender Law & Policy* 15 (2008): 365; Atwood. *The Handmaid's Tale*, 304.

31. H. N. Sallam and N. H. Sallam, "Religious Aspects of Assisted Reproduction," *Facts, Views, & Visions in ObGyn* 8, no. 1 (2016): 34.

32. Sallam and Sallam, "Religious Aspects of Assisted Reproduction," 35.

33. Sallam and Sallam, "Religious Aspects of Assisted Reproduction," 36.

34. Sallam and Sallam, "Religious Aspects of Assisted Reproduction," 33.

35. Jean-Louis Brugues, "Assisted Procreation and IVF-ET," in *Lexicon: Ambiguous and Debatable Terms regarding Family Life and Ethical Questions* (2006), 1.

36. Brugues, "Assisted Procreation and IVF-ET," 3.

37. For more information, see Rebecca Skloot, *The Immortal Life of Henrietta Lacks* (New York: Broadway Paperbacks, 2010).

38. "The Legacy of Henrietta Lacks," Johns Hopkins Medicine, https://www.hopkinsmedicine.org/henriettalacks/index.html.

39. Erin Y. Hisano, "Gestational Surrogacy Maternity Disputes: Refocusing on the Child," *Lewis & Clark Law Review* 15, no. 2 (2011): 517.

40. For more information, see Rosa J. Castro, "Mitochondrial Replacement Therapy: The UK and US Regulatory Landscapes," *Journal of Law and the Biosciences* 3, no. 3 (2016): 726–35.

41. Hisano, "Gestational Surrogacy Maternity Disputes: Refocusing on the Child," 531–32.

42. Anita J. Catlin and Deborah Volat, "When the Fetus Is Alive but the Mother Is Not," *Critical Care Nursing Clinics of North America* 21 (2009): 268.

43. For example, see Nicola S. Peart, A. V. Campbell, Alex R. Manara, S. A. Renowden, and Gordon M. Stirrat, "Maintaining a Pregnancy Following Loss of Capacity," *Medical Law Review* 8(2000): 275–99.

44. Daniel Sperling, "Maternal Brain Death," *American Journal of Law and Medicine* 30 (2004): 453.

45. Sperling, "Maternal Brain Death," 495–96.

46. For example, see Timothy F. Murphy, "Sperm Harvesting and Post Mortem Fatherhood," *Bioethics* 9, no. 4 (1995): 380–98.

47. Adrian Blomfield, "Family Given Permission to Extract Eggs from Ovaries of Dead Daughter in World First," *The Telegraph*, August 8, 2011.

48. Alessandro Stasi, "Protection for Children Born Through Assisted Reproductive Technologies Act, B.E. 2558: The Changing Profile of Surrogacy in Thailand," *Clinical Medicine Insights: Reproductive Health* 11(2017): 1.

49. Stasi, "Protection for Children Born Through Assisted Reproductive Technologies Act, B.E. 2558," 2.

50. Cris Shore, "Virgin Births and Sterile Debates: Anthropology and the New Reproductive Technologies," *Current Anthropology* 33, no. 3 (1992): 301.

51. Atwood, *The Handmaid's Tale*, xvii.

52. Atwood, *The Handmaid's Tale*, 305.

53. Daniel McLaughlin, "Legacy of Romania's Contraception Ban Lives On," *The Irish Times,* August 28, 2007.

54. Lyerly, "Marking the Fine Line," 687.

WORKS CITED

Atwood, Margaret. *The Handmaid's Tale*. New York: Anchor Books, 1998 [1985].

Barreca, Alan, Oliver Deschenes, Melanie Guldi. "Maybe Next Month? Temperature Shocks, Climate Change, and Dynamic Adjustments in Birth Rates." *National Bureau of Economic Research Working Paper* 21681, October 2015.

Blomfield, Adrian. "Family Given Permission to Extract Eggs from Ovaries of Dead Daughter in World First." *The Telegraph*, August 8, 2011. Accessed July 1, 2018. http://www.telegraph.co.uk/health/healthnews/8689479/Family-given-permission -to-extract-eggs-from-ovaries-of-dead-daughter-in-world-first.html.

Brugues, Jean-Louis. "Assisted Procreation and IVF-ET." In *Lexicon: Ambiguous and Debatable Terms regarding Family Life and Ethical Questions,* 1–8. Front Royal: Human Life International, 2006.

Carré, Julie, Nicolas Gatimel, Jessika Moreau, Jean Parinaud, and Roger Léandri. "Does Air Pollution Play a Role in Infertility?: A Systematic Review." *Environmental Health*, July 28, 2017. Accessed 1 July 2018. https://doi.org/10.1186 /s12940-017-0291-8.

Castro, Rosa J. "Mitochondrial Replacement Therapy: The UK and US Regulatory Landscapes." *Journal of Law and the Biosciences* 3, no. 3 (2016): 726–35.

Catlin, Anita J., and Deborah Volat. "When the Fetus Is Alive but the Mother Is Not." *Critical Care Nursing Clinics of North America* 21 (2009): 267–76.

Chandra, Anjani, Casey E. Copen, and Elizabeth Hervey Stephen. "Infertility and Impaired Fecundity in the United States, 1982–2010: Data from the National Survey of Family Growth." *National Health Statistics Reports* 67 (2013): 1–18.

Hisano, Erin Y. "Gestational Surrogacy Maternity Disputes: Refocusing on the Child." *Lewis & Clark Law Review* 15, no. 2 (2011): 517–53.

Levine, Hagai, Niels Jørgensen, Anderson Martino-Andrade, Jaime Mendiola, Dan Weksler-Derri, Irina Mindlis, Rachel Pinotti, and Shanna H. Swan. "Temporal Trends in Sperm Count: A Systematic Review and Meta-Regression Analysis." *Human Reproduction Update* 23(2017): 646–59.

Lyerly, Anne Drapkin. "Marking the Fine Line: Ethics and the Regulation of Innovative Technologies in Human Reproduction." *Minnesota Journal of Law, Science and Technology* 11, no. 2 (2010): 685–712.

McLaughlin, Daniel. "Legacy of Romania's Contraception Ban Lives On." *The Irish Times*, August 28, 2007. Accessed July 1, 2018. https://www.irishtimes.com/news /health/legacy-of-romania-s-contraception-ban-lives-on-1.958842.

Murphy, Timothy F. "Sperm Harvesting and Post Mortem Fatherhood." *Bioethics* 9, no. 4 (1995): 380–98.

Nicolaou, Elena. "What Caused Infertility in *The Handmaid's Tale*, Anyway?" *Refinery 29*, April 24, 2018. Accessed July 1, 2018. https://www.refinery29 .com/2018/04/197236/infertility-cause-handmaids-tale-pollution-virus.

Office on Women's Health. "Infertility." May 22, 2018. Accessed July 1, 2018. https://www.womenshealth.gov/a-z-topics/infertility.

Ombelet, W., and J. Van Robays. "Artificial Insemination History: Hurdles and Milestones." *Facts, Views, & Visions in ObGyn* 7, no. 2 (2015): 137–43.

Peart, Nicola S., A. V. Campbell, Alex R. Manara, S. A. Renowden, and Gordon M. Stirrat. "Maintaining a Pregnancy Following Loss of Capacity." *Medical Law Review* 8 (2000): 275–99.

Sallam, H. N., and N. H. Sallam. "Religious Aspects of Assisted Reproduction." *Facts, Views, & Visions in ObGyn* 8, no. 1 (2016): 33–48.

Shore, Cris. "Virgin Births and Sterile Debates: Anthropology and the New Reproductive Technologies." *Current Anthropology* 33, no. 3 (1992): 295–314.

Skloot, Rebecca. *The Immortal Life of Henrietta Lacks.* New York: Crown, 2010.

Sperling, Daniel. "Maternal Brain Death." *American Journal of Law and Medicine* 30(2004): 453–500.

Stasi, Alessandro. "Protection for Children Born Through Assisted Reproductive Technologies Act, B.E. 2558: The Changing Profile of Surrogacy in Thailand." *Clinical Medicine Insights: Reproductive Health* 11(2017): 1–7.

"STDs & Infertility." *Centers for Disease Control*, October 6, 2017. Accessed July 1, 2018. https://www.cdc.gov/std/infertility/default.htm.

Stopler, Gina. "'A Rank Usurpation of Power' – The Role of Patriarchal Religion and Culture in the Subordination of Women." *Duke Journal of Gender Law & Policy* 15(2008): 365–97.

"The Legacy of Henrietta Lacks." Johns Hopkins Medicine. Accessed 1 July 2018. https://www.hopkinsmedicine.org/henriettalacks/.

Wade, Nicholas. "Pioneer of In Vitro Fertilization Wins Nobel Prize." *New York Times*, October 4, 2010. Accessed July 1, 2018. https://www.nytimes.com/2010 /10/05/health /research/05nobel.html.

Walsh, Bryan. "Male Infertility Crisis in U.S. Has Experts Baffled." *Newsweek*, September 12, 2017. Accessed July 1, 2018. http://www.newsweek.com/2017/09/22 /male-infertility-crisis-experts-663074.html.

FILM AND TELEVISION

The Handmaid's Tale. "A Woman's Place." Season 1. Episode 6. Directed by Floria Sigismondi. Written by Wendy Straker Hauser. Hulu, May 17, 2017.

Chapter Ten

"I'm Ravenous for News"

Using The Handmaid's Tale *to Explore the Role of Journalism*

Theodora Ruhs

Margaret Atwood says that her 1985 book, *The Handmaid's Tale*, was built on clippings from newspapers.[1] She writes, "One of my rules was that I would not put any events into the book that had not already happened in what James Joyce called the 'nightmare' of history, nor any technology not already available."[2] Events, small and big, from around the world showed Atwood a picture of a potential future as reporters uncovered struggles over religion, women's rights, and the politics of both.

News can tell us about the world, uncover the unseen, and, in this and many other cases, warn us. When news is suppressed and controlled by those in power, or even when it is ignored or distrusted, Atwood shows us we lose our ability to have a say in those struggles. As such, her book and the 2017–2018 television show based on the book are fertile ground for exploring the role of journalism in a democratic society and to consider what that society might look like without it.

The most common theme discussed regarding *The Handmaid's Tale* is that of repression of women in an authoritarian regime. Offred, also called June,[3] played by Elisabeth Moss in the show, is kept in servitude and forced to serve couples as a potential producer of babies. Her identity prior to the birth of the nation of Gilead, the fictional government that takes over the United States, is taken from her. She faces threats of punishment and death and is cut off from the world beyond her immediate sphere. Enabling this repression is the suppression and manipulation of the press by the powers that be. This control of information is a key element in destroying the democratic system that came before and in maintaining power. Elisabeth Moss, a producer as well as an actress for the show, says in an interview, "There's also a scene that addresses journalism in Gilead. It's really intense. But it needs to be addressed.

Because, what would have happened to journalists?"[4] Yes, what would have happened to journalists and journalism?

In season 2, episode 2, "Unwomen,"[5] the audience is shown that Gilead has literally killed off journalists with bodies hanging in a now silent newspaper building, supposedly of *The Boston Globe*. In a sense, this can be read as killing democracy. The people of Gilead no longer have free access to information, something that would give them power to navigate and make decisions based on facts and other points of view. This is the role of a public sphere where there is a free exchange of information for participation in public discourse and active citizenship.[6]

Journalism has been attacked in *The Handmaid's Tale* just as echoes of this can be found in our reality. Around the world, there are examples of attacks on journalists. As in the Hulu television series, this can be brutal murder.[7] The attack on journalism can also show up in more subtle ways: discrediting journalists, removing access to the resources they need to do their job, and creating an environment that makes it difficult to discern the validity and credibility of news.

What does a society, a culture, a country become when it no longer has a free press? The media, once primarily the press and now expanding platforms as technology evolves, is one of the ways we learn about what is happening in our communities and in our world. There have been and are current examples of places where the media is less than free to varying degrees.[8] There we can see the control that those in power gain by controlling knowledge. *The Handmaid's Tale* gives us a way to examine the importance of information for an authoritarian government.

There is a connection between how free the press is in a country and how authoritarian that country is.[9] Yet, even in countries with laws protecting news media and without direct government censorship, it can be undermined with potentially real consequences for what news is reported, how it is reported, and what is believed. In the United States, in 2018, there is growing concern about the treatment of journalists and their access to the White House to do their job. We have a president who frequently belittles and discredits journalists, which some see as opening the door to curtailing press freedoms.[10] Donald Trump calls news media he does not like "fake news," sowing distrust of the news media.[11] Around the world, countries are inundated with actual fake news whereas the actual news is deemed fake. While this is not new, with the advent of social media, there is anxiety about the reach of fake news and misinformation.[12] One of the worries is the impact on elections,[13] one of the foundations of democracy. A functioning journalistic sphere is necessary for a functioning democracy.

This chapter examines how and why a robust public sphere, of which a free press is an integral part, is necessary to a functioning democracy and how fragile both are when facing the fall of a free press explicitly and implicitly. We will reflect on how the control of information in Gilead is a contrast to that function. While a dystopian example, this approach to *The Handmaid's Tale* can be a jumping-off point for reflection on journalistic ideals. It may also further illuminate the role and importance of journalism in a democratic society.

DISMANTLING OF THE PUBLIC SPHERE

In the original book, Offred remembers the steps the architects of Gilead took to consolidate their power:

> Things were in that suspended animation for weeks, though some new things did happen. Newspapers were censored and some were closed down, for security reasons they said. The road blocks began to appear, and Identipasses.[14] Everyone approved of that, since it was obvious you couldn't be too careful. They said that new elections would be held, but that it would take some time to prepare for them. The thing to do, they said, was to continue as usual.[15]

This is the dismantling of the public sphere. To succeed, Gilead must control the press. The democratic service of news media can be understood as aiding citizens in their maintenance of a democratic government. The public sphere is the space in which citizens do this work, where they come together to critically debate public issues. For contemporary Scandinavian media scholar Peter Dahlgren, this concept of the public sphere provides an ideal to guide citizen participation in democratic political debate and adds that, "close familiarity with what is said and not said, and how it is said—the topics, the coverages, the debates, the rhetoric, the modes of address, etc.—are a prerequisite not only for an enhanced theoretical understanding but also for concrete political involvement within—and with—the public sphere."[16] It is also where citizens can monitor and hold those in power accountable. In order to do this, citizens must have open access to accurate information.

A stark contrast to Gilead is provided by the fictional Canada in the television show (see the chapter 21 by Janis L. Goldie about Canada as a mythical country in this volume). In the episode "Smart Power,"[17] Mr. and Mrs. Waterford (Joseph Fiennes and Yvonne Strahovski) are visiting their neighbor in the North on a diplomatic mission. During the visit, a bundle of letters from women in Gilead is smuggled out and given to Luke (O-T Fagbenle), June's husband, now living in Canada. June's friend, Moira (Samira Wiley), discussing the letters, says she thought that instead of letters, the package they came in would have "something to make Gilead go boom." "This could go boom," another friend, Erin (Erin Way), says in response.[18] With the release of the letters, there is a public outcry forcing Canadian officials to act, asking the Waterfords to leave. There is still a free flow of information, a space for people to speak out and encourage action. People are paying attention.

While journalism is sometimes conflated with the public sphere and democracy, the media is not the public, nor do they create the public, but are part of the process of maintaining both in that news draws attention to and fosters common interests. For German sociologist and philosopher Jürgen Habermas, access to information is integral to a public sphere where people can discuss and debate public issues freely.[19] Journalism provides this access. As American sociologist and journalism professor Michael Schudson says, "This is the place of news in fostering democratic politics."[20] The function of journalism is to provide that information to citizens so that they can engage within the public sphere and democracy. American sociologist Herbert Gans writes, "The country's democracy may belong directly or indirectly to its citizens, but the democratic process can only be truly meaningful if these citizens are informed. Journalism's job is to inform them."[21] Information is necessary for sovereignty. While Gans admits this is an ideal that leaves out large portions of the reality of our democracy,[22] it is a goal to strive toward.

While the primary job of journalists is to inform, journalism's democratic function must be more. In their book, *The Elements of Journalism* (2001),[23] American journalists and researchers Bill Kovach and Tom Rosenstiel list a number of things that are needed for good journalism. The ones most relevant to the examples here are independence from those covered by journalists, an obligation to truth and verification, and independent monitoring of those in power, often called the watchdog role of journalism.

Without information from an independent source of news, it becomes more difficult to hold Gilead accountable. People are unable to freely debate and work toward common interests outside of the official channels. Sharing unsanctioned information eventually becomes a transgression, with the excuse of safety and security.[24] Elections were put off indefinitely, most likely because Gilead was able to maintain the story that they will be held at some future time. Meanwhile, the government members consolidated their power. There was no longer a press that could provide information critical of this story. Schudson states, "When a society enjoys an elected legislature and an independent press, the consequences can be great"[25]—and vice versa. Democracy in Atwood's fictionalized United States is in a large part derailed through the dismantling of the free press.

This is not to say that news no longer exists; it does. In the book, Offred is allowed to watch television news, and there are several examples where the audience sees glimpses of television live coverage in the TV series. However, the impetus to engage with the news is removed. Instead, it has other functions, which can also be seen in real-world examples of varying degrees of authoritarian governments.[26] It can act to create a passive and compliant audience, unquestioning and uncritical. The only information that exists is that which supports the status quo. It is highly controlled and full of propaganda, allowing the government to control the narrative.[27]

Women are further put in this role of passive audience. Their role in Gilead is intrinsically tied to their removal from the public sphere.[28] They are not allowed to read or write or to discuss anything that is not approved, including the Bible. Their access to anything that would allow them to think for themselves is limited. Attempts to rebel against these restrictions are severely punished. Symbolically, Mrs. Waterford, who was integral to the founding of Gilead, is beaten, incarcerated, and has her finger severed for her attempts to ask female children and women to regain participation through reading and writing.[29] This is shown to be necessary for those in power to maintain their unquestioned societal order.[30]

However, the need for information does not go away. In the book, while walking with another Handmaid telling her the latest news from the fight against terrorism, Offred says, "Sometimes I wish she would just shut up and let me walk in peace. But I'm ravenous for news, any kind of news; even if it's false news, it must mean something."[31] Offred's consumption of any news, whether word of mouth or from the little television news she is allowed to watch,[32] leaves her in a state of uncertainty. It provides a warped view, but she consumes it anyway. Not only must information be from an independent press, it must be reliable information. Unreliable news leaves a state of uncertainty, making it difficult to act. Offred/June ultimately runs away only because someone else makes the decision for her, someone with more knowledge.

A public is unable to use incorrect, false, or unreliable information for debate or action.[33] Because decisions based on unusable information are flawed, this type of information defeats the ability of citizens to rule themselves in a democracy. While this type of information is ineffective for making decisions, it does not stop the formation of opinions. This can be seen in the references to characters in both the book and the show that are "true believers," participating in the goals of those in power. Walter Lippmann, a journalist and public philosopher writing in the first half of the twentieth century, wrote that if facts are not known, "false ideas are just as effective as true ones, if not a little more effective."[34] There are many examples of this around the world.

A recent analogy might be drawn to the "alternative facts," as they have been called by counselor to the president Kellyanne Conway.[35] While this information is false or misleading, as Lippmann says, it is compelling.

Today, social media adds another component. The structure of social media platforms such as Facebook, Twitter, or reddit allows stories and information to be shared without the filter of traditional journalism's editorial process. Certain types of fake news have been found to be shared more widely on social media than actual news stories and to be believed by many of those who view them,[36] potentially influencing public opinion. It is easily accessible for manipulation by those who wish to spur ordinary citizens to action.[37] There are concerns that people's use of social media and the internet, in this way, are threatening democracy.[38]

In the book, the Commander's wife, Serena Joy Waterford, lets her household watch television news while waiting for Commander Fred Waterford to arrive. She describes the scenes of war that are happening in so many places and that Gilead is winning: "they only show us victories, never defeats."[39] Insurgents are blown up and captured. Spies are routed out. The Gilead soldiers are heroic. Children are rescued. "Such as it is: who knows if any of it is true? It could be old clips, it could be faked. But I watch it anyway, hoping to be able to read beneath it. Any news, now, is better than none," Offred says.[40] As she points out, she is now like "a child being allowed up late with the grown-ups."[41] Gilead is the parent.

This is not much different than any government or military would have its country's citizens believe: they are the good guys, others the bad. But the democratic ideals of a free press call for it to take a watchdog role, keeping those in power accountable to the public. Questions should be asked, research should be done, other voices heard. It should be an examination of not just what is said but of the impact of what is said. It should make visible the unseen machinations of society. In these ways, journalism can put pressure on those in power, not just the government, to change and become more transparent. Journalism can play a substantive role when it acts as a watchdog, critiquing government and other positions of power, taking them to task. While an exposé on a government institution may gain more interest from the audience, it certainly gains the interest of that institution. In a democracy, those in power must consider how this will impact elections or policy. Investigative journalists often provide an example of this such as, famously, the Watergate scandal that eventually lead to the resignation of President Nixon.[42]

A press that engages the public, creates public forums, is a vigilant watchdog, and always provides accurate, reliable, independent information is an essentially idealized concept of how journalism should function in the public sphere. There are many examples of how journalism fails in its charge, but there are also times that point to a closer realization of this ideal function. In Gilead, this function is dismantled.

LESSONS FROM STUDYING *THE HANDMAID'S TALE*

The Handmaid's Tale should be read and watched for its portrayal of the oppression of women in Gilead. It should also be read for its underlying look at how the fictional United States falls into authoritarianism and becomes Gilead. One of the first acts of those who take over, other than indefinitely postpone elections, is to censor and close newspapers. Curtailing the news media is a path toward authoritarianism.[43] If journalists are afraid to do their job, they are less likely to criticize those who threaten them, though journalists around the world continue to work in harrowing circumstances.

It is clear to see that free independent journalism does not exist in Gilead. It is also clear that most of its citizens, especially women, have no say, no power to act. There is no public sphere in which they can participate in political discourse and promote democratic participation in governing. A free press is an essential part of the public sphere that fuels democracy. If journalists are not free to be critical, either from government suppression or other means, journalism loses its function in democracy and citizens lose their power.

A free press is a fragile thing. The episodes "Unwomen"[44] and "Baggage"[45] in the second season of the Hulu TV show put this in a stark light by showing the audience the consequences for a fictionalized *The Boston Globe* in the wake of the Gilead rise to power. After escaping from her position as a Handmaid, June finds herself hidden away at the now closed newspaper, taken there by an old truck driver (Phillip Craig). He says it's been empty since before the "war," which Gilead's Commanders have undertaken against those who threaten them. He is unwilling to stay, not wanting to be seen with a fugitive. He leaves her with a flashlight to make her way through the building. The printing presses she walks past are still, blank reels of paper, old issues stacked and unread. The offices are unoccupied, but mementos are left behind from journalists no longer there, all reminders of what once was: a Red Sox pennant, photos of families, an art project from a child saying "I love you Mom," a woman's high heel left behind perhaps in haste. Women now oppressed were once part of this newsroom, working alongside the men as respected journalists.

She also finds nooses, though empty, still hanging, reminders of what happens to enemies of the government, deemed criminals for transgressing the new order.[46] Walls are covered with blood and strewn with bullet holes. There lies the other high heeled shoe. "Do you know what this is?" June

In season 2, June finds herself hiding in an abandoned newspaper's office. Walls are covered with blood and strewn with bullet holes.
Screenshot from Hulu television series.

says to Nick (Max Minghella), the Commander's driver who becomes June's lover and orchestrates her escape. "Do you know what happened here? It's a slaughter house."[47]

This scene, not part of the book but a continuation of the story under the consultancy of Margaret Atwood, draws our attention to just how easily the press can be deterred through violence. That isn't the only fragility. Press repression and press manipulation can both be problematic, as seen above. In order for the press to fulfill its functions within a democracy, it must also be supported by that democracy, by maintaining it as a free and functional enterprise. The First Amendment in the U.S. Constitution is one such support. In the period of martial law leading up to the establishment of Gilead, there isn't that support as the extreme violence explicitly shows. Journalists can now be labeled criminals and enemies of the state.

It is poignant that *The Boston Globe* is used for this scene. This paper is known for reporting on the Catholic Church's cover-up of child abuse by priests,[48] something that could be seen as an attack on religion, the basis for the new Gilead government. They are also one of many papers who put out an editorial criticizing the current U.S. president's treatment of the press and his calling of many journalists as "enemies of the people."[49]

The reception of news can also create additional problems. Yes, the ultimate death of the journalists was expedient, but, as June finds out, there was help getting to that point. Waiting at *The Boston Globe* to be taken to the next leg of her escape, she starts gathering newspaper clippings left behind from old issues of the paper. She pieces them together on the wall, tracing the dissolution of democracy through the evidence in the reporting. She is "grasping at straws," she says, "trying to piece together what happened. It was there all along, but we missed it."[50] The signs of the takeover by those who founded Gilead were there in the news, but were people paying attention? Were the connections being drawn?

There can be a failing of the audience, of citizens. While news and information are available, the public cannot be made to engage with it. As June/Offred points out in her voice-over in the Hulu TV series, something may be missed and the ability to do something about it may be given up. This can be seen as a bleak picture of journalism's role in promoting democracy through any impact on public opinion and action. These are similar themes we can follow when studying the current U.S. news media. Audiences for traditional news outlets have continued to shrink, leading to downsizing and closing of newspapers.[51] Additionally, there has long been a decline in trust of news media overall among the public.[52] Ironically, those who distrust the media are more likely to believe fake news.[53]

If citizens don't utilize what journalists have to offer, they may also lose their power. Once that power is lost, as it is in Gilead, suppression and control of information is a key part of maintaining the position of the government. There is no longer a democratic public sphere, and citizens no longer have access to, or even the ability to consume, real journalism. Instead, the news media becomes only the mouthpiece for the official story, with no other competing story line. The people of Gilead need to know what is happening in their world, but they have no other way of knowing than through official channels. As Offred says, there is a need to know, to have some bearing on the world. When information that is available could be true or false, and it is difficult to tell the difference, people are left in an uncertain position. A society is at the whim of those who determine what its citizens know.

NOTES

1. Rebecca Mead, "Margaret Atwood, the Prophet of Dystopia," *The New Yorker*, April 17, 2017, https://www.newyorker.com/magazine/2017/04/17/margaret-atwood-the-prophet-of-dystopia.

2. Margaret Atwood, "Margaret Atwood on What 'The Handmaid's Tale' Means in the Age of Trump," *The New York Times*, March 10, 2017, https://www.nytimes.com/2017/03/10/books/re view/margaret-atwood-handmaids-tale-age-of-trump.html.

3. I will refer to the character from the book as Offred and from the television show as June.

4. Jane Mulkerrins, "Elizabeth Moss on *The Handmaid's Tale*: 'This is happening in real life. Wake up, people,'" *The Guardian*, May 5, 2018, https://www.theguardian.com/tv-and-radio/2018/may/05/elisabeth-moss-handmaids-tale-this-is-happening-in-real-life-wake-up-people.

5. *The Handmaid's Tale*, "Unwomen," Season 2, Episode 2, directed by Mike Barker, Hulu, April 25, 2018, https://www.hulu.com/series/the-handmaids-tale -565d8976-9d26-4e63-866c-40f8a137ce5f.

6. Using here Jürgen Habermas's conception of a public sphere as private citizens coming together in public to engage in rational, critical debate. He provides examples of how, when the public sphere is open and maintains a diversity of discourse, it can promote the common public good and hold in check forces with too much power. Participation in the ideal public sphere is interaction with and access to a diverse public, universally accessible (*The Structural Transformation of the Public Sphere: An Inquiry into a Category of Bourgeois Society* [Cambridge, MA: MIT Press, 1989]).

7. Atwood is quoted saying, "Some country, somewhere, should make a monument to murdered journalists around the world. There's been quite a few of them" (Olivia Aylmer, "Margaret Atwood Says *The Handmaid's Tale* Season 2 Is a Call to Action," *Vanity Fair*, April 16, 2018, https://www.vanityfair.com/hol lywood/2018/04/the-handmaids-tale-season-2-margaret-atwood-interview). A recent example that has garnered attention is the death of Jamal Khashoggi, a columnist for *The Washington Post*. See David Ignatius, "How a Chilling Saudi Cyberwar Ensnared Jamal Khashoggi," *The Washington Post*, December 7, 2018, https://www.washingtonpost.com/opinions/global-opinions/how-a-chilling -saudi-cyberwar-ensnared-jamal-khashoggi/2018/12/07/f5f048fe-f975-11e8-8c9a -860ce2a8148f_story.html?utm_term=.c34671a1842d. See also "Killed in 2018," Committee to Protect Journalists, accessed December 7, 2018, https://cpj.org/data /killed/2018/?status=Killed &motiveConfirmed%5B%5D=Confirmed&type%5B%5 D=Journalist&start_year=2018&end_year=2018&group_by=location.

8. It is worth noting that only 13 percent of the world is considered as having a free press according to *Freedom House*. Among those with little to no freedom of the press include Russia and China. For further details see "Press Freedom's Dark Horizon," *Freedom of the Press* 2017, Freedom House, accessed December 7, 2018, https://freedomhouse.org/report/freedom-press/freedom-press-2017; "2018 World Press Freedom Index," Reporters Without Borders, accessed December 7, 2018, https://rsf.org/en/ranking/2018.

9. Sebastian Stier, "Political Determinants of Media Freedom," in *The Routledge Companion to Media and Human Right*, edited by Howard Tumber and Silvio Waisbord (Abingdon, Oxon: Routledge, 2017), 149–57.

10. For examples see Philip Bump, "Trump Eliminates the Middleman in His War against Journalists," *The Washington Post*, October 1, 2018, https://www.wash ingtonpost.com/politics /2018/10/01/trump-eliminates-middleman-his-war-against -journalists/?utm_term=.d7a1b06a11 eb; Rebecca Morin, "Trump Draws Rebukes for Scolding Female Reporters of Color," *Politico*, November 9, 2018, https://www .politico.com/story/2018/11/09/trump-cnn-white-house-access-980280; Michael M. Grynbaum, "Trump Threatens to Retaliate against Reporters Who Don't Show 'Respect,'" *The New York Times*, November 9, 2018, https://www.nytimes.com/2018/11 /09/business/media/trump-retaliation-reporters-april-ryan.html.

11. For discussion see Andrew S. Ross and Damian J. Rivers, "Discursive Deflection: Accusation of 'Fake News' and the Spread of Mis- and Disinformation in

the Tweets of President Trump," *Social Media and Society* 4, No. 2 (April 2018): 1–12, https://doi.org/10.1177/2056305118776010; John Wagner and Felicia Sonmez, "About 80 Percent of the Media Are 'the Enemy of the People,' Trump Says," *The Washington Post*, August 22, 2018, https://www.washingtonpost. com/politics about-80-percent-of-the-media-are-the-enemy-of-the-people-trump-says/2018/08/22 /d7d5710c-a635-11e8-a656-943eefab5daf_story.html?utm_term=.688f3f999f57; Jennifer Rubin, "What a New Poll About Trump and 'Fake News' Really Says." *Washington Post*, April 9, 2018, https://www.washingtonpost.com/blogs/right -turn/wp/2018/04/09/what-a-new-poll-about-trump-and-fake-news-really-says/?utm_ term=.75312508d048.

12. See Jackie Mansky, "The Age-Old Problem of 'Fake News,'" *Smithsonian .com*, May 7, 2018, https://www.smithsonianmag.com/history/age-old-problem-fake -news-180968945/.

13. For examples see Joe Parkinson and Georgi Kantchev, "In Depth: Document: Russia Meddles in Elections—Rigged Polls and Fake News Are Part of Playbook, Bulgarian Officials Say," *Wall Street Journal*, March 24, 2017, Eastern edition, ProQuest; Gabriel Pereira and Iago Bojczuk, "Zap Zap, Who's There? WhatsApp and the Spread of Fake News during the 2018 Elections in Brazil," Blog, *Global Media Technologies and Cultures Lab*, November 9, 2018, http://globalmedia .mit.edu/2018/11/09/zap-zap-whos-there-whatsapp-and-the-spread-of-fake-news -during-the-2018-elections-in-brazil/; James Reinl, "'Fake News' Rattles Taiwan ahead of Elections," *Al Jazeera*, November 22, 2018, https://www.aljazeera.com /news/2018/11/news-rattles-taiwan-elections-181123005140173.html; Nick Summers, "The UK Is Worried Fake News Will Impact General Election Results," *Engaget*, April 26, 2017, https://www.engadget.com/2017/04/26/uk-mp-facebook- fake-news-general-election/. There are arguments, however, that, at least in the U.S. election, fake news was not seen by enough people to have a significant impact on the election (Hunt Allcott, and Matthew Gentzkow, "Social Media and Fake News in the 2016 Election," *Journal of Economic Perspectives* 31, no. 2 [2017]: 211–36).

14. Indentipasses is the term Atwood uses for special identification required by the new regime.

15. Margaret Atwood, *The Handmaid's Tale* (New York: Anchor Books, 1998), 174.

16. Peter Dahlgren, introduction to *Communication and Citizenship: Journalism and the Public Sphere in the New Media Age*, eds. Peter Dahlgren and Colin Sparks (London: Routledge, 1991), 1–26.

17. *The Handmaid's Tale*, "Smart Power," Season 2, Episode 9, directed by Jeremy Podeswa, Hulu, June 13, 2018, https://www.hulu.com/series/the-handmaids -tale-565d8976-9d26-4e63-866c-40f8a137ce5f.

18. *The Handmaid's Tale*, "Smart Power."

19. Habermas, *The Structural Transformation of the Public Sphere*. It is also worth noting here that Habermas was involved in what is called the "Historikerstreit" that took place in West Germany in the 1980s. This was a debate over the legacy of fascism and the Holocaust. Habermas argued for a commitment to democratic politics

in the face of this history, criticizing those who would take an apologetic view of the past.

20. Michael Schudson, *The Sociology of News*, 2nd ed. (New York: W. W. Norton & Company, 2011), 203.

21. Herbert Gans, *Democracy and the News* (Oxford: Oxford University Press, 2003), 1.

22. Gans admits that this concept raises questions about what kind of news citizens are consuming and what kind of participation is taking place, saying it may be wishful thinking. News exists even where democracy does not.

23. Bill Kovach and Tom Rosenstiel, *The Elements of Journalism* (London: Atlantic Books, 2003).

24. An example of this tactic can be found in Turkey. See "Turkey Profile: Freedom of the Press 2017," Freedom House, accessed December 7, 2018, https://freedomhouse.org/report/freedom-press/2017/turkey.

25. Schudson, *The Sociology of News*, 188.

26. For a discussion of the role of news in authoritarian regimes, see Christopher Walker and Robert W. Orttung, "Breaking the News: The Role of State-Run Media," *Journal of Democracy* 25, no. 1 (2014): 71–85, https://muse-jhu-edu.ccsu.idm.oclc.org/article/535537.

27. Government control of the media isn't the only way this can happen. Habermas was also critical of the potential commercial nature of news media and the impact it could have on the public sphere. For further interesting discussion along these lines see Robert W. McChesney, *Corporate Media and the Threat to Democracy* (New York: Seven Stories Press, 1997).

28. Women have been excluded from the public sphere throughout history with their position being relegated to private matters and have not been allowed to participate in politics, including voting. It is recently that women have made gains in some parts of the world.

29. *The Handmaid's Tale*, "Women's Work," Season 2, Episode 8, directed by Kari Skogland, Hulu, June 6, 2018, https://www.hulu.com/watch/4acc571a-58ce-4685-8885-3ba46acd514d; *The Handmaid's Tale*, "The Word," Season 2, Episode 13, directed by Mike Barker, Hulu, July 11, 2018, https://www.hulu.com/watch/f2bf3935-49ee-4904-9142-2abcde6341be.

30. There is growing concern about the treatment of female reporters, especially black women, in the United States by the president. See Paul Farhi, "'What a Stupid Question': Trump Demeans Three Black Female Reporters in Three Days," *The Washington Post*, November 9, 2018, https://www.washingtonpost.com/lifestyle/style/what-a-stupid-question-trump-demeans-three-black-female-reporters-in-two-days/2018/11/09/272113d0-e441-11e8-b759-3d88a5ce9e19_story.html?utm_term=.5189377dffbb

31. Atwood, *The Handmaid's Tale*, 20.

32. The strict control of information has led to an underground spreading of information through word-of-mouth network. Written during the height of the Soviet Union, this article provides an interesting discussion on how word-of-mouth works in this type of environment: Raymond A. Bauer and David B. Gleicher, "Word-of-

Mouth Communication in the Soviet Union," *The Public Opinion Quarterly* 17, no. 3 (Autumn 1953): 297–310.

33. Keep in mind that in many situations, the government isn't the only potential source of unreliable information.

34. Walter Lippman, *Liberty and the News* (New Brunswick, NJ: Transaction Publishers, 1995), 64–65.

35. Rebecca Sinderbrand, "How Kellyanne Conway Ushered in the Era of 'Alternative Facts,'" *The Washington Post*, January 22, 2017, https://www.washington post.com/news/the-fix/wp/2017/01/22/how-kellyanne-conway-ushered-in-the-era-of -alternative-facts/?utm_term=.5e29304b4871.

36. Craig Silverman, "This Analysis Shows How Viral Fake Election News Stories Outperformed Real News on Facebook," *Buzzfeed*, November 16, 2016, https://www .buzzfeednews.com/article/craigsilverman/viral-fake-election-news-outperformed -real-news-on-facebook.; Craig Silverman and Jeremy Singer-Vine, "Americans Who See Fake News Believe It, New Survey Says," *Buzzfeed*, December 6, 2016, https:// www.buzzfeednews.com/article/craigsilverman/fake-news-survey; See also Gordon Pennycook, Tyrone D. Cannon, and David G. Rand. 2018. "Prior Exposure Increases Perceived Accuracy of Fake News." *Journal of Experimental Psychology: General* 147 (12): 1865–80. doi: 10.1037/xge0000465.supp

37. The Russian use of fake news and social media manipulation is a good example. Deepa Seetharaman and Georgia Wells, "More Russian Social-Media Posts Found—Facebook, Google and Twitter Find the Scope of Manipulation Was Broader Than Thought," *The Wall Street Journal*, October 31, 2017, ProQuest; Claire Allbright, "A Russian Facebook Page Organized a Protest in Texas. A Different Russian Page Launched the Counterprotest," *The Texas Tribune*, November 1, 2017, https:// www.texastribune.org/2017/11/01/russian-facebook-page-organized-protest-texas -different-russian-page-l/

38. Nathaniel Persily, "The 2016 U.S. Election: Can Democracy Survive the Internet?" *Journal of Democracy* 28, no. 2 (2017): 63-76, https://muse.jhu.edu /article/653377.

39. Atwood, *The Handmaid's Tale*, 83.

40. Atwood, *The Handmaid's Tale*, 82.

41. Atwood, *The Handmaid's Tale*, 82.

42. This story was later made into a film: *All the President's Men*, directed by Alan J. Pakula (1976; Burbank, CA: Warner Bros.). Another example, also made into a movie, is that of the release of the Pentagon Papers: *The Post*, directed by Steven Spielberg (2017; Universal City, CA: Amblin Entertainment).

43. Again, Turkey makes an interesting example. See "Not So Free; The Press in Turkey," *The Economist*, April 06, 2013, ProQuest; Zia Weise, "How Did Things Get So Bad for Turkey's Journalists?" *The Atlantic*, August 23, 2018, https:// www.theatlantic.com/international/archive/2018/08/destroying-free-press-erdogan -turkey/568402/.

44. *The Handmaid's Tale*, "Unwomen," directed by Mike Barker.

45. *The Handmaid's Tale*, "Baggage," Season 2, Episode 3, directed by Kari Skogland, Hulu, May 2, 2018, https://www.hulu.com/watch/67517156-6a63-42ce-96d4-0d99b2ef4849.

46. In both the book and the television show, hanging is showed as the sentence for those who are in violation of the ideals of Gilead, such as those who commit adultery or "gender treachery," for example, are gay. This also includes intellectuals who question the order of things. Nooses are also associated with lynching, deeply connected to racism and a response to the freedom of black people. This is a reminder of a bigoted society.

47. *The Handmaid's Tale*, "Unwomen," directed by Mike Barker.

48. This investigation was turned into a movie: *Spotlight*, directed by Tom McCarthy (2015; Los Angeles, CA: Participant Media).

49. "Journalists Are Not the Enemy," editorial, *The Boston Globe*, August 16, 2018, http://apps.bostonglobe.com/opinion/graphics/2018/08/freepress/; Tom Kludt, "'We Are Not the Enemy': 16 Must-Read Editorials That Capture the Spirit of a Free Press," *CNN Business*, August 16, 2018, https://money.cnn.com/2018/08/16/media/free-press-trump-editorials/index.html.

50. *The Handmaid's Tale,* "Baggage," directed by Kari Skogland.

51. "Digital News Fact Sheet," *State of the News Media* (2018), Pew Research Center, updated June 6, 2018, http://www.journalism.org/fact-sheet/digital-news/

52. "Indicators of News Media Trust," Knight Foundation, updated September 11, 2018, https://www.knightfoundation.org/reports/indicators-of-news-media-trust; "'My' Media versus 'The' Media: Trust in News Depends on Which News Media You Mean," American Press Institute, updated May 24, 2017, https://www.americanpressinstitute.org/publications/reports/survey-research/my-media-vs-the-media/.

53. "How the Public, News Sources, and Journalists Think about News in Three Communities." ASU News Co/Lab, Report, 2018, https://newscollab.org/2018/11/19/how-the-public-news-sources-and-journalists-think-about-news-in-three-communities/.

WORKS CITED

Allbright, Claire. "A Russian Facebook Page Organized a Protest in Texas. A Different Russian Page Launched the Counterprotest." *The Texas Tribune*, November 1, 2017. https://www.texastribune.org/2017/11/01/russian-facebook-page-organized-protest-texas-different-russian-page-l/.

Allcott, Hunt, and Matthew Gentzkow. "Social Media and Fake News in the 2016 Election." *Journal of Economic Perspectives* 31, no. 2 (2017): 211–36.

American Press Institute. "'My' Media versus 'The' Media: Trust in News Depends on Which News Media You Mean." Updated May 24, 2017. https://www.americanpressinstitute.org/publications/reports/survey-research/my-media-vs-the-media/.

ASU News Co/Lab. "How the Public, News Sources, and Journalists Think about News in Three Communities." Report, 2018. https://newscollab.org/2018/11/19/how-the-public-news-sources-and-journalists-think-about-news-in-three-communities/.

Atwood, Margaret. *The Handmaid's Tale*. New York: Anchor Books, 1998.

———. "Margaret Atwood on What 'The Handmaid's Tale' Means in the Age of Trump." *The New York Times*, March 10, 2017, https://www.nytimes.com/2017/03/10/books/review/margaret-atwood-handmaids-tale-age-of-trump.html.

Aylmer, Olivia. "Margaret Atwood Says *The Handmaid's Tale* Season 2 Is a Call to Action." *Vanity Fair*, April 16, 2018. https://www.vanityfair.com/hollywood/2018/04/the-handmaids-tale-season-2-margaret-atwood-interview.

Bauer, Raymond A., and David B. Gleicher. "Word-of-Mouth Communication in the Soviet Union." *The Public Opinion Quarterly* 17, no. 3 (1953): 297–310.

The Boston Globe. "Journalists Are Not the Enemy." August 16, 2018. https://apps.bostonglobe.com/opinion/graphics/2018/08/freepress/?p1=HP_special

Bump, Philip. "Trump Eliminates the Middleman in His War Against Journalists." *The Washington Post*, October 1, 2018. https://www.washingtonpost.com/politics/2018/10/01/trump-eliminates-middleman-his-war-against-journalists/?utm_term=.d7a1b06a11eb.

Committee to Protect Journalists. "Killed in 2018." Accessed December 7, 2018. https://cpj.org/data/killed/2018/?status=Killed&motiveConfirmed%5B%5D=Confirmed&type%5B%5D=Journalist&start_year=2018&end_year=2018&group_by=location.

Dahlgren, Peter. Introduction to *Communication and Citizenship: Journalism and the Public Sphere in the New Media Age*, edited by Peter Dahlgren and Colin Sparks, 1–15. London: Routledge, 1991.

The Economist. "Not So Free; The Press in Turkey." April 6, 2013, ProQuest.

Farhi, Paul. "'What a Stupid Question': Trump Demeans Three Black Female Reporters in Three Days." *The Washington Post*, November 9, 2018. https://www.washingtonpost.com/lifestyle/style/what-a-stupid-question-trump-demeans-three-black-female-reporters-in-two-days/2018/11/09/272113d0-e441-11e8-b759-3d88a5ce9e19_story.html?utm_term=.5189377dffbb.

Freedom House. "Press Freedom's Dark Horizon." Accessed December 7, 2018. https://freedomhouse.org/report/freedom-press/freedom-press-2017.

Gans, Herbert. *Democracy and the News*. Oxford: Oxford University Press, 2003.

Grynbaum, Michael M. "Trump Threatens to Retaliate against Reporters Who Don't Show 'Respect.'" *The New York Times*, November 9, 2018. https://www.nytimes.com/2018/11/09/business/media/trump-retaliation-reporters-april-ryan.html.

Habermas, Jürgen. *The Structural Transformation of the Public Sphere: An Inquiry into a Category of Bourgeois Society*. Cambridge, MA: MIT Press, 1989.

Ignatius, David. "How a Chilling Saudi Cyberwar Ensnared Jamal Khashoggi." *The Washington Post*, December 7, 2018. https://www.washingtonpost.com/opinions/global-opinions/how-a-chilling-saudi-cyberwar-ensnared-jamal-khashoggi/2018/12/07/f5f048fe-f975-11e8-8c9a-860ce2a8148f_story.html?utm_term=.c34671a1842d.

Kludt, Tom. "'We Are Not the Enemy': 16 Must-Read Editorials That Capture the Spirit of a Free Press." *CNN Business*, August 16, 2018. https://money.cnn.com/2018/08/16/media/free-press-trump-editorials/index.html.

Knight Foundation. "Indicators of News Media Trust." Updated September 11, 2018. https://www.knightfoundation.org/reports/indicators-of-news-media-trust.

Kovach, Bill, and Tom Rosenstiel. *The Elements of Journalism*. London: Atlantic Books, 2003.

Lippmann, Walter. *Liberty and the News.* New Brunswick, NJ: Transaction Publishers, 1995.

McChesney, Robert W. *Corporate Media and the Threat to Democracy*. New York: Seven Stories Press, 1997.

Mansky, Jackie. "The Age-Old Problem of 'Fake News.'" *Smithsonian.com*, May 7, 2018. https://www.smithsonianmag.com/history/age-old-problem-fake -news-180968945/.

Mead, Rebecca. "Margaret Atwood, the Prophet of Dystopia." *The New Yorker*, April 17, 2017. https://www.newyorker.com/magazine/2017/04/17/margaret-atwood -the-prophet-of-dystopia.

Morin, Rebecca. "Trump Draws Rebukes for Scolding Female Reporters of Color." *Politico*, November 9, 2018. https://www.politico.com/story/2018/11/09/trump -cnn-white-house-access-980280.

Mulkerrins, Jane. "Elisabeth Moss on *The Handmaid's Tale*: 'This is happening in real life. Wake up, people.'" *The Guardian*, May 5, 2018, https://www.theguard ian.com/tv-and-radio/2018/may/05/elisabeth-moss-handmaids-tale-this-is-happen ing-in-real-life-wake-up-people.

Parkinson, Joe, and Georgi Kantchev. "In Depth: Document: Russia Meddles in Elections—Rigged Polls and Fake News Are Part of Playbook, Bulgarian Officials Say." *Wall Street Journal,* March 24, 2017, Eastern edition. ProQuest.

Pennycook, Gordon, Tyrone D. Cannon, and David G. Rand. 2018. "Prior Exposure Increases Perceived Accuracy of Fake News." *Journal of Experimental Psychology: General* 147, no. 12: 1865–80. doi:10.1037/xge0000465.supp.

Pereira, Gabriel, and Iago Bojczuk. "Zap Zap, Who's There? WhatsApp and the Spread of Fake News during the 2018 Elections in Brazil." Blog. *Global Media Technologies and Cultures Lab*, November 9, 2018. http://globalmedia .mit.edu/2018/11/09/zap-zap-whos-there-whatsapp-and-the-spread-of-fake-news -during-the-2018-elections-in-brazil/.

Persily, Nathaniel. "The 2016 U.S. Election: Can Democracy Survive the Internet?" *Journal of Democracy* 28, no. 2 (2017): 63–76. https://muse.jhu.edu /article/653377.

Pew Research Center. "Digital News Fact Sheet." *State of the News Media* (2018). Updated June 6, 2018. http://www.journalism.org/fact-sheet/digital-news/.

Reinl, James. "'Fake News' Rattles Taiwan ahead of Elections." *Al Jazeera*, November 22, 2018. https://www.aljazeera.com/news/2018/11/news-rattles -taiwan-elections-181123005140173.html.

Reporters Without Borders. "2018 World Press Freedom Index." Accessed December 5, 2018. https://rsf.org/en/ranking/2018.

Ross, Andrew S., and Damian J. Rivers. "Discursive Deflection: Accusation of 'Fake News' and the Spread of Mis- and Disinformation in the Tweets of President Trump." *Social Media and Society* (April, 2018). doi:10.1177/2056305118776010.

Rubin, Jennifer. "What a New Poll about Trump and 'Fake News' Really Says." *The Washington Post*, April 9, 2018.

Schudson, Michael. *The Sociology of News*, 2nd ed. New York: W. W. Norton & Company, 2011.

Seetharaman, Deepa, and Georgia Wells. "More Russian Social-Media Posts Found—Facebook, Google and Twitter Find the Scope of Manipulation Was Broader Than Thought." *Wall Street Journal*, October 31, 2017. ProQuest.

Silverman, Craig. "This Analysis Shows How Viral Fake Election News Stories Outperformed Real News on Facebook." *Buzzfeed*, November 16, 2016. https://www.buzzfeednews.com/article/craigsilverman/viral-fake-election-news-outperformed-real-news-on-facebook.

Silverman, Craig, and Jeremy Singer-Vine. "Americans Who See Fake News Believe It, New Survey Says." *Buzzfeed*, December 6, 2016. https://www.buzzfeednews.com/article/craigsilverman/fake-news-survey.

Sinderbrand, Rebecca. "How Kellyanne Conway Ushered in the Era of 'Alternative Facts.'" *The Washington Post*, January 22, 2017. https://www.washingtonpost.com/news/the-fix/wp/2017/01/22/how-kellyanne-conway-ushered-in-the-era-of-alternative-facts/?utm_term=.5e29304b4871.

Stier, Sebastian. "Political Determinants of Media Freedom." In *The Routledge Companion to Media and Human Right*, edited by Howard Tumber and Silvio Waisbord, 149–57. Abingdon, Oxon: Routledge, 2017.

Summers, Nick. "The UK Is Worried Fake News Will Impact General Election Results." *Engaget*, April 26, 2017. https://www.engadget.com/2017/04/26/uk-mp-facebook-fake-news-general-election/.

Wagner, John, and Felicia Sonmez. "About 80 Percent of the Media Are 'the Enemy of the People,' Trump says." *The Washington Post*, August 22, 2018. https://www.washingtonpost.com/politics/about-80-percent-of-the-media-are-the-enemy-of-the-people-trump-says/2018/08/22/d7d5710c-a635-11e8-a656-943eefab5daf_story.html?utm_term=.688f3f999f57.

Walker, Christopher, and Robert W. Orttung. "Breaking the News: The Role of State-Run Media." *Journal of Democracy* 25, no. 1 (2014): 71–85. https://muse-jhu-edu.ccsu.idm.oclc.org/article/535537.

Weise, Zia. "How Did Things Get So Bad for Turkey's Journalists?" *The Atlantic*, August 23, 2018. https://www.theatlantic.com/international/archive/2018/08/destroying-free-press-erdogan-turkey/568402/.

FILM AND TELEVISION

The Handmaid's Tale. "Baggage." Season 2, Episode 3. Directed by Kari Skogland. Written by Dorothy Fortenberry. Hulu, May 2, 2018.

The Handmaid's Tale. "Smart Power." Season 2, Episode 9. Directed by Jeremy Podeswa. Written by Dorothy Fortenberry. Hulu, June 13, 2018.

The Handmaid's Tale. "The Word." Season 2, Episode 13. Directed by Mike Barker. Written by Bruce Miller. Hulu, July 11, 2018.

The Handmaid's Tale. "Unwomen." Season 2, Episode 2. Directed by Mike Barker. Written by Bruce Miller. Hulu, April 25, 2018.

The Handmaid's Tale. "Women's Work." Season 2, Episode 8. Directed by Kari Skogland. Written by Nina Fiore and John Herrera. Hulu, June 6, 2018.

Chapter Eleven

Women's Health in *The Handmaid's Tale* and the Marginalization of Women

Rati Kumar

As a teenager living in India, my introduction to Margaret Atwood's novel of *The Handmaid's Tale* was likely not as harrowing as it might have been for my counterparts halfway across the world. In retrospect, partly this reaction resulted from a lack of life experience, but also due to witnessing the veneer of respectability beneath which women in India were routinely subject to systemic misogyny. While the graphic imagery presented by Atwood was disturbing, the subtext and implication of stripping women of their health rights[1] was a routine occurrence witnessed in countless interactions in a society chillingly unwilling to recognize its biases as such. Majda Gama, an American poet of Saudi origin, describes a similar experience of womanhood in Saudi Arabia, and says "One woman's dystopia is another woman's reality," noting how she was unable to share intimate thoughts with her Caucasian friends about her lived experiences similar to those sketched by Atwood.[2]

With the resurgence of these issues presented by Atwood, in the Hulu TV series, these reflections have come back into sharp relief for many women, including myself, now as a mother, scholar, academic, and health advocate, living in the United States. Given the Trump-era political climate, women's rights, and consequently women's healthcare policies, are not merely a theoretical luxury but a reality which can threaten our daily existence if we fail to protect these rights. Dialogic spaces need to widen into arenas for action by utilizing popular culture as a catalyst for change.

However, in doing so, we must remember the intersectionalities of class, race, and nationality which converge on women's bodies. Women's health advocates should make it a critical practice to refer to health experiences not in monolithic terms, but as a spectrum on which all of us reside as partners. Instead of assuming the identical lived experiences of all women, we need to unearth both the differences and connections among various groups. An example of this would be to avoid dismissing the ways in which health issues affecting women in minority groups, women of lower socioeconomic status, and women of different nationalities are in fact tied into the mainstream, and to engage with this recognition meaningfully. We must avoid the reductionist tendency to think of these issues as nonimminent, or succumb to American rhetoric about exceptionalism, by remembering that women in the United States are subject to some of the objectively worst women's health policies in the world as noted in an annual State of the World's Mothers Report in 2015.[3] According to Jessica Ravitz, a senior health reporter at CNN, 49 percent of countries provide paid leave to both new parents, including Saudi Arabia— the United States does not, not even for new mothers, let alone their partners.[4] This chapter aims to add to such a discussion of the intersectionalities and divergences of women's health encounters both where we live and the effect of our seemingly localized policies on international health, drawing on *The Handmaid's Tale* as a frame of reference. I hope it serves as a warning for vigilance of trespasses on women's bodies, encompassing both a national and international perspective on women's health and communication practices, demonstrating the entwined nature of the same, across international and within national borders.

HANDMAIDS AND "COMMODITY" CULTURE

Atwood explores the notion of the female body as a space for male intervention and enforcement of what qualifies a woman to avail of the benefits of medical structures. The Handmaids are treated as commodities, albeit precious ones, and receive instant access to medical care as a precaution against harm to their physical bodies affecting their ability to procreate for their masters, the Commanders of Gilead. The women are not merely kept as independent agents for procreation, but are ascribed affluent male, predominantly Caucasian, elderly and middle-aged patrons, many of whom are sterile. It becomes evident that these caveats are not merely tied into a woman's fertility per se, but in her fertility servicing the promotion of the upper-class male lineage. For example, the Handmaid Janine (Madeline Brewer), despite the mental trauma she has to endure, receives excellent physical healthcare. Particularly poignant is her excitement postpartum at her ability to eat ice cream, since she knows that once her baby is weaned, the value of her body will depreciate until she gets pregnant again, most likely from another Commander, if ever.[5]

Alison Steube, a Professor at the University of North Carolina School of Medicine, describes this phenomenon as the mom being treated like a candy wrapper. She says the baby is the candy, the precious commodity, "And once the candy is out of the wrapper, the wrapper is cast aside."[6] There is sufficient evidence in the United States to demonstrate such a discrepancy between new-born and postpartum care. According to an American College of Obstetricians and Gynecologists report, there is a severe lack of postpartum care and support for women, focusing primarily on the baby or fetus and comparatively much less on the woman post childbirth.[7] *ProPublica* in a special series on postpartum maternal care and mortality in the United States entitled "Lost Mothers" reports that "more than 700 women die every year in this country from causes related to pregnancy and childbirth and more than 50,000 suffer life-threatening complications, among the worst records for maternal health in the industrialized world."[8] Thus, across the spectrum, American women suffer from a lack of infrastructural resources as a whole for postpartum care, giving credence to the status of women as second-class citizens within the legislative sphere.

INTERSECTIONS OF GENDER AND CLASS

While there is a global, transnational commonality of experience of women's bodies servicing the male agenda, there is also a divergence—for example between India and the United States—in terms of how privilege and consequent access can disproportionately affect certain women more deeply than others. This intersectionality of gender and class, often overlooked in the discussion of women's health policy, while not explicitly discussed in *The Handmaid's Tale*, is evident in the structure of the story. While women as a group are sub-servient to men, distinct class demarcations exist between the Commander's Wives, their Handmaids, and other categories of women such as the "Marthas," housekeepers; the "Aunts," who sadistically train the Handmaids in so-called "Red Centers"; the prostitutes in the Jezebel brothel (many of whom have previously worked in academia); the so-called "Econo-Wives" who live on the periphery of Gilead; and finally, the outcasts of society, many of which are either women of color, political opponents, or "gender traitors," forced to work themselves to death by cleaning up toxic waste in the colonies. In the second Hulu TV season teenage wives are introduced who are paired with younger men to procreate in arranged marriages that are deprived of love. Women whose bodies are considered worthy of protection (even though they are Other) are subsumed into a kind of "Us"- ness, living in the same household under the patronage of the man, and are also within Gilead. Women who are "fallen"—such as the prostitutes, or the women who are unworthy because they are "gender traitors," postmenopausal, or political activists—are at a literal and metaphorical distance from men in power, in the colonies.

The current policy climate in the United States (as was so obviously displayed during the Matt Kavanaugh Senate hearings to pave his way to the Supreme Court), dominated by upper-class white men, reflects this particular lack of consideration of the needs of single mothers, low-socioeconomic-status women, and minority women who often get circumvented or ignored as the "out group" similar to the lived experiences of marginalized women in Atwood's Gilead.[9]

An analysis of the current women's health policies, including a paring back of support for organizations such as *Planned Parenthood* and other Title X funded clinics, often used by minorities and women of color in "medically underserved" communities cannot preclude a discussion of the politics enacted on these women's bodies.[10] With the current policies surrounding women's health, the choice of having a child, especially for single or unmarried mothers (who often structurally tend to be women of color, due to high incarceration rates as noted by the Bureau of Justice Statistics for 2016[11]) are drastically narrowed, along with the inability to earn an income while on maternity leave. Nearly one-third of female-headed single-mother families tended to be Black in 2010, and nearly 20 percent of the same were Hispanic families. Working single mothers are disproportionately more likely to live in poverty. Thirty-nine percent of low-income working families across the nation are managed by a single mother, and that number is heavily influenced by factors like race: 65 percent of African-American low-income working families, 31 percent of Latino low-income working families, and 45 percent of low-income working families of other races are under the helm of single women.[12]

This points to the necessity to have a male patron in some form, either as spouse or financial partner, reminiscent of the necessity of patronage in Atwood's Gilead to protect one's health as a woman, with her fertility serving as an access point for such protections. According to a 2018 American College of Physicians position paper by Hilary Daniel, Shari Erickson, and Sue Bornstein,[13] while analyzing women's health policy in the United States, note that family planning access serves as such "an entry point to the health care system," paving the way for related services such as cancer and sexually transmitted infection (STI) screenings, breast and pelvic exams, and contraception provision. Thus, oftentimes the ability of lower-class women to ensure good health for themselves stems not just from their ability to procreate, but to do so under the patronage of upper-class white men, either as spouses, partners or policy makers.

Thus, coupled with the unfriendly policies which have recently further shrunk women's rights to reproductive health access and related screenings such as for cancer and STIs, and amputated healthcare provision, women of all classes in the United States fare among the lowest in the world in terms of women's rights in the health arena. Additionally, according to a *Status of Women in the States* report in 2018, while women overall have lower earnings, financial security, and representation in political office and specific adverse health outcomes compared to men in the United States, "certain population groups—including women of color, low-income women, recent immigrants, and women living in rural and inner city areas—are disproportionately affected."[14]

Feminism, with all its fourth wave promises and social media movements, often gets aligned with the needs of upper-class white women living in safe suburbs with access to insured healthcare and under the direct or indirect patronage of men in power, making or influencing policies as first-class citizens.[15] Even women who have insurance may have these benefits as a result of access to employment for themselves or their spouses, which, in itself, may be a result of the privilege of education.

Being mindful of such evidence then, female scholars and activists, while speaking of the health experiences of women, must pay due deference to the dichotomies that may exist under this umbrella. On a metatheoretical level, we—including the author—also need to acknowledge our own privileges, giving us the platform to speak for a diversity (accurately or inaccurately) of female health experiences.

SOLIDARITY AND THE POLITICS OF RESPECTABILITY AND DESIRE

While acknowledging the differences in the lived experiences of women, we must also draw strength from the unity of certain health experiences that women across the globe endure in the suppression of their agency, as well as look at ways in which we can support women globally. Briefly looking at the condition of the United States as a local context, and expanding to a case study of women's health rights in India, will demonstrate the oppressive politics of respectability and desire spanning a variety of contexts. Being cognizant of the need to represent the spectrum of women's health rights issues globally and in a transnational context, such analysis will reflect both the similarities and differences between women's experiences, as well as the effect that our national policies and electoral process can have on women's health across the globe.

In the United States, decisions about physical and mental health choices for women continue to be made by a white-male majority (a trend which has disturbingly gained momentum under the new Trump administration since 2017), undoing what little policy progress had been made in this area by women's rights activists in the country.[16] Women further face difficult choices when considering major health decisions such as contraception and abortion, so much so that the aforementioned report on the Status of Women ranks the United States as one of the lowest in the world when it comes to protecting the health of its female citizens. This derives from laws such as the ones currently in place which do not require all full-time employers to cover contraception costs,[17] and the push to reduce the number of abortion clinics across the country with states like Arkansas, Kentucky, and West Virginia steadily declining since 2014[18] (approximately 98 percent of their counties did not have a clinic), with more recent estimates putting seven states (Kentucky, West Virginia, Missouri, Wyoming, South Dakota, North Dakota, and Mississippi) with only one clinic remaining for the entire state.[19] This is happening concomitantly with social notions of desirability focused on altering the female body through medical interventions such as cosmetic surgery which are enshrined through cultural practices and popular media as well as social media platforms. Such practices have gained significant ground without any critical examination.[20] While veiled as a space of choice, these avenues also continue to serve as restrictive spaces subject to the male gaze of what womanhood should look like or of how women should act.

Within the United States, while the notion of respectability may not always be encased in the context of familial organizations like in India (further discussed below), they tend to have a stronghold in professional spaces. Oftentimes, the safety of women's bodies is compromised in an attempt for men in privilege to save face. Innumerable examples of such harm to female dignity and their bodies have exploded into the mainstream conscience as a result of the #MeToo movement. There are anecdotes and revelations abound where despite safeguarding mechanisms in place, people failed to enact the guarantees of safety to women's bodies and minds within such professional structures, in an attempt to prevent the disruption of power in traditionally male spaces. The widespread accounts of sexual assault in industries ranging from entertainment to sports and politics, and in other public spaces women occupy on a day-to-day basis like on public transportation and in work spaces, have brought into focus the numerous aggressions the female body encounters as part of its everyday experience.

In India, the deeply troubling issue of sexual assault on women, while finally coming to light, still faces gaslighting by religious and political factions, eager to use conspiracy theories to dispel such numbers as rumor-mongering by the media.[21] While the numbers presented in the National Crime Records Bureau Report [22] of 2016 generated by the Indian government each year, are quite high in terms of Crimes against Women (estimates show that a woman is raped every fifteen minutes in India), they still do not cover the plethora of assault and violent crimes which go unreported each day.[23] Within the country there exists differences between urban and rural women which markedly affect their lived experiences. A majority of India's population (almost 70%) lives rurally, and women comprise approximately half (48%) of this count, making it reasonable to extrapolate that a majority of women in India live in villages, many of whom tend to have poorer health outcomes than urban women. It is found that women in mid-level neighborhoods in rural areas and poor neighborhoods in urban areas are most at-risk for negative health outcomes.[24] As one example of this discrepancy, total fertility rates are higher for rural women, and contraception use is lower.[25]

Speaking specifically from an international Indian perspective, the politics of respectability and saving face such as those demonstrated in Gilead by the Wives' submissive behavior (the episode where the Mexican ambassador, Mrs. Castillo played by Zabryna Guevara, comes to visit) are deeply enshrined in societal fabric, making it difficult for many women to assert their authority against deeply held beliefs. For example, the concept of honor, while superficially a woman's honor (which in itself is defined narrowly in terms of controlling her body primarily through protection of her virginity, or controlling her verbal, mental, and physical behavior within the bounds of decorum defined patriarchally), when threatened is considered a penalty upon patriarchal legacy (i.e., the honor of the family, and more specifically that of the father).[26]

Desirability, while also promoted through popular media notions such as those present in the United States, with a uniquely Indian twist, focus on the physical attributes of women, especially in the wedding marketplace of arranged marriages. Brands such as *Fair & Lovely*, a bleach cream immensely popular in India, are market leaders in cosmetics, outlining very specific markers of desire for femininity. Such cosmetic treatments, while ubiquitous and used across generations, are known to have high levels of heavy metals and steroids, with dangerous carcinogenic effects in some cases.[27]

Thus women's bodies are erased of any agency, and are only considered worthy insofar as they are desirable objects defined within patriarchal parameters as obedient and attractive.[28] Such objectification of women either as prostitutes, Wives, or Handmaids, specifically only for their physical desirability and submissive behavior to the male patriarch is a constant theme echoed throughout *The Handmaid's Tale*. For example, during the visit of the Mexican diplomat, Serena Joy's (Yvonne Strahovski) past as an educated social activist comes to light, but we see the subsumption of her previous identity into a secondary role in her household serving primarily to bolster her husband's political agenda.[29]

In the Indian context, this presents an interesting study, where education itself has become constructed as another marker of desire and superficial modernity, but veils patriarchal notions of desire. An educated woman, often touted as a sign of emancipation, is used as a token for modernism on the marriage market. Women are encouraged to be educated enough to be married, thus demonstrating sufficient genetic proclivity to intelligence to be considered marriage and procreation-worthy, but upon being married are relegated to domesticity within the traditional confines of gender roles.[30]

These gender roles include subsumption of the female body in service to the status quo. To keep such male-dominated structures in place, women's bodies, like in Gilead, are primarily for procreation and service, both of which are threatened by access to education, and consequently knowledge of and access to contraception, both of which are again denied to the Handmaids. These issues often discussed in mainstream media as infrastructural gaps are in fact tumors deeply ingrained in the cultural imagination. The dignified discourse surrounding lack of education for women hides beneath it the chronic underreporting of sexual assault, domestic violence, societal pressure to birth male children at risk to maternal health, and an overall stripping of agency when it comes to control over and the well-being of one's health. The Indian government's program, Beti Bachao Beti Padhao (Save the girl child, educate the girl child), while a policy bandaid, faces numerous challenges in the form of data manipulation by local administrators as cultural norms surrounding the desirability of a male child still continue to hold strong sway.[31]

LOCAL POLITICS, GLOBAL EFFECTS

When trying to find ways to stand in solidarity with women across the globe in the fight for access to better healthcare, we need to analyze our domestic policy stances, emerging from our support for our elected officials. It must be noted that current health policies not only serve to restrict access to healthcare for women in the United States (abortion, lack of clinics, etc.), but they also cast a long shadow, affecting international aid for millions of women globally, with devastating consequences.

Most recently, U.S. president Donald Trump reinstated and expanded a long-held Republican policy called the Mexico City Policy, which forbids international nongovernmental organizations not only from using U.S. federal aid for providing abortion counseling or advocating for liberalization of abortion laws as part of family planning services in their own countries, but for all practical purposes also forbids the use of the NGO's own funds to engage in any of the above, or risk losing its foreign aid.[32] While the overall umbrella of aid to India from the United States approximates roughly $20 million[33] in particular, this will severely hamper the work of agencies like USAID among others which have a long-standing tradition of working alongside Indian NGOs to address issues of child and maternal death, tuberculosis, HIV/AIDS, as well as other infectious diseases.[34]

Human Rights Watch paints the following scenario when looking at the conflict facing numerous organizations relying on U.S. aid around the world:

> For example, take the case of a foreign nongovernmental organization receiving 50 percent of its funds from non-US sources to provide sexual and reproductive health services, including counseling, referrals, or services related to abortion, and the other 50 percent from the US to provide vaccinations for babies, nutritional supplements, or treatment for HIV/AIDS, malaria, and TB. Under this rule, that group must now choose between losing its US funding—slashing its operating budget in half—or restricting or cutting its reproductive health programs. Those that comply with the restrictions must also set aside some of their resources to meet additional compliance and reporting requirements.[35]

Thus, this expansion of the funding restriction will withdraw funding from not only reproductive health services but from all health services NGOs provide, including disease screening (such as breast and cervical cancer) and intervention or nutrition programs for mothers and young children in rural areas which need them the most. Kalpana Apte, head of the Family Planning Association of India (FPAI), serving upward of two million people a year, says that this unprecedented move will go beyond family planning funds and that "programmes which address HIV, maternal and child health, cervical cancer screening, addressing gender based violence and other health and disease areas will now be affected."[36] Further, Apte says that while her organization does not receive direct funding from USAID, they receive it through the International Planned Parenthood Federation, whose core grants will be affected as a result of such policy.[37]

Such withdrawal of funds will also affect sorely needed women's access to contraception, family planning education, and safe abortions often falling to NGOs at the community level. These organizations serve the important function of educating people against the prevalent norm of numerous births or unsafe sex-selective abortions in pursuit of a male child. In India, seven million abortions are conducted annually, nearly half of which are estimated to be illegal.[38] Indian women have a complex relationship with abortion due to the prevalent female foeticide. On the one hand, abortions are used as a tool to strip women of agency within traditional structures which demand male heirs, and on the other, they also serve the purpose of providing women choice in case of unwanted pregnancies and sexual assault, acting as a health service.

In terms of the former, women are often forced to get sex-selective abortions in favor of bearing male children. While such practice is illegal in India and rules surrounding abortion are theoretically strictly controlled within medical structures, these women often resort to back-alley abortions.[39] Both sets of circumstances, nonetheless, warrant the need for safe abortions which do not mortally endanger the women's health at the very basic level. Such further restriction on access to safe abortions, while superficially preventing female foeticide, will potentially create severe maternal health risks as a result of uncertified practitioners engaging in unsafe medical interventions, as well as strip voluntary choice from those who should choose to get abortions for other reasons. The significant reduction of maternal mortality rates in India[40] could also suffer greatly as a result of such rollbacks as well, which will affect contraception provision, family planning, and prenatal and postpartum education.

As discussed above, the time and need for a politics of change aimed toward a reinvigorating of the discussion of women's health in its varied aspects should be ignored only at the risk of a negative domino effect for women across the globe. *The Handmaid's Tale* serves both as a reminder of the vulnerabilities and the inherent agency of women's bodies and minds in the face of insurmountable odds through its themes of disenfranchisement and empowerment and as a foreboding dystopia arising from a false complacency about our place in society. Finally, and most poignantly, Atwood's Gilead serves as a mirror for recognizing the collective platform we occupy in uncomfortable yet transformative spaces, across a spectrum of lived experiences as women with and without privilege.

NOTES

1. Health experiences here are defined as encompassing physical and mental safety and the overall well-being of women, in addition to medical interventions for disease prevention.

2. Mona Eltahawy, "Why Saudi Women Are Literally Living the Handmaid's Tale," *New York Times*, May 24, 2017, https://www.nytimes.com/2017/05/24/opin ion/why-saudi-women-are-literally-living-the-handmaids-tale.html?_r=1.

3. Save the Children, "16th Annual State of the World's Mothers Report: The Urban Disadvantage," Save the Children, 2015, https://www.savethechildren.org /content/dam/usa/reports/advocacy/sowm/sowm-2015.pdf.

4. Jessica Ravitz, "Women in the World: Where the U.S. Falters in Quest for Equality," *Cable News Network*, April 16, 2015, https://www.cnn.com/2015/04/16 /us/american-women-world-rankings/index.html.

5. *The Handmaid's Tale*, "Late," Season 1, Episode 3, directed by Reed Morano, written by Bruce Miller, Hulu, May 2, 2018.

6. Nina Martin, "Redesigning Maternal Care: OB-GYNs Are Urged to See New Mothers Sooner and More Often," National Public Radio, April 23, 2018, https://www.npr.org/2018/04/23/605006555/redesigning-maternal-care-ob-gyns-are-urged-to-see-new-mothers-sooner-and-more-o.

7. American College of Obstetricians and Gynecologists, ACOG Committee Opinion No. 736, "Optimizing Postpartum Care," May 2018, https://www.acog.org/Clinical-Guidance-and-Publications/Committee-Opinions/Committee-on-Obstetric-Practice/Optimizing-Postpartum-Care.

8. ProPublica, "Lost Mothers: Maternal Care and Preventable Deaths," ProPublica, https://www.propublica.org/series/lost-mothers; Katherine Ellison and Nina Martin, "Nearly Dying in Childbirth: Why Preventable Complications Are Growing in U.S.," *National Public Radio*, December 22, 2017, https://www.npr.org/2017/12/22/572298802/nearly-dying-in-childbirth-why-preventable-complications-are-growing-in-u-s.

9. Paul Krugman, "The Angry White Male Caucus: Trumpism Is All about the Fear of Losing Traditional Privilege," *New York Times*, October 1, 2018, https://www.nytimes.com/2018/10/01/opinion/kavanaugh-white-male-privilege.html.

10. "US: New Threats to Women's Health: Health Legislation Should Not Slash Essential Services," Human Rights Watch, April 11, 2017, https://www.hrw.org/news/2017/04/11/us-new-threats-womens-health.

11. United States Bureau of Justice Statistics, "Prisoners in 2016 Summary," *Bureau of Justice Statistics*, January 2018, https://www.bjs.gov/content/pub/pdf/p16_sum.pdf.

12. The Working Poor Families Project, "Low-Income Working Mothers and State Policy: Investing for a Better Economic Future," Policy Brief, Winter 2013–2014," Working Poor Families Project, 2014, https://www.workingpoorfamilies.org/wp-content/uploads/2014/02/WPFP_Low-Income-Working-Mothers-Report_021214.pdf.

13. Hilary Daniel, Shari M. Erickson, and Sue S. Bornstein, "Women's Health Policy in the United States: An American College of Physicians Position Paper," *Annals of Internal Medicine* 168, no. 12 (2018): 874–75, doi: 10.7326/M17-3344.

14. Status of Women in the States, "About the Institute for Women's Policy Research," *Status of Women in the States*, accessed December 4, 2018, https://statusofwomendata.org/about/.

15. Constance Grady, "The Waves of Feminism, and Why People Keep Fighting Over Them, Explained," *Vox*, July 20, 2018, https://www.vox.com/2018/3/20/16955588/feminism-waves-explained-first-second-third-fourth; fourth wave feminism is distinguished from the other waves by its characteristic digitally driven nature.

16. Robert Pear, "13 Men, and No Women, Are Writing New G.O.P. Health Bill in Senate," *New York Times*, May 8, 2017, https://www.nytimes.com/2017/05/08/us/politics/women-health-care-senate.html.

17. "Trump Administration Allows Employers to Take Birth Control Coverage Away from Women," National Women's Law Center, October 13, 2017, accessed December 4, 2018, https://nwlc.org/resources/trump-administration-allows-employers-to-take-birth-control-coverage-away-from-women/.

18. Guttmacher Institute, *Data Center Table for Arkansas, Kentucky, West Virginia,* accessed December 4, 2018, https://data.guttmacher.org/states/table?topics=57 +58+59&dataset=data&state=WV+AR+KY.

19. Allison McCann, "The Last Clinics," *Vice News,* May 23, 2017, https://news .vice.com/en_us/article/paz4bv/last-clinics-seven-states-one-abortion-clinic-left.

20. Ariana E. Cha, "Plastic Surgery Is Surging in America—The Trends in Six Simple Charts," *Washington Post,* March 2, 2016, https://www.washingtonpost .com/news/to-your-health/wp/2016/03/01/the-surge-in-butt-implants-in-america -and-other-plastic-surgery-trends-in-5-simple-charts/?utm_term=.785136c8b38a.

21. Soutik Biswas, "Why India's Rape Crisis Shows No Signs of Abating," British Broadcasting Corporation, April 17, 2018, https://www.bbc.com/news/world-asia -india-43782471.

22. National Crime Records Bureau, Government of India, *Crime in India 2016: Statistics,* accessed December 4, 2018, http://ncrb.gov.in/StatPublications/CII /CII2016/pdfs/NEWPDFs/Crime%20in%20India%20-%202016%20Complete%20 PDF%20291117.pdf.

23. Annie Gowen, "In India It's Not Easy to Report on Rape," *Washington Post,* December 21, 2016, https://www.washingtonpost.com/world/asia_pacific/its-not-easy -to-report-on-rape-in-india/2016/12/20/fab13528-c0b1-11e6-b527-949c5893595e _story.html?utm_term=.e0f26d95c91c; Pramit Bhattacharya and Tadit Kundu, "99% Cases of Sexual Assaults Go Unreported, Govt. Data Shows," livemint, April 24, 2018, https://www.livemint.com/Politics/AV3sIKoEBAGZozALMX8THK/99 -cases-of-sexual-assaults-go-unreported-govt-data-shows.html; Anusha Venkat, "Why Most Rapes Go Unreported in India," *Asia Times,* January, 5, 2017, http:// www.atimes.com/article/rapes-go-unreported-india/.

24. Shweta Singh, Ru Zhou, Xiong Li, Liping Tong, "The Complex Relationship with Health: Rural and Urban 'Poor' Women," *International Social Work* 59, No. 1 (January 2016): 32–46, https://doi.org/10.1177/0020872813503862.

25. Victoria A. Velkoff and Arjun Adlakha, "Women of the World: Women's Health in India," *U.S. Department of Commerce,* December 1998, https://www.cen sus.gov/content/dam/Census/library/publications/1998/demo/wid98-3.pdf.

26. Deepa Narayan, "India's Abuse of Women Is the Biggest Human Rights Violation on Earth," *Guardian,* April 27, 2018, https://www.theguardian.com/com mentisfree/2018/apr/27/india-abuse-women-human-rights-rape-girls.

27. Center for Science and Environment, *Data Charts,* January 15, 2014, accessed December 4, 2018, https://www.cseindia.org/data-charts-5291.

28. Narayan, "India's Abuse of Women Is the Biggest Human Rights Violation on Earth."

29. *The Handmaid's Tale,* "A Woman's Place," Season 1, Episode 6, directed by Floria Sigismondi, written by Wendy Straker Hauser, Hulu, May 17, 2017.

30. Rohini Pandey and Charity Troyer Moore, "Why Aren't India's Women Working?" *New York Times,* August 23, 2015, https://www.nytimes.com/2015/08/24 /opinion/why-arent-indias-women-working.html; Maitreyi B. Das, "Do Traditional Axes of Exclusion Affect Labor Market Outcomes in India?" *World Bank South Asia*

Series 97 (2006), http://documents.worldbank.org/curated/en/195941468034790110 /Do-traditional-axes-of-exclusion-affect-labor-market-outcomes-in-India.

31. Wamika Kapur, "Why the Beti Bachao Beti Padhao Scheme Has Failed on Several Counts," The Wire, May 4, 2017, https://thewire.in/education/beti-bachao -beti-padhao-scheme-failed.

32. "Trump's 'Mexico City Policy' or 'Global Gag Rule,'" Human Rights Watch, February 14, 2018, accessed December 5, 2018, https://www.hrw.org /news/2018/02/14/trumps-mexico-city-policy-or-global-gag-rule.

33. Sushmi Dey, "Trump's 'Global Gag Rule' to Financially Affect Health Programs in Country," *Times of India*, January 29, 2017, https://timesofindia.indiatimes.com india/trumps-global-gag-rule-to-financially-affect-health-programmes-in-country /articleshow/56845675.cms.

34. United States Agency for International Development, "Ending Preventable Maternal Mortality: USAID Maternal Health Vision for Action Evidence for Strategic Approaches," *USAID,* January 15, 2017, https://www.usaid.gov/sites/default /files/documents/1864/MH%20Strategy_web_red.pdf.

35. "Trump's 'Mexico City Policy' or 'Global Gag Rule,'" Human Rights Watch.

36. Katie Forster, "Global Gag Rule: Unsafe Abortions Kill One Woman Every Two Hours in India—Donald Trump Will Make This Worse," *The Independent*, February 2, 2017, https://www.independent.co.uk/news/world/asia/unsafe-abortions -kill-woman-india-two-hours-donald-trump-global-gag-rule-mexico-city-policy-for eign-a7559781.html.

37. Dey, "Trump's 'Global Gag Rule' to Financially Affect Health Programs in Country."

38. Dey, "Trump's 'Global Gag Rule.'"

39. Ministry of Health and Family Welfare, Government of India, "District Level Household and Facility Survey 2007–2008," accessed December 5, 2018, http:// rchiips.org/pdf/INDIA_REPORT_DLHS-3.pdf; BBC, "Where Are India's Millions of Missing Girls?" British Broadcasting Corporation, May 23, 2011, https://www.bbc .com/news/world-south-asia-13264301; BBC, "Unsafe Abortions Killing Thousands in India," British Broadcasting Corporation, April 17, 2013, https://www.bbc.com news/world-asia-india-22119447.

40. Poonam K. Singh, "India Has Achieved Ground-Breaking Success in Reducing Maternal Mortality," World Health Organization, accessed December 6, 2018, http://www.searo.who.int/mediacentre/features/2018/india-groundbreaking-sucess -reducing-maternal-mortality-rate/en/.

WORKS CITED

American College of Obstetricians and Gynecologists. "Optimizing Postpartum Care," ACOG Committee Opinion No. 736 (2018). https://www.acog.org/Clin ical-Guidance-and-Publications/Committee-Opinions/Committee-on-Obstetric -Practice/Optimizing-Postpartum-Care.

BBC. "Where Are India's Millions of Missing Girls?" British Broadcasting Corporation, May 23, 2011. https://www.bbc.com/news/world-south-asia-13264301.

———. "Unsafe Abortions Killing Thousands in India." British Broadcasting Corporation, April 17, 2013. https://www.bbc.com/news/world-asia-india-22119447.

Bhattacharya, Pramit, and Tadit Kundu. "99% Cases of Sexual Assaults Go Unreported, Govt. Data Shows." livemint, April 24, 2018. https://www.livemint.com/Politics/AV3sIKoEBAGZozALMX8THK/99-cases-of-sexual-assaults-go-unreported-govt-data-shows.html.

Biswas, Soutik. "Why India's Rape Crisis Shows No Signs of Abating." *British Broadcasting Corporation*, April 17, 2018. https://www.bbc.com/news/world-asia-india-43782471.

Center for Science and Environment. *Data Charts,* January 15, 2014, accessed December 4, 2018, https://www.cseindia.org/data-charts-5291.

Cha, Ariana E. "Plastic Surgery Is Surging in America—The Trends in Six Simple Charts." *Washington Post*, March 2, 2016. https://www.washingtonpost.com/news/to-your-health/wp/2016/03/01/the-surge-in-butt-implants-in-america-and-other-plastic-surgery-trends-in-5-simple-charts/?utm_term=.785136c8b38a.

Das, Maitreyi B. "Do Traditional Axes of Exclusion Affect Labor Market Outcomes in India?" *World Bank South Asia Series* 97 (2006), http://documents.worldbank.org/curated/en/195941468034790110/Do-traditional-axes-of-exclusion-affect-labor-market-outcomes-in-India._

Daniel, Hilary, Shari M. Erickson, and Sue S. Bornstein. "Women's Health Policy in the United States: An American College of Physicians Position Paper." *Annals of Internal Medicine* 168, no. 12 (2018): 874–75. doi: 10.7326/M17-3344.

Dey, Sushmi. "Trump's 'Global Gag Rule' to Financially Affect Health Programs in Country." *Times of India*, January 29, 2017. https://timesofindia.indiatimes.com/india/trumps-global-gag-rule-to-financially-affect-health-programmes-in-country/articleshow/56845675.cms.

Eltahawy, Mona. "Why Saudi Women Are Literally Living the Handmaid's Tale." *New York Times*, May 24, 2017. https://www.nytimes.com/2017/05/24/opinion/why-saudi-women-are-literally-living-the-handmaids-tale.html?_r=1.

Ellison, Katherine, and Nina Martin. "Nearly Dying in Childbirth: Why Preventable Complications Are Growing in U.S." National Public Radio, December 22, 2017. https://www.npr.org/2017/12/22/572298802/nearly-dying-in-childbirth-why-preventable-complications-are-growing-in-u-s.

Forster, Katie. "Global Gag Rule: Unsafe Abortions Kill One Woman Every Two Hours in India—Donald Trump Will Make This Worse," *The Independent*, February 2, 2017. https://www.independent.co.uk/news/world/asia/unsafe-abortions-kill-woman-india-two-hours-donald-trump-global-gag-rule-mexico-city-policy-foreign-a7559781.html.

Gowen, Annie. "In India It's Not Easy to Report on Rape." *Washington Post*, December 21, 2016. https://www.washingtonpost.com/world/asia_pacific/its-not-easy-to-report-on-rape-in-india/2016/12/20/fab13528-c0b1-11e6-b527-949c5893595e_story.html?utm_term=.e0f26d95c91c.

Grady, Constance. "The Waves of Feminism, and Why People Keep Fighting over Them, Explained." *Vox*, July 20, 2018. https://www.vox.com/2018/3/20/16955588 /feminism-waves-explained-first-second-third-fourth.

Guttmacher Institute. *Data Center Table for Arkansas, Kentucky, West Virginia,* accessed December 4, 2018. https://data.guttmacher.org/states/table?topics=57+58 +59&dataset=data&state=WV+AR+KY.

Human Rights Watch. "Trump's 'Mexico City Policy' or 'Global Gag Rule.'" February 14, 2018. https://www.hrw.org/news/2018/02/14/trumps-mexico-city-policy-or -global-gag-rule.

———. "US: New Threats to Women's Health: Health Legislation Should Not Slash Essential Services." April 11, 2017. https://www.hrw.org/news/2017/04/11/us -new-threats-womens-health.

Kapur, Wamika. "Why the Beti Bachao Beti Padhao Scheme Has Failed on Several Counts." The Wire, May 4, 2017. https://thewire.in/education/beti-bachao-beti -padhao-scheme-failed.

Krugman, Paul. "The Angry White Male Caucus: Trumpism Is All about the Fear of Losing Traditional Privilege." *New York Times*, October 1, 2018. https://www .nytimes.com/2018/10/01/opinion/kavanaugh-white-male-privilege.html.

McCann, Allison. "The Last Clinics." *Vice News*, May 23, 2017. https://news.vice .com/en_us/article/paz4bv/last-clinics-seven-states-one-abortion-clinic-left.

Martin, Nina. "Redesigning Maternal Care: OB-GYNs Are Urged to See New Mothers Sooner and More Often." National Public Radio, April 23, 2018. https://www.npr .org/2018/04/23/605006555/redesigning-maternal-care-ob-gyns-are-urged-to-see -new-mothers-sooner-and-more-o.

Ministry of Health and Family Welfare, Government of India. "District Level House-hold and Facility Survey 2007–2008." Government of India, accessed December 5, 2018. http://rchiips.org/pdf/INDIA_REPORT_DLHS-3.pdf.

Narayan, Deepa. "India's Abuse of Women Is the Biggest Human Rights Violation on Earth." *Guardian*, April 27, 2018. https://www.theguardian.com/commentis free/2018/apr/27/india-abuse-women-human-rights-rape-girls.

National Women's Law Center. "Trump Administration Allows Employers to Take Birth Control Coverage Away from Women." *National Women's Law Center*, October 13, 2017. https://nwlc.org/resources/trump-administration-allows -employers-to-take-birth-control-coverage-away-from-women/.

National Crime Records Bureau, Government of India. *Crime in India 2016: Statis-tics.* Accessed December 4, 2018. http://ncrb.gov.in/StatPublications/CII/CII2016 /pdfs/NEWPDFs/Crime%20in%20India%20-%202016%20Complete%20 PDF%20291117.pdf.

Pandey, Rohini, and Charity T. Moore. "Why Aren't India's Women Working?" *New York Times*, August 23, 2015. https://www.nytimes.com/2015/08/24/opinion/why -arent-indias-women-working.html.

Pear, Robert. "13 Men, and No Women, Are Writing New G.O.P. Health Bill in Senate." *New York Times*, May 8, 2017. https://www.nytimes.com/2017/05/08/us /politics/women-health-care-senate.html.

ProPublica. "Lost Mothers: Maternal Care and Preventable Deaths." ProPublica. Accessed December 5, 2018. https://www.propublica.org/series/lost-mothers.

Ravitz, Jessica. "Women in the World: Where the U.S. Falters in Quest for Equality." *Cable News Network*, April 16, 2015. https://www.cnn.com/2015/04/16/us/american-women-world-rankings/index.html.

Save the Children. "16th Annual State of the World's Mothers Report: The Urban Disadvantage." Save the Children, 2015. https://www.savethechildren.org/content/dam/usa/reports/advocacy/sowm/sowm-2015.pdf.

Singh, Poonam K. "India Has Achieved Ground-Breaking Success in Reducing Maternal Mortality." World Health Organization. Accessed December 6, 2018. http://www.searo.who.int/mediacentre/features/2018/india-groundbreaking-sucess-reducing-maternal-mortality-rate/en/.

Singh, Shweta, Ru Zhou, Xiong Li, and Liping Tong. "The Complex Relationship with Health: Rural and Urban 'Poor' Women." *International Social Work* 59, no. 1 (January 2016): 32–46, https://doi.org/10.1177/0020872813503862.

Status of Women in the States. "About the Institute for Women's Policy Research." *Status of Women in the States.* Accessed December 4, 2018. https://statusofwomendata.org/about/.

United States Agency for International Development. "Ending Preventable Maternal Mortality: USAID Maternal Health Vision for Action Evidence for Strategic Approaches." *USAID,* January 15, 2017. https://www.usaid.gov/sites/default/files/documents/1864/MH%20Strategy_web_red.pdf.

United States Bureau of Justice Statistics. "Prisoners in 2016 Summary." *Bureau of Justice Statistics*, January, 2018. https://www.bjs.gov/content/pub/pdf/p16_sum.pdf.

The Working Poor Families Project. "Low-Income Working Mothers and State Policy: Investing for a Better Economic Future" Policy Brief Winter, 2013–2014, The Working Poor Families Project, 2014. https://www.workingpoorfamilies.org/wp-content/uploads/2014/02/WPFP_Low-Income-Working-Mothers-Report_021214.pdf.

Velkoff, Victoria A., and Arjun Adlakha. "Women of the World: Women's Health in India." *U.S. Department of Commerce*, December 1998. https://www.census.gov/content/dam/Census/library/publications/1998/demo/wid98-3.pdf.

Venkat, Anusha. "Why Most Rapes Go Unreported in India." *Asia Times*, January 5, 2017. http://www.atimes.com/article/rapes-go-unreported-india/.

TELEVISION

The Handmaid's Tale. TV series. Season 1. MGM Television / Hulu. USA, 2017.

The Handmaid's Tale. "A Woman's Place." Season 1, Episode 6. Directed by Floria Sigismondi. Written by Wendy Straker Hauser. Hulu, May 17, 2017.

The Handmaid's Tale. "Late." Season 1, Episode 3. Directed by Reed Morano. Written by Bruce Miller. Hulu, April 26, 2017.

Chapter Twelve

Resist!

Racism and Sexism in The Handmaid's Tale

Charisse Levchak

Some may interpret Margaret Atwood's *The Handmaid's Tale's* Gilead as implausible, while others in this unfortunate political, social, and cultural moment may see it as a possible future for us. Reading[1] and watching[2] the horrors that Atwood imagined is anxiety producing and downright horrific when we imagine the possibility that our friends, family, associates, or selves could one day be oppressed in the manners depicted in *The Handmaid's Tale*. Our voices: silenced. Our bodies: controlled. Our spirits: broken.

Those not convinced that such horrors could happen in the contemporary United States need only look to the countless past *and* current examples of cruelty, violence, and brutality that people of color and women have and continue to experience. As noted in my past research on racist and sexist microaggressions,[3] "the seeds of American racism and sexism that were planted at the country's inception and that were sustained by the blatant subjugation of people of color and women continue to generate race-based and gender-based oppression within present-day American society."[4] In a later work, I note:

The country was established and developed because of the coercion, cruelty, tyranny, subjugation, exploitation, repression, and oppression of people of color. We see this in the past and present maltreatment of American Indians and people of African descent within America. For centuries, Americas' First Peoples were dominated, subjugated, and had their land stolen.[5] Similarly, for centuries, Africans and their descendants were enslaved, abused, slaughtered, and forced to provide free labor to ensure the growth and prosperity of this nation.[6] After slavery was abolished, restrictive laws and practices were enforced to ensure that African Americans remained subjugated and oppressed scholastically, professionally, financially, and socially.[7] Presently, even with the elimination of such overtly racist laws, people of color are still mistreated and disadvantaged because of racist ideologies and practices throughout society.[8]

Women have been, and continue to be, subjugated and marginalized in public and private spaces. In some instances, our work and voices are ignored, and on other occasions some men and horizontally oppressive women attempt to take credit for our efforts and ideas. For some of us, our bodies have been exoticized, harmed, disparaged, and violated by family, friends, strangers, and acquaintances.

Fortunately, there have been some impressive developments as it relates to addressing racism and sexism. Notably, some contemporary social movements have empowered activists and advocates to name injustices, to seek an end to domination, and to hold violators accountable—as seen in the Movement for Black Lives, the #MeToo Movement, and the Time's Up Movement. However, more work needs to be done. More of us must use our voices, power, and privilege to serve as allies, to actively stand in solidarity with those under attack, and to name, challenge, and work to eradicate *all* systems of oppression (not just the ones that impact us, or those we care about). Our active work and participation in movements to dismantle oppression is vital, especially since lives are at stake and since some members of dominant and targeted groups deliberately work to maintain systems of oppression in the United States and around the world.

However, there are lessons that we can learn from Atwood's dystopia, and these lessons should not be taken lightly since they can empower individuals to actively work toward dismantling racism and sexism, which will undoubtedly help us avoid Atwood's dystopia becoming our reality. Below, I highlight some points and lessons from *The Handmaid's Tale* that will be useful as we work toward social justice in our daily lives. I then close the chapter by providing assignment ideas for social justice educators.

Prevention and resistance. These two words come to mind when thinking of *The Handmaid's Tale*. Regarding prevention, what could have been done to stop Gilead, the toxic regime in Atwood's dystopia, from gaining momentum and power and from implementing sexist and racist policies, procedures, and practices? The *people* in pre-Gilead America were key in preventing the oppressive regime from rising, just as *we* are key in preventing tyrannical, racist, and sexist powers from rising in our society. Several scenes from the Hulu TV adaptation, and specifically the episode titled "Late"[9] are quite powerful as they relate to prevention and resistance. In "Late," we see a powerful scene in which June and Moira are at a protest to oppose Gilead and its ideals (which we'll revisit later).

However, prior to the protest scene were manifestations of horizontal and vertical aggression throughout the pre-Gilead society. June (Elisabeth Moss) and Moira (Samira Wiley) first experienced horizontal aggression from a woman who stared menacingly at them as they were out jogging in clothes that the woman seemingly deemed "too revealing." It should be noted that the aggressor in this scene wore several layers of clothing as well as a turtle neck, which is in line with the "modest" clothing style worn by Gilead women. Moira and June also experienced vertical aggression from a male cashier (Dan Beirne), a Barista at a coffee shop who hurled sexist slurs at them, forcing them to leave the establishment. These are examples of the social climate shifting in a direction that tolerated open aggression toward people—and especially women who did not conform to sexist and racist Gilead ideals such as submissiveness, modesty in behavior and appearance, and expectations of interracial interactions—that oftentimes resulted in segregation.

More disturbing is the scene with the coffee shop Barista, not just because of his disgusting comments toward June and Moira, but because of the *silence* and *inaction* of others in the shop who *said nothing* and *did nothing* to challenge his behavior or to advocate for Moira and June. We can prevent larger manifestations of oppression, by challenging smaller ones. We can stop macroaggressions by challenging microaggressions. We can prevent the implementation of sexist and racist policies, procedures, and practices by using our voice, privilege, and power when injustices, both great and small, occur. But we must first be willing to act.

In a monologue, June/Offred reflects on the gradual changes Gilead implemented, as well as the lack of resistance efforts among everyday people, like you and me, to stop Gilead from gaining too much power and influence:

> Now I'm awake to the world. I was asleep before. That's how we let it happen. When they slaughtered Congress, we didn't wake up. When they blamed terrorists, and suspended the Constitution, we didn't wake up then either. They said it would be temporary. Nothing changes instantaneously. In a gradually heating bathtub, you'd be boiled to death before you knew it.[10]

June's flashbacks in this episode also show major setbacks for the world as we know it and significant gains for Gilead, such as: the suspension of bank accounts owned by women, the implementation of a law that banned women from owning property, and the dismissal of women from workplaces. The dismissal scene was sobering and shows another major shift toward Gilead solidifying its power (see Jaqueline Maxwell's chapter in this volume). Again, there was silence and inaction. This time it came from male coworkers and a male manager who shared that he "didn't have a choice" regarding the firing of women employees (since there were armed enforcers present to ensure that all women left and would be threatened if they attempted to return). While the dismissal scene was horrific in its own right because of the sense of impending doom, it is my estimation that the silence of men in the face of sexism, as seen in the coffee shop (where there *was not* a threat of force), is what is more disturbing. Men in the pre-Gilead world showed apathy toward milder forms of oppression *not* backed by force, and this paved the way for oppression *bolstered* by the threat of force. In other words, their lack of concern about the sexist ideals peddled by Gilead and their indifference when women were verbally assaulted in public was a major building block to the rights of women being eroded. As June points out, we have to be "awake to the world" because nothing "changes instantaneously." Furthermore, the lesson here is that we all must challenge the sexism and racism that we see *in our everyday lives* otherwise we may find the rights of women and people of color further eroded.

The protest scene in "Late" is one of the most memorable scenes of the series. The scene displays the raw emotions of protest and resistance. The unruly shouting and interactions of the protestors, against the well-organized paramilitary deployed by Gilead leadership. The cries of concern and passion, against the menacing enforcers with emotionless faces. It is a reminder that we must not only speak out against the injustices we see in our daily lives, but we must organize against and resist oppression and oppressors in our world. We must face them bravely, and let them know, unwaveringly, that they cannot have our world or us; and maybe, when we use our voices, power, and privilege, we will inspire others to do the same. "Late" applies to other circumstances in the story that I will not reveal here. However, it is also a subtle hint that due to complacency and apathy, the efforts to keep Gilead from gaining control were too "late" for the people of Atwood's world. While it was too late for them, it is not too late for us. Consequently, we must take care of ourselves and others, and bravely resist through individual action such as committing to being more aware, voting, being an ally, running for office, and committing to social justice education and efforts; as well as collective action, such as engaging in peaceful protests and supporting those who are involved in daily efforts of resistance.

NOTES

1. Margaret Atwood, *The Handmaid's Tale* (Anchor Books: New York, 1986).

2. *The Handmaid's Tale*, TV series, Created by Bruce Miller, Season 1, MGM Television / Hulu. USA, 2017.

3. Charisse Camilla Levchak, *An Examination of Racist and Sexist Microaggressions on College Campuses* (University of Iowa, 2013).

4. Levchak, *An Examination*, 1.

5. Kimberly Roppolo, "Symbolic Racism, History, and Reality: The Real Problem with Indian Mascots," in *Genocide of the Mind: New American Indian Writing*, ed. M. Moore (New York: Nation Books, 2003).

6. Ta-Nehisi Coates, "Slavery Made America: The Case for Reparations: A Narrative Bibliography," *The Atlantic*, https://www.theatlantic.com/business/archive/2014/06/slavery-made-america/373288/.

7. Steve J. Gold, "A Critical Race Theory Approach to Black American Entrepreneurship," *Ethnic and Racial Studies* 39, no. 9 (2016).

8. Levchak, *An Examination*, 8.

9. *The Handmaid's Tale*, "Late," Season 1, Episode 3, directed by Reed Morano, written by Bruce Miller, Hulu, April 26, 2017.

10. *The Handmaid's Tale*, "Late," Season 1, Episode 3.

WORKS CITED

Atwood, Margaret. *The Handmaid's Tale*. Anchor Books: New York, 1986.

Coates, Ta-Nehisi. "Slavery Made America: The Case for Reparations: A Narrative Bibliography." *The Atlantic*, https://www.theatlantic.com/business/archive/2014/06/slavery-made-america/373288/.

Gold, Steve J. "A Critical Race Theory Approach to Black American Entrepreneurship." *Ethnic and Racial Studies* 39, no. 9 (2016): 1697–718.

Levchak, Charisse Camilla. *An Examination of Racist and Sexist Microaggressions on College Campuses*. University of Iowa, 2013.

Roppolo, Kimberly. "Symbolic Racism, History, and Reality: The Real Problem with Indian Mascots." In *Genocide of the Mind: New American Indian Writing*, edited by M. Moore. New York: Nation Books, 2003.

FILM AND TELEVISION

The Handmaid's Tale. TV Series. Season 1. MGM Television / Hulu. USA, 2017.

The Handmaid's Tale. "Late." Season 1, Episode 3. Directed by Reed Morano. Written by Bruce Miller. Hulu, April 26, 2017.

Chapter Thirteen

Erasing Race in *The Handmaid's Tale*

Paul Moffett

In the literary tradition of utopian writing, both utopias and dystopias are reactions to concerns in the present: dystopias serve as warnings, utopias as aspirations. Although dystopian fiction can include personal triumphs for characters, and can even end on a hopeful note, any world element depicted in a dystopia is liable to be read as a projection of either the author's own fears[1] or more generally of the presumed fears of a target audience. It is in this spirit that I want to look at the depiction of race in *The Handmaid's Tale,* both the book and especially the two seasons of the Hulu television adaptation. What are the fears and desires related to race that *The Handmaid's Tale* dramatizes?

There are many avenues of inquiry with which to approach race in *The Handmaid's Tale*. I am approaching this chapter from my academic perspective as a literature scholar interested in dystopia. I have mostly focused on the representation of Moira (Samira Wiley), the character of color given the most narrative attention in the TV series and therefore the character in whom we might expect to see the racial perspectives of the TV show most strongly exemplified. Additionally, since her character is white in the novel, the changes between her representation in the novel and her representation in the TV series are likely to be illuminating.[2]

RACE IN THE NOVEL

Margaret Atwood's dystopian novel, *The Handmaid's Tale* explicitly depicts a monochromatically white world. A news report Offred[3] watches midway through the novel refers to the "Resettlement of the Children of Ham,"[4] by which the book means the segregation and deportation of people of color, drawing off of a religious tradition popularized in the Southern United States in the mid-nineteenth century that associated Noah's three sons Japheth, Shem, and Ham with Europe, Asia, and Africa respectively. In Genesis Noah curses the children of Ham into servitude, and this text was used as a religious justification of the African slave trade in the United States.[5] An allusion to the Children of Ham is more than just a conveniently biblically-valanced reference for Atwood; it is an allusion to the political history of the United States, a political history whose ramifications persist.

In the novel *The Handmaid's Tale,* the all-white world is an assertion that the dystopian world of Gilead has a racial component. Atwood's novel is conscious of the racial implication of control of reproduction. In the "Historical Notes" section of the novel, Pieixoto describes the historical buildup to Gilead as "an age of plummeting Caucasian birth rates, a phenomenon observable not only in Gilead but in most northern Caucasian societies of the time,"[6] and a few sentences later refers to "the differing statistics among Caucasians and non-Caucasians."[7] While the premise of the TV series is an ecologically triggered universal drop in birthrates worldwide, or at least throughout North America, the novel posits only a fall in Caucasian birth rates. Paranoia about decreasing Caucasian birth rates and a consequent shift in the demographic makeup of the United States continue to pervade white-supremacist rhetoric, and this is usually what is meant by allusions to white genocide:[8] not the murder of whites, but their proportionate decrease through a combination of immigration and disproportionately small population growth due to a falling birth rate. Quite aside from the racist ideas of one's "own kind," the anxiety expressed here is that a future for white children is in some kind of jeopardy. Pieixoto also refers to Gilead's "racist policies" which were "firmly rooted in the pre-Gilead period,"[9] demonstrating—in case readers missed it—that Atwood is aware of the racial component of rhetoric surrounding reproduction.[10]

Finally, Pieixoto alludes to "racist fears [that] provided some of the emotional fuel that allowed the Gilead takeover to succeed as well as it did."[11] In other words, the dystopia of the book's Gilead is not only an incidentally white one; it is white by design, by practice, and by motivation. It was the desire to create and maintain a white state that was part of the impetus behind the creation of the book's Gilead, and the whiteness of the book's world is part of what makes it dystopian.

Since race is a culturally constructed and mediated phenomenon, cultural shifts not only allow for but necessitate an adjustment in the understanding and representation of race.[12] Furthermore, the adaptation of a novel into a TV show is a transformation. Attempts to reproduce the novel exactly would be misguided; if we wanted to experience the novel exactly, we would read the novel. That is to say that the adaptation of *The Handmaid's Tale* into a TV series (and previously into a film) rightly changes the text's conception of race. Therefore, a TV show has metatextual and production issues to consider that a novel does not, and the ethical considerations are necessarily different. As showrunner Bruce Miller asked in a *Time* magazine interview: "What's the difference between making a TV show about racists and making a racist TV show where you don't hire any actors of color?"[13] Having made the appropriate choice to include actors of color, the TV series is then faced with the choice of how to represent the experiences of those people once they were on the screen, and here I think it disappoints. *The Handmaid's Tale* treats race as almost entirely irrelevant.

MOIRA AS A HANDMAID AND RACE ERASURE

Moira (Samira Wiley) is a problem for the first season of *The Handmaid's Tale*. Moira is a fellow Handmaid-in-training whom June encounters at the Red Center, and she and June were best friends before Gilead. We are introduced to her at the Red Center and almost simultaneously in flashbacks at a party where she is flirting with a woman. Moira helps June to navigate the autocracy of Gilead, encouraging June to join the Handmaids in blaming Janine for her own sexual assault.[14] She escapes the Red Center but is later captured and becomes a prostitute at Jezebel's. Ultimately Moira flees to Canada, where she takes on a role welcoming and supporting other refugees from Gilead. In the TV show as in the book Moira is depicted as a lesbian, but in the TV show she is black while in the book she is white. Her presence in Gilead as a woman of color coupled with her role as a Handmaid raises issues that it is to the show's detriment to ignore, preeminent among which is that her race is completely uncommented upon. Whether it is used as the justification for her slavery or as a rationale for excluding her as a suitable parent, Moira's race should matter.

We should note that the social problem that Gilead seeks to solve through the use of handmaids is not a problem of infertility. The issue not the *existence* of children but their *distribution.* Socially mandated ritual rape is not a real solution to infertility, even when the moral issues are dismissed. For example, in both the novel and the show it is strongly implied that Commander Waterford (Joseph Finnes) is sterile. No amount of legal or social permission for him to rape anyone is going to solve that problem. The presumption that the society would ignore existing racial prejudice on pragmatic terms in the service of increased fertility suggests that the social structure of Gilead is actually a solution to decreased fertility, which it is not. What the social structure of Gilead—the premise of their society—is a "solution" to is the distribution of fertility and of children along biological rather than classed lines. In other words, the fundamental program of Gilead is using women's uteruses and the babies that come from them as a natural resource which they then redistribute. The end result of the program is not that more babies exist, but that the babies that do exist are in the hands of the (primarily white) people who the regime has determined deserve them. We see this dramatized when Gilead shows their children to the Mexican ambassador Mrs. Castillo (Zabryna Guevara). These children are symbolically—and to a great degree literally—the property of the state. A version of this policy is in practice in the United States as I write this chapter, where children who crossed the southern border with their parents have been separated from those parents and given to (primarily white) American parents instead.[15]

The point here is not just that the racisms of America's past are too entrenched to be plausibly irrelevant in Gilead; it is that in a world where birth rates have fallen precipitously, race becomes more important, not less. It is unclear whether misogyny fuels white supremacy or vice versa, but the two are unavoidably interconnected within a political or social context where white men hold the balance of power or even historically *have held* the balance of power. As criminologist Barbara Perry, an expert in hate crimes, argued in 2004, "Racial purity cannot be sustained without strict adherence to rigid constructions of appropriate gender and sexual behavior. All white women must fulfill their role as procreators of the race, all white men must fulfill their role as white saviors, all white people must be protected from the evils of nonwhite, non-Christian, non-heterosexual Others."[16] This implies a converse, that when we follow strict adherence to rigid constructions of gender and sexual behavior, it is wise to look for racial purity as a motivating factor.

It is implausible that Gilead would use Moira and the other unseen racialized women she symbolizes as Handmaids without attaching any significance to their race, because as Carlos A. Hoyt has argued, "the critical distinction between race and other forms of social identity group classification is *the presumption of immutability.*"[17] Although gender, sexuality, and class are all commonly understood by politically progressive ideologies to be flexible and by politically conservative ideologies to be static, race is conceived of as immutable by the mainstream of both progressive and conservative ideologies. The logic of biology would say that Moira's theoretical baby would be no less biologically connected to the Commander's Wife than June's (Elizabeth Moss) would be to Serena (Yvonne Strahovski), but since race is a cultural and not a biological reality, and since whiteness is understood by the dominant racial metanarratives as being the generic nonrace, and furthermore since race is culturally constructed as immutable, any baby Moira might theoretically have would be read as black. The infamous "one drop rule," whereby "a black is any person with *any* known African black ancestry"[18] has a lasting effect.[19] Davis notes that this definition "was generally accepted by whites and blacks alike . . . taken for granted as readily by judges, affirmative action officers, and black protesters as it is by Ku Klux Klansmen."[20] Remember, "twenty-two states, including many Northern states, still had anti-miscegenation laws in the early 1960s"[21] until the federal Supreme Court ruled such laws unconstitutional in 1967, which incidentally means that such laws were in effect when both Margaret Atwood (b. 1939), and director Bruce Miller (b. 1965) were children.

The proverbial elephant in the room of the first season of *The Handmaid's Tale* is that historically, in the United States, black slave women were raped by white men, and babies that were born out of these assaults were not taken into the house by the white plantation wives. In his article in *The Verge*, Noah Berlatsky opines that "in Western fiction, dystopic stories often ask, 'What if this atrocity had happened to white people instead?'"[22] This may be problematic, but it is explicitly Atwood's project in the novel, and she has repeatedly defended the realism of the book by asserting that in writing it she "made a rule for [her]self: [she] would not include anything that human beings had not already done in some other place or time."[23] Although the novel makes these choices consciously, the show seems to make them unconsciously. Moira's story line is much expanded from the book, but it is still as a secondary character, and her identity as a woman of color is not relevant to either her character or to the development of the plot. June is still white, and the experiences of Moira and the other Handmaids of color are given less narrative weight than June's. The core story of the TV series is still about what happens when a white person experiences the atrocities that have historically happened to nonwhite people.

The result of the first season of *The Handmaid's Tale* ignoring the historical and theoretical implications of race is that the show ignores or undervalues the realities of the lived experiences of people of color, and how systemic injustice disproportionately affects them. Charles Gallagher, a sociologist specializing in social inequality, has argued many times, in one way or another, that "embracing color-blind egalitarianism as a way of understanding racial hierarchy allows individuals to inhabit a skin color but to view race as not conferring any relative social privilege or disadvantage. Within this perspective, there is no such thing as white privilege."[24]

Both the privileges and the liabilities of social identities are stackable and magnify one another, so that a black gay woman experiences the negative social effects of being a woman, of being gay, and of being black, but also the social effects of being a gay woman, of being a black woman, and of being gay and black, and finally the effect of wearing all those social identities at once. *The Handmaid's Tale* recognizes this in its treatment of homosexuality, and Emily's (Alexis Bledel) experience in Gilead is comparatively worse than June's because Emily experiences all the oppression of being a white woman in Gilead *as well as* all the oppression of being a lesbian in Gilead. While we see some expression of Moira sharing Emily's specific oppression as a "gender traitor," we do not see any expression of the relevance of her racial identity. Moira's experiences in Gilead are different from June's—her experience in Jezebel's, for example, dramatizes an alternative path of objectification to the one June experiences—but without either any comment on her race or any implicit racializing of Jezebel's in general (by casting mostly women of color as the prostitutes, for example), Moira's unique experiences are not clearly relevant to her race. In other words, the show does not recognize that Moira's experience in Gilead should be distinct from either Emily's or June's *by virtue of her blackness*.

We may wish that her representation had been handled differently, but what are the implications of Moira's narrative as it is in fact presented, leaving hypotheticals to the side? This line of inquiry, incidentally, highlights a pitfall that accompanies representation in media: since people of color are still a minority on screen in *The Handmaid's Tale*, the symbolic significance of each individual is drastically heightened. Moira is not the only woman of color in *The Handmaid's Tale*, but she is by far the woman of color to whom the narrative of the show gives the most attention, and as such, she is saddled with the interpretive weight of having to be representative of women of color in general. The solution to this pitfall, obviously, is a greater presence of people of color on television in general—the problem is systemic.[25] If there were thirty TV series currently airing that featured nonwhite leads, then the symbolic stress on Moira would be substantially diminished. But since that is not the case, creators of media (whether they be books, movies, TV shows, YouTube programs, music videos, or anything else) should be especially careful about the implications of their representation of underrepresented people, and it would be both intellectually dishonest and also unethical of us as people who watch and analyze those media artifacts to pretend that the race of the characters does not mean that that character signifies disproportionately about the nature of race in general.

MOIRA'S ROLE IN THE TV SERIES

Moira is introduced to the Hulu TV viewers in *The Handmaid's Tale* as a Handmaid-in-training. As she does in the novel, Moira stages a daring escape from the Red Center, kidnapping an Aunt and exchanging clothes with her in a bid for escape to a safe house in Boston. In the show, however, unlike in the book, June accompanies Moira in her attempted escape.[26] The effect is to decentralize Moira. In the book, the white Moira is the protagonist of the escape subplot, but in the show the black Moira is recast as the guide who almost-but-not-quite leads the protagonist June to safety. Instead of Moira being a character with a story of her own, she becomes a character who guides June. The racial resonances here should not be overlooked. The woman of color is sidelined so that her story can be used instead to add dramatic tension and emotional resonance to the white woman's story.

When we next meet Moira, she is in Jezebel's, having been offered the choice between that and the invariably deadly physical labour in "the Colonies." [27] Moira chooses Jezebel's because it is comparatively physically safe; she says there are "a few good years before your pussy wears out," [28] which implies that the Colonies are more physically dangerous and demanding.[29] In Jezebel's, Moira tells June the story of her near-escape, with the help of the "Underground Femaleroad." [30] The Underground Femaleroad is a clear allusion to the historical Underground Railroad that transported black slaves from the Southern United States into the North or further north to Canada. Here what was troubling in the novel is compounded and magnified by the choices of the TV show. Moira, a woman of color, is the character into whose mouth *The Handmaid's Tale* places the narrative of and the phrase "Underground Femaleroad," but neither, she nor any other character, acknowledges the historical precedent.

When Moira does escape from Jezebel's,[31] she does it through her own daring, without the help of the Underground Femaleroad. The likely intention here is well meaning. Moira's escape on her own increases her personal agency, which gives her a more active role in the plot. The symbolic effect, however, is firstly to suggest that it is a lack of courage or of will that keeps slaves enslaved, and secondly to vicariously undermine the importance of the historical Underground Railroad. To the show's credit, though, it does attempt to reassert the importance of the Underground Femaleroad in the finale of season 2, when the Underground Femaleroad orchestrates Emily's escape and June's near-escape.

NOT JUST BLACK AND WHITE

Just as there is a tendency, especially in American conversations about race, to revert to or implicitly endorse myths of white purity, there is also a tendency to think of race in terms of black and white. That is, not only has the dominant discourse historically assumed that race is a binary where a person either belongs to a race or does not, but also the racial discussion in the United States is dominated by black and white thinking, with less critical attention focused on other racial identities. Let's focus for a moment on how nonwhite nonblack race is represented in *The Handmaid's Tale*.

By far the most prominent examples of nonblack people of color in *The Handmaid's Tale* are Rita (Amanda Brugel), the Waterfords' Latina Martha, and the Mexican ambassador, Mrs. Castillo. Rita's presence and experience are notable because of the prevailing filmic stereotype of Latina housekeepers and household staff.[32] Rita's character could lift into a realistic contemporary

drama with almost no changes. This should stand as a caustic indictment of
the depiction of Latinas on film and in American culture generally: a dystopian regime constitutes no measurable change in their lived experience as it
is depicted on screen.[33]

The Mexican ambassador Mrs. Castillo adds another perspective to this
picture. At first, Mexico appears in the series as a possible source of hope
for June and the other Handmaids of Gilead, but when June takes the risk of
telling Ambassador Castillo that she and the other Handmaids are unwilling,
Ambassador Castillo reveals that Mexico is desperate and will trade with
Gilead nevertheless.[34] The question this raises is Why is there a distinction drawn here between Mexico and Canada? Why is Canada independent
and self-reliant, but Mexico is desperate? Why is Canada a safe haven, but
Mexico is susceptible to the lure of Gilead? Later in the series, Commander
Waterford and Serena travel to Canada on a trade delegation of their own,[35]
and the Canadian government rejects Gilead's diplomatic overtures and ex-
pels the Waterfords from the country. Although Canada is (appropriately) not
depicted as uniformly white, the difference between Mexico and Canada and
their respective reactions to Gilead follows tropic stereotypes of Latin America as corrupt. This difference hinges on perceptions of race. Mexico and by
extension Mexicans are depicted as morally compromised and corrupt, and
as less capable of managing their resources than Northern countries are. The
ambassador chooses not to help June, but her assistant Mr. Flores (Christian
Barillas) secretly informs June that her husband is alive and offers to pass a
written message on to him from June. In plot terms this moment is ambiguous—it is not clear if Mr. Flores is acting with or without his employer's
approval. Symbolically, however, we see corruption and powerlessness associated with the darker-skinned woman, Mrs. Castillo, and benevolent action
associated with the lighter-skinned man, Mr. Flores.

The second season of *The Handmaid's Tale* does not constitute a substantial shift in the show's representation of race. Leading into the second season
of the show, Bruce Miller commented on the topic of race in the show: "We
let our characters be the guide. How much does it impact them? And when
it impacts them a lot you want to show those stories and when it doesn't you
also want to show those stories."[36] This might justifiably lead viewers to
expect that season two of *The Handmaid's Tale* would include stories where
race impacts the characters "a lot," but the increased engagement with race
in the second season primarily features the insertion of Luke's first wife Annie (Kelly Jenrette), the insertion of Dr. Hodgson (Karen Glave), the black
neonatologist-turned-Martha who tries to save the life of baby Charlotte/
Angela,[37] and the presence of Omar (Yahya Abdul-Mateen II).[38]

It is hard to see why Annie's presence would be read as an improvement on
the racial politics of the first season, since the show's utopian color blindness
continues with regard to her, and Dr. Hodgson represents another squandered

opportunity to textually address the politics of race in Gilead. The in-world controversy surrounding Dr. Hodgson centers around her status as both a doctor and a woman, and neither she nor any of the characters ever acknowledges her race in any way.

Omar, however, is worth a bit more attention. Although the show never acknowledges Omar's race textually, he typifies the central racial problem with both the show and the book. In his story line he rescues June and hides her (Season 2, Episolde 3) and afterward is presumably caught and executed (Season 2, Episode 4). Omar and his white wife Heather (Joanna Douglas) are implied to be Muslims—while hiding in their apartment, June discovers a prayer mat and Qur'an—but neither Omar's race nor the family's religion is the reason for Omar's eventual arrest and Heather's reassignment as a Handmaid nor for their son's forced adoption to another family. All of this comes as a result of their helping June. Symbolically, Omar's body shields and protects June, the white woman, and the show uses his suffering to protect and motivate its white protagonist.

John Carey's working definition of dystopia and utopia states that "to count as a utopia, an imaginary place must be an expression of desire. To count as dystopia, it must be an expression of fear."[39] In this sense *The Handmaid's Tale* TV series is a feminist dystopia but a racial utopia, predicated on a desire that racial difference and prejudice can simply be erased, that when faced with greater challenges, race can become irrelevant. That desire is laudable in the abstract, but in the context of dystopian fiction it is radically out of place, and when the showrunners suggest that people of color might benefit from the subjugation of white women, they exacerbate an antagonism between white feminism and sexist racial activism, leaving women of color to the side, and they tacitly exclude women of color from feminism in general. None of this, I think, is deliberate, but is the consequence of unexamined attitudes about race that are the special privilege of whiteness; I think that they do not notice when they do. The whiteness of June is invisible to them. But as Sara Ahmed has said, "whiteness is only invisible for those who inhabit it."[40]

NOTES

1. There is a strong aversion in literary theory to hypothesising about the author's intention, both because it is fundamentally unknowable even to the author and also because the intention of the author is ultimately irrelevant since the artifact we react to is the text that exists, not an imaginary text that was intended. But utopias and dystopias are unavoidably didactic genres, and as a result it is, I think, a mistake for critics to twist themselves into rhetorical knots to avoid invoking an authorial intent that is obviously relevant. For the purpose of this chapter let's agree that when I refer to the intentions of any of the creators—of the show or of the novel—I'm referring to my presumptions about intent, while acknowledging the limits of those presumptions.

2. I want to very briefly mention some issues that readers should be aware of but which this chapter does not have time to address. Dorian Cironne wrote compellingly in 2001 about the significance of colonies in feminist dystopian fiction, including in the novel *The Handmaid's Tale.* Cironne's thoughts would certainly be fruitful for further interrogation of race in the TV show as well. Colonizing bodies is a metonymy for colonizing land, and that colonialism is inextricably tied to notions of race and racial superiority, and vice versa, and this merits more engagement than I can give it here. Luke (O-T Fagbenle), Offred's/June's husband in the TV show, the representation of his character, the nuances that arise from him being portrayed by a biracial man, and the significance of his escape to Canada are also rich veins of inquiry I leave untapped. I touch very briefly in this chapter on the treatment and representation of nonblack people of color in the TV series, but this also merits much more attention than I am able to give it in this context. My focus on Moira also largely leaves to the side discussions of stereotypical assumptions of black women as "stronger" (both physically and emotionally) than white women, and therefore able to survive worse treatment—a myth that has historically been used to justify that treatment and that coincides with a myth that black men are stronger and feel less pain than white men, which is a narrative that has been used to justify police violence against black men. I also leave mostly unexplored the idea that black women are unusually sexual or lascivious, which Moira's presence in Jezebel's reinforces. Both the stereotype of black women's strength and of their "excessive" sexuality stem from a fundamental animalizing—racist discourses have historically associated black people with bodily passions and dissociated them from dispassionate rationality. My minimal engagement with these threads does not indicate that I give them little importance, just that it was necessary to make choices in writing this chapter and to leave some important things unsaid for now.

3. The choice of what name to use to refer to the titular Handmaid is obviously loaded. Offred is not her name, but a mark of her dehumanization and subjugation. I think it is one of the show's better choices to insist on referring to the main character as "June" in the credits and promotional materials. The main character of the book, however, is not explicitly named "June," we can only infer that that is likely her name. Atwood leaves the main character unnamed. I have therefore decided to refer to the book character by the only name we definitely have for her, "Offred," and to refer to her screen counterpart as June.

4. Margaret Atwood, *The Handmaid's Tale* (Toronto: Emblem, 2015), 94.

5. Stephen R. Haynes, "Race, National Destiny, and the Sons of Noah in the Thought of Benjamin M. Palmer," *The Journal of Presbyterian History (1997–)* 78, no. 2 (2000): 127, accessed October 30, 2018, http://www.jstor.org/stable/23335423.

6. Atwood, *The Handmaid's Tale*, 349.

7. Atwood, *The Handmaid's Tale*, 349.

8. White genocide is a conspiracy theory with too many popular and historical incarnations to cite fully. Sociologist Andrew Wilson wrote in 2018 about the use of the hashtag #whitegenocide on twitter, for example ("#whitegenocide, the Alt-right and Conspiracy Theory: How Secrecy and Suspicion Contributed to the Mainstreaming of Hate," *Secrecy and Society* 1, no. 2 [2018], accessed November 7, 2018, http://hdl.handle.net/10545/622321).

9. Atwood, *The Handmaid's Tale*, 350–51.

10. In interviews Atwood has pointed to other historical precedents for the reproduction programs in Gilead, including Napoleon, who banned abortions because "he wanted offspring—for cannon fodder," and Hitler, who "stole his children, blond ones, hoping that he could turn them into blond Germans." See Margaret Atwood, interview by Jennifer Vineyard, *New York Times*, June 14, 2017, https://www.ny times.com/2017/06/14/watching/the-handmaids-tale-tv-finale-margaret-atwood.html for the comment about Napoleon, and Margaret Atwood, interview by Patt Morrison, *Los Angeles Times*, April 19, 2017, http://www.latimes.com/opinion/op-ed/la-ol -patt-morrison-margaret-atwood-hulu-handmaiden-20170419-htmlstory.html for the comment about Hitler.

11. Atwood, *The Handmaid's Tale*, 351.

12. The idea of race as culturally constructed rather than biological is commonplace and accepted by most theorists of race. Further suggested readings on the topic include Franz Fanon, *Black Skin, White Masks* (New York: Grove Weidenfeld, 1982); Geraldine Heng, *The Invention of Race in the European Middle Ages* (Cambridge: Cambridge University Press, 2018); Carlos A. Hoyt Jr., *The ARC of a Bad Idea: Understanding and Transcending Race* (New York: Oxford University Press, 2016).

13. Bruce Miller, interview by Eliana Dockterman, *Time*, April 25, 2017.

14. There is a very fruitful line in inquiry here that I have left mostly unexplored because of limitations of the scope of this chapter.

15. "Deported Parents May Lose Kids to Adoption, Investigation Finds," NBC News online, last modified October 8, 2018, https://www.nbcnews.com/news/latino /deported-parents-may-lose-kids-adoption-investigation-finds-n918261.

16. Barbara Perry, "'White Genocide': White Supremacists and the Politics of Reproduction," in *Home-Grown Hate: Gender and Organized Racism*, ed. Abby Ferber, (New York: Routledge, 2004), 72.

17. Carlos A. Hoyt Jr., *The ARC of a Bad Idea: Understanding and Transcending Race.* (New York: Oxford University Press, 2016), 39 (emphasis in original).

18. Floyd James Davis, *Who Is Black? One Nation's Definition* (University Park: Pennsylvania State University Press, 2001), 5.

19. The one drop rule is a rule of social convention that has had various manifestations in law, but as historian Winthrop D. Jordan explains, "expressions in formal law appear later than evidence of perceptions and practices that were customary long before they were written down." The earliest expression of the rule, according to Jordan, is in 1790, and it has always been "particularly American" ("Historical Origins of the One-Drop Racial Rule in the United States," *The Journal of Critical Mixed Race Studies* 1, no. 1 [2014]: 103).

20. Davis, *Who Is Black? One Nation's Definition*, 5.

21. Davis, *Who Is Black? One Nation's Definition*, 68.

22. Noah Berlatsky, "Both Versions of The Handmaid's Tale Have a Problem with Racial Erasure," *The Verge,* June 15, 2017, https://www.theverge .com/2017/6/15/15808530/handmaids-tale-hulu-margaret-atwood-black-history -racial-erasure.

23. Margaret Atwood, "Margaret Atwood on How She Came to Write The Handmaid's Tale," *Literary Hub*, accessed November 1, 2018, https://lithub.com /margaret-atwood-on-how-she-came-to-write-the-handmaids-tale.

24. Charles A. Gallagher, "Color-blind Egalitarianism as the New Racial Norm," in *Theories of Race and Ethnicity: Contemporary Debates and Perspectives*, ed. Karim Murji and John Solomos (Cambridge: Cambridge University Press, 2015), 45.

25. According to a report by UCLA and put out in 2017, in the 2015–2016 season whites made up 66 percent of all roles in broadcast scripted shows, compared to 17 percent for blacks, and 17 percent for all other minority groups combined. Cable scripted shows in the same time period had a greater proportion of white cast members, with 74.6 percent of those casts being white, compared to 13.3 percent black and 12.1 percent for all other minority groups combined. Whites make up 61.3 percent of the actual population and are therefore overrepresented, even if we naively discount historical realities and consider the present as a blank slate (UCLA College, "Hollywood Diversity Report 2018," accessed November 20, 2018, https://socialsciences .ucla.edu/hollywood-diversity-report-2018/).

26. *The Handmaid's Tale,* "Nolite Te Bastardes Carborundorum," Season 1, Episode 4, directed by Mike Barker, written by Leila Gerstein, Hulu, May 3, 2017.

27. *The Handmaid's Tale,* "Jezebel's," Season 1, Episode 8, directed by Kate Dennis, written by Kira Snyder, Hulu, May 31, 2017.

28. *The Handmaid's Tale,* "Jezebel's," Season 1, Episode 8.

29. We see the Colonies directly when Emily is sent there, and the physical danger and hardship of it do seem to live up to Moira's expectations. *The Handmaid's Tale,* "Unwomen," Season 2, Episode 2, directed by Mike Barker, written by Bruce Miller, Hulu, April 25, 2018.

30. *The Handmaid's Tale,* "Jezebel's," directed by Kate Dennis; Also Atwood, *The Handmaid's Tale*, 285.

31. *The Handmaid's Tale,* "The Bridge," Season 1, Episode 9, directed by Kate Dennis, written by Eric Tuchman, Hulu, June 7, 2017.

32. Yajaira M. Padilla, "Domesticating Rosario: Conflicting Representations of the Latina Maid in U.S. Media," *Arizona Journal of Hispanic Cultural Studies* 13 (2009): 42, accessed October 31, 2018, http://www.jstor.org/stable/20641946.

33. See, for example, *Dharma and Greg* (1997–2002), *My Name Is Earl* (2005), *Will and Grace* (1998–2007), and *Arrested Development* (2003–2006; 2013–2018), all of which feature Latina housekeepers or domestic help. These are only a handful of arbitrary examples—Padilla cites "Chicana actress Lupe Ontiveros [who] estimated having played the role of a maid in both theatre and film some 300 times" "Domesticating Rosario," 54, accessed November 20, 2018, http://www.jstor.org/ stable/20641946).

34. *The Handmaid's Tale,* "A Woman's Place," Season 1, Episode 6, directed by Floria Sigismondi, written by Wendy Straker Hauser, Hulu, May 17, 2017.

35. *The Handmaid's Tale,* "Smart Power," Season 2, Episode 9, directed by Jeremy Podeswa, written by Dorothy Fortenberry, Hulu, June 13, 2018.

36. Bruce Miller, interview by Baraka Kaseko and Marah Eakin, AV/TV Club, April 25, 2018, https://tv.avclub.com/the-handmaid-s-tale-showrunner-bruce-miller -says-theyre-1825535699.

37. *The Handmaid's Tale,* "Women's Work," Season 2, Episode 8, directed by Kari Skogland, written by Nina Fiore and John Herrera, Hulu, June 2, 2018.

38. *The Handmaid's Tale,* "Baggage," Season 2, Episode 3, directed by Kari Sk-ogland, written by Dorothy Fortenberry, Hulu, May 2, 2018.

39. John Carey. *The Faber Book of Utopias* (London: Faber, 1999), xiii.

40. Sarah Ahmed, "A Phenomenology of Whiteness," *Feminist Theory* 8, no. 2 (2007); 157, accessed November 1, 2018, doi: 10.1177/1464700107078139.

WORKS CITED

Ahmed, Sarah. "A Phenomenology of Whiteness." *Feminist Theory* 8, no. 2 (2007): 149–68. Accessed November 1, 2018. doi: 10.1177/1464700107078139.

Atwood, Margaret. "Margaret Atwood on How She Came to Write The Handmaid's Tale." *Literary Hub*, 2012. Accessed November 1, 2018. https://lithub.com/margaret-atwood-on-how-she-came-to-write-the-handmaids-tale/.

———. *The Handmaid's Tale*. Toronto: Emblem, 2014.

———. Margaret Atwood Annotates Season 1 of 'The Handmaid's Tale.'" Interview with Jennifer Vineyard. *New York Times*. June 14, 2017. https://www.nytimes.com/2017/06/14/watching-the-handmaids-tale-tv-finale-maraget-atwood.html.

———. "Margaret Atwood on why 'The Handmaid's Tale' is More Relevant Now Than Ever." Interview with Patt Morrison. *Los Angeles Times*. April 19, 2017. http://www.latimes.com/opinion/op-ed/la-ol-patt-morrison-maragaret-atwood-hulu-handmaiden-201707119.htmlstory.html.

Berlatsky, Noah. "Both Versions of The Handmaid's Tale Have a Problem with Racial Erasure." *The Verge,* June 15, 2017. https://www.theverge.com/2017/6/15/15808530/handmaids-tale-hulu-margaret-atwood-black-history-racial-erasure.

Carey, John. *The Faber Book of Utopias*. London: Faber, 1999.

Cirrone, Dorian. "Millennial Mothers: Reproduction, Race, and Ethnicity in Feminist Dystopian Fiction." *Femspec* 3, no. 1 (2001): 4–11.

Davis, F. James. *Who Is Black? One Nation's Definition*. University Park: Pennsylvania State University Press, 2001.

"Deported Parents May Lose Kids to Adoption, Investigation Finds." NBC News online, October 8, 2018. https://www.nbcnews.com/news/latino/deported-parents-may-lose-kids-adoption-investigation-finds-n918261.

Dockterman, Eliana. "'The Handmaid's Tale' Showrunner on Why He Made Some Major Changes from the Book." *Time*, April 25, 2017. http://time.com/4754200/the-handmaids-tale-showrunner-changes-from-book/.

Ferber, Abby L. *White Man Falling: Race, Gender, and White Supremacy*. Lanham, MD: Rowman & Littlefield, 1998.

Gallagher, Charles A. "Color-blind Egalitarianism as the New Racial Norm." In *Theories of Race and Ethnicity: Contemporary Debates and Perspectives,* edited by Karim Murji and John Solomos, 40–56. Cambridge: Cambridge University Press, 2015.

Haynes, Stephen R. "Race, National Destiny, and the Sons of Noah in the Thought of Benjamin M. Palmer." *The Journal of Presbyterian History (1997–)* 78, no. 2 (2000): 125–43. http://www.jstor.org/stable/23335423.

"Hollywood Diversity Report 2018." UCLA College, February 2, 2018. Accessed November 20, 2018. https://socialsciences.ucla.edu/hollywood-diversity-report-2018/.

Hoyt, Carlos A. Jr. *The ARC of a Bad Idea: Understanding and Transcending Race.* New York: Oxford University Press, 2016.

Jordan, Winthrop D. "Historical Origins of the One-Drop Racial Rule in the United States." *The Journal of Critical Mixed Race Studies* 1, no. 1 (2014): 98–132.

Kaseko, Baraka, and Marah Eakin. "'The Handmaid's Tale' showrunner Bruce Miller says they're aware of the show's mishandling of race." AV/TV Club, April 25, 2018. https://tv.avclub.com/the-handmaid-s-tale-showrunner-bruce-miller-says -theyre-1825535699.

Morrison, Patt. "Margaret Atwood on Why 'The Handmaid's Tale' Is More Relevant Now Than Ever.'" *Los Angeles Times,* April 19, 2017. http://www.latimes.com/opin ion/op-ed/la-ol-patt-morrison-margaret-atwood-hulu-handmaiden-20170419-html story.html.

Padilla, Yajaira M. "Domesticating Rosario: Conflicting Representations of the Latina Maid in U.S. Media." *Arizona Journal of Hispanic Cultural Studies* 13 (2009): 41–59. http://www.jstor.org/stable/20641946.

Perry, Barbara. "'White Genocide': White Supremacists and the Politics of Reproduction." In *Home-Grown Hate: Gender and Organized Racism*, edited by Abby Ferber, 71–91. New York: Routledge, 2004.

Vineyard, Jennifer. "Margaret Atwood Annotates Season 1 of 'The Handmaid's Tale.'" *New York Times*, June 14, 2017. https://www.nytimes.com/2017/06/14 /watching/the-handmaids-tale-tv-finale-margaret-atwood.html.

Wilson, Andrew F. "#whitegenocide, the Alt-right and Conspiracy Theory: How Secrecy and Suspicion Contributed to the Mainstreaming of Hate." *Secrecy and Society* 1, no. 2 (2018). http://hdl.handle.net/10545/622321.

FILM AND TELEVISION

The Handmaid's Tale. "A Woman's Place." Season 1, Episode 6. Directed by Floria Sigismondi. Written by Wendy Straker Hauser. Hulu, May 17, 2017.

The Handmaid's Tale. "Baggage." Season 2, Episode 3. Directed by Kari Skogland. Written by Dorothy Fortenberry. Hulu, May 2, 2018.

The Handmaid's Tale. "Jezebels," Season 1, Episode 8, directed by Kate Dennis, written by Kira Snyder, Hulu, May 31, 2017.

The Handmaid's Tale. "Nolite Te Bastardes Carborundorum," Season 1, Episode 4, directed by Mike Barker, written by Leila Gerstein, Hulu, May 3, 2017.

The Handmaid's Tale. "Smart Power." Season 2, Episode 9. Directed by Jeremy Podeswa. Written by Dorothy Fortenberry. Hulu, June 13, 2018.

The Handmaid's Tale. "The Bridge." Season 1, Episode 9. Directed by Kate Dennis. Written by Eric Tuchman. Hulu, June 7, 2017.

The Handmaid's Tale. "Unwomen," Season 2, Episode 2, directed by Mike Barker, written by Bruce Miller, Hulu, April 25, 2018.

The Handmaid's Tale. "Women's Work." Season 2, Episode 8. Directed by Kari Skogland. Written by Nina Fiore and John Herrera. Hulu, June 2, 2018.

Chapter Fourteen

Women, Complicity, and
The Handmaid's Tale

Jessica Greenebaum and Beth Merenstein

The intent of this chapter is to use a sociological and feminist analysis to highlight the similar religious, political, and cultural ideologies and laws that permit forced motherhood, rape culture, and compulsory heterosexuality in both our current society and in *The Handmaid's Tale* television series adaptation on Hulu. Patriarchal power is often misinterpreted as the power of individual men rather than a set of ideologies that values men, masculinity, and the degradation of women and femininity.[1] In this chapter, we will emphasize how patriarchal power relies on the complicit actions of women in their quest for either power or survival in the patriarchal environment.

Using the two Hulu television series from 2017 and 2018 as a text, we juxtapose forms of gendered social control under Gilead to the current sociopolitical climate in the United States. Although *The Handmaid's Tale* represents a dystopian future, we warn the reader from viewing the series as total fantasy. In fact, so does Margaret Atwood, who wrote *The Handmaid's Tale* in the 1980s after the election of Ronald Regan. The book was written in reaction to the Christian evangelical movement's promotion of "family values" on the backs of women, particularly poor women of color and members of the LGBTQ community. According to a synopsis of Atwood in the New Yorker, "In writing *The Handmaid's Tale*, Atwood was scrupulous about including nothing that did not have a historical antecedent or a modern point of comparison."[2]

REPRODUCTIVE RIGHTS UNDER ATTACK
IN THE UNITED STATES

Although the television series was under production before Trump won the Electoral College in 2016, viewing the series under the Trump/Pence administration makes this allegory even more chilling.[3] How easy could it be to freeze women's bank accounts, fire them from their jobs, gun them down at protests, and strip them of their reproductive and human rights, as seen in series one, episode three?[4] While many people may scoff at the idea that women would be raped by the state and face a forced pregnancy, many women currently lack control over their reproduction. For example, Republican legislators on a state level are decimating reproductive rights protected under Roe v. Wade (1973). States have mandated transvaginal and/or transabdominal ultrasounds, instituted biased counseling and waiting periods, and targeted restrictions on abortion providers not required for other medical procedures.[5] None of these recent laws are based on medical evidence or practice nor on provider-patient decisions. Many states have attempted to pass personhood status bills that give rights to fertilized eggs, embryos, and fetuses in order to outlaw abortion, although it is against the recommendation of the American Congress of Obstetricians and Gynecologists since 50 percent of pregnancies result in a spontaneous abortion or miscarriage.[6] On May 4, 2018, Iowa governor Kim Reynold signed into the law the "heartbeat bill,"[7] which bans abortion after six weeks when the fetus has a detectable heartbeat but before most women know they are even pregnant.[8] The Ohio House of Representatives has proposed a "personhood bill" that, if passed, will criminalize abortion and potentially punish both women who have abortions as well as the doctors who perform the surgery with the death penalty.[9]

Reproductive health is also under attack as Trump passed a gag order to restrict Title X funding to programs, such as Planned Parenthood, that provide abortions or any organizations that refer patients to abortion providers.[10] On June 26, 2018, the Supreme Court upheld a ruling, based on free speech, to allow Crisis Pregnancy Centers to refuse informing women, who are seeking their care, about their birth control and abortion options provided by the state of California. In addition, although Crisis Pregnancy Centers often deceptively pose as medical centers, they do not need to disclose the lack of licensed medical providers on site.[11] The 2017 documentary, *Birthright; A War Story,* explores how the religious right is not just weakening abortion access and rights, but is also controlling the birth process of poor, vulnerable women. Catholic hospitals dominate across the country and women are denied life-saving medical care, such as Dilation & Curettage (D&C), even when women miscarry or experience nonviable pregnancies.[12]

The increased visibility of women in the conservative right party has coincided with the increased visibility of women in the pro-life movement; both of which have become more prominent in the last decade. Most recently, it was notable when Tomi Lahren, a prominent far-right conservative spokesperson in the United States, came out arguing against overturning Roe v. Wade. She was immediately lambasted from her party, her followers, and other prominent women in the movement.[13] Many of these women are introduced to the movement from their religious communities and follow the belief that women are victims of the sexual revolution and their own selfishness due to a disconnect with God. "Pro-woman" organizations, such as Feminists for Life (FFF) and Democrats for Life of America (DLA) take a nonreligious stance in their opposition to abortion. It is debatable whether one can be pro-life and a feminist, but it would require a commitment to support efforts that would reduce the need for abortion, such as affordable and accessible contraception and comprehensive sex education; ending sexual, emotional, and physical violence against women; as well as social, sexual, and economic equality.[14] Although FFF claims that "abortion is a reflection that we have not met the needs of women" and blames the feminization of poverty, they claim "preconception" issues are beyond their mission.[15] Thus, organizations such as FFF and DLA use their power and positionality to uphold misogynistic and patriarchal ideologies that deny women control over their reproductive, professional, and sexual lives.

While it is likely that Roe v. Wade will be overturned now that Brett Kavanaugh[16] is sitting on the Supreme Court, the plot of *The Handmaid's Tale* seems implausible to most people living in the contemporary United States. The dystopia genre can be easily dismissed as fantasy or women's hysteria, but for many women reading the book today the premise feels too real. All women living under a patriarchal political climate are valued by their ability to service and serve men in the public and private sphere. However, the primary value of women is their ability to reproduce and mother. Under a patriarchy, motherhood becomes the source of women's power and the reason for their oppression.[17]

The premise behind the revolution that takes place to create Gilead is the idea that reproduction has been threatened by climate change and by the "sins" of women. In this context, and under this premise, the male (predominantly white, middle-aged) leaders in Gilead feel justified in taking over full control of women's reproductive rights. All women in Gilead lose the ability of choice—whether to be a mother to their own child, whom to fall in love with, or to control their own bodies in any way. In Gilead, this complete control over women's lives and bodies happens relatively quickly and easily. In one scene, we see that June (Elisabeth Moss) must get her husband Luke's

(O-T Fagbenle) signature to refill her birth control prescription.[18] It's a small, quick, scene but it gives us a glimpse to how easy and subtle this control over women's lives would be. While both June and her husband comment on the idea that she needs his "permission" to take birth control, we see how they have also resigned themselves to this state control.

Why are we controlling women's reproduction today in the United States and in *The Handmaid's Tale's* Gilead? Because it is the ultimate form of control over women in a patriarchal society. In order to keep women dependent on men, and to maintain their place in society, women cannot be allowed to control the reproduction that maintains this society. They cannot be allowed to freely express their sexuality, have total control over their bodies, or be allowed to make decisions about when, or if, to reproduce at all. It is in this way that women learn their place, as subjugated controlled beings, in a patriarchal Western society. In order for a patriarchal society to successfully control women and their sexuality, women need to accept this—to accept this subjugated position and contribute to maintaining the patriarchal system.

BARGAINING WITH PATRIARCHY IN THE UNITED STATES

For any power structure to succeed, women need to be complicit to its ideology. Patriarchy is understood as the rule of father or rule of men as exemplified in Gilead. Currently, we live in a modified patriarchy in the United States that simultaneously promotes an ideology of gender equality while reinforcing a culture that values traits, behaviors, and activities associated with men and masculinity. In a modified patriarchy, women have to navigate being a woman in a man's world. They need to navigate both hostile sexism, which is overt in its misogyny, and benevolent sexism, which values feminine attributes associated with passivity and nurturance, as well as sexual appeal and beauty. In a modified patriarchy, women face a "double bind," having to highlight their femininity and distinguish themselves from men, while also being forced to work under the standards set by and for men.[19] This is amply signified in the role of the Commander's wife Serena Joy Waterford (Yvonne Strahovski) who is depicted as a former right-wing activist who helped write the script for Gilead and promote her ideologies on public campus talks. When she suggests to her husband and his tribunal of like-minded leaders in season 2 that their (adopted) daughter be allowed to read, her husband Fred Waterford (Joseph Fiennes) has Serena captured by the paramilitary forces and her finger cut off as punishment for her transgression.[20]

Serena is a picture book example of women in a modified patriarchy, who secure power and control over themselves and others, but are not liberated. To gain power, women engage in a patriarchal bargain, "a decision to accept gender rules that disadvantage women in exchange for whatever power one can wrest from the system. It is an individual strategy designed to manipulate the system to one's best advantage, but one that leaves the system itself intact."[21]

Women learn their subjugated role in both contemporary society and Gilead through socialization and "education" in so-called "Red Centers" where "Aunts" teach them the rules of submission, including the ritual of sanctified monthly sexual assault by the Commanders. Socialization is the process by which individuals learn the ways of a given society or social group so that they may function within it. A critical element of socialization in a patriarchal society is learning the power of men, the value in masculinity, and learning your "place" as a woman.[22] The internalization of this culture and this ideology is part of a process of hegemony, whereby all parts of society work to maintain this dominance. Any unequal system requires all levels of the hierarchy to support the system in order to maintain it.

In both our current environment, as well as in *The Handmaid's Tale*, men succeed at this dominance by controlling the social, cultural, ideological, and economic spheres. But for this dominance to be truly effective, women must accept and internalize it. In Gilead, men use military and violent sanctions, as well as the dominant ideology, to control women. In this way, most women go along with the extreme patriarchy out of fear, but many, like Aunt Lydia (Ann Dowd) who trains the Handmaids in the Red Center and also watches over executions, go along with it because they truly believe in it. In the United States, we see the ideology as a stronger force, but fear—of losing more rights, of less control over our bodies, of repercussions in our jobs or our homes, of violence from men—also serves to maintain our patriarchy.

BARGAINING WITH PATRIARCHY IN GILEAD

In the current economic sphere, for example, we witness the control women have over other women on the hierarchy of class. Educated, upper-class women, while still subjugated by men in all areas of their lives, use their economic power to further dominate over other women. They use their economic privilege to hire other women to be nannies for their children, to clean their homes, to work as their assistants, all while maintaining their own class privilege. Furthermore, this class privilege means some women will be protected from the challenges to our reproductive rights. For example, some states, such as South Dakota, have one abortion provider serving the entire state. For poor women, this essentially means they have no access to abortions. For wealthy women, they still have some—albeit smaller—choice. With men largely absent in these power relationships, women in economic power are further cementing the dominance of men in the larger political and economic worlds, while continuing to place all women in a submissive position.

Similar in many ways to our current patriarchal society, women are doing a majority of the work necessary to make society function. Women continue to do the nurturing, and therefore, devalued work in both societies. We can only understand how this can occur if we understand the ways in which women must be complicit in patriarchy for it to succeed. Women care for the children; they are predominant in the health field, working as nurses, health care aides, nursing home attendants; they are the majority of elementary school teachers; they clean the homes, wash the clothes, and make the meals.[23]

Upper-class women hold similar limited powers in Gilead. Although these class issues are largely absent in *The Handmaid's Tale*, we still see glimpses of it in the roles of the Marthas and the Econowives. In this way, the upper-class women, such as Serena Joy, maintain power over other women, yet hold no true power in a patriarchal society.

In Gilead, men hold most positions of power and authority, but women run the patriarchy. This is an important reminder that a patriarchal society does not rely on the actions of individual men or a collection of men, and it does not require people to have "oppressive personalities." But the patriarchy "is a society organized around certain kinds of social relationships and ideas."[24] Thus, women are not just passive victims within the system. As one author notes,

> It's easy to rest the blame of the horrors of Gilead solely at the feet of men like Commander Fred Waterford. But no system this deeply entrenched and high functioning could survive without help. Fred and other Commanders need women to internalize their doctrine so they police themselves. The very people suffering from oppressive systems become the most valuable tools of enforcement by those in power. *The Handmaid's Tale* is at its most potent when it interrogates the ways women participate in systems that exploit them, holding onto power that is ultimately transitory.[25]

Serena Joy, the wife of Commander Fred Waterford, helped plan the terrorist attack against the government and helped create Gilead. According to the backstory, she promoted a fundamentalist religious theocracy and wrote a book called "A Woman's Place," which contained the line, "Do not mistake a woman's meekness for weakness."[26] On a book tour to a college campus, she encountered hostile protestors and was shot in the abdomen and lost her ability to reproduce. Once the revolution took place, her political aspirations were thwarted and she was pushed aside from the power elite. Consistent with a true patriarchal society, Serena Joy needed to remember that she could never hold any real power in a world dominated by men. In this new regime, Serena is expected to remember what she wrote, that a woman's place is in the home, which is emphasized in the scene when her book is thrown in the trash.[27] What happens when you overstep your boundaries as you bargain with the patriarchy? Your husband beats you with a belt in front of your Handmaid.[28] In her new role as the Wife of the Commander, Serena Joy's only power is to delegate chores to the (female) servants in her household and wait for her Handmaid, Offred (Moss), to give birth to a child she cannot conceive. She uses violence to cope with her resentment of Offred's ability to reproduce and having to share Offred with her husband during the ritual rape.

Aunt Lydia is the most powerful woman in the series, who uses violence and coercion to indoctrinate the Handmaids in their new role by any means necessary. She pits Handmaids against each other. She forces the girls to blame Janine (Madeline Brewer) for her rape, expects her peers later to stone Janine to death and help hang a fellow Handmaid for her indiscretion (sleeping with her Ob-Gyn who suggested to Offred before that he could "help" her get pregnant which she refuses), and punishes the Handmaids for not complying by threating mass execution by hanging.[29] She uses various forms of torture to punish Handmaids, including, but not limited to: shocking the girls with cattle prods, removing Ofwarren's/Janine's eye for yelling profanities,[30] and delegating orders for Ofglen/Emily (Alexis Bledel) to undergo genital mutilation for being a "gender traitor" by having an affair with another woman.[31] As of this writing, we lack a backstory of Aunt Lydia but in season 2, episode 1, we see her weeping in the bell tower as she rings the bell announcing a Handmaid's pregnancy, hinting at her status as a true believer in the goals and promise of Gilead.[32]

CONCLUSION

In watching *The Handmaid's Tale*, it would be relatively easy to allow ourselves the luxury of believing this dystopian world is far away from our own. We would be wrong. In our view, the first way to achieve this extreme form of patriarchal control is by controlling women's reproductive rights. In the past decade or so, the men in the increasingly conservative Republican party have realized that in order to achieve this, they need the support and help of women in their party. Putting conservative women in the forefront—as news anchors on Fox News, political nominees, and as the spokespersons predominantly—serves to reassure all women that the conservatives have our interests in mind. Getting more women to buy into the ideology of male control, allows for the next steps in the extreme patriarchal system. Once a new Supreme Court takes over, it is likely Roe v. Wade will be overturned or weakened, and reproductive rights will become a state-by-state issue. Just like in Gilead, where you are born will dictate the level of control, or lack thereof, you have over your own body. This tale is not just a story any longer—it is quickly becoming our new reality.

NOTES

1. Allan G. Johnson, *The Gender Knot: Unraveling Our Patriarchal Legacy* (Philadelphia University Press, 2005), 78.

2. Rebecca Mead, "Margaret Atwood, The Prophet of Dystopia," *New Yorker*, April 17, 2017. https://www.newyorker.com/magazine/2017/04/17/margaret-atwood-the-prophet-of-dystopia.

3. Twenty-two women have accused the president of the United States of sexual misconduct. Furthermore, in his campaign for the presidency, Donald Trump exclaimed in an interview that "there has to be some form of punishment for women who choose abortion." To get the Evangelical Christian vote, he chose Mike Pence, an anti-abortion advocate who has passed anti-choice legislation as the governor of Indiana to be vice president. For more information, see Eliza Relman, "The 22 Women Who Have Accused Trump of Sexual Misconduct," *Business Insider*, September 26, 2018, https://www.businessinsider.com/women-accused-trump-sexual-misconduct-list-2017-12; Matt Flegenheimer and Maggie Haberman, "Donald Trump, Abortion Foe, Eyes 'Punishment' for Women, Then Recants," *The New York Times*, March 30, 2018, https://www.nytimes.com/2016/03/31/us/politics/donald-trump-abortion.html; Miriam Berg, "8 Outrageous Facts about Mike Pence's Record on Reproductive Rights," *Planned Parenthood*, July 20, 2016, https://www.plannedparenthoodaction.org/blog/8-outrageous-facts-about-mike-pencerecord-reproductive-rights.

4. *The Handmaid's Tale*, "Late," Season 1, Episode 3, directed by Reed Morano, written by Bruce Miller, Hulu, April 26, 2017.

5. For more information on state legislation see: https://www.prochoiceamerica.org/laws-policy/state-government.

6. ACOG Practice Bulletin, "Early Pregnancy Loss," May 2015, https://www.acog.org/Clinical-Guidance-and-Publications/Practice-Bulletins/Committee-on-Practice-Bulletins-Gynecology/Early-Pregnancy-Loss?IsMobileSet=false.

7. Rewire, "Personhood," November 7, 2017, https://rewire.news/legislative-tracker/law-topic/personhood.

8. Sasha Inger, "Iowa Bans Most Abortions As Governor Signs 'Heartbeat' Bill," NPR, May 5, 2018, https://www.npr.org/sections/thetwo-way/2018/05/05/608738116/iowa-bans-most-abortions-as-governor-signs-heartbeat-bill.

9. AJ Willingham, "A Proposed Ohio Law Would Redefine a Person to Include 'Unborn Humans' and Could Treat Abortion like Murder," CNN, November 21, 2018, https://www.cnn.com/2018/11/21/us/ohio-abortion-ban-bill-criminal-law-trnd/index.html.

10. Julie Hirschfeld Davis and Maggie Haberman, "Trump Administration to Tie Health Facilities' Funding to Abortion Restrictions," *New York Times*, May 17, 2018, https://www.nytimes.com/2018/05/17/us/politics/trump-funding-abortion -restrictions.html?hp&action=click&pgtype=Homepage&clickSource=story-head ding&module=first-column-region&region=top-news&WT.nav=top-news.

11. Mark Sherman and Jessica Gresko, "Supreme Court Says Crisis Pregnancy Centers Do Not Have to Provide Women Abortion Information," *Chicago Tribune*, June 26, 2018, http://www.chicagotribune.com/news/nationworld/ct-supreme-court -pregnancy-center-abortion-ruling-20180626-story.html.

12. *Birthright: A War Story*, DVD, directed by Civia Tamarkin (New York: Women, Make Movies, 2017).

13. Jenny Kutner, "Tomi Lahren Champions Choice, Much to Conservative Chagrin," *Vogue*, March 21, 2017, https://www.vogue.com/article/tomi-lahren-pro -choice-suspended-conservative-backlash.

14. Jennifer Baumgardner, *Abortion and Life* (New York: Akashic Books, 2008), 64–65.

15. "Frequently Asked Questions," Feminists for Life, accessed July 2, 2018, http://www.feministsforlife.org/faq/#abstinence.

16. Kavanaugh's appointment to the Supreme Court was controversial because he was accused of sexual misconduct. Kavanaugh, and his accuser, Dr. Christine Blasey Ford, both gave testimony (Sheryl Gay Stolberg and Nicholas Fandos. "Kavanaugh and Christine Blasey Ford Duel with Tears and Fury," *New York Times*, September 27, 2018, https://www.nytimes.com/2018/09/27/us/politics/brett-kavanaugh-confir mation-hearings.html). He was confirmed after the Senate hearing. American women were outraged, and as a result, approximately one hundred women, many of whom are racial and religious minorities, ran and won congressional seats during the 2018 midterm elections (Mary Jordan, "Record Number of Women Heading to Congress," *The Washington Post*, November 8, 2018, https://www.washingtonpost.com/poli tics/record-number-of-women-appear-headed-for-congress/2018/11/06/76a9e60a -e1eb-11e8-8f5f-a55347f48762_story.html?utm_term=.90389318d792).

17. Adrienne Rich, *Of Women Born: Motherhood as Experience and Institution* (New York: W.W. Norton & Company, Inc., 1995).

18. *The Handmaid's Tale*, "June," Season 1, Episode 1, directed by Mike Barker, written by Bruce Miller, Hulu, April 25, 2018.

19. Lisa Wade and Myra Marx Feree, *Gender: Ideas, Interactions, Institutions* (New York: W.W. Norton & Company, Inc., 2015), 305–6.

20. *The Handmaid's Tale*, "The Word," Season 2, Episode 13, directed by Mike Barker, written by Bruce Miller, Hulu, July 11, 2018.

21. Deniz Kandiyoti, "Bargaining with Patriarchy," *Gender and Society* 2 (1988), 274–90; Lisa Wade, "Serena Williams's Patriarchal Bargain," *Sociological Images*, May 22, 2011, https://thesocietypages.org/socimages/2011/05/22/women-damned-if -you-do-damned-if-you-dont.

22. Candace West and Don H. Zimmerman, "Doing Gender," *Gender and Society* 1 (1987): 125–51; Judith Lorber, *Paradoxes of Gender* (New Haven: Yale University Press, 1994).

23. Louise Howe, *Pink Collar Workers: Inside the World of Women's Work* (New York: Putnam 1977); Barbara Reskin and Patricia Roos, *Job Queues, Gender Queues* (Philadelphia: Temple University Press, 1990).

24. Johnson, *The Gender Knot*, 78.

25. Anjelica Jade Bastien, "Why the Female Villains on *The Handmaid's Tale* Are So Terrifying," *Vulture,* May 17, 2017, http://www.vulture.com/2017/05/the -handmaids-tale-aunt-lydia-serena-joy-female-villains.html.

26. *The Handmaid's Tale*, "A Woman's Place," Season 1, Episode 6, directed by Floria Sigismondi, written by Wendy Straker Hauser, Hulu, May 17, 2017.

27. *The Handmaid's Tale*, "A Woman's Place," Season 1, Episode 6.

28. *The Handmaid's Tale*, "Women's Work," Season 2, Episode 8, directed by Kari Skogland, written by Nina Fiore and John Herrera, Hulu, June 2, 2018.

29. *The Handmaid's Tale*, "June," directed by Mike Barker.

30. *The Handmaid's Tale*, "Offred," Season 1, Episode 1, directed by Reed Morano, written by Bruce Miller, Hulu, April 26, 2017.

31. *The Handmaid's Tale*, "Late," directed by Reed Morano.

32. *The Handmaid's Tale*, "June," directed by Mike Barker.

WORKS CITED

ACOG Practice Bulletin. "Early Pregnancy Loss," May, 2015. https://www.acog.org /Clinical-Guidance-and-Publications/Practice-Bulletins/Committee-on-Practice -Bulletins-Gynecology/Early-Pregnancy-Loss? IsMobileSet=false.

Bastien, Anjelica Jade. "Why the Female Villains on *The Handmaid's Tale* Are So Terrifying." *Vulture*, May 17, 2017. http://www.vulture.com/2017/05/the-hand maids-tale-aunt-lydia-serena-joy-female-villains.html.

Baumgardner, Jennifer. *Abortion and Life*. New York: Akashic Books, 2008.

Berg, Miriam. "8 Outrageous Facts about Mike Pence's Record on Reproductive Rights." *Planned Parenthood*, July 20, 2016. https://www.plannedparenthood action.org/blog/8-outrageous-facts-about-mike-pencerecord-reproductive-rights.

Davis, Julie Hirschfeld, and Maggie Haberman, "Trump Administration to Tie Health Facilities' Funding to Abortion Restrictions." *The New York Times,* May 17, 2018. https://www.nytimes.com/2018/05/17/us/politics/trump-funding-abortion -restrictions.html?hp&action=click&pgtype=Homepage&clickSource=story-head ing&module=first-column-region&region=top-news&WT.nav=top-news.

Feminists for Life. "Frequently Asked Questions." Accessed July 2, 2018.

Flegenheimer, Matt, and Maggie Haberman. "Donald Trump, Abortion Foe, Eyes 'Punishment' for Women, Then Recants." *The New York Times*. March 30, 2018. https://www.nytimes.com/2016/03/31/us/politics/donald-trump-abortion.html.

Howe, Louise. *Pink Collar Workers: Inside the World of Women's Work.* New York: Putnam, 1977.

Inger, Sasha. "Iowa Bans Most Abortions As Governor Signs 'Heartbeat' Bill." National Public Radio, May 18, 2018. https://www.npr.org/sections/thetwoway /2018/05/05/608738116/iowa-bans-most-abortions-as-governor-signs-heartbeat -bill.

Johnson, Allan G. *The Gender Knot: Unraveling Our Patriarchal Legacy.* Philadelphia: Philadelphia University Press, 2005.

Jordan, Mary. "Record Number of Women Heading to Congress." *The Washington Post*, November 8, 2018. https://www.washingtonpost.com/politics/record-num ber-of-women-appear-headed-for-congress/2018/11/06/76a9e60a-e1eb-11e8-8f5f -a55347f48762_story.html?utm_term=.90389318d792.

Kandiyoti, Deniz. "Bargaining with Patriarchy." *Gender and Society* 2 (1988): 274–90.

Kutner, Jenny, "Tomi Lahren Champions Choice, Much to Conservative Chagrin." V*ogue*, March 21, 2017, https://www.vogue.com/article/tomi-lahren-pro-choice -suspended-conservative-backlash.

Lorber, Judith. *Paradoxes of Gender*. New Haven: Yale University Press, 1994.

Mead, Rebecca. "Margaret Atwood, The Prophet of Dystopia." *New Yorker*, April 17, 2017. https://www.newyorker.com/magazine/2017/04/17/margaret-atwood -the-prophet-of-dystopia.

Prochoice America. "State Government." Accessed December 4, 2018. https://www .prochoiceamerica.org/laws-policy/state-government.

Relman, Eliza. "The 22 Women Who Have Accused Trump of Sexual Misconduct." *Business Insider*, September 26, 2018. https://www.businessinsider.com/women -accused-trump-sexual-misconduct-list-2017-12.

Rewire. "Personhood." Accessed June 23, 2018. https://rewire.news/legislative -tracker/law-topic/personhood.

Reskin, Barbara, and Patricia Roos. *Job Queues, Gender Queues*. Philadelphia: Temple University Press, 1990.

Rich, Adrienne. *Of Women Born: Motherhood as Experience and Institution*. New York: W.W. Norton & Company, Inc., 1995.

Sherman, Mark, and Jessica Gresko. "Supreme Court Says Crisis Pregnancy Centers Do Not Have to Provide Women Abortion Information." *Chicago Tribune*, June 26, 2018, http://www.chicagotribune.com/news/nationworld/ct-supremecourt -pregnancy-center-abortion-ruling-20180626-story.html.

Stolberg, Sheryl Gay, and Nicholas Fandos. "Kavanaugh and Christine Blasey Ford Duel With Tears and Fury." *New York Times,* September 27, 2018. https://www .nytimes.com/2018/09/27/us/politics/brett-kavanaugh-confirmation-hearings.html.

Wade, Lisa, "Serena Williams's Patriarchal Bargain." *Sociological Images*, May 22, 2011. https://thesocietypages.org/socimages/2011/05/22/women-damned-if-you -do-damned-if-you-don't.

Wade, Lisa, and Myra Marx Feree. *Gender: Ideas, Interactions, Institutions.* New York: W.W. Norton & Company, Inc., 2015.

West, Candace, and Don H. Zimmerman. "Doing Gender." *Gender and Society* 1 (1987): 125–51.

Willingham, AJ. "A Proposed Ohio Law Would Redefine a Person to Include 'Unborn Humans' and Could Treat Abortion like Murder." CNN, November 21, 2018. https://www.cnn.com/2018/11/21/us/ohio-abortion-ban-bill-criminal-law-trnd /index.html.

FILMS AND TELEVISION

Birthright: A War Story. DVD. Directed by Civia Tamarkin (New York: Women, Make Movies, 2017).

The Handmaid's Tale. "A Woman's Place." Season 1, Episode 6. Directed by Floria Sigismondi. Written by Wendy Straker Hauser. Hulu, May 17, 2017.

The Handmaid's Tale, "June." Season 1, Episode 1. Directed by Mike Barker. Written by Bruce Miller. Hulu, April 25, 2018.

The Handmaid's Tale. "Late." Season 1, Episode 3. Directed by Reed Morano. Written by Bruce Miller. Hulu, April 26, 2017.

The Handmaid's Tale. "Offred." Season 1, Episode 1. Directed by Reed Morano. Written by Bruce Miller. Hulu, April 26, 2017.

The Handmaid's Tale. "The Word." Season 2, Episode 13. Directed by Mike Barker. Written by Bruce Miller. Hulu, July 11, 2018.

The Handmaid's Tale. "Women's Work." Season 2, Episode 8. Directed by Kari Skogland. Written by Nina Fiore and John Herrera. Hulu, June 2, 2018.

Chapter Fifteen

"Discards, all of Us"

Representations of Age in The Handmaid's Tale

Christina Barmon

We live in an age-segregated society in which we spend most of our time with similarly aged people and much of what we learn about aging or older people is through books and television.[1] Even among feminists, who seek to eliminate the inequality and misrepresentations of marginalized people, ageism is often ignored, or at worst employed.[2] In this chapter, I use a feminist gerontological lens to analyze depictions of age in Margaret Atwood's *The Handmaid's Tale*[3] and the recent TV adaptation on Hulu.[4] I analyze how age intersects with gender, how they are represented in both the book and the recent television adaptation, and how these representations change in moving from the book to the television adaptation. In addition, I focus on what is missing from these representations as that can be just as powerful in its effects.[5]

Feminist gerontology is a critical theoretical perspective that situates gender as central to how members of society age, how we think about age, and aging on both an individual and institutional level.[6,7] It is not limited to examining the experiences of older women, nor does it assume the experiences of older, white women are universal, but views both gender and age as relational and born of power dynamics and social interactions within a patriarchal system that values youth and devalues femininity.[8] In addition, feminist gerontology is intersectional. A feminist gerontological approach recognizes that how we age and the consequences of systems of inequality vary depending not only on age and gender, but also on race, class, sexuality, and ability.[9,10] It is useful not only in highlighting how women in patriarchal societies are disadvantaged as they age, but also in looking at the implications for how men age in a patriarchal society, and how they must work to maintain masculine privilege and power as they age in a society that values youth.[11]

Both the original book by Margaret Atwood and the Hulu TV adaptations present depictions of age and gender that simultaneously challenge and reinforce ageist ideology. An important way that Atwood's 1985 book challenges ageism is that it critiques an oppressive society in which younger women are valued for their reproductive potential and older women are cast aside. Young women who are not in the privileged position of being married to a powerful man, a Commander, lose their names, their identities, and become used for reproduction while the majority of older women in Gilead are sent to the Colonies with the other undesirable "unwomen." There are a variety of colonies where the unwomen go to farm, bury dead bodies, or in the worst case, clean up toxic waste that ultimately kills them. This is explained in the middle of the book and in season 2 of the Hulu TV adaptation. When Offred (Elisabeth Moss) and her best friend Moira (Samira Wiley) find each other, Moira tells her that she found out that Offred's mother (Cherry Jones) was sent to the Colonies to clean up toxic waste.

She discovered this by seeing her in a documentary about the Colonies that was shown to the Handmaids as a warning of what would happen if they didn't behave. "It's old women, I bet you've been wondering why you haven't seen too many of those around anymore, and Handmaids who've screwed up their three chances, and incorrigibles like me. Discards, all of us. They're sterile of course. If they aren't that way to begin with, they are after they've been there for a while."[12] An exception in the book, but not the televi-

Offred's mother is discovered to have been sent to the Colonies after she appears in a documentary warning the Handmaids of their fate if they misbehave. Screenshot from Hulu television series.

sion adaptation, is that the privileged Wives of Commanders are allowed to be older. They are the heads of households, there to eventually raise the children born by their raped Handmaids. They fought for this oppressive society, but now find themselves bored and without purpose. In Gilead, where women are primarily valued for reproduction, other aspects of their identity and other talents become unimportant. Women, aside from reproduction, become useless, and their contributions from older women devalued.

Although *The Handmaid's Tale* critiques an ageist society, it also draws on ageist stereotypes to invoke fear or hatred. Having been banished to the Colonies, there were very few older characters in the book or the TV series. Thus, their stories are not told. The only older women characters in the book were decidedly unsympathetic. One of the few older characters in the book was Offred's mother who is only seen in Offred's memories. She was a radical second wave feminist (see chapter 5 by Heather Munro Prescott in this volume). Some saw her character as a warning against extremism—both religious fundamentalism and radical feminism.[13,14] She participated in pornography burnings, was too radical, too man-hating, and too strident. Her friends were too rowdy. She said that "a man is just a woman's strategy for making other women."[15] She did not like her daughter being married to a man, and Luke Bankole (O-T Fagbenle), June's husband in the time before, would often tease her by espousing gender essentialist ideas. Offred is shown in the television adaptation as being ashamed of her mother. She wanted a mother who was more like the other mothers she knew. June thought she dressed too young for her age, overreacted, and was embarrassed by her. In one scene, June is still a child when she witnesses her mother during a book burning. She is intimidated by her mother's passion. Another conflict emerges when Offred becomes pregnant and wants her mother to be present during the birth of her first grandchild. June suffers from having been neglected by her mother who sacrificed her personal life to the cause of feminism, raising June in a commune with other women.

Atwood uses the character of Offred's mother as a critique of elements of Second Wave feminism.[16] Atwood has long tried to distance herself from feminisms that she found too proscriptive.[17] However, her work can also be viewed as a commentary on the dismissal of the achievements by previous generations of feminists, taking for granted the reproductive rights for which they fought, and how ageism informs that discourse. Feminist poet and activist Audre Lorde argues that ageism is at the root of generation gaps and is an important tool for oppressive societies.[18] According to Lorde, by forgetting, disregarding, or not listening to the lessons learned by our mothers, we are doomed to repeat them and to continually have to find new solutions to the same problem. The character of Offred's mother expresses this frustration and refers to it on multiple occasions. She is bitter about the lack of recognition and credit given to her generation for the rights that current generations assume. She says, "You young people don't appreciate things. . . . You don't know what we had to go through, just to get you where you are. Look at him [Luke cooking], slicing up the carrots. Don't you know how many women's lives, how many women's *bodies*, the tanks had to roll over just to get that far?"[19] Offred seemed to recognize this phenomenon too late and regrets it. She misses her mother when she becomes aware that her mother most likely perished in the Colonies. She finally realizes "they didn't do badly by one another."[20] She regrets that they missed all the warning signs of the impending totalitarian society and became complacent. She says, "We lived as usual, by ignoring. Ignoring isn't the same as ignorance, you have to work at it."[21] Atwood is simultaneously critiquing radical Second Wave feminism, while acknowledging the dangers of dismissing it and assuming that all rights have been won. Additionally, she highlights the ageism that is at the root of dismissing earlier generations of feminists as outdated and unnecessary.

Regardless of where one stands in relation to debates between feminisms, these are necessary conversations and contribute to ageism when ignored or the gains of earlier feminist movements are disregarded. This conversation disappears from the Hulu TV adaptation almost entirely. In the television series, Offred is not alienated by her mother's feminism, but by the need for maternal approval. Her mother was not a radical feminist. Her feminism was made palatable for TV. Rather than burning pornography, rioting, and overtly hating men, Offred's mother became an abortion clinic escort, took part in "Take Back the Night" vigils, and worried that June might be too dependent on men and might be wasting her creativity. June was less embarrassed by her and merely seemed more hurt that her mother didn't approve of her having a traditional marital relationship with her husband and would rather she had been working on the resistance and women's rights issues than working as a copy editor for a magazine at a desk job downtown.

June/Offred clearly craved her mother's approval in the TV show in a way that is not as apparent in the book. Ultimately, it was the memories of her strong mother that helped her survive birthing her second child alone in the dead of winter, supposedly born of rape by Commander Fred Waterford (Joseph Fiennes) but fathered clandestinely by his chauffeur Nick Blaine (Max Minghella). Making her mother a more palatable uncontroversial feminist in the television show renders invisible an important conversation between feminists of different generations and calls attention to the contribution of ageism to this conversation.

AGEIST STEREOTYPES OF OLDER ADULTS

Although Atwood highlights important debates within feminist movements and critiques an ageist society, she still draws upon ageist stereotypes of older adults. Older women are often depicted as weak, bitter, vindictive, and witchy. The age of Serena Joy Waterford (Yvonne Strahovski), the Commander's wife, is never explicit in the book, but she is not young—rather menopausal; she cannot bear children anymore. From the description, she could be anywhere from forty to seventy and bears a striking similarity to Tammy Fay Bakker, who along with her husband, was a television evangelist in the 1980s and 1990s known for heavy makeup and excessive crying. Bakker and her husband built an evangelical television empire and amassed a fortune until a very public downfall that included fraud, adultery, and divorce.

In the book, Offred recognizes Serena Joy Waterford from seeing her throughout her childhood. She started out as a gospel singer on the "Growing Souls Gospel Hour," which was a children's television show in which they told bible stories and sang. "She could smile and cry at the same time."[22] Later, she and Luke would see her on television and laugh, "Luke and I would watch her sometimes on the late-night news. Bathrobes, nightcaps. We'd watch her sprayed hair and her hysteria, and the tears she could still produce at will, and the mascara blackening her cheeks. By that time she was wearing more makeup. We thought she was funny."[23]

In the description of their first meeting in chapter 3, it is evident that Serena Joy is older because Offred describes her as how she looked when she was young compared to how she looks now: "her blue waist, thickened, her left hand on the ivory head of her cane, the large diamonds on the ring finger, which must once have been fine and was still finely kept, the fingernail at the end of the knuckly finger."[24] She goes on:

> A little of her hair was showing, from under her veil. It was still blonde. . . . Her eyebrows were plucked into thin arched lines, which gave her a permanent look of surprise, or outrage, or inquisitiveness . . . but below them her eyelids were tired-looking. . . . Her nose must once have been what was called cute but now was too small for her face. Her face was not fat but it was large. Two lines led downwards from the corners of her mouth; between them was her chin, clenched like a fist. [25]

Additionally, we find out a little later in the book that she has arthritis, one of the most common disabilities among older adults.[26] She also spends her time on hobbies that are stereotypical of older women—knitting and gardening. During the first ritualized rape, "the Ceremony," Offred uses ageist and ableist descriptions of her entrance,

> We hear Serena coming, down the stairs along the hall, the muffled tap of her cane on the rug. Thud of the good foot. She hobbles through the doorway. . . . She's in one of her best dresses—sky blue with embroidery in white along the edges of the veil, flowers and fretwork. Even at her age, she still feels the need to wreathe herself in flowers. No use for you, I think at her, my face unmoving, you can't use them anymore, you're withered. They're the genital organs of plants. I read that somewhere, once.[27]

Here, Offred reinforces the idea that a woman's beauty and value is tied to age and fertility in the same way that the system that is oppressing her is only valuing her for her fertility. But these stereotypes are also drawn on to make Serena Joy Waterford scarier, in a scene in which she is meant to be terrified—about to be raped. Additionally, the parallels to Tammy Faye Bakker add not only to the fear but also to the preposterousness of her character. Thus, Atwood is using ageist stereotypes in order to create more fear and loathing for the women of Gilead.

In moving from the book to the Hulu television adaptation, with the exception of Aunt Lydia (Ann Dowd), whose character is the archetype of a witch, the sadistic authority figure in charge of regulating and punishing the innocent Handmaids, the majority of characters become younger. Serena Joy becomes just Serena, when played by Yvonne Strahovski. She loses the association with Tammy Faye Bakker. She is no longer a caricature of an older, bitter, arthritic woman. Rather, she is tall, thin, and has long blond hair. She is approximately the same age as Offred. Rather than being infertile due to menopause, it is inferred that she is infertile because of a violent clash with protestors. We lose the stereotypes, but this makes age even more invisible. In an interview with Bruce Miller, the producer of the Hulu television series, he said he had two reasons for making Serena younger.[28] The first was that Serena Joy was elderly and he wanted the series to go on for years. The second reason for a younger Serena was that he thought it would be more interesting if she and her Handmaid were closer in age. He says, "The element that was missing for me was the direct competition between the two women."[29] These notions that women should be competing for the same man, that this competition would not be possible with an older woman, and that a dialogue between an older woman and a younger woman would not hold interest for years is both ageist and sexist.

DEPICTION OF OLD AGE IN THE MEDIA

One of the most persistent ageist stereotypes is that older adults are asexual. According to the stereotype, they are neither desirous of sex, or desired. Older adults are assumed to have outgrown their sexuality. Older women in the media are often portrayed as caring grandmothers who exist for other people—or hags. When older men are presented in the media as sexual, it is often as a sexual predator—the creepy old man. These stereotypes for both older men and women are inaccurate. The majority of older adults are interested in and continue to engage in sexual activity.[30] However, the television writers assumed that Serena would not be seen as viable competition for a man. In the Commander's eyes, the younger woman would automatically win, because she is more beautiful, sexual, and fertile, which disregards a lifetime of relationship history between the Commander and his wife Serena. This was a missed opportunity by the TV series creators to portray an older woman as a complicated multifaceted sexual being.

Feminist gerontology is important as a way to look at how the patriarchy structures aging not only for women but also for men. Atwood's novel and the Hulu TV adaptation are both useful for examining how older men maintain power as they resist ageist stereotypes regarding potency and frailty. In Gilead, the Commanders went to great lengths to maintain the illusion of power and control. They used younger men as guards, who are portrayed as more volatile, to exert violence while they were the rational intellectuals in charge. By law, it was impossible for a man to be infertile; if there was a fertility problem, it was a woman's fault. Finally, in the series, this is illustrated in the physical punishments given to Serena when she stepped out of the bounds of the restrictive role of woman in the second season after her adoptive daughter has been born. The Commander not only spanks her violently, but when she begins to advocate for women being allowed to read, he orders that one of her fingers be amputated as punishment. He feels threatened and needs to exert authority over women in order to maintain masculinity as he ages. The Commander also feels entitled to assert his power in front of the other members of the government who had gotten to know Serena as one of the founders of the autocratic movement; she wrote the script and is now written out of it. Serena is not even allowed to own a pen.

In conclusion, feminist gerontology provides a lens with which to analyze intersections of gender and age. I found that although *The Handmaid's Tale*—both the novel and the television adaptation—is critiquing a society that values women primarily for youth and reproduction, it is also drawing on ageist and sexist stereotypes about older women. Furthermore, ageism is not just about discrimination against individuals or the perpetuation of individual stereotypes. It is also ageist to denigrate and dismiss of the ideas and contributions of previous generations.

NOTES

1. Gunhild O. Hagestad and Peter Uhlenberg, "The Social Separation of Old and Young: A Root of Ageism," *Journal of Social Issues* 61, no. 2 (2005).

2. Toni Calasanti, Kathleen F. Slevin, and Neal King, "Ageism and Feminism: From 'Et Cetera' to Center," *NWSA Journal* 18, no. 1 (2013).

3. Margaret Atwood, *The Handmaid's Tale* (Anchor Books: New York, 1986).

4. *The Handmaid's Tale*, TV series, created by Bruce Miller, MGM Television/Hulu. USA, 2017.

5. Gillian Rose, *Visual Methodologies: An Introduction to Researching with Visual Material* (Thousand Oaks: Sage, 2016).

6. T. M. Calasanti and K. F. Slevin, *Gender, Social Inequalities, and Aging* (Walnut Creek, CA: AltaMira Press, 2001).

7. Ruth E. Ray, "A Postmodern Perspective on Feminist Gerontology," *The Gerontologist* 36, no. 5 (1996).

8. Calasanti and Slevin, *Gender, Social Inequalities, and Aging*.

9. Calasanti and Slevin, *Gender, Social Inequalities, and Aging*.

10. Ray, "A Postmodern Perspective on Feminist Gerontology."

11. Toni Calasanti, "Feminist Gerontology and Old Men," *The Journals of Gerontology Series B: Psychological Sciences and Social Sciences* 59, no. 6 (2004).

12. Atwood, *The Handmaid's Tale*, 248.

13. Barbara Ehrenreich, "Feminism and Religious Fundamentalism Merge in *The Handmaid's Tale*," in *Women's Issues in Margaret Atwood's* The Handmaid's Tale, ed. David Erik Nelson (Farmington Hills, MI: Greenhaven Press, 2012).

14. Fiona Tolan, "Feminist Utopias and Questions of Liberty: Margaret Atwood's *The Handmaid's Tale* as Critique of Second Wave Feminism," *Women: A Cultural Review* 16, no. 1.

15. Tolan, "Feminist Utopias," 121.

16. Tolan, "Feminist Utopias."

17. Rebecca Mead, "The Prophet of Dystopia," *The New Yorker* 93, no. 9 (2017).

18. Audre Lorde, *Sister Outsider* (U.S.A.: Ten Speed Press, 1984, 2007).

19. Atwood, *The Handmaid's Tale*, 121.

20. Atwood, *The Handmaid's Tale*, 181.

21. Atwood, *The Handmaid's Tale*, 56.

22. Atwood, *The Handmaid's Tale*, 16.

23. Atwood, *The Handmaid's Tale*, 46.

24. Atwood, *The Handmaid's Tale*, 14.

25. Atwood, *The Handmaid's Tale*, 15.

26. Richard F. Loeser, "Osteoarthritis Year in Review 2013: Biology," *Osteoarthritis and Cartilage* 21, no. 10 (2013).

27. Atwood, *The Handmaid's Tale*, 81.

28. Kim Renfro, *Showrunners*, Podcast Audio, "Bruce Miller talks 'The Handmaid's Tale,'" 2017.

29. Renfro, *Showrunners*.

30. Stacy Tessler Lindau et al., "A Study of Sexuality and Health among Older Adults in the United States," *New England Journal of Medicine* 357, no. 8 (2007).

WORKS CITED

Atwood, Margaret. *The Handmaid's Tale*. Anchor Books: New York, 1986.

Calasanti, Toni. "Feminist Gerontology and Old Men." *The Journals of Gerontology Series B: Psychological Sciences and Social Sciences* 59, no. 6 (November 1, 2004). S305–S14.

Calasanti, T. M., and K. F. Slevin. *Gender, Social Inequalities, and Aging*. Walnut Creek, CA: AltaMira Press, 2001.

Calasanti Toni, Kathleen F. Slevin, and Neal King. "Ageism and Feminism: From 'Et Cetera' to Center." *NWSA Journal* 18, no. 1 (2013): 13–30.

Ehrenreich, Barbara. "Feminism and Religious Fundamentalism Merge in *The Handmaid's Tale*." In *Women's Issues in Margaret Atwood's* The Handmaid's Tale, edited by David Erik Nelson. Farmington Hills, MI: Greenhaven Press, 2012.

Hagestad, Gunhild O., and Peter Uhlenberg. "The Social Separation of Old and Young: A Root of Ageism." *Journal of Social Issues* 61, no. 2: 343–60.

Lindau, Stacy Tessler, L. Philip Schumm, Edward O. Laumann, Wendy Levinson, Colm A. O'Muircheartaigh, and Linda J. Waite. "A Study of Sexuality and Health among Older Adults in the United States." *New England Journal of Medicine* 357, no. 8 (2007): 762–74.

Loeser, Richard F. "Osteoarthritis Year in Review 2013: Biology." *Osteoarthritis and Cartilage* 21, no. 10 (2013): 1436–42.

Lorde, Audre. *Sister Outsider*. U.S.A.: Ten Speed Press, 1984, 2007.

Mead, Rebecca. "The Prophet of Dystopia." *The New Yorker* (2017): 38–47.

Ray, Ruth E. "A Postmodern Perspective on Feminist Gerontology." *The Gerontologist* 36, no. 5 (October 1, 1996): 674–80.

Renfro, Kim. *Showrunners.* Podcast audio. "Bruce Miller talks 'The Handmaid's Tale.'" 2017.

Rose, Gillian. *Visual Methodologies: An Introduction to Researching with Visual Material*. Thousand Oaks: Sage, 2016.

Tolan, Fiona. "Feminist Utopias and Questions of Liberty: Margaret Atwood's *The Handmaid's Tale* as Critique of Second Wave Feminism." *Women: A Cultural Review* 16, no. 1: 18–32.

FILM AND TELEVISION

The Handmaid's Tale. TV Series. Created by Bruce Miller. MGM Television / Hulu. USA, 2017.

Section III:

PRODUCTION, CINEMATIC TECHNIQUES, AND FILM ADAPTATIONS

Chapter Sixteen

No Light without Shadow

The Question of Realism in Volker Schlöndorff's The Handmaid's Tale *and Hulu's TV Series*

Eileen Rositzka

Shortly after its release in 2017, several websites listed ways in which Hulu's TV series, *The Handmaid's Tale,* feels "way too real." Marianne Eloise, one of many online bloggers sharing this opinion, wrote in May 2017: "Like all good dystopian visions, the brilliant TV adaptation of Margaret Atwood's seminal novel is not all that far from reality."[1] But where to find the source for this impression beyond plot and narrative? If we take a closer look at the aesthetics of the TV series, the most striking feature is its color palette and lighting: washed-out sepia tones and natural light dominate the scenes, with said light from outside casting long shadows on all interior spaces (in the most literal sense). Both features almost add a persisting "Victorian hue" to the images, qualifying the dystopian idea of Gilead not only as an image of reactionary social structures, but as a regime of forced interiority, of captivation, and institutionalized symmetry.

The colors and textures characterizing the series (which include fabric, dust, and object surfaces) not only express all sorts of restrictions and the female characters' confinement to the domestic sphere and to spaces of institutional collectivization, but moreover, this scheme places the plot within the framework of another medium: realist art. This aesthetic choice provides another limitation in itself, as it virtually puts the action into the frames of countless paintings. Through the almost expressionistic use of light, on the other hand, *The Handmaid's Tale* insinuates a palpable threat that eventually turns the image space into a subjective space of experience—an experience of fear, humiliation, and objectification.

Not only present in the television series, this effect is also achieved in Volker Schlöndorff's 1990 film adaptation of Margaret Atwood's book, albeit by different means. Here, several interior spaces are frequently illuminated by cold artificial light in the colors of blue, green, and red. Not only does this seem to move the plot closer to the realm of dystopian science fiction, but, even more importantly, it articulates the persistence and effects of a self-destructive society—like a prism dissecting the light into its single components.

Seen in this way, both Schlöndorff's film and the *Handmaid's Tale* TV series can be analyzed in terms of their contrasting notions of genre and realism—specifically in their connection to realist art of the Victorian age, or in their evocation of subjective realities through color and lighting. Questions of realism—whether in relation to specific visual styles, atmospheres, production contexts, or matters of authenticity—have been a vital component of media-historical debates and film criticism. However, only few approaches elaborate on realism as an aesthetic experience that actually aims at establishing a shared perspective of/on the world through cinematic images. As I hope to show, a comparison of the two adaptations of *The Handmaid's Tale* in this regard can demonstrate in what ways cinematic (or televisual) realism can create an experiential space in which an idea of society and interiority is made graspable in relation to both characters and spectators.

WHAT REALISM?

The very first episode of the first season of the TV series opens with an escape on a treacherously idyllic fall afternoon: A biracial family—Caucasian mother (Elisabeth Moss), black father (O-T Fagbenle), and their biological child (Jordana Blake)—tries to flee from the menacing sound of police sirens when suddenly their car slides off the street. The mother and her child run into the woods while the father stays behind. A couple of gunshots and some minutes of silence later they are found and violently separated, and the beaten mother is dragged out of the frame before being shoved into a van. Then, within the millisecond of a cut, and with the brutal sound of a slamming door, we (the spectators) are thrown into a dark attic bedroom, dimly lit by pale sunlight that falls through the curtains and outlines the frozen silhouette of a—presumably different—woman. She sits on the window sill, hands folded in her lap, facing the camera, but her body is obscured by shadows. She is wearing a bonnet and a plain dress—an outfit that would make her a contemporary of the Victorian era, if we were to guess and judge only from the looks of her costume and her spatial surroundings. A voice sets in: "A chair, a table, a lamp. There's a window with white curtains, and the glass is shatterproof, but . . . it isn't running away they're afraid of. A handmaid wouldn't get far."

It soon becomes clear that, when the camera zooms in on the woman and we recognize her face, that she is the young mother we saw earlier, that she had a name once, but one that is forbidden now—like so many other things "these days." Within these few minutes of screen time, two very different portrayals of the same woman place her between seemingly opposed images of time and space: between an escape scenario that could easily be set in present day (with landscape features, vehicles, and clothes familiar to the contemporary viewer) and a domestic scene from a more distant past (one that the viewer would imagine based on written and painted accounts of bygone times). Ironically, in the narrative universe of *The Handmaid's Tale*, this chronology is reversed: the failed escape turns out to be a flashback, and "present day" or, in other words, "a not too distant future," is the time of Offred, a Handmaid and former loving mother and wife, June—of the woman in the window.

Yet, however opposed these images and their temporal dimensions might be, they are connected by the very same natural sunlight that breaks through the trees in the episode's first shots, and that falls through the window in Offred's chamber a few moments later, although the fighting mother from before has seemingly become an object among objects frozen in time: a chair, a table, a lamp, a Handmaid.

When the voice-over (as an evocation of Margaret Atwood's original writing) thus establishes an order of things in which the body of a woman is—quite literally—"objectified," this narrative strategy alone could be identified as continuing the prosaic tradition of realist storytelling. In this context,

In one of the opening scenes of the Hulu series, Offred's silhouette is visible against daylight streaming in through her window. Screenshot from Hulu's television series.

however, realism is not to be reduced to accurate representations of objects, people, and landscapes, or, in other words, to renditions of pure objectivity on the part of the author, as it is bound to a certain notion of "truth"—a truth which reveals not reality itself but "the order inscribed in particular discourses."[2]

While such implications are undoubtedly at work in *The Handmaid's Tale*, such a reading has to account for the aesthetic patterns and complexities of audiovisual media: That is, when it comes to describing the peculiar "reality effect" of Hulu's TV series, this effect must necessarily arise from the interplay between expressive qualities beyond spoken language. In this vein, lighting and color design in *The Handmaid's Tale* not only contribute to the show's stylistic recognition value; what is more, they link the story's specific rendition of the past with its specific present and future, ultimately marking said temporal layers as distinctly located in the present of the viewer. If this is what makes the show feel considerably more "real," this perception is rooted in what has pervaded various art forms to this day as a sense of "realism"—as "a specific relationship between media texts and their viewers."[3]

While the main agenda of nineteenth-century realist movements in visual art and literature had been a call to artists to be true to oneself as well as to the social reality of one's time,[4] and thus to reach personal and universal liberation, this approach was to take on various aesthetic styles and forms. After so-called "genre paintings" had provided the frame for the casual depiction of everyday life leading to the formation of naturalist and social realist traditions of the twentieth century, film history alone brought about several variations of realism, ranging from French poetic realism and Italian neorealism to magic realism—whereas particular documentary movements have grounded their respective idea of "reality" in treating the camera as an impartial observer. In concrete cinematic terms, and for what concerns fictional films, nuances of realism can be detected in matter-of-fact narration or nonprofessional acting, and, perhaps most notably, in the portrayal of class struggles and social disillusionment—which does not exclude lyrical motifs and elements (as in French poetic realism[5]) or the invasion of the surreal into the everyday (as in magic realism[6]).

In a broader theoretical sense, cinematic realism, both in its poetic and political dimension, does not only concern plots, themes, and other matters of representation, but is also established through a film's (or a TV show's) interaction with the sensing and feeling bodies of its spectators. As German film scholar Hermann Kappelhoff writes:

> [C]inema spectators [. . .] embody film images so that the world of the film becomes fused with a spectator's world as though the audience participated with

the film in a shared *reality*. The interplay or fusion of these worlds is encapsu-
lated in a single word that has long dominated the aesthetics of film: *realism*.[7]

He continues to describe film as a media practice that addresses viewers in
two specific ways with regard to their everyday life and environment:

> Spectators are encouraged, on the one hand, to be artists, to turn the film's
> sounds and signs, bodily arrangements and spatial fragments, rhythms and figu-
> rations of movement into an imagined world of reality, and, on the other, to be
> participants in a political community. Combining the poetic and political allows
> spectators to imagine worlds that could be different from everyday lived reality.
> [. . .] Cinematic realism is just the dynamic tension between poetics and politics
> that allows films and their audiences endlessly to make new worlds.[8]

In the case of Hulu's *The Handmaid's Tale*, the world that is created for and
by the audience is one of resistance despite acts and signs of suppression,
separation, and pseudo-archaic law enforcement, which is brought to effect
by the depiction of bodies caught up in choreographed rituals and ceremonies that brutally contrast the series' overall lack of bodily movement when
it comes to its depiction of Gilead. This world, in all its facets of categorized
anonymity (faceless architecture, nameless streets, color-coded costumes and
uniforms, standardized names and speech acts) is in itself a highly artificial
construct; nevertheless, its unsettling intensity stems from the fact that this
world is precisely not presented as an unlikely dystopia set in a distant future.
On the contrary: Gilead is always not more than a cut away from those scenes
that portray our world and society as we know it.

While some flashbacks help to reconstruct the relationship between Of-
fred/June and her husband or to her friend Moira (Samira Wiley) by focusing
on intimate gestures, heated arguments, or family activities, others already
contain subtle hints of aggressive behavior, open protest, and even violent
outbreaks before the show suddenly cuts back to the dismal places of Gilead.
In any case, it is through the vitality of these scenes that we experience the
lifeless order of the republic even more intensely. Any form of optional motion, so it seems, is chained to the past—but to a past that had been a present
not too long ago.[9] The series' cinematic realism is thus based on the troubling
idea that any democratic society could straightforwardly deactivate the shared
moral values that had so far been their founding principle in order to revert
to a premodern strive for reproduction, thereby negating a whole history of
struggling for human and civil rights.[10]

As is made clear in *The Handmaid's Tale*, this history is not forgotten
but still alive in everyone's memory; it is not erased but silenced. Obviously,
such storytelling plays on the contemporary viewer's political consciousness

and his/her impulse to draw parallels between the fictional world of Gilead and the real-life politics of today. But in order to get to these conclusions, the silencing or overwriting of history has to be examined as an aesthetic strategy by means of which Offred's immediate surroundings become an abstract-allegorical space; a space in which political effects are made to be visible to the spectator through changes in a highly artificial setting.[11] Because Gilead is precisely not to be grasped in topographical terms (as there are no street signs or characteristic architectural features that would be worth memorizing), the interior of the Commander's house sets the stage for an intimate chamber play in which body politics are negotiated through postures, gestures, and objects. In a house like this, where everything has its place and order, every irregularity, every misplaced word, and every sign of an existing world outside these structures must disrupt this order—for example, when Offred notices a blood stain in her underwear that renders countless ceremonies fruitless; when Nick and Offred's fingers touch in secret moments; when the Commander begins to look at her differently during later ceremonies; or when she finds the mock Latin phrase her predecessor has carved into the wooden closet ("Nolite te bastardes carborundorum"[12]).

Both consoling and disturbing, these words inscribed into the "body" of the house are at the same time an effect of the violence that has been inflicted upon the previous Handmaid's body; thus, they form an arcane visual motif and plot element which, again, points to a sense of realism as we find it in fine art, and specifically in paintings by Edgar Degas: that is, if we also add in the show's characteristic representation of natural light from outside, as opposed to the rather weak, punctual light sources inside, it is especially the interior of the Commander's house which bears striking resemblance to Degas's "Interior" from 1868/1869. This oil painting, also known as "The Rape," shows a couple in a dimly lit bedroom. The woman has her back turned on the man who watches her from a distance. Some clothes are strewn across the floor, and part of the woman's dress is hanging from her shoulder. Whether or not a rape has occurred remains unclear; however, the relation between what is present and what is absent seems to transform the visual space of the painting into an inner space, an "interior" not only realistic in its faithful representation of the object world, but "real" in terms of what takes shape as a human drama in the beholder's perception and imagination. Jennifer Thompson from the Philadelphia Museum of Art traces this effect back to Degas's own notes:

> Despite a wealth of anecdotal detail, the drama unfolding between the couple represented in this painting by Edgar Degas remains a mystery. [. . .] An annotation in a notebook used by Degas in this period provides a clue as to his intentions: "Work a great deal on nocturnal effects, lamps, candles, etc. The fascinating thing is not always to show the source of light but rather its effect." The

softly diffused light from the table lamp and fire contribute much to the intimacy of the setting and divide the conflicted figures, whose faces are cast in shadows. Degas made numerous preparatory studies for the room and the figures in order to create a powerful psychological mood and convincing setting. He seems to have intentionally obscured the narrative in order to seduce the viewer with the suggestive power of his painting and its unrevealed secrets.[13]

Degas's realism thus seems to conceal and reveal social drawbacks by subordinating a potential narrative to insinuating aesthetic compositions. This strategy is very similar to Hulu's *The Handmaid's Tale* in that—beyond its obvious ties to nineteenth-century art—even the countless flashbacks do not reveal the reasons and motivations for certain events but consciously omit any sense of chronology and closure. Rather, these sequences break the pseudo-Victorian frame of Gilead in order to let the past shed its light on the present. These flashbacks, therefore, more likely form a narrative equivalent to the natural light which allows an exterior space to enter the show's many secluded interiors.

CHANGING PERSPECTIVES

By contrast, an exterior in this sense, let alone an emotionally charged interior, is never seen or felt in Volker Schlöndorff's 1990 film adaptation of *The Handmaid's Tale*. To a certain extent, this film's vision of Gilead is a highly abstract one, composed of stylized spaces and surfaces that seem to transport Atwood's story into another genre—namely that of the (erotic) thriller—and one whose overall very cold and clinical atmosphere largely derives from its expressive lighting. Several interior settings are bathed in neon green or blue light which does hardly leave any room for textures; otherwise, extremely bright off-screen light sources create sharp color contrasts and contoured shadows that recall the expressionist style of 1940s film noir. Throughout the film, Schlöndorff thus creates the look and feel of a hard-boiled police investigation requiring facts to be *shown* rather than *told*. Seen in this light, the Handmaid is not framed by means of painterly allusions; rather, she is "framed" in the sense of an alleged suspect under arrest. Therefore, both the psychological and physical violence inflicted upon Offred (played by Natasha Richardson) is linked to an order of high visibility, meaning that her character is subjugated not only to the patriarchic regime described in the story but also to the (male) gaze of the viewer—which becomes particularly evident through the film's repeated eroticization of Natasha Richardson's body.

Not only is this a fundamental change to Atwood's literary mode of storytelling, but—in addition to the director's numerous plot changes—also a shift in gender perspective: according to literary scholar Reingard M. Nischik, Schlöndorff "remasculinizes" the dystopian genre making a "his-story" of Atwood's "her-story"[14] in his attempt to streamline "the complexity of the book into an easily consumable film."[15] By consequence, Offred's character is eventually transformed into a *femme fatale* who takes murderous revenge on the Commander—a scene which makes up the graphic climax of the movie (and very clearly diverges from the book).

Given the fact that, before Schlöndorff got to shoot the first film version of *The Handmaid's Tale*, no Hollywood studio would adapt Harold Pinter's screenplay based on Atwood's novel,[16] this film's cinematic realism testifies to a problematic relationship between consumer-oriented media and their viewers: it alludes to the fact that genres are not only to be conceived of as stylistic frameworks but also as forms of formulaic communication; that is, the director's decision to change the story's perspective to that of the thriller seems to confirm that male fantasies can only be tackled and potentially over-turned within the generic codes of this fantasy itself in order to be acknowl-edged.[17] Within the Hollywood genre system, both the woman that falls victim to a radically patriarchic regime and the *femme fatale* that eventually turns against it are constructed images, two poles on a scale of female representa-tion defined and perpetuated by the film industry. Hence, the overt stylization of bodies and surfaces in Schlöndorff's *The Handmaid's Tale* not only attests to the apparent demands of a 1990s film industry and audience, but also to the artificiality of media images per se—a condition in which history, his-stories, and her-stories are more than often reduced to accustomed represen-tational codes, exchangeable surfaces and filters (in this case blue or green). In part, Schlöndorff's lighting concept can be said to relate to the style of other European directors such as Luchino Visconti, who, for his historical films, frequently made use of mirrors and colored artificial light to turn specific settings into sites of psychological and political negotiation. Yet Visconti's specifically constructed visual spaces articulate a certain process of inner decay, treating history as a "reconstruction of a human drama."[18] As Kappelhoff writes on *La caduta degli dei,* Visconti's film about the tragic downfall of a German industrial family:

> In the world of this film, history is something that changes the scene without this change ever becoming quite comprehensible. A shift in the lighting, a dis-harmonic zoom, an abrupt change in color—at first these are hardly noticeable, but in the end they represent a creeping devastation. History is the duration of this change; a time quite detached from the course of the plot, which can only be grasped in the gradually diminishing light, the changing of colors, the ever more vacant table.[19]

This specific temporal dimension is certainly missing in Schlöndorff's adaptation, as his film seems to reveal more about the time of its production than about the past and present fragments of a world that has become incomprehensibly unhinged. However, both Schlöndorff's film and Hulu's TV series consciously revert to specific media frameworks in order to expose the multiple framings of women in sociocultural contexts—one in favor of a distinctly male (and mainly voyeuristic) perspective, the other in an attempt to unravel this framework as an inner drama for characters and spectators alike.

NOTES

1. Marianne Eloise, "*The Handmaid's Tale* Is a Dystopia That Feels All Too Real," Dazed, May 29, 2017, accessed July 15, 2018, http://www.dazeddigital.com/artsand culture/article/36104/1/the-handmaids-tale-atwood-moss-dystopia.

2. As Hallam and Marshment elaborate, this has been claimed by post-structuralist critics such as Colin MacCabe, Stephen Heath, and Catherine Belsey. For further discussion, see Julia Hallam and Margaret Marshment, *Realism and Popular Cinema* (Manchester: Manchester University Press, 2000), 10.

3. Anne Jerslev, "Introduction," in *Realism and 'Reality' in Film and Media*, ed. Anne Jerslev (Copenhagen: Museum Tusculanum Press, University of Copenhagen 2002), 9.

4. J. H. Rubin, "Realism," Grove Art Online (2003), accessed July 15, 2018, http://www.oxfordartonline.com/groveart/view/10.1093/gao/9781884446054.001.0001/oao-9781884446054-e-7000070996.

5. For a more detailed description of poetic realism in French cinema, see, for instance, David A. Cook, "Poetic Realism, 1929–1934," in *A History of Narrative Film*, ed. Peter Simon (New York: W. W. Norton & Co., 2016), or Kristin Thompson and David Bordwell, "Poetic Realism," (in *Film History: An Introduction* (New York: McGraw Hill, 2010).

6. See, for instance, Fredric Jameson, "On Magic Realism in Film," *Critical Inquiry* 12, no. 2 (1986).

7. Hermann Kappelhoff, *The Politics and Poetics of Cinematic Realism* (New York: Columbia University Press, 2015), IX.

8. Kappelhoff, *The Politics and Poetics of Cinematic Realism*, X.

9. Margaret Atwood has made this point explicit in numerous statements on *The Handmaid's Tale*, and quite recently in an essay published in the *New York Times*: "Having been born in 1939 and come to consciousness during World War II, I knew that established orders could vanish overnight. Change could also be as fast as lightning. 'It can't happen here' could not be depended on: Anything could happen anywhere, given the circumstances" ("Margaret Atwood on What 'The Handmaid's Tale' Means in the Age of Trump," the *New York Times*, March 10, 2017, accessed July 15, 2018, https://www.nytimes.com/2017/03/10/books/review/margaret-atwood-handmaids-tale-age-of-trump.html).

10. This has also been described in an online blog post by Rebekah Valentine: "[. . .] it's the constant reminders and realizations as to just how close we might be to something like the Republic of Gilead, and the flashbacks showing the process of how things got that way in the first place. It hits painfully close to home, time and time again" ("10 Times *The Handmaid's Tale* Got Way Too Real," Culturess, 2017, accessed July 15, 2018, https://culturess.com/2017/05/10/10-times- handmaids-tale -got-way-real/).

11. See Kappelhoff, *The Politics and Poetics of Cinematic Realism*, 77.

12. "Nolite te bastardes carborundorum" is actually a made-up phrase in mock Latin, which would roughly translate to "Don't let the bastards grind you down."

13. Jennifer A. Thompson quoted on "Collections," Philadelphia Museum of Art, accessed July 15, 2018, http://www.philamuseum.org/collections/permanent/82556. html.

14. Reingard M. Nischik, *Engendering Genre* (Ottawa: University of Ottawa Press, 2009), 160.

15. Nischik, *Engendering Genre*, 150.

16. Initially, British-Czech director Karel Reisz was supposed to be in charge of the film adaptation, after he had already worked with Pinter on the screenplay. Yet, several film studios approached by producer Daniel Wilson turned it down, and Reisz eventually moved on to a different project. As journalist Sheldon Teitelbaum writes: "[. . .] Wilson would take the Pinter script to every studio in Hollywood, encountering a wall of ignorance, hostility and indifference" ("The Handmaid's Tale," *Cinefantastique* [1990]: 19).

17. On the differences between Atwood's novel, Pinter's screenplay, and Schlöndorff's film, see also Dennis Tredy's chapter in this volume.

18. Kappelhoff, *The Politics and Poetics of Cinematic Realism*, 77.

19. Kappelhoff, *The Politics and Poetics of Cinematic Realism*, 77.

WORKS CITED

Atwood, Margaret. "Margaret Atwood on What *The Handmaid's Tale* Means in the Age of Trump." *New York Times*, March 10, 2017. Accessed July 15, 2018. https://ww w.nytimes.com/2017/03/10/books/review/margaret-atwood-handmaids-tale -age-of-trump.html.

"Collections." Philadelphia Museum of Art. Accessed July 15, 2018. http://www .philamuseum.org/collections/permanent/82556.html.

Cook, David A. "Poetic Realism, 1929–1934." In *A History of Narrative Film*, edited by Peter Simon, 242–45. Fifth edition. New York: W.W. Norton & Co., 2016.

Eloise, Marianne. "*The Handmaid's Tale* Is A Dystopia That Feels All Too Real." Dazed, May 26, 2017. Accessed July 15, 2018. http://www.dazeddigital.com/arts andculture/article/361 04/1/the-handmaids-tale-atwood-moss-dystopia.

Hallam, Julia, and Margaret Marshment. *Realism and Popular Cinema*. Manchester: Manchester University Press, 2000.

Jameson, Fredric. "On Magic Realism in Film." *Critical Inquiry* 12, no. 2 (1986): 301–25. doi:10.1086/448333.

Jerslev, Anne. "Introduction." In *Realism and 'Reality' in Film and Media*, edited by Anne Jerslev, 7–9. Copenhagen: Museum Tusculanum Press, University of Copenhagen, 2002.

Kappelhoff, Hermann. *The Politics and Poetics of Cinematic Realism*. New York: Columbia University Press, 2015.

Nischik, Reingard M. *Engendering Genre: The Works of Margaret Atwood*. Ottawa: University of Ottawa Press, 2009.

Rubin, J. H. "Realism." Grove Art Online, 2003. Accessed July 15, 2018. http://www.oxfordartonline.com/groveart/view/10.1093/gao/9781884446054.001.0001/oao-97818844460 54-e-7000070996.

Teitelbaum, Sheldon. "The Handmaid's Tale." *Cinefantastique* 20, no. 4 (1990): 16–25.

Thompson, Kristin, and David Bordwell. "Poetic Realism." In *Film History: An Introduction*, 265–68. Third edition. New York: McGraw Hill, 2010.

Valentine, Rebekah. "10 Times *The Handmaid's Tale* Got Way Too Real." Culturess, 2017. Accessed July 15, 2018. https://culturess.com/2017/05/10/10-times-hand maids-tale-got-way-real/.

FILM AND TELEVISION

The Handmaid's Tale. Created by Bruce Miller. MGM Television / Hulu. USA, 2017.

The Handmaid's Tale. Directed by Volker Schlöndorff. USA / Germany, 1990.

The Handmaid's Tale. "Offred." Season 1, Episode 1. Directed by Reed Morano. Written by Bruce Miller. Hulu, April 26, 2017.

Chapter Seventeen

Shifting Perspectives and Reaccentuation

Adapting The Handmaid's Tale *as a Film in 1990 and as a Hulu TV Series in 2017/2018*

Dennis Tredy

In the relatively new field of adaptation studies, which seeks to create a common analytical approach to both a work of literature and its adaptation to film, theater or television,[1] Margaret Atwood's *The Handmaid's Tale* provides an excellent opportunity for scholars to better understand this dual approach to literature and other media, and to better comprehend the rather tenuous notion of "fidelity" behind that approach. The book was first adapted into a commercially unsuccessful film in 1990 by director Volker Schlöndorff and then into an extremely successful television series on Hulu that began in 2017, with two seasons having aired, each featuring ten one-hour episodes, and a third season scheduled for 2019. In addition, in a classroom, the novel's impact and controversial themes can fuel more technical discussions on the methods used to transpose and represent those same themes to the visual medium.

The 1990 film adaptation of *The Handmaid's Tale*, generally panned by critics and lovers of the novel alike, was also an astounding failure at the box office, grossing under $5 million for a $13 million budget, in spite of the hype that had come with news that respected German director Volker Schlöndorff would be adapting a screenplay written by the great Nobel Prize–winning British playwright Harold Pinter.[2] It is perhaps not surprising then that among the hundreds of essays and book-length studies devoted to *The Handmaid's Tale*, we rarely come across mention, let alone an analysis, of the doomed film.

In one of the rare articles available on how the film can be used in a classroom, by Mary K. Kirtz, an American professor specializing in Canadian literature, the focus is on how the film apparently draws the students' attention to the best elements of the novel simply because they realize that they are completely absent from the film![3] In other film studies that set out to compare *The Handmaid's Tale* to others in the dystopian genre, discussion of Atwood and her novel completely eclipses that of Schlöndorff and his film.[4] Yet, simply deeming a work as a "good" or a "bad" adaptation is very much a matter of personal taste and is of little interest in adaptation studies. What is more interesting is to try to understand the choices made when transposing the novel to a new medium, the strategies and intentions behind those choices, and the scope and impact of the final product—and to try to understand why one adaptation may have failed to appeal to fans of the novel while another adaptation might have them singing its praises. This is what this chapter will set out to do by going through some of the adaptation techniques used in the 1990 film—both those that could be attributed to Pinter as main screenwriter (plotlines, structural devices, and point of view) and those which would be more squarely Schlöndorff's contribution (stylistic devices and visual referencing)—and comparing them to those employed by Bruce Miller for the 2017/2018 TV series.

STORY, STRUCTURE, AND FIDELITY (OR LACK THEREOF)

In adaptation studies, the very notion of "fidelity" to the original work is problematic, though for most students and the general public it is the first aspect that comes to mind and often the litmus test for determining how successful an adaptation is. Not only does discussing fidelity often wrongly assume the superiority of the original over the new work derived from it, it too often assumes that an adaptation could indeed be 100 percent faithful, thereby forgetting the inherent differences in the two forms of storytelling, in the textual and in the visual medium. It is true that some adaptations seek to be as "faithful" as possible, creating a scene-by-scene transcription of a novel, like many BBC Masterpiece Theatre adaptations, for example, which are often used as a visual support for schoolchildren studying the source novel. Another such case might be Michael Radford's 1984 filmic adaption of George Orwell's dystopian narrative *1984*, which went so far in its scrupulous quest for fidelity as to shoot each scene on the very day and location on which the scenes in the novel took place.[5]

Yet such attempts seem to forget that transposing a novel to a visual medium requires enormous amounts of cutting, adding, and reshaping, and that one cannot judge an adaptation by simply ticking off a checklist of plot elements and scenes found in the novel. Determining the better of two adaptations by simply making such a checklist and comparing the number of what early adaptation specialist Brian McFarlane dubbed "narrative instances" (recognizable plot and character elements from the source work)[6] is indeed a fool's errand, for visual literalism is not the goal of a successful adaptation.

Take for example the fact that, in the 1990 film, Offred (Natasha Richardson) was a librarian before her life in Gilead, just as she was in the novel, yet in the Hulu TV series she was instead an editor at a major publishing house. While the film provides the more "faithful" choice, at first glance, the series creates a stronger contrast between the successful professional woman June/Offred (Elisabeth Moss) was and the repressed concubine she has become, more emphatically stressing the paradox of her (and other women) no longer being allowed to read or write. The TV episodes even allow for a second-season plotline in which she proves her worth to Serena Joy Waterford (Yvonne Strahovski) by helping her edit important government documents.[7] Similarly, in the film and in the novel, the key scene showcasing Serena's cruelty to Offred occurs when she shows her a photograph of her lost child (chapter 32 in Atwood's novel), but in the first season finale of the series, in one of the most gut-wrenching scenes of any episode, Serena takes Offred by car to get a glimpse of her daughter (Jordana Blake) in her new home but refuses to let her understandably hysterical mother get anywhere near the child; the series then comes back to the photo device much later, in season 2, though it is the Commander Fred Waterford (Joseph Fiennes) who uses it to try to solicit sexual favors from Offred. In both cases, the apparent deviations from Atwood's novel come off as being far more "faithful" to the spirit of the novel, and far more riveting for the new medium.

HAROLD PINTER'S CRAFTSMANSHIP

When setting out to adapt a dense three-hundred-page novel into a two-hour film, Pinter, like any screenwriter, inevitably had to cut down the source material. In terms of plot elements, his rule of thumb seems to have been to limit the story line to Offred's deplorable experience in Gilead, from her capture to her possible escape. However, Pinter, known for his minimalist style, simplified the complex, convoluted dramatic monologue of the novel and created a straightforward, linear chronology of Offred's time in Gilead. In fact, the only deviation from the novel's order of events involves Pinter's advancing both Offred's first secret encounter with the Commander from Atwood's chapter 23 and especially her first sexual encounter with Nick from chapter 40 so as to more immediately establish the sexual triangle she is involved in and allow for a stronger "love story" arc to be set up between Offred and the Commander's chauffeur, Nick Blaine (Max Minghella) who also works as an "Eye," a surveillance aid, for the Gilead government. (Nick is the father of Offred's second child.) Gone are thus the innumerable flashbacks we find in the novel and any connections to life before Gilead, and with them key secondary characters and their related themes. The lack of flashbacks to Offred's previous family life with Luke Bankole (O-T Fagbenle) and her child (Jordana Blake) thus deprives the character of a good deal of emotional depth (as well as freeing her up for the new romance), just as cutting out flashbacks to her mother's militant feminism and disappointment in her daughter's apathy strips away many of the pro-feminist bona fides we find in the novel.[8]

To make matters worse, Pinter was quite adamant about avoiding voice-over narration in all of his films,[9] and this screenplay was no exception. Schlöndorff agreed with this choice, only allowing voice-over for the epilogue and declaring that constant access to Offred's thoughts would be "unbearable for the audience and border on kitsch."[10] Thus Offred, in the film, not only has no recollections of the past but has no apparent consciousness either, reducing her to a silent and seemingly passive, repressed figure. The actress playing Offred, Natasha Richardson, daughter of the legendary Vanessa Redgrave, was thus nearly as stifled on set as her character was in Gilead, and could only rely on furtive and telling looks in the direction of other Handmaids or Nick, what Hans-Bernard Moëller, a specialist on Schlöndorff, praises as the film's "gaze structures,"[11] or dialogue scenes in which she is alone with Nick (Aidan Quinn) or with Moira (Elizabeth McGovern). We thus have no access to Offred's inner thoughts, her inner strength, and her inner struggle not only with self-doubt, loss, and despair, but also with her often conflicted feelings regarding feminism and the inhumanity of her captors.

To show Offred's strength in spite of all these self-imposed restrictions, Pinter decided to take a few liberties with the plot. For example, he made Offred slightly more sarcastic when speaking to the Commander Fred Waterford (Robert Duvall) or had her actively aid in Moira's attempt to escape from the Red Center (though, without voice-over, viewers will never know why she did not escape with her). More importantly, Pinter's sharpest break from the novel occurs at the end of the film, when Offred actively joins the Mayday resistance group, and, at their behest, assassinates her repulsive Commander, whose character had been established as far more unequivocally evil than in the novel so that the viewer might rejoice in the catharsis of her attack. However, that show of strength is greatly undercut by the film's epilogue, in which we see a pregnant Offred, now simply named "Kate," in the rebel-controlled mountains and *finally* have access to her thoughts through voice-over narration, only to learn that she is waiting there to be saved by a man (Nick) and to raise his baby with him.

So much for her becoming a feminist icon. . . . Is it any wonder that the American feminist critic Marianne Barnett, at an MLA convention during the film's release in 1990, blasted the male director and screenwriter for creating a weak, nonthinking protagonist obsessed with a new love affair and with sexual satisfaction?[12] By flattening both the story line and the main character, by cutting it down to her experience in Gilead while cutting out her point of view and inner self, and by overplaying the "love story" between Offred and Nick, Pinter's attempt at "fidelity" to the novel inevitably fell short. "Faithfully" following her Gilead plotline was not nearly enough.

BRUCE MILLER'S ADAPTATION TECHNIQUES

When writing the initial 2017 TV series for Hulu, showrunner Bruce Miller was well equipped to avoid the pitfalls that befell Pinter. As TV series have grown in the past twenty years to have production values and "cinematic" features comparable to those of feature films, Miller and his team were essentially writing a ten-hour film for each of the two seasons that have been released, a luxury that allows for far less cutting and flattening during the adaptation process. In fact, one could argue that Miller has decided to do everything, in terms of narrative structure and point of view, that Pinter and Schlöndorff could not, or would not, do. While the film limited the presentation to Offred's experience in Gilead, the TV series branches out and goes far beyond the scope of the novel, bringing in parallel story lines on Emily/Ofglen (Alexis Bledel) in early episodes, before devoting nearly entire episodes successively to the plight and memories of Serena Joy, Luke, Moira, and Nick,[13] all while providing nearly all of Offred's story line from the novel within the first season. Granted, Miller takes more liberties than Pinter in terms of the order of narrative events.

Most of the novel's plot elements that occur during the first thirty-five chapters can be found in the first five episodes, with later chapters relating Offred's trip to Jezebel's (chapters 36–39) and her final arrest after Serena learns of it (chapters 45–46) staged for the last two episodes of the season, after the new story lines for other characters have been laid out. Within that framework, the order of events is often quite different from the novel—for example, the gruesome public execution the Handmaids are made to take part in near the end of the novel (chapter 43) is moved up to the very first episode, so as to have more impact on viewers and give them a broader view of the depraved world of Gilead from the start. Very few plot elements are left out of the first season, which ends on the very last lines of the novel, as if completing the adaptation. When writing the second TV season, most of which is not from the novel, Miller cleverly culled the few events he had skipped over in the first season and found ways to give them more impact—for example, the Prayvaganza ceremony to stage the marriages of child brides (chapters 33–34) is picked up in the fifth episode of season 2 ("Seeds") and given far more impact, as it is through this ceremony that Serena and the Commander, seeing Nick's affection for Offred, surprise him with a young virgin bride, Eden (Sydney Sweeney), whose presence will greatly disrupt life at the Waterfords' household.

In addition, in the series as in the novel, flashbacks abound, and time is anything but linear. This is particularly true of the first five episodes, two of which are dominated by eight flashback sequences for Offred;[14] in the second half of the season, the flashbacks continue but are more often memories by other characters (four for Serena in episode 6 of each season; an extended flashback for Luke in season 1, episode 7 that itself contains five smaller flashbacks; four for Nick in season 1, episode 8; and 5 for Moira in season 2, episode 7). Offred's flashbacks gradually disappear over time, once the series has moved far beyond the content of the novel and the focus has broadened to include many characters besides Offred.

Also, while the film had no voice-over narration, the series has it in spades, allowing full access to June/Offred's inner thoughts and struggles and making her appear even stronger than the often ambivalent Offred of the novel. Much like the use of flashbacks, voice-over narration dominates earlier episodes, but once the series moves onto new story lines for other characters, Offred's narration often only bookends an episode,[15] to then disappear completely from many later episodes,[16] again as the series breaks away from the novel and becomes a more independent work. Similarly, for the first nineteen episodes only Offred's character is permitted voice-over, clearly in keeping with the novel's first-person format, though by the tenth episode of season 2 ("The Last Ceremony") even this cardinal rule is broken when Emily, now Ofroy, is briefly allowed voice-over. Structurally, then, the series' showrunners sought strong "fidelity" on several levels *besides* plotline (time shifts, subjective point of view, exposure to Offred's inner struggle, etc.), while making the protagonist even stronger and more decidedly feminist, and opening the story up to the experiences, past and present, of many other characters.

HITTING THE MARK (OR NOT) THROUGH AESTHETICS AND REFERENCING

There are other aspects of the 1990 film that have less to do with Pinter and the screenplay and more to do with aesthetic and directorial choices made by Schlöndorff, and though the intentions may have been noble, again the results were quite disappointing. Aesthetically, the film would have surely been quite different had the original director, award-winning British filmmaker Karel Reisz, stayed on the project. Reisz, who had successfully worked with Pinter on the award-winning film adaptation of *The French Lieutenant's Woman* in 1981, wanted this adaptation to be one of dark realism,[17] perhaps more in line with the dark dystopian world of Radford's then-recent *1984* and with his own trademark style of uncompromising realism. When Reisz was unable to get funding for the thousands of extras he wanted for the Salvaging scene, he left the project, and Pinter soon followed suit, leaving his screenplay in the hands of Schlöndorff and of Atwood for eventual rewrites.[18]

Schlöndorff replaced Reisz and had in mind a more cost-effective "expressionist" approach.[19] He thus chose to use setting, lighting, costumes, and color coding to delineate characters and their emotions, along with ubiquitous symbols and visual patterning (including many new logos for the castes in Gilead and the all-seeing Eye of Providence, no longer simply on the back of the dollar bill but at the center of the flag of Gilead and noticeably in the background during certain rituals involving the Handmaids). Schlöndorff even brought in the renowned American neo-expressionist artist Jennifer Bartlett for conceptual advice on the film. The result, which often borders on the aesthetics of an expressionist morality play that turns into a somewhat hackneyed love story between Offred and Nick, is a far cry from the dark, disturbing realism and uncomfortable scenes of oppression and abuse that characterize the recent TV series.

Finally, another key difference between Schlöndorff's approach and that of Miller is the extent to which each adaptation is also grounded in social issues of its own time. The American film scholar Robert Stam stresses the importance of this phenomenon in all adaptations, going so far as to define the very term *adaptation* as a "work of re-accentuation," for the ambient social discourse at the time of the adaptation inevitably colors content and social criticism found in the source work.[20] For example, to his credit, Schlöndorff, gives slightly more focus on the plight of African Americans in Gilead than we find in the novel, creating a disturbing new scene early in the film in which we see the so-called "Children of Ham" (black people) being separated from whites at a "sorting center," loaded like cattle onto buses and shipped off to their own territory—a scene surely meant to evoke images of the transport of Jews to concentration camps during the Holocaust and a strong metaphor to show history repeating itself with another ethnic group.[21]

The above-mentioned sorting scene is in fact part of a much larger trend in Schlöndorff's film, for the filmmaker on the whole does not seek to ground his work in the social strife of the time of filming—quite the contrary, as he sets up a vast network of visual referencing calling back to Nazi Germany. Schlöndorff was struck by the fact that themes he had dealt with in his earlier German films on World War II ("fascism, patriarchy, conformity, individualism and rebellion") were also the features of Atwood's Gilead.[22] Thus, as critic

Hans-Bernard Moëller points out, in addition to the aforementioned sorting scene that evokes the trainloads of Jews being sent to concentration camps, there are also guards overseeing hard laborers in drab clothes, searchlights around the Waterford's house, Nazi-inspired uniforms and insignias, and even the "cultificated tradition of family," which leads to a breeding program that is not that different from the Lebensborn project in Nazi Germany.[23]

Schlöndorff even went so far as to build a replica of the Berlin Wall on the set in North Carolina, though it was obscured by a blizzard that occurred on the day of filming—its connection to the real Berlin Wall that had just been brought down in 1989 being his main tie to current events.[24] The Nazi subtext is even used to transform the Commander into a far less ambiguous villain than in the novel, as the film version repeatedly brags to Offred about cleansing society of those who are "impure," "unfit," or in a word "garbage"—thereby turning the Commander into a makeshift SS Neo-Nazi avatar.

Due to the importance given to the Nazi subtext and to the limited scope that resulted from the many structural choices discussed above—and possibly a dose of self-censorship—nearly all the controversial social topics of the 1980s that the novel broaches are completely absent from the film. Atwood's novel was, of course, deeply rooted in the events of the year it was written: 1984, with all its dystopian undertones. She saw the sharp rise of pro-life movements under Republican U.S. president Ronald Reagan and the notorious "backlash" against 1970s feminists, led by conservative women much like the Commander's wife Serena Joy Waterford who used religious justification and the mantra of "family values" to fight sexual liberation and feminist advances in general. As Heather Latimer, a Canadian specialist in Women's Studies, points out, it was a time that saw pro-life bombings of women's health clinics, and states voting to restrict pornography and not only access to abortions but even information on abortions[25]—and traces of all these events can be found in the novel, but not at all in Schlöndorff's film.

CURRENT POLITICAL ECHOES IN THE TV ADAPTATION

The current TV series, on the other hand, is fully grounded in today's social strife, and particularly with struggles in the United States under Donald Trump's presidency. More in line with today's world of African American and the Black Lives Matter protests, and the #MeToo movement, themes of racism and interracial marriage as well as sexual violence are brought to the forefront in the series through the many African American characters on screen—from Luke and their daughter Hannah, to Moira, to the nurse who births Hannah, to the female police officer who saves the child from kidnapping (all in the first episode of season 1), to the gay nun who helps Luke escape (in episode 7), to the country's foremost neonatologist, now forced to be a Martha, who is called on to save Janine's child (in season 2, episode 8). Similarly, the recent passage into law of same-sex marriage, the resulting conservative backlash, and controversy over adoption by same-sex couples are put into the foreground, notably through the new story lines given to Moira and Emily, and often pop up in minor characters in season 2, including a Canadian statesmen or two lonely women Emily befriends in the Colonies. The current Alt-Right movement is there as well, and Serena Joy's second-season flashbacks to her career as a conservative spokesman are a clear nod to Ann Coulter and Tomi Lahren and other far-right female talking heads speaking on college campuses and sparking violent protest.

Of course, the feminist movement reflected in the series is not that of the 1970s, but of the current #Me Too and Time's Up movements, along with the Pussy Hat Protests and the Women's Marches after President Donald Trump's election, as are the current attacks on Planned Parenthood Clinics and closings of abortion clinics under his presidency. The series is "woke" in a way the 1990 film could never have dared to be, and this "re-accentuation" firmly grounds the 1985 novel in 2017 and thereafter. As if to drive this point home, the series inserts modern-day references into Atwood's masterpiece (including Tinder apps, online banking, and Airbnb) and adds a few metafictional touches, including a lightning-quick cameo by Atwood herself as an Aunt who violently slaps a disobedient June on her first day at the Red Center (in the very first episode) and Offred later remembering one of the author's most famous quotes ("Men are afraid women will make fun of them. Women are afraid men will kill them"), without specifying the source.[26] The target audience of the series seems to be those with an acute awareness of today's social struggles and of Atwood's recognition as a figurehead for those struggles.[27]

Comparing the 1990 film to the 2017/2018 series, in a classroom or elsewhere, may not seem like much of a fair fight. Among other things, the series' showrunners benefit from higher production values, far more screen-time than a two-hour movie, and a more permissive film and television landscape that allows for starker depictions of the sex, violence, and the controversial social themes of the novel. Yet, Pinter and Schlöndorff had a system in place and fidelity in mind, demonstrating that even a so-called "bad adaptation" is worth taking a look at, as it highlights the difficulty anyone making an adaptation faces—How does one deal with subjective point-of-view and time shifts? What should be cut and what should be kept, and in what order? Should new story lines or symbols or subtexts be added, and if so which ones? How much "re-accentuation" of the source work would allow for an adaptation that both rings of fidelity with the original novel and is an independent work grounded in its own time? Miller and his team, when creating the current Hulu series, seem to have found effective answers to all these questions, whereas Pinter and Schlöndorff—much like Atwood's character Serena Joy—seem to have allowed the noblest of intentions to trap them in a system that ended up undermining the very ideals that they had fought for.

NOTES

1. Though the field of adaptation studies first came into the fore circa 1996, notably with the publication of Brian McFarlane's *Novel to Film: An Introduction to the Theory of Adaptation* (Oxford: Clarendon Press), it was nearly ten years later that it gained worldwide attention, notably with the publication of seminal works by Robert Stam (*Literature and Film: A Guide to the Theory and Practice of Film Adaptation* [Malden, MA: Blackwell Publishing, 2005]) and Linda Hutcheon (*A Theory of Adaptation* [New York & London: Routledge, 2006]), among many other scholars, all of whom seek to create a common language and methodology with which to analyze both a literary work and its subsequent adaptations, thereby blurring the traditional boundaries between literary theory and film theory, while opening up the notion of adaptation to any other chosen medium.

2. The independent and international dimension to the film was the result of a very problematic production process from the start. Atwood sold the rights to adapt her best-seller almost immediately, in 1986, to little-known producer Daniel Wilson, mainly because Wilson had secured British playwright Harold Pinter as screenwriter and Karel Reisz, a famous Czechoslovakian refugee turned British filmmaker, as director. The pair had been the toast of Hollywood a few years prior with their adaptation of *The French Lieutenant's Woman*, which starred Meryl Streep and Jeremy Irons and garnered five Oscar nominations in 1981. However, as Canadian journalist Sheldon Teitelbaum explains, Wilson was met with "a wall of ignorance, hostility and indifference" when he proposed the project to major American film studios, who saw the project as too overtly feminist and felt it would result in "a film for and about women [that] would be lucky to make it to video" let alone the big screen (Sophie Gilbert, "The Forgotten *Handmaid's Tale*," *The Atlantic*, March 24, 2015). In the end, Wilson managed to get funding from Cinecom Entertainment group and a handful of other small production companies, ensuring a low-budget film. This in turn resulted in Reisz, who had planned a big-budget film with thousands of extras, quitting the project, soon followed by Pinter who claimed he was too "exhausted" to rework his screenplay for a new director and instead left the script in the hands of Atwood herself, confident she would not betray her own masterpiece (Steven Gale, *Sharp Cut*, 318–19). Wilson then found a replacement director in Volker Schlöndorff, a famed icon of the New German Cinema, who both felt a strong affinity to themes in the novel and hoped to use the English-language film project to break into Hollywood (Gilbert). He would soon learn that Hollywood had little interest in the project, and was disheartened when the actress first slated to play Offred, Sigourney Weaver,

dropped out due to pregnancy, and no other American star would agree to take on the role, most pointing to their "fear of the stigma of being associated with such an explicitly feminist work" (Gilbert). In the end, Schlöndorff gave up on finding a Hollywood star for the role and took on British actress and activist Natasha Richardson to play Offred.

3. Mary K. Kirtz, "Teaching Literature through Film: An Interdisciplinary Approach to *Surfacing* and *The Handmaid's Tale*," in *Approaches to Teaching Atwood's The Handmaid's Tale and Other Works*, edited by Sharon R. Wilson, Thomas B. Friedman, and Shannon Hengen (New York: MLA, 1996), 141.

4. See for example E. Ann Kaplan's *Climate Trauma: Foreseeing the Future in Dystopian Film and Fiction* (New Brunswick, NJ: Rutgers UP, 2016), 59–78, or Heather Latimer's *Reproductive Acts: Sexual Politics in North American Fiction and Film* (Montreal: McGill-Queen's University Press, 2013), 32–53.

5. Radford's film proudly touts this feat in its closing credits: "This film was photographed in and around London during the period April-June 1984, the exact time and setting imagined by the author." See also I. Q. Hunter's *British Science Fiction Cinema* (London: Routledge, 1999), 157.

6. Brian McFarlane, *Novel to Film: An Introduction to the Theory of Adaptation* (New York: Oxford University Press, 1996), 12.

7. *The Handmaid's Tale*, "After," Season 2, Episode 7, directed by Kari Skogland, written by Lynn Renee Maxcy, Hulu, May 30, 2018; and *The Handmaid's Tale*, "Women's Work," Season 2, Episode 8, directed by Kari Skogland, written by Nina Fiore and John Herrera, Hulu, June 6, 2018.

8. In both the novel and the TV series, Offred's pre-Gilead memories of her mother and their decidedly different takes on feminism are a key vehicle to allowing the reader/viewer access to the main character's (and perhaps Atwood's) nuanced notions of feminism and seem to represent the ideological clash that occurred between second- and third-wave feminists in the late twentieth century. In the novel, there are five chapters presenting at least one flashback to Offred's relationship with her mother: memories of walks in the park with her as a child and her mother's activism (chapter 7); a memory of her first days at the Red Center, when she spotted her mother in a documentary about supposedly dangerous feminists before the purge, which reminds her how much she misses arguing with her mother about feminism (chapter 20); a flashback to watching a Holocaust documentary with her mother on the wife of a Nazi who did not see her spouse as a monster (chapter 24); another of her mother in a feminist march in the 1970s (chapter 28); and finally a moment when Moira informs her, in a restroom at Jezebel's, that she has seen a video of her mother among many "Unwomen" struggling in the Colonies, which leaves Offred both happy to learn she is alive and sad to imagine how her exile must have destroyed her fighting spirit (chapter 39). The first season of the TV series, which covered most events of the novel, had conspicuously left June's mother out of the story, with only an oblique reference to her as Mr. Whitford (Tim Ransom), who nearly succeeds in getting June and her family across the Canadian border before getting caught and hanged, is said to be a friend of her mother's (*The Handmaid's Tale*, "The Other Side," Season 1, Episode 7, directed by Floria Sigismondi, written by Lynn Renee Maxcy, Hulu, May 24,

2017). The second season of the series fills that gap, however, bringing in respected Broadway actress Cherry Jones in the role of Holly Maddox, June's mother, for two separate episodes. In the third episode of the second season ("Baggage"), most of the above-mentioned flashbacks from the novel find their way into the series, as Holly is seen taking her young daughter to a Take Back the Night feminist march in the 1970s, later showing her disapproval at both June's career choice (an editor rather than an activist) and her decision to marry a soon-to-be-divorced Luke, and then, in a memory of one of June's first days at the Red Center, is seen by Moira and her daughter in a documentary on "Unwomen" suffering in the Colonies (thereby combining elements of chapters 20 and 39 of the novel). The series then takes her mother's importance to June one step further in the eleventh episode of the second season—indeed entitled "Holly"—though the new flashbacks to Holly's support during June's first pregnancy and Hannah's birth, and the character's renewed importance, culminate in June's naming her new baby, birthed on her own in the worst possible circumstances, "Holly." One wonders if, in the coming third season, the series will continue to reinforce the character of Holly by having her found to be alive and well and fighting the good fight in the Colonies. Schlöndorff's film, however, by completely stripping the story of Offred's mother—which film critic Hans-Bernard Moëller feels is the film's most regrettable omission (261)—leaves no possibility for such nuanced discussion of feminism.

9. Steven Gale, *Sharp Cut: Harold Pinter's Screenplays and the Artistic Process* (Lexington: University Press of Kentucky, 2003), 239. Gale notes how this lack of voice-over worked for his 1981 adaptation of *The French Lieutenant's Woman* but resulted in Adrian Lyne rejecting Pinter's screenplay for *Lolita* in 1996. Like Atwood's novel, those of Fowles and of Nabokov rely heavily on internal monologue.

10. Volker Schlöndorff, Interview with Jochen Schütze, *Volker Schlöndorff's Cinema: Adaptation, Politics and the 'Movie-Appropriate,'* edited by Hans-Bernard Moëller and George Lellis (Carbondale: Southern Illinois Press, 2002), 79, 253.

11. Moëller and Lellis, *Volker Schlöndorff's Cinema*, 260.

12. Marianne Barnett, "Atwood's Seduction: *The Handmaid's Tale,*" Rocky Mountain MLA Convention (University of Utah, Salt Lake City, October 12, 1990), 9–12.

13. *The Handmaid's Tale*, "A Woman's Place," Season 1, Episode 6, directed by Floria Sigismondi, written by Wendy Straker Hauser, Hulu, May 17, 2017; "The Other Side," Season 1, Episode 7; "Jezebel's," Season 1, Episode 8, directed by Kate Dennis, written by Kira Snyder, Hulu, May 31, 2017.

14. *The Handmaid's Tale*, "Offred," Season 1, Episode 1, directed by Reed Morano, written by Bruce Miller, Hulu, April 26, 2017; and "Nolite Te Bastardes Carborundorum," Season 1, Episode 4, directed by Mike Barker, written by Leila Gerstein, Hulu, May 3, 2017.

15. *The Handmaid's Tale*, "A Woman's Place," "The Other Side," and "Night," Season 1, Episode 10, directed by Kari Skogland, written by Bruce Miller, Hulu, June 14, 2017.

16. *The Handmaid's Tale*, "The Bridge," Season 1, Episode 9, directed by Kate Dennis, written by Eric Tuchman, Hulu, June 7, 2017; "Seeds," Season 2, Episode 5,

directed by Mike Barker, written by Kira Snyder, Hulu, May 16, 2018; "First Blood," Season 2, Episode 6, directed by Mike Barker, written by Eric Tuchman, Hulu, May 23, 2018; "After."

17. Gale, *Sharp Cut*, 318.

18. Gale, *Sharp Cut*, 319.

19. Expressionism—a modernist technique that can be found in painting, literature, dance, drama, and film—seeks to move away from concrete representation of external reality and find more abstract and symbolic ways of outwardly depicting the subjective inner world of emotions. Edvard Munch's famous 1893 painting *The Scream* is often cited as an early work of expressionism. In expressionist films, symbolic settings and costumes, abstract dialogue and referencing, and scores of other stylistic devices distance us from any concrete or straightforward representation of the "real." Schlöndorff's adaptation employs many such stylistic devices.

20. Stam, *Literature and Film*, 46.

21. Though some may find Schlöndorff's use of strong images evoking the Jewish Holocaust experience to stress the plight of African Americans in general and white women in particular somewhat problematic, the film has not been accused of cultural appropriation on that point, perhaps because the subtext of the Jewish plight is so strong and pervasive in the film as to seem to be included among its themes. The same, however, cannot be said for Atwood's novel. Though the novel more openly deals with the plight of Jews in Gilead—who are given the possibility to go to Israel, convert to Christianity, or risk death by hanging in the public square wearing a yellow Star of David (chapter 31)—it is Atwood's supposed cultural appropriation of the experience of black slaves for white Handmaids and Marthas, without focusing on the plight of blacks, that has drawn ire among some critics. Ben Merrimon, a professor of sociology at the University of Chicago, calls the novel "a politically hazardous fantasy" for that very reason, a fantasy "fraught with white privilege" (*Women's Issues in Margaret Atwood's* The Handmaid's Tale, ed. David E. Nelson, [Farmington Hills, MI: Greenhaven Press, 2012], 42–45). The recent TV series, to its merit, adds scores of black characters and makes the plight of African Americans a key focus.

22. Moëller and Lellis, *Volker Schlöndorff's Cinema*, 248.

23. Moëller and Lellis, *Volker Schlöndorff's Cinema*, 249–50.

24. Brian Johnson, "Returning to a New Berlin," *MacLean's* (February 26, 1990), 44.

25. Latimer, *Reproductive Acts*, 39–40.

26. This popular quotation is in fact a slight paraphrasing of Atwood's recollection of a conversation she had with a male friend, whom she asked why men were afraid of women, to which he responded, "They are afraid women will laugh at them." Atwood later asked a group of women why they were afraid of men, and the response was "We're afraid of being killed." The anecdote is recounted in the *Minneapolis Star Tribune* (March 27, 1998), 20A, and it is referenced in the series in the eighth episode of the second season, entitled "Women's Work."

27. Margaret Atwood is often seen as a feminist icon, although she herself hesitates to use the label as she sees the term as rather ambiguous, and as she does not necessarily seek to advance the feminist cause when she writes a novel. Atwood is

more than a novelist—she is also a poetess, a literary critic, an inventor, and a political activist for both feminist and environmentalist causes. In most interviews, like one with Maya Oppenheimer for *The Independent* in 2017, Atwood claims there are as many varieties of feminism as there are of Christianity, and that there are many feminists whose views she cannot tolerate—such as those who think women are always right or are better than men, or those who espouse right-wing politics on other matters [Maya Oppenheimer, "Margaret Atwood: Feminism Is Not About Believing Women Are Always Right," *The Independent* (July 18, 2017)]. However, in spite of her reluctance to take up the mantle of today's feminism, readers have long been drawn to the feminist dimensions of her novels—from early proto-feminist works such as *The Edible Woman* (1969) and *Surfacing* (1972), to more openly feminist works such as *The Handmaid's Tale* (1985) and *Alias Grace* (1996), both of which depict strong women fighting against a starkly repressive patriarchy (the latter in the nineteenth century, the former in a dystopian future), and both of which have gained wide exposure through 2017 adaptations as television series. Since 2016, *The Handmaid's Tale*'s renewed popularity and return to the best-seller list—prompted as much by excitement over the Hulu series as by the rise of Donald Trump and his misogynist worldview—have been co-opted by the #MeToo movement and feminist protests worldwide—with, for example, the appearance of silent protestors dressed as Handmaids at the U.S. Senate confirmation hearings for Supreme Court Justice Brett Kavanaugh in 2018, or of actresses like Emma Watson, who hid copies of the novel around Paris in the summer of 2017 as a strong pro-feminist gesture. The result is that Atwood is now perceived as the figurehead of modern-day feminism, in spite of her personal caveats.

WORKS CITED

Atwood, Margaret. *The Handmaid's Tale*. London: Jonathan Cape Ltd., 1986.

Barnett, Marianne. "Atwood's Seduction: *The Handmaid's Tale.*" Rocky Mountain MLA Convention, University of Utah, Salt Lake City, October 12, 1990.

Gale, Steven H. *Sharp Cut: Harold Pinter's Screenplays and the Artistic Process*. Lexington: University Press of Kentucky, 2003.

Gilbert, Sophie. "The Forgotten *Handmaid's Tale*" *The Atlantic*, March 24, 2015.

Johnson, Brian. "Returning to a New Berlin" *MacLean's* (February 26, 1990): 44–45.

Kaplan, E. Ann. *Climate Trauma: Foreseeing the Future in Dystopian Film and Fiction*. New Brunswick, NJ: Rutgers University Press, 2016.

Kirtz, Mary K. "Teaching Literature through Film: An Interdisciplinary Approach to *Surfacing* and *The Handmaid's Tale.*" In *Approaches to Teaching Atwood's The Handmaid's Tale and Other Works*. Edited by Sharon R. Wilson, Thomas B. Friedman, and Shannon Hengen, 140–145. New York: MLA, 1996.

Latimer, Heather. *Reproductive Acts: Sexual Politics in North American Fiction and Film*. Montreal: McGill-Queen's University Press, 2013.

McFarlane, Brian. *Novel to Film: An Introduction to the Theory of Adaptation.* New York: Oxford University Press, 1996.

Merrimon, Ben. "*The Handmaid's Tale* Addresses Sexism and Ignores Racism." In *Women's Issues in Margaret Atwood's* The Handmaid's Tale, edited by David E. Nelson, 42–45. Farmington Hills, MI: Greenhaven Press, 2012.

Moëller, Hans Bernhard, and George Lellis. *Volker Schlöndorff's Cinema: Adaptation, Politics and the 'Movie-Appropriate.'* Carbondale: Southern Illinois Press, 2002.

Schlöndorff, Volker. "Weinen ist so billig! Interview mit v. Schlondorff." Int. 1990: 78–79.

Stam, Robert. *Literature and Film: A Guide to the Theory and Practice of Film Adaptation.* Malden, MA: Blackwell Publishing, 2005.

FILM AND TELEVISION

The Handmaid's Tale. Directed by Volker Schlöndorff. USA / Germany, 1990.

The Handmaid's Tale. "After." Season 2, Episode 7. Directed by Kari Skogland. Written by Lynn Renee Maxcy. Hulu, May 30, 2018.

The Handmaid's Tale. "A Woman's Place." Season 1, Episode 6. Directed by Floria Sigismondi. Written by Wendy Straker Hauser. Hulu, May 17, 2017.

The Handmaid's Tale. "First Blood." Season 2, Episode 6. Directed by Mike Barker. Written by Eric Tuchman. Hulu, May 23, 2018.

The Handmaid's Tale. "Jezebel's." Season 1, Episode 8. Directed by Kate Dennis. Written by Kira Snyder. Hulu, May 31, 2017.

The Handmaid's Tale. "Night." Season 1, Episode 10. Directed by Kari Skogland. Written by Bruce Miller. Hulu, June 14, 2017.

The Handmaid's Tale. "Nolite Te Bastardes Carborundorum." Season 1, Episode 4. Directed by Mike Barker. Written by Leila Gerstein. Hulu, May 3, 2017.

The Handmaid's Tale. "Offred." Season 1, Episode 1. Directed by Reed Morano. Written by Bruce Miller. Hulu, April 26, 2017.

The Handmaid's Tale. "Seeds." Season 2, Episode 5. Directed by Mike Barker. Written by Kira Snyder. Hulu, May 16, 2018.

The Handmaid's Tale. "The Bridge." Season 1, Episode 9. Directed by Kate Dennis. Written by Eric Tuchman. Hulu, June 7, 2017.

The Handmaid's Tale. "The Other Side." Season 1, Episode 7. Directed by Floria Sigismondi. Written by Lynn Renee Maxcy. Hulu, May 24, 2017.

The Handmaid's Tale. "Women's Work." Season 2, Episode 8. Directed by Kari Skogland. Written by Nina Fiore and John Herrera. Hulu, June 6, 2018.

Chapter Eighteen

The Handmaid's Tale
The Optics of Dystopia

Ellen Grabiner

Wordplay peppers the pages of Margaret Atwood's 1985 novel, and not in the least because access to words is one of the many freedoms wrenched from women in her dystopian tale. When protagonist June is invited to join Commander Fred Waterford, her sanctioned rapist, in a game of scrabble, she luxuriates in the long-unused combinations of letters that might result in the highest scores. Atwood writes,

> Larynx, I spell. Valance. Quince. Zygote. I hold the glossy counters with their smooth edges, finger the letters. The feeling is voluptuous. This is freedom, an eyeblink of it.[1]

Voluptuousness is precisely, then, what cinematographer, Colin Watkinson, achieves in the first season of Hulu's TV adaptation of *The Handmaid's Tale*. Life in Gilead, a nation-state in which an appropriation of the biblical story of Rachel serves as the justification for state-prescribed rape and the enslavement of women, is brought into sharp relief through his singularly stunning cinematography. The series affords a glimpse into an imagined reality that today seems both frighteningly prescient and at the same time utterly impossible. Watkinson's deft handling of the filmic frame and all that it contains achieves for the eye what Atwood's protagonist had tasted in her "eyeblink" of freedom. It is my assertion that his aesthetic treatment of the series is rendered performative: the composition of each exquisite frame, the use of diffuse light and saturated color, jarring juxtapositions and temporal fluctuations together serve to adumbrate the dystopia Atwood so deftly delineated.

In the first season of the series, as well as in the novel on which it was based, the narrative begins in medias res. The worst has already happened. Women's rights—to work and own property, to read and write, to be known by one's own name, to control one's own body—were first eroded and then extinguished as a solution to a planet-wide plague of infertility. In the first episode, we are dropped into a horrifyingly vivid scene where June (Elizabeth Moss), her husband Luke (O-T Fagbenle), and their young daughter Hannah (Jordana Blake) are fleeing to Canada to escape the madness. June is captured, her child torn from her, and her husband shot.

Like any rootstock narrative, *The Handmaid's Tale* offers multiple ways in: it can be read as science fiction or a foreboding feminist fairy tale. We could attempt to untangle its twisted Old Testament hermeneutics or deconstruct its ambivalent relationship with technology. What follows here, however, is an exploration of the ways in which in this adaptation the figural speaks.[2] As Thomas Elsaesser and Malta Hagener claim in their book *Film Theory: An Introduction through the Senses*, "The eye is the privileged point of convergence for various structures of visibility."[3] In Atwood's cautionary tale, the literal and metaphorical eye are harnessed to maintain structures of appearance and to ensure the control and captivation of the women of Gilead. In Hulu's lush TV series, the cinematic eye shows us how.

SEEING: STRUCTURES OF APPEARANCE

The structures of appearance which Atwood employed in her narrative have deep philosophical antecedents, first and foremost in the thinking of Michel Foucault, specifically in his engagement with visibilities and their concomitant links to epistemology. Additionally, the thinking of Hannah Arendt and of her protégé Elizabeth Minnich also figures prominently in this analysis. Before undertaking an exploration of the ways in which those structures were concretized cinematically, I would like to briefly explore how, by imposing controls over what could be seen and what could be said, those in power in Gilead hoped to consequently control that which was not visible: thought.

In her book *Life of the Mind*, Arendt took to task the entrenched metaphysical premise that "mere" appearance masks "true" being. In her 1971 treatise, Arendt radically suggests that appearance not only doesn't obscure our true being, but rather our true being is that we are, by nature, creatures who appear.

"In this world which we enter, appearing from a nowhere, and from which we disappear into a nowhere, Being and Appearing coincide."[4] "To be alive means to be possessed by an urge toward self-display."[5] Arendt posits that we not only have the urge to show ourselves, but that we are also the requisite recipients of these necessary appearances.

Those charged with the design of Gilead's new order were only too aware of this intrinsic urge to present one's self, to be seen, but also to be the recipient of myriad appearances. If we accept Arendt's contention that our capacity to witness is an essential element of who we are, by extension, removing that ability removes access to our being.

At the Red Center, where Handmaids were indoctrinated, they were first instructed to keep their gaze down; they were told not to "look," and were forbidden from making eye contact with each other and with the Aunts who were complicit in their programming. Walking, talking, eating, they were to always train their focus to the ground. The only exception to this perpetual downward gaze was enacted during the monthly ceremony. Restrained by the wrists, head pressed to the groin of the commander's barren wife, their eyes flew heavenward, averting a visual collision with the man who was "ritually" pummeling them.

By design, the white wings the Handmaids were required to wear functioned like blinders. Blinkered, they were cut off from one another as they walked side by side on their way to the market. Not only could they not see each other as they promenaded along the river, but according to Arendt, they were consequently also cut off from themselves and ultimately from their own ability to think.

If Arendt is correct, rubbing out our ability to appear erases our humanity. The men of Gilead took great pains to impose these structures that would ensure the impossibility that any woman—Handmaid, Wife, Martha, Aunt, or Jezebel—could think for herself.

Yet paradoxically, there were some appearances the Handmaids were forced to receive. The wall along the river where they sometimes walked on their way to and from the market was rife with the rotting corpses of those who had transgressed. Because words—writing and reading—were forbidden to women, groceries in the marketplace were denoted by colorful illustrations. So, too, the decaying bodies, were marked with simple signs to communicate the particularity of their crimes. This one a priest, this one a "gender traitor," this one a doctor who continued to perform abortions, and so on.

SAYING

If the structures of appearance, the ones forced and the ones forbidden, work in tandem in the service of oppression, then the artifice of stipulated social intercourse ensures that no human connection is possible. This dehumanization begins as the Handmaid's names were taken from them: they are known only as "of" their commander; for example, Offred, Ofglen, Ofwarren, etcetera.

When Offred/June (Elisabeth Moss) and her shopping partner Ofglen, (Alexis Bledel) greet each other each morning, the conversation is always the same.

"May the Lord Open."

"Blessed be the fruit."

"We've been sent good weather."

"Which I receive with Joy."

"The war is going well."

"By his hand."

And the ubiquitous parting quip, "Under His Eye."[6]
Rote phrases, like "Praised be his bounty" when there are oranges to be had in the market, serve to maintain a level of banality that Elizabeth Minnich suggests enables and perpetuates evil.

There are all sorts of conventional banalities ready to hand that work very well . . . in service of larger systems. . . . Evils . . . thrive when places, peoples, meanings have become enclosed, by walls, logics, bureaucracies, authoritative "knowledge." These enablers too, turn out to be seeded in everyday life.[7]

*Handmaids are grateful and excited to have oranges available for purchase.
Screenshot from Hulu television series.*

Sanctioned snippets exemplify those enclosed exchanges; banalities buttressed by a bevy of armed enforcers; everywhere the Handmaids turn are "guardians" packing automatic weapons, lest the Handmaids turn intractable. Along with these machine guns, the lack of authentic generative language keeps the Handmaids isolated, alone, unknown, and unthinking. If we presume Foucault's notion that we construct knowledge by combining what is uniquely visible and what we are uniquely able to articulate, in this fictional historical stratum, knowing becomes impossible. When conversation consists of only contrivances, each Handmaid believes the other to be "a pious little shit,"[8] and neither has any real knowledge of the other's being.

Ironically, while the coincidence of appearance and being is out of reach, surveillance is at hand. As Offred thinks of her partner Ofglen, "She is my spy, and I am hers."[9] Handmaids not only held suspicions about their partners, but were also aware of the ubiquitous "Eyes," as the official Gilead spies were called. Bypassing the centrally placed watcher reminiscent of Bentham's Panopticon, an "Eye" was embedded in every household, on every street. Known to be ever present if never actually identified, the constant surveillance of the Eyes took its toll.

CINEMATOGRAPHIC EYE

Detailing the extensive dehumanization of the Handmaids—the "red tagging" of fertile women, eyes and limbs removed as archaic punishments meted out and rationalized by scripture, and so on—is beyond the scope of this chapter, so I want now to shift the focus and to look at the ways in which the cinematographic choices of Colin Watkinson perform these structures of appearance and entice/invite the audience into the evil of their banality.

Watching the first season of the Hulu TV series, I was left breathless; simply wowed. As I watched and rewatched episodes, hoping to deconstruct, to understand what I was seeing, I would find myself in the same place—a wordless, thoughtless place, where my only impulse was to grab a pencil and draw what I was seeing. I felt compelled to map the ways in which Watkinson had rigidly composed each shot. In my continued efforts to understand what the cinematographer had accomplished, it occurred to me that I was experiencing the effect of inhabiting Benjamin's unconsciously penetrated space. I couldn't access it on the conscious level, most immediately because I found it stunning. In other words, I was stunned. Things of rare and overwhelming beauty take our breath away. They stun us speechless. Watkinson's taut and luscious imagery, in effect, as Benjamin suggests, bypasses our intellect and reaches for the part of us that is beneath or beyond words, and consequently thought. When Watkinson shifts the temporality to show us rain, the ceremonious rape, or a salvaging[10] in slow motion, we are captivated. Captivated in the sense of beguiled, entranced, but more importantly, like the Handmaids, taken captive. All we can do is respond viscerally to what we are seeing.

Riveted and at the mercy of our senses, we are doubly stunned as we recoil at the horrors perpetrated against these women, and thrice again, as we witness the literal stunning—the use of cattle-prods to control and constrain the Handmaids. Confronted by the formality of rigidly structured, tight shots, we find ourselves in so close that there is no room for thoughts to form. Just as we begin to catch our stunned breath, Watkinson jump-shifts to a birds-eye view, offering long shots of serried Handmaids. The formations of white-capped, red figures evoke Descartes's contemplation from his window of the man on the street below. How is it, he wonders, that we can be sure that what we are seeing are not automatons? The red and white shapes, now abstracted and reduced, work in conjunction with one another on a purely figural level, and point to the dehumanization of these Handmaids, and the resultant loss of their value as individuals, in the face of a concerted, coordinated attack on all that they had been.

Watkinson is so taken with geometry that he often arranges his shots with perfect symmetry, yet somehow manages to avoid the expected static result. The monthly rape ceremony is shot in a canopied bed, framed by vulva-shaped draperies and a headboard, flanked by the phallic four-posts. His camera angles and unexpected intrusion of ultra slo-mo render the ritualized rape ludicrous, especially in juxtaposition to the majestic stateliness of the marital suite. Many of his establishing shots, both straight on and from above, depict inkblot compositions, marked by a flash of red, to tip the balance.

Watkinson employs juxtapositions like Foucault might have, giving us before and after pictures.[11] These alert the viewer to what had been "ordinary" before, and what, inconceivably, has now become the ordinary, as Aunt Lydia (Ann Dowd) from the Red Center warned. Revealing how things were once made visible, how things were given to be seen, Watkinson demonstrates the ways in which slippage occurs, moving us from one system of thought to another. We watch a vibrant June the first time she makes love to her husband, Luke, laughing playfully above a tinkling piano score, and then, with a rupture in the sound track, we are abruptly brought to present-day Gilead. Nick Blaine (Max Minghella), the Waterfords' driver and an Eye, has been recruited to add his sperm into the mix and assumes the position in a starkly silent scene, broken only by the sound of his belt buckle clanking and the creaking of the bedsprings.

The citizenry of Gilead is acutely aware of the extent to which visibilities inform epistemologies. When the Mexican delegation comes to Boston to finalize a trade agreement—fertile women are being exchanged for Mexican chocolates—Handmaids are enlisted to scrub the blood off the wall where the bodies have been hanging. Corpses whose sole purpose was to deter rebellion are removed. On some level the Leaders of the Faithful remember a time when this was not ordinary. Transfixed by the blood of those who have stained it, Ofwarren (Madeline Brewer) claims that the wall "looks kinda' weird without all those dead bodies on it, doesn't it? I guess you get used to things being one way."[12]

Recognizing the importance of how things seem and their connections to what can be known, Mrs. Serena Joy Waterford (Yvonne Strahovski) insists that Aunt Lydia remove the damaged Handmaids from the banquet hall before the delegates arrive. Those who had a limb severed or an eye gouged out would make plain the horrors of their reality. When Lydia pleads for them to be allowed to attend the fete, Mrs. Waterford explains, "You don't put the bruised apples at the top of the crate? Do you?"[13]

While there is much more left to unpack—the amazing score and sound track, for example—in a thorough discussion of this adaptation, there was one aesthetic treatment that gave me pause, and I'd like to address it here. Throughout the series, Watkinson consistently employs diffuse light: it streams in the windows of the Waterfords' home, it ignites the insects abuzz along the wall by the river; it obscures, reveals, softens. The way the light barely illuminates the kitchen, Offred's bedroom, the bath, evokes a Vermeer painting. This treatment was so insistent and pervasive, I struggled to understand its import. What, precisely, was Watkinson attempting to signify with this misty, mote-filled lighting? Other than the fact that it was, without a doubt, visually stunning. I inadvertently stumbled, then, upon this quote from Gilles Deleuze, writing on Foucault:

> We must break things open. Visibilities are not forms of objects, nor even forms that would show up under light, but rather forms of luminosity which are created by the light itself and allow a thing or object to exist only as a flash, sparkle or shimmer.[14]

If luminosity is diminished or extinguished, as Minnich warns, things, ideas remain enclosed. There is no flash or sparkle or shimmer for the imprisoned women of Gilead. To ensure that we see this, Watkinson has no choice but to visually break things open.

EPILOGUE: *THE HANDMAID'S TALE*, SEASON 2

As of this writing, Hulu's *The Handmaid's Tale* has just finished airing the
last episode of season 2. Colin Watkinson, director of cinematography and
winner of the Emmy for Outstanding Cinematography for a Single-camera
Series for season 1, continues to construct visually breath-taking frames in
season 2. Even as the writers have left the armature of Atwood's story behind,
Watkinson does not disappoint. He pulls together new palettes to articulate
life in the Colonies, the hospital, and the ritual of a mass Handmaid funeral.
However, in addition to relying on a sumptuous slow and close cinematography to continue to uncover Atwood's imagined dystopian landscape, Watkinson elevates his filmic craft, utilizing visibilities to reveal the humanity of
the characters caught in Gilead's web.

There are many such smaller narrative arcs sitting within the larger story—
for example, the volumes articulated in one small momentary juxtaposition
of the Handmaid's mouths muzzled as they are led to the gallows, while the
guard dogs' jaws snarl freely. Here I'd like to focus on one standout vignette
that occurs during the time June is hiding out at *The Boston Globe* facility,
awaiting transport out of Gilead.[15] Alongside the powerful symbolism of the
now defunct New England paper of record, and the larger implications of
"words" being literally stopped and hidden away, June discovers that *The
Globe* Offices doubled as a slaughterhouse (see chapter 10 by Theodora Ruhs
in this volume).

In a disturbing and wordless series of scenes, we watch June explore the
very human, very individual spaces in which *Globe* employees worked.
Walking from desk to desk, June encounters photos, mementos, favorite
mugs, children's artwork, all the flotsam and jetsam one would expect to be
tacked to the cubicle walls in which one spends one's workday. Only a single
high-heeled shoe, left lying on the floor, as if an office Cinderella had to make
a run for it, hints at anything other than a normal workplace.

Juxtaposed to this quotidian scene, is one in which June comes across a pa-
rade of nooses strung from the rafters and a bullet-riddled wall against which
the stains of numbers of people's blood remains.

At first, horrified, June can't bear the thought of remaining in this place
where so many lives were taken. But slowly, over time, June gathers the
unremarkable treasures from each desk, bringing them together at the foot of
the bloody wall. There, she arranges photos, stuffed animals, and the other
trappings of an ordinary life barely remembered; amid candles, she creates a
shrine to those whose lives ended in the service of collecting, editing, and dis-
seminating the news. In one particularly poignant moment, Watkinson shows
June scooping up the matching high-heeled shoe beneath the wall where the

*June creates a shrine for those who once worked in the newspaper's office
to commemorate their lives.
Screenshot from Hulu television series.*

executions took place. She tenderly places the two shoes next to one another in the circle of items that point to lives once lived. When the two shoes are rejoined, something broken is made whole again. Watkinson's deft visual storytelling is already the prayer that June utters as she brings lights into the circle of her shrine.

NOTES

1. Margaret Atwood, *The Handmaid's Tale* (Toronto: McClelland and Stewart, 1985).

2. Thomas Elsaesser and Malte Hagener, *Film Theory: An Introduction through the Senses* (New York: Routledge, 2010), 82–107.

3. Elsaesser and Hagener, *Film Theory*, 83.

4. Hannah Arendt, *Life of the Mind* (San Diego, New York, London: Harcourt Brace & Company, 1971), 9.

5. Arendt, *Life of the Mind*, 21.

6. *The Handmaid's Tale*, Season 1, created by Bruce Miller, Hulu, April, 26, 2017.

7. Elizabeth Minnich, *The Evil of Banality: On the Life and Death Importance of Thinking* (Lanham, MD: Rowman and Littlefield, 2016), 12.

8. *The Handmaid's Tale*, Season 1, Episode 1, created by Bruce Miller.

9. *The Handmaid's Tale*, Season 1, Episode 1, created by Bruce Miller.

10. The salvaging was a ceremony in which someone convicted of a crime—rape, endangering a child—was ritually stoned by the community of Handmaids.

11. John Rajchman, "Foucault's Art of Seeing," *October* 44, (Spring 1988): 90.

12. *The Handmaid's Tale*, "A Woman's Place," Season 1, Episode 6, directed by Floria Sigismondi, written by Wendy Straker Hauser, Hulu, May 17, 2017.

13. *The Handmaid's Tale*, "A Woman's Place," Season 1, Episode 6.

14. Gilles Deleuze, *Foucault* (Minneapolis: University of Minnesota Press, 1986), 52.

15. *The Handmaid's Tale*, "Unwomen," Season 2, Episode 2, directed by Mike Barker, written by Bruce Miller, Hulu, April 25, 2018.

WORKS CITED

Arendt, Hannah. *Life of the Mind*. San Diego, New York, London: Harcourt Brace & Company, 1971.

Atwood, Margaret. *The Handmaid's Tale*. Toronto: McClelland and Stewart, 1985.

Benjamin, Walter. "The Work of Art in the Age of Mechanical Reproduction." In *The Continental Aesthetics Reader*, edited by Clive Cazeaux, 322–43. New York: Routledge, 2000.

Deleuze, Gilles. *Foucault*. Minneapolis: University of Minnesota Press, 1986.

Elsaesser, Thomas, and Malte Hagener *Film Theory: An Introduction through the Senses*. New York: Routledge, 2010.

Minnich, Elizabeth. *The Evil of Banality: On the Life and Death Importance of Thinking*. Lanham, MD: Rowman and Littlefield, 2016.

Rajchman, John. "Foucault's Art of Seeing." *October* 44 (Spring 1988).

FILMS AND TELEVISION

The Handmaid's Tale. Created by Bruce Miller. Seasons 1–2. Hulu, 2017/2018.

The Handmaid's Tale. "A Women's Place." Season 1, Episode 6. Directed by Floria Sigismondi. Written by Wendy Straker Hauser. Hulu, May 17, 2017.

The Handmaid's Tale. "Unwomen." Season 2, Episode 2. Directed by Mike Barker. Written by Bruce Miller. Hulu, April 25, 2018.

Section IV:

INTERDISCIPLINARY LESSONS
LEARNED FROM
THE HANDMAID'S TALE

Chapter Nineteen

Offred's Journey through Gilead

Subverting Oppositional Discourse through First Person Performed Narrative

Sheila Siragusa

The #MeToo[1] and Time's Up[2] movements have burst upon the national scene and created an unprecedented shift of attitude toward the acceptability of violence against women. How can we use live theater to keep up the momentum of this radical change in American culture? The extremity of our political moment has created a climate in which the possibility of discourse about opposing viewpoints has become severely compromised.[3] Using the example of the two Hulu TV series' adaptations of Margaret Atwood's *The Handmaid's Tale* (2017 and 2018),[4] this chapter explores the use of a first person narrator whose survival relies upon strict observation of critical silence to subvert the problem of more direct discussion addressing violence against women. Theater's[5] innate capacity to create an immediate and empathic journey for the viewer is the perfect medium through which this form of first person performed narrative can continue to awaken audiences.

In October 2017, the *New York Times* released an article reporting that producer and cofounder Harvey Weinstein of the Weinstein Company paid out settlements for accusations of sexual misconduct by three women over a twenty-year period.[6] What resulted was an explosion of reports against Weinstein and an enormous number of leaders in the entertainment industry,[7] in politics, banking, sports, and publishing, to name just a few. It sparked an unprecedented social media movement in which millions of women joined together to stand in solidarity against the power of a culture that has accepted and even protected behaviors that harm women. In the process, the #MeToo and the Time's Up movement educated us about the prevalence of sexual violence against women. Men saw their sisters, mothers, wives, and daughters add their names to the ever-growing list of women who said, "Me too." Social media platforms ignited with compassionate posts.

This awareness was a long time in coming. It wasn't until 1975 that the term sexual harassment was coined.[8] Since then, women have continued to shine a light on the problem of sexual violence of all kinds, often at the cost of their careers and livelihood. Today there are a significant number of organizations dedicated to assisting women who have been violated.[9] Tarana Burke, the Senior Director of Girls for Gender Equity in Brooklyn and the originator of the Me Too movement, reports that at one of her first Me Too workshops at a high school in Alabama twelve years ago, twenty out of the thirty girls in the workshop reported having been violated in some way. Still, as we have seen exemplified in much public discourse about treatment of peoples that are limited by marginalized status, it is hard to fully comprehend the scope of a plight that is not one's own. As a result, violence against women has continued in epidemic proportions,[10] and yet the conversation has stayed largely between women themselves. However, the seeming miracle of instant exposure that social media can provide has visited its magic on the issue and moved it into a level of focus merited by its cultural urgency.

Now that the issue is receiving its proper attention, we are faced with the problem of keeping it from falling into the graveyard of the twenty-four-hour news cycle. The movement is still growing rapidly enough to populate headlines, but how do we keep the conversation going?

THE DIFFICULTY OF POLITICAL DISCOURSE ABOUT VIOLENCE AGAINST WOMEN

When considering how to effect lasting change on peoples' opinions about social issues, we know that one's exposure to differing experiences and points of view can come largely from other individuals in family and community.[11] Indeed, the most significant statistics on this subject suggest that putting a face on discrimination and social bias can create the most profound change in social thought. In a study about a Los Angeles–based organization called Leadership Lab, it was determined that conversations with transgender volunteers who canvassed a neighborhood talking with voters about LGBTQ rights were "found to be successful in reducing transgender prejudice, the effect of which persisted even months later."[12]

However, the #MeToo movement comes at a time when the possibility of discourse about political and social issues has become unusually compromised. Marked extremes in political thought, combined with our knowing consumption of curated social media information that exclusively reinforces our existing viewpoints, conspire to keep us from engaging with one another.[13] We live in a culture in which the mere mention of a controversial point of view can clear a room. This necessarily means that much of our learning about social issues will be limited during this time of curtailed exchange.

It is for this very reason that the performing arts are so important to a society; they can expose us to points of view we might otherwise never have the opportunity to inhabit. So it is that artists, in particular, are positioned to speak and persuade during this difficult historical moment. American philosopher John Dewey shone a light on this idea of the artist as a voice of social enlightenment in his lectures on *Art as Experience* in the 1930s, saying that through art we "install ourselves in modes of apprehending nature that at first are strange to us [and] . . . our own experience is reoriented. . . . Barriers are dissolved [and] limiting prejudices melt away. . . . [It is] far more efficacious than the change effected by reasoning."[14] This is exactly what Hulu's TV adaptation of Margaret Atwood's *The Handmaid's Tale* does.[15] It puts us in the driver's seat experientially. It reorients our experience through the use of first person performed narrative.

FIRST PERSON PERFORMED NARRATIVE

The first-person voice through literature, in which the story is told to us from the point of view of a single character, allows us to experience the world through the eyes of that character, often with direct narration. A character tells us what happens and what he or she thinks about what happens. In first person performed narrative we are also in every way *with* the character, but the character might not ever speak to us directly. The adaptation into film or television imagery allows us to not only read or hear about it but to *see* it through the character's eyes.

The Handmaid's Tale takes place in a dystopian future where America is ruled by a violent, misogynistic, totalitarian, and extremist Christian regime called "The Republic of Gilead." The TV series invites us into the daily life of its main character named Offred (Elisabeth Moss). We quickly learn that Offred (Of Fred) is so named because she is the property of the Commander Fred Waterford (Joseph Fiennes) and his wife, Serena Joy Waterford (Yvonne Strahovski). Offred is one of a social caste of female slaves called Handmaids whose sole function is to bear children for the couples in ruling power who are unable to have children of their own. In this way, Gilead will be repopulated with children raised by the ruling class.

We encounter Gilead through Offred's eyes. Through her lens we witness a culture in which violence against women is normalized. In Gilead, women are no longer allowed to read or write (a stricture to which the women in the ruling class have voluntarily subjected themselves), and as the Handmaids walk through the city, we see symbols on signs instead of text, put there to ensure that this is enforced. We see dissenters of all kinds publicly killed and their bodies hung up for all to see. The dissenters are individuals who have committed so-called moral crimes—people who engage in sexual intercourse for anything other than procreation, adulterers, or individuals who in any way resist the rules of the regime. We witness the constant threat that disobedient Handmaids are exposed to: those who can no longer conceive for the Commanders will be sent to a work camp that is contaminated by radioactivity to perform hard labor until they die. Children are traded into marriage for social status. Homosexuals (so-called "gender traitors") are desexualized or hung, and people who try to escape Gilead or harbor those who are escaping are shot and killed on the spot. Mass media is shut down, effectively silencing voices of dissent.

A central part of the creative construct of the series is that Offred is unable to voice her opinion to anyone because speaking out is likely to get her killed. At the beginning of the series the Handmaids don't even speak to each another. It is simply too much of a risk to speak to another Handmaid. Perhaps they are loyal and faithful members of Gilead. It is not until well into the second episode[16] that the Handmaids speak to one another, and by then we have seen the dangerous consequences of not complying. We see repeated images of bodies swinging and men with guns, called the Eyes, threatening the Handmaids in order keep them silent.

This is the brilliance of Hulu's translation of *The Handmaid's Tale*. We don't get to hear what Offred really feels about what is surrounding her because it is far too dangerous. We have constant awareness of that very real threat. Rather, the adaptation *shows* us and we watch with her, horrified that what we/she feels cannot be spoken or she will die. By this method, as we walk with Offred—*as* Offred—through this world in silence, we experience what she might plead with us to understand if she were free as we, the viewers, are.

COERCION AND THE DISPLAY OF POWER

A particular chilling example of this first person performed narrative can be found in season 1, episode 10,[17] in which Offred finally sees that her daughter Hannah (Jordana Blake) is alive. In the episodes preceding this one, we have seen flashbacks showing us that Hannah was taken from her on the day she, her husband Luke Bankole (O-T Fagbenle), and her daughter were fleeing to Canada as the men of Gilead first came into power. In episode 10, Offred has no idea what they have done to Hannah or if she is even alive.

Once Offred has been supposedly impregnated by Commander Waterford (the true father is the chauffeur Nick Blaine, played by Max Minghella), Serena Joy Waterford begins to fear Offred's power to somehow keep the baby from them. To solve this problem, Serena Joy decides to bring Offred to see that Hannah is alive and has been given to an infertile couple in the ruling class, whereby Serena Joy makes it clear to Offred that if she keeps the new baby safe, Serena Joy will keep Hannah safe. In the sequence, Offred doesn't know she is going to get to see Hannah, and we are, with Offred, watching through the window from the carriage. When Serena Joy goes to the door of a private home and Hannah is brought out, we see her for the first time at the same moment that Offred sees her. With Offred we go through the joy of recognition that she is alive and then the desperation and horror that she cannot get to Hannah or touch her or even make Hannah hear her, trapped as she is in the enclosed carriage. It is a profoundly moving sequence, during which we share Offred's desperation.[18]

Had someone spoken to us directly about the issues of morality around separation of children and their families, our own attachments and existing political positions might cloud our ability to listen and understand one another. When we consider the issue as an experience, we are affected just as John Dewey purports that we might be. The barriers are removed and our prejudices melt away. It is far more persuasive than a reasoning debate could be. Through this first person performed narrative we have effectively *experienced* the issue.

Offred is devastated as she is able to see her lost child, but not communicate with her. Screenshot from Hulu television series.

The trauma of being separated from one's children has been utilized memorably in other films as well. During the film *Sophie's Choice*[19] (1983) we fall in love with the complex and deeply traumatized Sophie (Meryl Streep). The narrative reveals she is a Holocaust survivor, and we watch as she struggles to live with trauma she cannot speak aloud. As we become increasingly attached to her own emotional survival, we begin to feel as viewers that the filmmaker is walking us toward an inevitable dramatic revelation; a breakdown of her defenses that somehow allows her to voice her pain, thereby releasing its hold on her. When we finally arrive at the moment of revelation, the filmmaker beautifully puts us into a first person performed narrative that delivers the full impact of her trauma in a way to which words would be unequal.

It happens in a flashback. We see Sophie on a crowded train platform with Nazi soldiers attempting to separate and transport Jews to concentration camps. Sophie is there with her two children, a boy and a girl. She is trying to keep them safe as the soldiers prowl through the crowd. An obviously high-ranking official (Karlheinz Hakl) approaches her and asks if she is a "Polack" and a Communist. Sophie says she is a Christian and that her children are pure blooded. He says to her, "Do you believe in Christ, the Redeemer? Didn't he say, 'suffer the little children?'"[20] Then he tells her she can keep only *one* of her children. She stands there, astonished and pleads with him to not make her choose. He calls for someone to come and take them both and, as they are grabbing both of the children she screams, "Take the girl! Take my little girl!!" and hands her over. There is a long shot of the soldier walking away with the girl, who is screaming for her mother.

The trauma of a parent being separated from a child has been explored in many other stories, such as the film Sophie's Choice *(1983).*

No amount of teaching about the inhumanity of the Nazi regime could be more persuasive than watching the *experience* of this trauma on film. To be with Sophie during this horrific choice effectively gives us a glimpse of the true size of that inexplicable inhumanity.

LIVE THEATER AND SOCIAL CHANGE

Live theater enjoys a long, proud history of making an enormous impact on the community it serves, and it can be inextricably linked to the politics of the day. If we listen to Dewey, we know that an equitable society can come only from a revolution that appeals to the imagination and emotional experience of the people.[21] But there is no need to look to the philosophy of art to drive this point home. For a lesson on American nationalism and how it was finding its expression in the theater, we need only look at the Astor Place Riots of 1849. During this uprising twenty-two citizens were killed amongst the thousands who protested the casting of William Charles Macready, a British Shakespearean actor beloved by the upper class in America, to play the role of Macbeth at the Astor Opera House instead of Edwin Forrest, the American Shakespearean actor with whom Macready had a professional rivalry.[22] This was a class riot. Forrest was an American actor and epitomized a particularly American performance style. The working people who went to the theater regularly in New York would do just fine with their own beloved actor and didn't need someone to come over from England to show them how. They did not need the British, nor did they need the wealthy owner class who seemed to find the British culturally superior.

Vital social discourse finds its way into the theater in modernity as well. This was epitomized by an event during the curtain call of Lin Manuel Miranda's play *Hamilton*[23] (2016) when the actors pleaded with Vice President Mike Pence, who was attending the play that evening, saying, "We are the diverse America who are alarmed and anxious that your new administration will not . . . defend us and uphold our inalienable rights, Sir. But we truly hope this show has inspired you to uphold our American values and work on behalf of all of us."[24] Theater has the potential to change the world, and by extension, so do television and film.

Live theater's distinction among narrative media is that the audience experiences the performance live. All of us are there, together. An audience is there to complete a kind of circuit relied upon by the playmakers to complete the event. Theater is necessarily about the experience in the present moment. It depends on an exchange between the actors and the audience members who are responding to the performances.

This does not, however, mean that any point of view is always expressed through the use of first person performed narrative. The kinds of arguments employed in theater are legion, encompassing styles that range from theatrical movement with very little use of text, as in Bill T. Jones's *Still/Here*[25] (1994) to a La Teatro de Campesino's first work that sprung from the picket lines of the Farm Workers' Union in the 1970s, which educated and entertained audiences with its *Agitprop* (agitation and propaganda) theater.[26]

THE HANDMAID'S TALE SPEAKS TO OUR TIME

In this historic moment, we must ensure that this great evolution in understanding about the worldwide epidemic of violence against women will not slip through our grasp. Again, we can risk losing our ground in the whirl of failing political discourse or find another way. Theater makers can utilize the style of first person performed narrative that is so central to the success of *The Handmaid's Tale.* We can find plays, write plays, or create plays that place us in the position of the people who, like Offred, experience silencing, violence, and oppression.

There are so many plays that can serve us well in this regard. But we must shine an intensified light on the experience of this violence. It is all over the text of Shakespeare's *Hamlet* (1599–1602), for example, that Ophelia is used as a pawn by those around her and the world she experiences at the hands of those she trusts is too much for her to bear. Yet, in production after production of the play you find this unhandled and relegated to the background. We remember so well that Claudius and Polonius decide Hamlet is crazy after they witness the violence of the nunnery scene,[27] but do we remember the collapsed and ruined Ophelia left there, unconsoled by any of the men? We can take a lesson from Offred's story and stage these scenes from Ophelia's point of view so that *we* are brutalized by Hamlet and ignored by Polonius and the King; so that *we* are left to wander, disoriented until we are submerged by the weight of her grief.

We can stage the work of women playwrights; plays that steep us in the rich and varied viewpoints of half the world; plays by Caryl Churchill and Lynn Nottage, Paula Vogel and Sarah Ruhl, Sarah Kane and Susan Lori-Parks, Aphra Ben and Sor Juana, and let them shift the perspective lens through which we experience life.

NOTES

1. Emma Brocks, "Me Too Founder Tarana Burke: 'You have to use your privilege to serve other people,'" *Guardian* (US Edition), January 15, 2018. https://www.theguardian.com/world/2018/jan/15/me-too-founder-tarana-burke-women-sexual-assault. Senior Director of Girls for Gender Equity Tarana Burke coined this phrase in 2006 as a shared signal among survivors of sexual assault. Within days of the October 2017 *New York Times* article exposing Harvey Weinstein's payoffs to a number of women over a twenty-year period (Jodi Kantor and Megan Twohey, "Harvey Weinstein Paid Off Sexual Harassment Accusers for Decades," October 5, 2017), actress Alyssa Milano called for women who had been subject to sexual aggression to speak out with #MeToo. Within ten days #MeToo had been posted over twelve million times and generated an avalanche of cultural response, including a subsequent *New York Times* article in which seventy-one men in high-profile positions, many in media and entertainment were accused of sexual misconduct (Sarah Almukhtar, Michael Gold, and Larry Buchanan, "After Weinstein: 71 Men Accused of Sexual Misconduct and Their Fall from Power," February 8, 2018).

2. Cara Buckley, "Powerful Women Unveil Anti-Harassment Action Plan," *New York Times,* January 1, 2018, https://www.nytimes.com/2018/01/01/movies/times-up-hollywood-women-sexual-harassment.html. The Time's Up movement was launched in response to the #MeToo movement and the record number of reports of sexual misconduct that followed. It is a three-tiered initiative that includes a legal defense fund for women of lesser means, legislation to hold organizations and companies responsible for conduct in the workplace and a push toward gender parity in the film industry.

3. Melanie Green, "Why Is It So Stressful to Talk Politics with the Other Side?" *The Conversation*, April 6, 2018, http://theconversation.com/why-is-it-so-stressful-to-talk-politics-with-the-other-side-92391.

4. Margaret Atwood, *The Handmaid's Tale* (New York: Houghton Mifflin Company, 1986.)

5. I am using theater as a term indicative of performing art in this chapter. Although an actor's performance in theater and his or her performance in film are different in essential ways (most profoundly in theater's ability to provide a live audience/actor interchange), they share vast similarity by virtue of performing an experience into which a viewer can enter and relate their own life experience.

6. Kantor and Twohey, "Weinstein Paid Off."

7. Almukhtar, Gold, and Buchanan, "After Weinstein."

8. Lin Farley, *Sexual Shakedown: The Sexual Harassment of Women on the Job* (New York: McGraw Hill, 1975).

9. "Directory of Organizations," National Sexual Violence Resource Center, accessed July 12, 2018, https://www.nsvrc.org/organizations?field_organizations_target_id=All&field_states_territories_target_id=All&page=21.

10. NSRVC, "Statistics," https://www.nsvrc.org/statistics. In the United States one in three women experience some sort of contact sexual violence in their lifetime.

11. Green, "Stressful."

12. Benoit Denizet-Lewis, "How Do You Change Voters' Minds? Have a Conversation," *New York Times Magazine,* April 7, 2016, https://www.nytimes .com/2016/04/10/magazine/how-do-you-change-voters-minds-have-a-conversation .html.

13. Kirk Kovach, "On Discourse and Disagreement," *Carolina Political Review*, May 2018. https://www.carolinapoliticalreview.org.

14. John Dewey, *Art as Experience* (New York: Minton, Balch & Company, 1934), 134.

15. *The Handmaid's Tale*, TV series, Created by Bruce Miller, MGM Television/ Hulu, USA, 2017.

16. *The Handmaid's Tale,* "Birth Day," Season 1, Episode 2, directed by Reed Morano, written by Bruce Miller, Hulu, April 26, 2017, https://www.hulu.com /watch/1069120.

17. *The Handmaid's Tale*, "Night," Season 1, Episode 10, directed by Kari Skogland, written by Bruce Miller, Hulu, June 14, 2017, https://www.hulu.com /watch/1092255.

18. The scene is particularly relevant today. In the United States, the children of undocumented migrants are regularly being detained, causing irreparable damage to both children and parents.

19. *Sophie's Choice,* directed by Alan J. Pakula, Lions Gate, March 4, 1983, Amazon. https://www.amazon.com/Sophies-Choice-Meryl-Streep/dp/B075DWX HZF/ref=sr_1_1?ie=UTF8&qid=1532885646&sr=8-1&keywords=sophie %27s+choice. This film is based on the novel by William Styron, screenplay by Alan J. Pakula, featuring Meryl Streep, Kevin Kline, and Peter MacNicol.

20. *Sophie's Choice,* Pakula.

21. Tom Leddy, "Dewey's Aesthetics," *The Stanford Encyclopedia of Philosophy* (Winter 2016 edition), edited by Edward N. Zalta, https://plato.stanford.edu/cgi-bin /encyclopedia/archinfo.cgi?entry=dewey-aesthetics.

22. Oscar Brockett, *The History of the Theatre* (Boston: Allyn and Bacon 1999).

23. *Hamilton: An American Musical,* music and lyrics by Lin Manuel-Miranda, directed by Thomas Kail, Richard Rogers Theatre, New York, February 2, 2016.

24. Ashley Lee and Jennifer Konerman, "'Hamilton' Broadway Cast Addresses Mike Pence in Audience: 'Work on Behalf of All of Us," *The Hollywood Reporter,* November 18, 2016.

25. *Still/Here*, created by Bill T. Jones, video score by Gretchen Bender, Brooklyn Academy of Music, 1994.

26. *Actos,* directed by Luiz Valdez, featuring members of the Farm Workers Union, 1965.

27. William Shakespeare, *The Tragedy of Hamlet, Prince of Denmark* (London: The Folio Society, 1954), Act 3; Scene 1.

WORKS CITED

Almukhtar, Sarah, Michael Gold, and Larry Buchanan. "After Weinstein: 71 Men Accused of Sexual Misconduct and Their Fall from Power." *New York Times,* February 8, 2018, https://www.nytimes.com/interactive/2017/11/10/us/men-accused -sexual-misconduct-weinstein.html.

Atwood, Margaret. *The Handmaid's Tale.* New York: Houghton Mifflin Company, 1986.

Brockett, Oscar. *The History of the Theatre.* Boston: Allyn and Bacon, 1999.

Brocks, Emma. "Me Too Founder Tarana Burke: 'You have to use your privilege to serve other people.'" *Guardian* (US Edition), January 15, 2018. https://www theguardian.com/world/2018/jan/15/me-too-founder-tarana-burke-women-sexual -assault.

Buckley, Cara, "Powerful Women Unveil Anti-Harassment Action Plan." *New York Times,* January 1, 2018, https://www.nytimes.com/2018/01/01/movies/times-up -hollywood-women-sexual-harassment.html.

Denizet-Lewis, Benoit, "How Do You Change Voters' Minds? Have a Conversation." *New York Times Magazine,* April 7, 2016, https://www.nytimes.com/2016/04/10 /magazine/how-do-you-change-voters-minds-have-a-conversation.html.

Dewey, John. *Art as Experience.* New York: Minton, Balch & Company, 1934.

"Directory of Organizations." National Sexual Violence Resource Center. Accessed July 12, 2018, https://www.nsvrc.org.

Farley, Lin. *Sexual Shakedown: The Sexual Harassment of Women on the Job.* New York: McGraw Hill, 1975.

Green, Melanie. "Why Is It So Stressful to Talk Politics with the Other Side?" The Conversation, April 6, 2018, http://theconversation.com/why-is-it-so-stressful-to -talk-politics-with-the-other-side-92391.

Jones, Bill T. *Still/Here.* Video score by Gretchen Bender, Brooklyn Academy of Music, 1994.

Kantor, Jodi, and Megan Twohey. "Harvey Weinstein Paid Off Sexual Harassment Accusers for Decades." *New York Times,* October 5, 2017. https://www.ny times .com/2017/10/05/us/harvey-weinstein-harassment-allegations.html.

Kovach, Kirk. "On Discourse and Disagreement." *Carolina Political Review*, May 2018. https://www.carolinapoliticalreview.org.

Leddy, Tom. "Dewey's Aesthetics." *The Stanford Encyclopedia of Philosophy* (Winter 2016 edition), edited by Edward N. Zalta. https://plato.stanford.edu/cgi-bin /encyclopedia/archinfo.cgi?entry=dewey-aesthetics.

Lee, Ashley, and Jennifer Konerman. "'Hamilton' Broadway Cast Addresses Mike Pence in Audience: 'Work on Behalf of All of Us.'" *The Hollywood Reporter,* November 18, 2016, https://www.hollywoodreporter.com/news/hamilton-broad way-cast-addresses-mike-pence-audience-work-behalf-all-us-949075.

Manuel-Miranda, Lin. *Hamilton: An American Musical.* Directed by Thomas Kail, Richard Rogers Theatre. New York, February 2, 2016.

Shakespeare, William. *The Tragedy of Hamlet, Prince of Denmark,* London: The Folio Society, 1954.

Valdez, Luis. *Actos.* Featuring members of the Farm Workers Union, 1965. https://www.nsvrc.org/organizations?field_organizations_target_id=All&field_states_territories_target_id=All&page=21.

TELEVISION AND FILM

The Handmaid's Tale. TV series. Created by Bruce Miller. MGM Television / Hulu, USA, 2017.

The Handmaid's Tale. "Birth Day." Season 1, Episode 2. Directed by Reed Morano. Written by Bruce Miller. Hulu, April 26, 2017, https://www.hulu.com/watch/1069120.

The Handmaid's Tale. "Night." Season 1, Episode 10. Directed by Kari Skogland. Written by Bruce Miller. Hulu, June 14, 2017, https://www.hulu.com/watch/1092255.

Sophie's Choice. Directed by Alan J. Pakula. Lions Gate, 1983. https://www.amazon.com/Sophies-Choice-Meryl-Streep/dp/B075DWXHZF/ref=sr_1_1?ie=UTF8&qid=1532885646&sr=8-1&keywords=sophie%27s+choice.

Chapter Twenty

The Artist and Her Art

An Examination of Elisabeth Moss as Peggy Olson and June Osborne through a Feminist Lens

Jacqueline Maxwell

The word of the year for 2017 was "feminism,"[1] but 2018 has consisted of similar, if not more emotionally charged, conversations regarding gender inequality, including many academic discussions about whether it is possible to separate artists from their art. In the wake of the #MeToo movement, this question has been predominantly asked of celebrity male artists, many of whom are straight and white, who have been accused of abusing their power in various ways. While the public has witnessed some celebrities start to be held accountable for their actions, it is important to remember that viewers have the responsibility to determine who should or shouldn't hold power through their support of celebrities and their work. Therefore, while some find the question whether or not we can separate the art and the artist too complicated to reach a clear conclusion, many are also reconsidering their support for accused artists and their creative works. In this chapter, I would like to explore the argument that the artist and the art are intrinsically linked, and this examination is critical to our role as responsible consumers of pop culture and media. This discussion is one that is also important in the classroom when teaching students to think critically and demonstrate social responsibility by encouraging them to be self-aware when creating, consuming, and analyzing works of art.

The Handmaid's Tale by Margaret Atwood, as well as the Hulu TV adaptations,[2] allow for discussions about what it means to be a feminist, as well as a feminist who considers herself to be an artist. I would like to consider the main actor of the television series, Elisabeth Moss, and her relationship to two of her arguably feminist television characters and alter egos, most notably June Osborne and Peggy Olson from *The Handmaid's Tale* and *Mad Men*, respectively. *Mad Men,* a television show that takes place predominantly at an advertising agency during the 1960s in New York, highlights gender inequity, and stars many strong female characters, such as Elisabeth Moss's character, Peggy, who fight against societal conventions in order to break the glass ceiling and succeed in the workplace.

Moss also identifies as a feminist in her private life, although she has been criticized by some audiences due to her affiliation with the Church of Scientology,[3] as well as her insistence that *The Handmaid's Tale* is not a feminist television show. A *Vanity Fair* article from April 2017 called into question *The Handmaid's Tale* actors' reluctance to associate with feminism, and Moss was asked about similarities between her characters in *Mad Men* and *The Handmaid's Tale.* She responded, "Well, they're both human beings. They're the same height," adding later, "For me, [*The Handmaid's Tale* is] not a feminist story. It's a human story because women's rights are human rights. So, for me it's, I never intended to play Peggy as a feminist. I never intended to play Offred as a feminist."[4] Nevertheless, most viewers would say that she does.

Despite the fact that Moss didn't intend to portray both of these characters as feminists, I would like to examine the feminist connection between Peggy Olson, a white, working-class woman in the 1960s and 1970s fighting for gender equality, in contrast to Moss's dystopian character, June Osborne or Offred, a white Handmaid in an apocalyptic, theocratic society. More specifically, I will demonstrate the feminist connection that links these two characters by comparing the iconic scene of Peggy in *Mad Men,* in which Moss carries a box of her belongings into her new job, juxtaposed to the scene from *The Handmaid's Tale* in which June, of course also played by Moss, is left with a box that is nearly empty after losing her job. By examining these two female roles and their representation in these hierarchical societies, I will demonstrate just how pertinent it is to recognize one's own agency in oppressive environments, and I will suggest how students can learn from these women. Ultimately, they might feel empowered to understand these systems and fight oppression as critical thinkers and conscious consumers.

PEGGY AND THE PATRIARCHY

In this section, I would like to first examine the relationship between Elisabeth Moss's iconic character in *Mad Men*, Peggy Olson, and feminism, in order to better determine how the feminism of the 1960s and 1970s differs from what feminism looks like in *The Handmaid's Tale.* Peggy is introduced at the very start of the television series and is portrayed as an earnest, inexperienced, and naïve young woman who longs to make it in the competitive and unforgiving advertising world in Manhattan, dominated by men. In the first episode of *Mad Men,* "Smoke Gets in Your Eyes,"[5] Joan, a secretary and Peggy's superior (played by Christina Hendricks), explains to Peggy that her job is not just being a secretary for Donald Draper (played by Jon Hamm), because "most of the time [the men] are looking for something between a mother and waitress."[6] Joan suggests that the men might be looking for some kind of sexual relationship "the rest of the time," although she doesn't say so in this conversation. Joan tells Peggy to go home and cut eyeholes in a paper bag, examine herself in the mirror, and "really evaluate where [her] strengths and weaknesses are, and really be honest."[7] Even before Peggy has met Donald Draper, her boss, she is introduced to the sexist nature of the agency, including the scrutiny she will have to endure from other women who are not her allies. By giving her what she thinks is good advice, Joan reinforces the norms of the patriarchal society outside the walls of the advertising agency "Sterling and Cooper."

However, Peggy is an example of a character who initially listens to the advice of her employers, but almost immediately begins to question and challenge the role she has been given. She takes to writing, she argues with the role that Joan and her coworkers have determined for her, and she begins to move up as a copywriter in the company. Her outward ambition was unheard of for women in the 1960s, as women were expected to be tending to domestic duties at home, rather than seeking to acquire power in the workplace. Peggy's complex relationship with Joan demonstrates that some of the challenges of feminism are also presented by other women, potentially because feminism, especially second-wave feminism, was not inclusive of all women, based on characteristics such as class and race. Not to mention, women like Joan have been taught to use their bodies to gain men's favor because the agency's culture is such that the only way for women to be noticed or acknowledged is to act as highly sexualized in this environment.

In one of Peggy's iconic scenes, in the third-to-last episode of the final season of *Mad Men,*[8] she walks into her new agency with a spring of confidence in her step, which was empowering for marginalized women everywhere; however, in terms of the history of feminism in the workplace, this was still second-wave feminism, and the movement was not as inclusive as it would later come to be. Additionally, Peggy also might be outwardly fighting the norms of a patriarchal society, but she's still buying into the capitalist system in order to make her way to the top.

PEGGY JUXTAPOSED TO JUNE

Peggy has socially worked against the familial norms of the patriarchal society (such as having children or being a stay-at-home mother) by dating without the end goal of marriage and working in a male-dominated field. Peggy even has a quiet pregnancy and gives her child up for adoption in exchange for her career goals in advertising. Unlike Peggy, Offred, formerly known as June Osborne, is left with little autonomy, especially in regards to her choice to mother a child. While June has the ability and opportunity to be a parent to Hannah (Ayomi Jonas) prior to her life in Gilead, Offred is not only stripped of that agency, but is also sent back to the norms of life prior to feminism, as she is routinely raped in the hopes of producing a child for the Commander and his wife. In the episode "Late" in the first season of *The Handmaid's Tale* on Hulu,[9] Offred is learning how to survive in a totalitarian society in which she functions as a Handmaid, where she is seen for the sole purpose of bearing children for the Commander, Fred Waterford (played by Joseph Fiennes), and his wife, Serena Joy Waterford (played by Yvonne Strahovski).

Offred is seen in her new home in Gilead, but there are many flashbacks that unpack the narrative that brought her to her role as a Handmaid. These flashbacks demonstrate how quickly June, a confident and independent woman in the workplace as a copy editor in a magazine, loses any sense of agency in only a matter of minutes for the audience. In just one day June is denounced for her appearance by a Barista (Daniel Beirne) who refuses to serve her and her friend Moira (played by Samira Wiley), is denied access to her bank account in a coffee shop, and is stripped of her job based solely on her gender. The viewer is, therefore, forced to consider how all these events happen so quickly and leave June so powerless, which begs the audience to grapple with the harsh reality that the systems that rob June of her agency possibly already exist in our own world in 2018. In other words, we are also a part of systems that could potentially, and already do, quickly remove the rights of marginalized groups or groups that don't have the privilege that the straight, white men of Gilead do. Similar to June's experience, women are stripped of their rights to control not only their work spaces but also their reproductive organs in a society where religiously motivated conservatism is attempting to intimidate women into subordinate roles in the private as well as public sphere.

In *We Were Feminists Once*, Andi Zeisler,[10] the cofounder of Bitch Media, focuses on Peggy's success in her career and her opportunity to advertise women's cigarettes. In the final season of *Mad Men*, Peggy has worked her way up to the top, and is tasked with advertising cigarettes to women. This apparent success for Peggy is also helping her play into what Zeisler describes as "marketplace feminism," in which women might feel empowered by choosing cigarettes made specifically for them. However, Zeisler's reading of this calls to attention the ideas of third-wave feminism, which is more intersectional, and critiques neoliberalism, in that women are only under the impression that they are independent consumers; in reality, they are being coerced into buying products that are targeting them specifically. *The Handmaid's Tale* also highlights these neoliberalist ideas when the Commander offers Offred, entirely deprived of any form of luxury, an officially forbidden fashion women's magazine, and he assumes that she's been dreaming of this kind of consumption while locked away in her room.[11]

In addition to the role that third-wave feminism plays in both texts, I would like to call attention to the parallels between the scene that actor Elisabeth Moss has in season 1 of *The Handmaid's Tale*, in which June's character loses her job, and Peggy Olson, when she is walking into her new job in the last season of *Mad Men*. In *The Handmaid's Tale*, Offred's character has just lost access to her bank account, as well as her job, and continues to lose any kind of control over her own life. Similar to Peggy, she is holding a box with her belongings, walking out of the building with a look of frustration and confusion. The juxtaposition of Moss in these two iconic and feminist roles, in these specific moments, certainly seems like an intentional, intertextual statement by the writers of the television show. Now, even more than in 2016, when Zeisler wrote her text, these moments stand as statements about the lack of women's agency in the workplace, as well as capitalist America. This juxtaposition is yet another feminist warning: although Peggy is smirking with that cigarette in her mouth, we, as an audience, have to realize that this perceived success is only temporary in the 1970s. In other words, June's moment of leaving her work environment, escorted by paramilitary troopers with machine guns, serves as a warning that Peggy's buying into the capitalist, patriarchal world of advertising could also be the cause of her demise in 2018 (in her role as June Osborne), and we, as a society and as feminists, are setting ourselves up for a fate similar to Offred in Gilead.

TEACHING STUDENTS TO BE THOUGHTFUL ARTISTS AND CRITICAL CONSUMERS

If there's any hope to be had for resisting the dystopian future that Atwood and Miller outline for us, it is with the next generation. In the classroom, film and television can be employed as central texts or additional resources that help students to understand history as it repeats itself, as well as the complexities of modern-day issues. In the case of Elisabeth Moss and *The Handmaid's*

Tale, it is especially important to encourage students to examine the context in which the visual medium as a cultural artifact and "work of art" is made. Therefore, Elisabeth Moss as an artist and creative contributor to *The Handmaid's Tale* is someone whom students might examine as a public and private figure, especially as an individual who considers herself to be a feminist.

Elisabeth Moss has received and continues to receive many accolades for her role in the first and second seasons of *The Handmaid's Tale* on Hulu, such as the Emmy Award she received in 2017 and the Golden Globe Award she received for Best Performance by an Actress In A Television Series - Drama in 2018. As Moss receives more attention in the media for her acting, she also is receiving more criticism for her affiliation with the Church of Scientology, which has a reputation for being an exclusive, controversial religion that abuses its power and requires its members to pay their way to the top. Students may be encouraged to consider how Moss's social location as a hetero, able-bodied, white, upper-class Scientologist has affected her ability to invest in the television show, as well as her ability to star on highly successful television shows such as *The West Wing*, *Mad Men*, *Top of the Lake*, and *The Handmaid's Tale*. By doing so, class conversations can start by considering the text's commentary, and then move to the author's intentional and unintentional messaging made through casting, directorial, and cinematographic decisions.

Take, for example, the decision to cast Samira Wiley, a queer woman of color, in *The Handmaid's Tale* as June's closest friend, Moira. Despite this attempt to include a woman of color in the show, although the novel does not do so, Priya Nair, a writer for *Bitch Magazine,* criticized the novel and show for its "anti-blackness," arguing that "it is Offred's whiteness that ultimately allows her to escape the Commander's house and leave a record of her experience"[12] (see chapters by Charisse Levchak and Paul Moffett in this volume). She also notes that "being banned from reading, writing, or congregating, the spectacle of public lynchings, and the practice of naming people after their owners (Offred, or 'of Fred') were all methods used to control black people during (and after) slavery."[13] These statements demonstrate the power of using race as a lens when watching the show and would help students to reconsider Margaret Atwood, Elisabeth Moss, and all of the artists' choices based on their own influences, experiences, and biases.

Samira Wiley's character, Moira, is also important to think of in terms of an artist and her chosen art. Wiley is known for her character Poussey Washington on *Orange Is the New Black*,[14] an iconic character who is both black and queer, and struggles with depression. Unlike Poussey's character, who is killed during a peaceful protest in *Orange Is the New Black*, Moira fights against her designated role as Handmaid in Gilead, and works as a sex worker at Jezebel's while she plans her escape to Canada. Unlike Offred,

Moira has the strength to fight the system almost from the beginning of the story, and, as someone who has continuously fought against the intersections of both racism and sexism in her life pre-Gilead, she is not willing to trust the men in power as a means of escape. Instead, as someone who is working against multiple forms of oppression—including race, gender, and sexual orientation—she manages to escape Gilead, just as Wiley continues to serve as an icon in the world of media by representing marginalized groups, and introducing these narratives through mainstream media.

By teaching students to be responsible consumers of pop culture, they can observe the world through a critical lens to which they can connect their own identities and ultimately empower them to create their own artistic expressions. Similar to celebrity artists, students should also be taught to consider their own backgrounds, privileges, and implicit biases while studying television and visual media in class. By doing so, we will help mold a generation of individuals who can see themselves represented in a variety of narratives, and marginalized voices will hopefully be brought to light.

NOTES

1. "Merriam-Webster's 2017 Words of the Year," Merriam-Webster, accessed July 15, 2018, https://www.merriam-webster.com/words-at-play/word-of-the-year-2017-feminism/complicit.

2. Margaret Atwood and Bruce Miller, *The Handmaid's Tale*, Television series, Hulu, 2017.

3. Jessica Chasmar, "Scientologist Elisabeth Moss Branded a Hypocrite for Golden Globe Acceptance Speech," *The Washington Times*, January 8, 2018, accessed July 16, 2018, https://www.washingtontimes.com/news/2018/jan/8/elisabeth-moss-scientologist-branded-a-hypocrite-f/.

4. Laura Bradley, "Why Won't *The Handmaid's Tale* Cast Call It Feminist?" *Vanity Fair*, April 22, 2017, www.vanityfair.com/hollywood/2017/04/handmaids-tale-hulu-feminist-elisabeth-moss.

5. *Mad Men*, "Smoke Gets in Your Eyes," Season 1, Episode 1, directed by Alan Taylor, written by Matthew Weiner, AMC, July 15, 2007.

6. *Mad Men*, "Smoke Gets in Your Eyes," Season 1, Episode 1.

7. *Mad Men*, "Smoke Gets in Your Eyes," Season 1, Episode 1.

8. *Mad Men*, "Lost Horizon," Season 7, Episode 12, directed by Phil Abraham, written by Semi Chellas and Matthew Weiner, AMC, May 3, 2015.

9. *The Handmaid's Tale*, "Late," Season 1, Episode 3, directed by Reed Moreno, written by Bruce Miller, Hulu, April 26, 2017.

10. Andi Zeisler, *We Were Feminists Once: From Riot Grrrl to CoverGirl, the Buying and Selling of a Political Movement* (New York: Public Affairs, 2016).

11. *The Handmaid's Tale*, "Faithful," Season 1, Episode 5, directed by Mike Barker, written by Bruce Miller, Hulu, May 10, 2017.

12. Priya, "Anti-Blackness in 'The Handmaid's Tale,'" *Bitch Media,* April 14, 2017, accessed July 15, 2018, https://www.bitchmedia.org/article/anti-blackness -handmaids-tale.

13. Priya, "Anti-Blackness."

14. *Orange Is the New Black*, created by Jenji Kohan, Netflix, 2013.

WORKS CITED

Bradley, Laura. "Why Won't *The Handmaid's Tale* Cast Call It Feminist?" *Vanity Fair*, April 22, 2017. www.vanityfair.com/hollywood/2017/04/handmaids-tale -hulu-feminist-elisabeth-moss.

Chasmar, Jessica. "Scientologist Elisabeth Moss Branded a Hypocrite for Golden Globe Acceptance Speech." *The Washington Times*, January 8, 2018. Accessed July 16, 2018. https://www.washingtontimes.com/news/2018/jan/8/elisabeth-moss -scientologist-branded-a-hypocrite-f/.

"Merriam-Webster's 2017 Words of the Year." Merriam-Webster. Accessed July 15, 2018. https://www.merriam-webster.com/words-at-play/word-of-the-year -2017-feminism/complicit.

Priya. "Anti-Blackness in 'The Handmaid's Tale.'" *Bitch Media*, April 14, 2017. Accessed July 15, 2018. https://www.bitchmedia.org/article/anti-blackness-hand maids-tale.

Zeisler, Andi. *We Were Feminists Once: From Riot Grrrl to CoverGirl, the Buying and Selling of a Political Movement*. New York: Public Affairs, 2016.

FILMS AND TELEVISION

Mad Men. "Smoke Gets in Your Eyes." Season 1, Episode 1. Directed by Alan Taylor. Written by Matthew Weiner. AMC, July 15, 2007.

Mad Men. "Lost Horizon." Season 7, Episode 12. Directed by Phil Abraham. Written by Semi Chellas and Matthew Weiner. AMC, May 3, 2015.

Orange Is the New Black. Created by Jenji Kohan. Netflix, 2013 to present.

The Handmaid's Tale. "Late." Season 1, Episode 3. Directed by Reed Moreno. Written by Bruce Miller. Hulu, April 26, 2017.

The Handmaid's Tale. "Faithful." Season 1, Episode 5. Directed by Mike Barker. Written by Bruce Miller. Hulu, May 10, 2017.

The West Wing. Created by Aaron Sorkin. NBC. 1999 to 2006.

Top of the Lake. Created by Jane Campion and Gerald Lee, Sundance Channel. 2013 to present.

Chapter Twenty-One

"The Magical Land of the North"

Anti-Americanism and Canadian Identity *within* The Handmaid's Tale

Janis L. Goldie

The Handmaid's Tale, Hulu's hit television series based on the best-selling novel by Canadian author Margaret Atwood, has received much critical and academic attention for its themes of dystopia, feminism, and reproductive rights and technologies as is evident with our collection of interdisciplinary projects in this book and beyond.[1] Little has been said in this body of scholarship, however, about the explicit idealization of Canada which is presented as a stark national contrast to the totalitarian regime of Gilead.

One of the most notable geographical aspects of the repressive, autocratic Republic of Gilead is that it is set in the United States, specifically in the Boston, Massachusetts, area. The second Hulu series ends with Offred/June (Elisabeth Moss) handing over her newborn baby girl to her fellow Handmaid Ofglen/Emily (Alexis Bledel) who is ready to flee to Canada. The land to the North is the main migration route and promises those who escape successfully some relief from the traumatic events in Gilead. In the dystopic narrative that Atwood evokes, Canada offers a safe haven. As I will illustrate throughout this chapter, *The Handmaid's Tale* makes explicit the construction of Canada as an idyllic and stable moderate state and draws on persistent myths of Canadian national identity, such as tolerance and equality.[2] In essence, Canada is presented as the utopia within the dystopian narrative frame. From the initial episode where an escape across the border is the only possible hope for the protagonists, to references to Canadian liberal institutional stalwarts such as newspapers and immigration policies, *The Handmaid's Tale* presents an image of Canada as a pillar of liberal democracy and as a sanctuary for those wanting to escape the restrictive and oppressive laws experienced within Gilead. This is particularly the case for the women in the show, whose reproductive rights and basic freedoms are eliminated.

As a scholar of Communication and Cultural Studies—and as a Canadian national and coeditor of this volume—this television program is a fascinating site within which to study discourses of Canadian nationalism and identity in popular media culture. Relying on rhetorical narrative analysis,[3] this chapter unpacks the explicit references to Canada as safe haven and argues that there is a Canadian nationalist narrative underlying the production, one which draws on common Canadian myths and identity claims. The idealization of Canada that is constructed is even more interesting when one considers the transnational nature of the media product alongside the long history of cultural protectionism and anti-Americanism within Canada itself.

BEYOND BORDERS: *THE HANDMAID'S TALE* AS TRANSNATIONAL MEDIA PRODUCT

Hulu's production of *The Handmaid's Tale* is a unique transnational media product.[4] The novel on which the show is based on is written by a Canadian literary icon, Margaret Atwood, arguably the most recognized[5] and celebrated author in contemporary Canadian history, sometimes even referred to as "'*the*' voice of Canada."[6] Atwood originally published *The Handmaid's Tale* in 1985 and sold the rights to the novel to MGM in 1990 to make the film version (directed by Volker Schlöndorff), which was both financially and critically unsuccessful[7] (discussed in more detail in chapter 16 by Rositzka and chapter 17 Tredy in this volume). MGM later sold the rights to Hulu to make the television production in 2016,[8] and Atwood has indicated that despite being the original creative force, she hasn't received much financial compensation from the overwhelming success of the show.[9] As Atwood explains:

> I sold the rights to MGM in 1990 to make a movie—so when the TV rights were sold to Hulu, the money went to MGM. . . . We did not have a negotiating position. I did get brought on as an executive consultant, but that wasn't a lot of money. People think it's been all Hollywood glamour since the TV show happened, but that's not happening to me. But book sales have been brisk, so there's that.[10]

The majority of the production team behind the television show is American. The executive producer and writer of Hulu's adaptation, Bruce Miller, is American, and the majority of the major actors are also American, British, or Australian. The only exceptions are Amanda Brugel, who plays Rita, the Waterford's Martha, and Margaret Atwood herself who makes a brief cameo in season 1 as an Aunt.[11] The majority of the directors of the episodes have also been American.[12]

Despite the majority of the production team being American, the show was filmed entirely in Canada, specifically in Toronto and area including Cambridge, Oshawa, and Hamilton, even while setting up notable sites like Fenway Park or the Boston Globe.[13] As a result of its filming location in Canada, the television production relied on predominantly Canadian crews.[14] Further, in an interesting distribution twist, when the television program was initially released on April 26, 2017, Canadians couldn't actually view it. Hulu was initially the only network carrying the show, which Canadians couldn't access.[15] After Canadians publicly showed frustration at this, Bravo picked it up and began showing it a few days later on April 30, 2017, making *The Handmaid's Tale* the most-watched broadcast in Bravo history.[16]

In all, there is an interesting and complicated transnational media relationship present here. You have an original Canadian creator and literary work, re-created by an American media culture production team, and led by an American executive producer and writer. This American production is filmed and shot entirely in Canada—however—it is re-enacted by predominantly American, British, and Australian actors. The program is distributed by American media production companies and networks first, and then to Canadians, without significant financial compensation to the original creator. That Canada and America are so starkly represented within the narrative of the show, despite the joint production effort, indicates that nationalism within transnational media production is still very relevant and needs to be closely examined.

DEFINING BORDERS: CANADA AS TOLERANT SANCTUARY

Despite the transnational nature of the cultural production, there are very clear national boundaries drawn between Canada and Gilead/America in the discourse of the show itself.[17] One of the main ways Canada centers into the plot is via the emphasis on, and importance of, the border. The central goal of the protagonists over both seasons is to first get to the Canadian-American (now Canadian-Gileadian) border and then successfully cross the border as a refugee. Thus, the major plot driver thus far in *The Handmaid's Tale* is for the characters to move *out of Gilead* and *into Canada*. We can see this clearly in the initial episode of season 1, where the program opens to Luke (O-T Fagbenle), June, and Hannah (Jordanna Blake) racing down an icy road in their vehicle, trying to get closer to the border before crossing. When we eventually learn the backstory of their escape, we hear the man who is helping them, Mr. Whitford (Tim Ransom), tell them that he'll get them to the "Magical Land of the North," implying both that they will be safe and that this is a charmed, almost dreamlike or unbelievable, site of refuge.

June's husband, Luke, later manages to get over the border via a boat crossing, despite serious casualties amongst his fellow refugees. Moira (Samira Wiley), June's best friend, also makes several attempts at escape to Canada throughout season 1, and eventually succeeds in episode 7. In a poignant scene, we see Moira crossing an icy, snowy, and windy field to stumble, exhausted, onto a farm where she uncovers a dusty Ontario license plate with its tagline, "Yours to Discover." She laughs deliriously on the floor of the barn in rejoicing that she has finally arrived in Canada, the "magical" destination where she is suddenly safe and her individual rights and freedoms protected. In season 2, June makes multiple failing escape attempts to get to the Canadian border, further motivated by her powerful desire to get her daughters out. In this way, a central motivating force behind three of the main protagonists' actions (June, Luke, and Moira) so far in the show has been to escape the horrors of Gilead, but also, importantly, to escape *to* Canada.

Notably, it is not a nameless fictional nation that viewers are presented with as an escape site. Just as it is explicitly constructed that the main plot site, Gilead, is the former Boston, the show explicitly constructs the site of refuge as Canada via images of Canadian flags, Ontario license plates, references to Toronto's Pearson airport, and liberal news institution *The Toronto Star,* among other direct verbal references to the North and Canada. It is Canadian officials who are predominantly represented to help refugees of Gilead, welcoming them at their immigration centers, helping with their transition, and allowing them to exist within their own cultural community, "Little America." It's not Britain officials that help, or the Mexican border that is the preferred destination for escape, for example. In this way, Canada is constructed as not only the ultimate—but the only—alternative destination possible for the main characters within *The Handmaid's Tale.*

The imagery of the borderlands is also notable within the show. With the exception of the diplomatic mission to Canada in which urban Toronto is pictured and the scenes of "Little America" where Moira and Luke reside after their escape, the remainder of the show displays the borderland area as wild and rural, as well as typically void of people. Most of the images of Canada, or when getting close to Canada, especially, are of woods, farms, trees, and open spaces—as well as snow. The wilderness is a traditional symbol of Canada and the North in Canadian literature and film as well as in the Canadian imagination.[18] In *The Handmaid's Tale,* the empty rural setting along the borderlands is heavily contrasted to the urban setting of Gilead, and further works to idealize Canada as a romantic, natural wilderness—empty of urbanization and potentially ripe for symbolic meaning as well as a new, freer, life.

Beyond acting as a central plot driver, there is an important emphasis on the border itself as a symbol of freedom, hope, and tolerance. One of the most interesting scenes to analyze comes in episode 10 of the first season when Moira arrives at the refugee center in Canada. Against a stark, large Canadian flag hanging as a back drop, Moira meets her refugee case worker (Andrew Moodie). He begins by apologizing ("Sorry, sorry") and further draws on Canadian stereotypes of politeness and kindness. He is constructed as helpful, caring, and friendly via his questions to Moira, asking her if she has everything she needs, and telling her that "I get to be your best friend" because she has no family there. His attitude is friendly, familiar, and informal, telling her about turkey tetrazzini night in a kind of coconspirator way. Further, he displays understanding, empathy, and a caring nature. By way of greeting, he says, "Welcome to Ontario. I wish it were under different circumstances but we're happy to have you here." That Canadians welcome, rather than refuse, refugees draws on one of the Canadian myths around tolerance, openness, and helpfulness in addition to policies toward immigrants.

This scene also displays an effective social support system for refugees. The alert texting system is mentioned, which notifies the family member if a person comes in. Further, the efficient and seamless way Moira is processed indicates that refugees are frequently dealt with and supported. Moira is given a refugee identification card, and a temporary case worker until a permanent one can be assigned. She is also given a cell phone which is paid for twelve months, with $200 for cabs, $470 in cash, a medical insurance card, a prescription drug card, and a bag of clothes. The emphasis on the healthcare coverage is an important signifier of Canada's universal health care. As Moira leaves the center, there is an "I support refugees" poster on the door in case the symbolism is lost on the viewer up until that point.

What is really notable in this scene is not perhaps the stereotypical representations of Canada as a polite, welcoming, helpful country with effective and efficient social support systems, but Moira's complete bewilderment of this treatment. She is dramatically overwhelmed and overcome by this drastic change in her situation. The shift from a state of absolute control and severely hampered personal freedoms (including working at a brothel), to one of absolute choice, is clearly shocking to Moira. The scene with the case worker concludes by him asking her what she would like to do next: "Eat? Shower? Grab a book and find someplace quiet? Whatever you want, it's completely up to you." The distinctions between America/Gilead and Canada are being very clearly constructed in this scene and this statement. While Moira experienced a setting of pure control and hampered individual freedoms—reproductive, sexually, and otherwise—in America/Gilead, in Canada she suddenly finds herself in a setting of individual choice and freedom, where one is greeted with politeness, food, universal healthcare, and social support systems. In this way, over the border and in the North, Canada is represented as a welcoming and open sanctuary where one's rights and freedoms are restored.

The Canadian border is also represented as a kind of defense mechanism for rights, such as women's rights and the rights of the LGBTQ community. For example, when Serena Joy (Yvonne Strahovski) and Fred Waterford (Joseph Fiennes) arrive in Canada on their diplomatic mission in season 2 (episode 9), they are greeted by a female Deputy Minister of Foreign Affairs (Carinne Leduc), an openly gay male Associate Deputy Minister for Immigration (José Arias), along with a member of the Prime Minister's Office (James Gilbert), all of whom have differing skin tones and, presumably, differing racial and ethnic backgrounds. Upon being introduced to the Waterfords, the Associate Deputy Minister tells the couple, "I was very fond of visiting the States before. With my husband." That this character directly challenges the Waterfords and publicly acknowledges his sexual preferences and family lifestyle indicates the social acceptance of sexual choice and diversity that is implied to exist within Canada. Further, that he is a high-ranking government official directly flies in the face of the situation in Gilead, where only heteronormative white males hold positions of any power.

Women's rights are also emphasized in this episode. The Waterfords are eventually asked to leave (i.e., return across the border) because they are "no longer welcome in Canada" once the letters from the women in Gilead are shared publicly. The Canadian government official tells them, "We believe the women," a powerful statement in light of the context of the #MeToo movement and women's rights. Scenes of protesting Canadians surrounding the cars in which the Gileadian diplomats travel is another powerful image of the contrasted social situation in Canada—where peaceful protests are permitted and there is a strong public support for women's rights. When the Waterfords are officially out of Canadian airspace, Moira and her fellow expats cheer and celebrate, highlighting the border as an important symbol of protection for the refugees. In the context of the #MeToo movement, this episode emphasizes myths of Canadian multiculturalism,[19] diversity, and equality for people of all races, ethnicities, sexual orientations, and genders.

Throughout *The Handmaid's Tale,* the Canadian-American border figures prominently as both a major plot driver as well as a symbolic site of liberal democratic values. As the ideal destination in the show, Canada is constructed as a tolerant sanctuary where multiculturalism and diversity exist. Further, because it is framed as the utopia in the dystopian narrative, Canada is also represented as a site of hope for the future. Not only is it a place to escape the harrowing lives led in Gilead, but it is a place where liberal democratic values such as openness, tolerance, multiculturalism, and the basic human rights of all people, including women and members of the LGBTQ community, are upheld and defended. It is a beacon of normality/rationality in a seemingly foreign/irrational new world for the protagonists.

If America as a whole, and Boston, MA, in particular, are the primary settings of this dystopian tale, then the construction of Canada as utopia in the Hulu adaptation (similarly to the novel) is compelling. Canada is a safe haven, a sanctuary, offering protection from the intolerant and restrictive laws dictated by religious fundamentalists in Gilead, laws enforced by an extreme military state and a trigger-friendly armed paramilitary force. By drawing on the importance of a physical and symbolic border between Canada and America, *The Handmaid's Tale* is emphasizing the duality of the nations in their existence and values. *The Handmaid's Tale* thus presents an idealized version of Canada as all that is "good" or desirable (freedom, sanctuary, social systems, tolerance, openness, reproductive and sexual rights, etc.) to all that is "bad" or undesirable in Gilead/America (militarized, ruled by religious fanatics, hypocrisy, intolerance, state-sanctioned sexual assault, women's rights stripped, etc.).[20]

PROTECTING BORDERS: CANADIAN NATIONALISM, ANTI-AMERICANISM, AND CULTURAL IMPERIALISM

Within studies on discourses of nationalism, it is frequently noted that rather than the anticipated demise of the importance of nations and nationhood for humanity as a result of various globalization processes, there has been a visible resurgence of nationalism in various parts of the world.[21] The work to define nation states is discursive, that is, nation states and their collective identities need to be coconstructed via discourse in order to remain.[22] In this way, what constitutes a nation is consistently constructed and renegotiated through the written, spoken, and visual discourses in and of a nation—via banal artifacts such as flags and currency, to official government documents or speeches, to news media stories, to the popular culture products of a nation.[23] All these texts work to coconstruct national identity among a vast and diverse collective and are the products of a flexible and dynamic process.[24]

An important way that Canadian national discourse has been presented within the popular imagination has been to rely on the discourse of difference[25]—that is, to emphasize its strongest difference/s with other nations, particularly the United States. This has often been tied to a long and colorful history of anti-Americanism.[26] In this way, because of the similarities between Canada and the United States, especially for Anglophone Canada, there is a tendency for Canada to be preoccupied with demonstrating to itself and others that it is separate and different from a larger, very-similar neighbor (similarly to New Zealand/Australia, Austria/Germany, and most of Central America/Mexico).[27] As Canadian political scientist Brian Bow argues, "These impulses may be especially powerful in Canada, because of the relatively shallow and profoundly contested nature of the country's sense of national identity: Canadians are forever casting about for markers of collective identification, but there are few at hand, apart from not being Americans."[28] This is where the border figures so prominently.

The Canada-U.S. border is both geographically and symbolically important for Canadian Anglophone cultural identity, as a way to maintain differences between "us" and "them," even though the identities are relational and intertwined.[29] As American literary and border studies scholar Evelyn P. Mayer explains, "The border as dividing line between Canadians and Americans is clearly a sanctuary line for Canadian culture as understood by Canadians."[30] The majority of Canadians live within 350 kilometers of the border, and this proximity plays an important role in self-identification and awareness of their more powerful Southern neighbor. Notably, the border acts as an important psychological and physical separation against assimilation. As a borderlands society, "The border penetrates deeply into the Canadian consciousness, identity, economy, and polity to a degree unknown and unimaginable in the United States."[31] It is the asymmetric relationship between Canada and the United States that leads to the border figuring so prominently within the Canadian national consciousness. The constant perceived threat of American cultural imperialism has meant that the border is frequently seen as a defense mechanism, so that "the border often symbolizes Canadian efforts to resist US cultural, economic, and political intrusions. The border thus functions as a bulwark for definitions of Canadian particularities, which are almost always conceptualized as differences from its southern neighbor."[32] James Loucky and Donald Alper, border studies specialists in anthropology and political science respectively, further elucidate, "For Canadians the border is central to identity. There is substantial concern over the influence of the United States on virtually every aspect of Canadian life. [. . .] Thus, the border is viewed somewhat optimistically, as a necessary if insufficient protective shield to help maintain Canadian sovereignty."[33]

The border as shield and defense against "what [Canadians] do not want to become"[34] is prominently displayed within *The Handmaid's Tale*. That the crux of the narrative revolves around the Canadian-Gileadian border—as the central motivating plot thrust, as the ultimate alternative nation, as a rural sanctuary, as a symbol and site of freedom, hope, tolerance, diversity, and equality with strong social support systems and peaceful protests, and as an important defense mechanism for individual rights and protection—is telling from a Canadian national discourse perspective. It is important to come full circle and remind ourselves that the original creator of the tale, Margaret Atwood, arguably a Canadian nationalist,[35] has indicated in interviews and other writings that part of her motivation behind writing *The Handmaid's Tale* was her understanding and concerns around fundamental religious movements in the United States.[36] That Atwood has constructed a tale which emphasizes the differences between Canada and America and acts as a warning against assimilation and the political and cultural tendencies to the south, and thus, uses the border as an important symbolic tool, is not necessarily surprising. Concerns of cultural imperialism have long been felt within the Canadian literary community as well as a perceived sense of inferiority.[37]

But what is particularly interesting around this overtly Canadian nationalist tale—is that it is produced, written, and wildly popular in America as a transnational media product. The Canadian nationalism has not been removed or lessened in Hulu's television adaptation. Why a tale that presents America as a dystopia to Canada as utopia is immensely popular in traditionally patriotic America is interesting and worthy of further research. Is it perhaps that Americans, as Canadians have long suspected, find Canada so inconsequential and unthreatening that it can be ignored? As Canadian literary scholars Arnold Davidson, Priscilla Walton, and Jennifer Andrews so aptly describe,

> Borders exist only to the degree that they are defended and . . . this imaginary line is especially defended by the way that each side imagines an identity *in relation to* the other across it—but differently. The asymmetrical working of the imaginary border is especially evident in the way Canadians tend, somewhat dubiously, to view Americans as the rampant example of what they do not want to become, whereas the American tendency is to see, just as dubiously, Canada as already so much like the United States (except less interesting) that it is hardly there at all.[38]

Alternatively, it is possible that Canada is increasingly seen as the kind of America that Americans want to reside in, indeed, as a kind of safe haven, amidst the extreme and violent political and cultural divides that currently exist within the nation. As we are concluding the manuscript in December 2018, border politics are a contentious and crucial issue. The United States is currently closing its border to Mexico[39] and gassing unwanted migrants, including children.[40] In contrast, the government of Canada has provided temporary refuge to migrants who are escaping perceived injustices in the United States, at a controversial estimated cost of $340 million.[41] The complicated relationship around the borders exists in the present day. Whatever the motivation or reason, one thing remains clear—Hulu's *The Handmaid's Tale* presents a strong Canadian nationalist discourse despite, or perhaps because of, its transnational production.

NOTES

1. See Heather Latimer, "Popular Culture and Reproductive Politics: Juno, Knocked Up and the Enduring Legacy of *The Handmaid's Tale*," *Feminist Theory* 10, no. 2 (August 1, 2009): 211–26; S. C. Neuman, "'Just a Backlash': Margaret Atwood, Feminism, and *The Handmaid's Tale*," *University of Toronto Quarterly* 75, no. 3 (July 17, 2006): 857–68; Allan Weiss, "Offred's Complicity and the Dystopian Tradition in Margaret Atwood's *The Handmaid's Tale*," *Studies in Canadian Literature/ Études En Littérature Canadienne* 34, no. 1 (January 1, 2009): 120–41.

2. Eva Mackey, *House of Difference: Cultural Politics and National Identity in Canada* (London: Routledge, 2005).

3. Sonja K. Foss, *Rhetorical Criticism: Exploration & Practice*, 2nd Edition (Prospect Heights, IL: Waveland Press, 2008).

4. Miyase Christensen, "TransNational Media Flows: Some Key Questions and Debates," *International Journal of Communication* 7 (2013): 2400–2418.

5. Ed Nawotka, "The Canadian Author Canadians Know Best? Margaret Atwood," *PublishersWeekly.com*, 2017. https://www.publishersweekly.com/pw /by-topic/international/international-book-news/article/74334-the-canadian-author -canadians-know-best-margaret-atwood.html.

6. Kiley Kapuscinski, "Negotiating the Nation: The Reproduction and Reconstruction of the National Imaginary in Margaret Atwood's Surfacing," *ESC: English Studies in Canada* 33, no. 3 (2007): 95–123, https://doi.org/10.1353/esc.0.0060.

7. David Michael Brown, "We Need to Talk about What Happened with 'The Handmaid's Tale' Movie," *Guide*, 2017. https://www.sbs.com.au/guide /article/2017/06/27/we-need-talk-about-what-happened-handmaids-tale-movie.

8. "Hulu Announces Straight-to-Series Order for *The Handmaid's Tale* from MGM Television – Hulu Press Site," Hulu, accessed October 17, 2018, https:// www.hulu.com/press/hulu-announces-straight-to-series-order-for-the-handmaids -tale-from-mgm-television/.

9. Hulu's *The Handmaid's Tale* has been immensely successful. It has received multiple awards including two Golden Globes, eight Emmy's, and AFI's television program of the year, among many others. "The Handmaid's Tale – Awards," *IMDb*, accessed October 10, 2018, https://www.imdb.com/title/tt5834204/awards.

10. Sian Cain, "Margaret Atwood Says Handmaid's Tale TV Show Profits Went to MGM, Not Her," *The Guardian*, February 1, 2018, sec. Books. https://www .theguardian.com/books/2018/feb/01/margaret-atwood-mgm-the-handmaids-tale-tv.

11. Atwood slaps Offred in the face after the Handmaid refuses to blame Janine (Madeline Brewer) for having been raped in high school by pointing a finger at her in

unison with all other Handmaids in "Offred," Season 1, Episode 1, directed by Reed Morano, written by Bruce Miller, Hulu, April 26, 2017.

12. Toronto-born director Jeremy Podeswa directed episodes 9 and 10 of season 2.

13. "The Handmaid's Tale (TV Series 2017 –) Filming & Production," *IMDb*, accessed October 10, 2018, https://www.imdb.com/title/tt5834204/locations?ref_=tt _dt_dt#filming_locations; Liz Shannon Miller, "'The Handmaid's Tale': Behind the Scenes of Season 2's Most Brutal Moments (So Far)," *IndieWire* (blog), April 26, 2018, https://www.indiewire.com/2018/04/handmaids-tale-fenway-park-friends -boston-globe-ear-season-2-spoilers-1201957434/.

14. David Fleischer, "Everything We Know (So Far) about the Second Season of *The Handmaid's Tale*," *Toronto Life* (blog), April 25, 2018, https://torontolife.com /culture/movies-and-tv/everything-know-far-second-season-handmaids-tale/.

15. Debra Yeo, *"The Handmaid's Tale* Finally Gets Canadian Distributor," thestar. com, March 27, 2017, https://www.thestar.com/entertainment/television/2017/03/27 /the-handmaids-tale-finally-gets-canadian-distributor.html.

16. "THE HANDMAID'S TALE Becomes Bravo's Most-Watched Broadcast, Ever," Cision, accessed October 10, 2018, https://www.newswire.ca/news-releases /the-handmaids-tale-becomes-bravos-most-watched-broadcast-ever-621996583.html.

17. In *The Handmaid's Tale*, the dystopian setting is the former United States, and specifically, the plot centers predominantly in the state of Massachusetts and in Boston. Miller, the executive producer and writer, has pointedly noted in various interviews the implied and intended connection to Boston, making overt references to sites such as the Harvard wall, Fenway Park, or the *Boston Globe*, for instance. See Dana Feldman, "Bruce Miller Talks 'The Handmaid's Tale': Season 2 Finale and What to Expect for Season 3," *Forbes*, July 11, 2018, accessed October 17, 2018, https://www.forbes.com/sites/danafeldman/2018/07/11/bruce-miller-talks-the -handmaids-tale-season-2-finale-and-what-to-expect-for-season-3/.

18. Margaret Atwood, *Survival: A Thematic Guide to Canadian Literature* (House of Anansi, 2012).

19. Canada is also represented as a multicultural and diverse nation by the exis-tence of "Little America." Various scenes throughout the show display Little America as similar to various communities in Toronto, such as Little Italy, for example, with people with similar backgrounds coming together. In the show, Little America has memorials, a bureaucratic site with which to operate, and former government officials are able to assist their former citizens. That the site is referred to as "Little America" is particularly interesting, however. It could just as easily have been termed Toronto or Canada. Instead, "Little America" indicates that this is America on Canadian soil. Or perhaps, it's a symbolic reference to Canada being Little America. In either case, the American bureaucrat tells Moira and Luke that "this isn't our country. In the end, we are guests of the Canadian government" ("Smart Power," Season 2, Episode 9, directed by Jeremy Podeswa, written by Dorothy Fortenberry, Hulu, June 13, 2018). The deference to Canada, and the indication of political and military powerlessness at the hands of Canada, is a particularly unusual balance of political power.

20. See Paul Moffett, "U for Utopia: The Dystopian and Eutopian Visions in Alan Moore and David Lloyd's V for Vendetta," *Journal of Graphic Novels and Comics*

8, no. 1 (January 2, 2017): 46–58, for a useful explanation of utopias/dystopia as dependent on the particular historical and cultural contexts in which they produce either desires and fears.

21. Ruth Wodak, "Discourses about Nationalism," in *The Routledge Handbook of Critical Discourse Studies*, edited by John Flowerdew and John Richardson (New York: Routledge, 2018) 403–20; Sabina Mihelj, *Media Nations: Communicating Belonging and Exclusion in the Modern World* (London: Palgrave Macmillan, 2011).

22. Wodak, "Discourses about Nationalism," 404.

23. Wodak and others from the Discourse Historical Approach (DHA) utilize, draw on, and build from important work on nationalism and the construction of national identity from authors like E. Gellner, *Nations and Nationalism* (Oxford: Blackwell, 1983); Benedict Anderson, *Imagined Communities: Reflections on the Origin and Spread of Nationalism* (London: Verso, 1995); T. Adorno, *Negative Dialektik* (Frankfurt/Main: Springer, 1966); Ulrich Beck, "We Do Not Live in an Age of Cosmopolitanism but in an Age of Cosmopolitisation. The 'Global Order' in Our Midst," *Irish Journal of Sociology* 19, no. 1 (2011): 16–35; and Michael Billig, *Banal Nationalism* (London: Sage, 1995). DHA's underlining premises are "that nations are primarily mental constructs, in the sense that they exist as discrete political communities in the imagination of their members; that national identity includes a set of dispositions, attitudes and conventions that are largely internalised through socialisation and create a 'national habitus', drawing on Bourdieu's concepts of habitus, capital, and field (1990); and, lastly, that nationhood as a form of social identity is produced, transformed, maintained and dismantled through discourse" (Wodak, "Discourses about Nationalism," 408).

24. Wodak, "Discourses about Nationalism," 409.

25. Wodak, "Discourses about Nationalism," 408–9.

26. Anti-Americanism is defined as "an attitude toward the United States and its people which is profoundly mistrustful—a prejudice that colors the way a person interprets Americans' choices, and consistently attributes them to negative values and purposes" (Brian Bow, "Anti-Americanism in Canada, before and after Iraq," *American Review of Canadian Studies* 38, no. 3 [October 2008]: 341).

27. Bow, "Anti-Americanism in Canada, before and after Iraq."

28. Bow, "Anti-Americanism in Canada," 342.

29. Evelyn P. Mayer. "Beyond Border Binaries: Borderline, Borderlands, and In-Betweenness in Thomas King's Short Story 'Borders,'" *International Journal of Canadian Studies* 43 (2011): 67–82.

30. Mayer, "Beyond Border Binaries," 72.

31. Roger Gibbins, *Canada as a Borderlands Society*, Borderlands Monograph 2 (University of Maine: Canadian-American Center, 1989), 2.

32. Claudia Sadowski-Smith, *Border Fictions: Globalization, Empire, and Writing at the Boundaries of the United States* (Charlottesville: University of Virginia Press, 2008), 12.

33. James Loucky and Donald K Alper, "Pacific Borders, Discordant Borders: Where North America Edges Together," in *Transboundary Policy Challenges in the*

Pacific Border Regions of North America, edited by James Loucky, Donald K Alper, and J. C. Day, 11–38 (Calgary: University of Calgary Press, 2008), 17.

34. Arnold Davidson, Priscilla L. Walton, and Jennifer Andrews, *Border Crossings: Thomas King's Cultural Inversions* (Toronto: University of Toronto Press, 2003), 16.

35. Paul Goetsch, "Margaret Atwood: A Canadian Nationalist," in *Margaret Atwood: Works and Impact*, edited by Reingard M. Nischik (Rochester, NY: Camden House, 2000), 166–79; Sandra Tomc, "'The Missionary Position': Feminism and Nationalism in Margaret Atwood's 'The Handmaid's Tale,'" *Canadian Literature* 138–39 (1993): 73–87.

36. Margaret Atwood, "Margaret Atwood on What 'The Handmaid's Tale' Means in the Age of Trump," *New York Times*, April 25, 2018, sec. Books. https://www.ny times.com/2017/03/10/books/review/margaret-atwood-handmaids-tale-age-of-trump .html.

37. In her Letter to America, Atwood explicitly links Americans to Romans and Canadians to Gauls in order to highlight Canadians' perceived inferior role in comparison with Americans. She states, "We're like Romanized Gauls—look like Romans, dress like Romans, but aren't Romans—peering over the wall at the real Romans" (Atwood in Mayer, 2013), presumably directly toward the powerful Southern neighbor in an asymmetric bilateral relationship in terms of economy, politics, the military, and population.

38. Davidson, Walton, and Andrews, *Border Crossings: Thomas King's Cultural Inversions*, 16.

39. Yesica Fisch, Julie Watson, and Norman Merchant, "U.S. Closes Busiest Mexico Border Crossing for Several Hours to Install New Barriers against Caravans, Migrants," *The Globe and Mail*, November 19, 2018, https://www.theglobeandmail. com/world/article-us-closes-busiest-mexico-border-crossing-for-several-hours-to/.

40. "Trump Defends Tear Gas on Mexico Border," *BBC News*, November 27, 2018, sec. US & Canada, https://www.bbc.com/news/world-us-canada-46355258.

41. Kathleen Harris, "Asylum Seekers Entering Canada outside Legal Border Points Cost an Average of $14K Each," *CBC News*, November 29, 2018, https:// www.cbc.ca/news/politics/pbo-budget-officer-asylum-seekers-costs-1.4924364.

WORKS CITED

Adorno, T. *Negative Dialektik*. Frankfurt/Main: Springer, 1966.

Anderson, Benedict. *Imagined Communities: Reflections on the Origin and Spread of Nationalism*. London: Verso, 1995.

Atwood, Margaret. "Margaret Atwood on What 'The Handmaid's Tale' Means in the Age of Trump." *New York Times*, April 25, 2018, sec. Books. https://www

.nytimes.com/2017/03/10/books/review/margaret-atwood-handmaids-tale-age-of
-trump.html.

———. *Survival: A Thematic Guide to Canadian Literature*. House of Anansi, 2012.

Beck, Ulrich. "We Do Not Live in an Age of Cosmopolitanism but in an Age of Cosmopolitisation. The 'Global Order' in Our Midst." *Irish Journal of Sociology* 19, no. 1 (2011): 16–35.

Billig, Michael. *Banal Nationalism*. London: Sage, 1995.

Bow, Brian. "Anti-Americanism in Canada, before and after Iraq." *American Review of Canadian Studies* 38, no. 3 (October 2008): 341–59. https://doi .org/10.1080/02722010809481718.

Brown, David Michael. "We Need to Talk about What Happened with 'The Handmaid's Tale' Movie." *Guide*, 2017. https://www.sbs.com.au/guide/arti cle/2017/06/27/we-need-talk-about-what-happened-handmaids-tale-movie.

Cain, Sian. "Margaret Atwood Says Handmaid's Tale TV Show Profits Went to MGM, Not Her." *The Guardian*, February 1, 2018, sec. Books. https://www.the guardian.com/books/2018/feb/01/margaret-atwood-mgm-the-handmaids-tale-tv.

Christensen, Miyase. "TransNational Media Flows: Some Key Questions and Debates." *International Journal of Communication* 7 (2013): 2400–2418.

Cision. "THE HANDMAID'S TALE Becomes Bravo's Most-Watched Broadcast, Ever." Accessed October 10, 2018. https://www.newswire.ca/news-releases/the -handmaids-tale-becomes-bravos-most-watched-broadcast-ever-621996583.html.

Davidson, Arnold E., Priscilla L. Walton, and Jennifer Andrews. *Border Crossings: Thomas King's Cultural Inversions*. Toronto: University of Toronto Press, 2003.

Feldman, Dana. "Bruce Miller Talks 'The Handmaid's Tale': Season 2 Finale and What to Expect for Season 3." *Forbes,* July 11, 2018. Accessed October 17, 2018. https://www.forbes.com/sites/danafeldman/2018/07/11/bruce-miller-talks -the-handmaids-tale-season-2-finale-and-what-to-expect-for-season-3/.

Fisch, Yesica, Julie Watson, and Norman Merchant. "U.S. Closes Busiest Mexico Border Crossing for Several Hours to Install New Barriers against Caravans, Migrants." *The Globe and Mail*, November 19, 2018. https://www.theglobe andmail.com/world/article-us-closes-busiest-mexico-border-crossing-for-several- hours-to/.

Fleischer, David. "Everything We Know (So Far) about the Second Season of *The Handmaid's Tale.*" *Toronto Life* (blog), April 25, 2018. https://torontolife.com /culture/movies-and-tv/everything-know-far-second-season-handmaids-tale/.

Foss, Sonja K. *Rhetorical Criticism: Exploration & Practice*, 2nd Edition. Prospect Heights, IL: Waveland Press, 2008.

Gellner, E. *Nations and Nationalism*. Oxford: Blackwell, 1983.

Gibbins, Roger. *Canada as a Borderlands Society*. Borderlands Monograph 2. University of Maine: Canadian-American Center, 1989.

Goetsch, Paul. "Margaret Atwood: A Canadian Nationalist." In *Margaret Atwood: Works and Impact*, edited by Reingard M. Nischik, 166–79. Rochester, NY: Camden House, 2000.

Harris, Kathleen. "Asylum Seekers Entering Canada outside Legal Border Points Cost an Average of $14K Each." *CBC News*, November 29, 2018. https://www.cbc.ca/news/politics/pbo-budget-officer-asylum-seekers-costs-1.4924364.

"Hulu Announces Straight-to-Series Order for *The Handmaid's Tale* from MGM Television—Hulu Press Site." Hulu. Accessed October 17, 2018. https://www.hulu.com/press/hulu-announces-straight-to-series-order-for-the-handmaids-tale-from-mgm-television/.

Kapuscinski, Kiley. "Negotiating the Nation: The Reproduction and Reconstruction of the National Imaginary in Margaret Atwood's Surfacing." *ESC: English Studies in Canada* 33, no. 3 (2007): 95–123. https://doi.org/10.1353/esc.0.0060.

Latimer, Heather. "Popular Culture and Reproductive Politics: Juno, Knocked Up and the Enduring Legacy of *The Handmaid's Tale*." *Feminist Theory* 10, no. 2 (August 1, 2009): 211–26. https://doi.org/10.1177/1464700109104925.

Loucky, James, and Donald K Alper. "Pacific Borders, Discordant Borders: Where North America Edges Together." In *Transboundary Policy Challenges in the Pacific Border Regions of North America*, edited by James Loucky, Donald K. Alper, and J. C. Day, 11–38. Calgary: University of Calgary Press, 2008.

Mackey, Eva. *House of Difference: Cultural Politics and National Identity in Canada*. London: Routledge, 2005. https://doi.org/10.4324/9780203981306.

Mayer, Evelyn P. "Beyond Border Binaries: Borderline, Borderlands, and In-Betweenness in Thomas King's Short Story 'Borders.'" *International Journal of Canadian Studies* 43 (2011): 67–82.

Mihelj, Sabina. *Media Nations: Communicating Belonging and Exclusion in the Modern World*. London: Palgrave Macmillan, 2011.

Miller, Liz Shannon. "'The Handmaid's Tale': Behind the Scenes of Season 2's Most Brutal Moments (So Far)." *IndieWire* (blog), April 26, 2018. https://www.indiewire.com/2018/04/handmaids-tale-fenway-park-friends-boston-globe-ear-season-2-spoilers-1201957434/.

Moffett, Paul. "U for Utopia: The Dystopian and Eutopian Visions in Alan Moore and David Lloyd's V for Vendetta." *Journal of Graphic Novels and Comics* 8, no. 1 (January 2, 2017): 46–58. https://doi.org/10.1080/21504857.2016.1233894.

Nawotka, Ed. "The Canadian Author Canadians Know Best? Margaret Atwood." *PublishersWeekly.com*, 2017. https://www.publishersweekly.com/pw/by-topic/international/international-book-news/article/74334-the-canadian-author-canadians-know-best-margaret-atwood.html.

Neuman, S. C. "'Just a Backlash': Margaret Atwood, Feminism, and *The Handmaid's Tale*." *University of Toronto Quarterly* 75, no. 3 (July 17, 2006): 857–68. https://doi.org/10.1353/utq.2006.0260.

Sadowski-Smith, Claudia. *Border Fictions: Globalization, Empire, and Writing at the Boundaries of the United States*. Charlottesville: University of Virginia Press, 2008.

"The Handmaid's Tale – Awards." *IMDb*. Accessed October 10, 2018. https://www.imdb.com/title/tt5834204/awards.

"The Handmaid's Tale (TV Series 2017 –) Filming & Production." *IMDb*. Accessed October 10, 2018. https://www.imdb.com/title/tt5834204/locations?ref_=tt_dt _dt#filming_locations.

Tomc, Sandra. "'The Missionary Position': Feminism and Nationalism in Margaret Atwood's 'The Handmaid's Tale.'" *Canadian Literature* 138–39 (1993): 73–87.

"Trump Defends Tear Gas on Mexico Border." *BBC News*, November 27, 2018, sec. US & Canada. https://www.bbc.com/news/world-us-canada-46355258.

Weiss, Allan. "Offred's Complicity and the Dystopian Tradition in Margaret Atwood's *The Handmaid's Tale*." *Studies in Canadian Literature/Études En Littérature Canadienne* 34, no. 1 (January 1, 2009): 120–41.

Wodak, Ruth. "Discourses about Nationalism." In *The Routledge Handbook of Critical Discourse Studies*, edited by John Flowerdew and John Richardson, 403–20. New York: Routledge, 2018.

Yeo, Debra. "*The Handmaid's Tale* Finally Gets Canadian Distributor." thestar.com, March 27, 2017. https://www.thestar.com/entertainment/television/2017/03/27 /the-handmaids-tale-finally-gets-canadian-distributor.html.

FILM AND TELEVISION

The Handmaid's Tale. "Night." Season 1, Episode 10. Directed by Kari Skogland. Written by Bruce Miller. Hulu, June 14, 2017.

The Handmaid's Tale. "Offred." Season 1, Episode 1. Directed by Reed Morano. Written by Bruce Miller. Hulu, April 26, 2017.

The Handmaid's Tale. "Smart Power." Season 2, Episode 9. Directed by Jeremy Podeswa. Written by Dorothy Fortenberry. Hulu, June 13, 2018.

The Handmaid's Tale. "The Other Side." Season 1, Episode 7. Directed by Floria Sigismondi. Written by Lynn Renee Maxcy. Hulu, May 24, 2017.

Chapter Twenty-Two

Suffering Motherhood, Sexuality, and Woman's Empowerment

Metropolis *and* The Handmaid's Tale

Clémentine Tholas

Director Fritz Lang's *Metropolis* (1927) and the first season of the Hulu TV adaptation of Margaret Atwood's *The Handmaid's Tale* (2017) deal with stories of control: control over the female body and sexuality, control of birth, and control of social divisions and hierarchies. Both the film and the series discuss the issue of a world divided along the lines of gender and class. The Hulu TV series is rather faithfully adapted from Margaret Atwood's speculative fiction published in 1986 and written in 1984 under the influence of George Orwell's work. As the author was a consultant on the Hulu show, the series directed by Bruce Miller obeys the principles of Atwood's literary production which requires that nothing is fabricated—the historical incidents and events mentioned have occurred at some point in history and in some place. With the release of the program in 2017, Atwood gave numerous interviews in which she explained: "All of the details have precedents in real life. . . . It's based on stuff that people have really done and therefore could do again."[1]

The Handmaid's Tale imagines "a dictatorship based on history and probability,"[2] inspired by what has been going on for several decades in alleged modern civilizations. We can wonder if the same rule applies to Thea Von Harbou's *Metropolis* adapted to the screen by her husband Fritz Lang in 1927. The preamble by Von Harbou rejects any specific reading of class struggle or social predictions but asserts the universalism of a tale: "This book is not of today or of the future. It tells no place. It serves no cause, party or class. It has a moral which grows on the pillar of understanding: the mediator between the brain and the muscle must be the heart." However, the spectators of the film cannot ignore the echoes of the Russian Proletarian Revolution of 1917 or the strikes and claims for social transformations in a Weimar Germany stifled by the Reparation payments of the First World War.

If *Metropolis* stages the oppression of laborers by demonic machines and wretched capitalists, *The Handmaid's Tale* focuses on the emotional and sexual exploitation of women whose role is to serve the leaders of the Republic of Gilead and their barren wives. *Metropolis* represents the absence of compassion in industrial rationalized modern life, while Gilead represents the United States if it were to become a totalitarian regime based on the literal reading of the Bible and using religion as "an excuse to be repressive."[3]

This chapter examines the power struggles stemming from the issue of maternity. It will ponder about the falsification of parenthood as well as the commodification of women and children before commenting on the representation of female sexuality on screen and the persistence of the hackneyed Madonna-whore dichotomy.

METROPOLIS AND GILEAD: CONTROLLING WOMEN AND CHILDREN

The prelude of *Metropolis* opens on a depiction of "The Club of the Sons," a portion of the city reserved to the progenies of the wealthy and devoted to leisure. The epicenter of this privileged world is "the miracle of the Eternal Gardens" filled with fancy courtesans and created—as the title card explains—by the Fathers to provide their sons with the pleasure of the flesh. In the motherless world of *Metropolis*, young males are kings celebrated and spoiled by their powerful fathers who encourage them to mingle only with women to satisfy their physical instincts. The master of the city Joh Fredersen (Alfred Abel) has lost Hel, the mother of his child Freder (Gustav Fröhlich), when she gave birth, and seems to have imagined a futuristic realm were women are scarcely needed. Patriarchal power is based on the absence of women among the dominant class (no wives, no daughters) and the vilification of women from the other classes, trapped in inferior roles such as industrial workers or prostitutes. On the other hand, in *The Handmaid's Tale*, women are more numerous and seem to outnumber men, but their life has been organized according to a rigorous patriarchal caste system discouraging any form of support and solidarity between women. No matter their social status, they are all made to serve men: the Wives are to take care of their homes and rule over other women;[4] the Aunts are to re-educate their fellow sisters into the new system; the Marthas are the domestic servants of the commanding families; the Handmaids are the child-bearers for the unfertile influential couples; the Jezebels are prostitutes in a government-controlled club; and the barren women refusing to obey the rules are called "Unwomen" and sent to the Colonies—a vast toxic wasteland. Considering the large proportion of women and their role in the preservation of human species in *The Handmaid's Tale*, Gilead could have been a matriarchy if women were not subjected to obliging men and had not accepted their dominion. As Alice Elaine Adams underlines, "in Atwood's Gilead the state is all Father."[5] The expression "Under His Eye" illustrates the constant surveillance and the omnipotence of the male gaze which seems to neutralize women, and it is clearly reminiscent of Big Brother's watch in *1984*. In season 1, episode 3, Offred underlines her passive complicity and how women's lack of vigilence validated the Theocratic Republic: "I was asleep before. That's how we let it happen. When they slaughtered Congress, we didn't wake up. When they blamed terrorists and suspended the Constitution, we didn't wake up then, either. Nothing changes instantaneously. In a gradually heating bathtub, you'd be boiled to death before you knew it."[6]

Male supremacy is asserted thanks to the power of naming. In *Metropolis*, in the name of the Father lies the identity of the son. In *The Handmaid's Tale*, the red servant, the Handmaid, is named after the Commander she is assigned to. Joh Fredersen, the master of *Metropolis*, called his son "Freder," as if to prove the young man has no identity of his own and is a little runt only able to live in the shadow of his father. Fredersen's project to entrap the sons of the wealthy in a club is a way to maintain them in a state of immaturity and dependence. They are kept in an ideal cocoon and not encouraged to discover the depths of the workers' city outside the protective fences of the upper city. The "Club of the Sons" operates as a golden cage in which young male adults are infantilized so that they don't disturb the rich men ruling *Metropolis*.

In the idle existence shaped for them by their genitors, Freder and the other sons are allowed to navigate between their childlike bedrooms, their sports activities at the club, the Eternal Gardens, and the Yoshiwara night club. Their lives are mapped by other people, and Freder's subversive encounter with Maria (Brigitte Helm) in the gardens disrupts the trajectory chosen by his father, as he will then venture in the workers' city and the catacombs to meet with this fascinating woman who seems liberated from any figure of authority. In *The Handmaid's Tale*, the Handmaids and the Good Women of Gilead also obey a specific routine which has been decided for them by the men to whom they belong. The main character, once called June (Elisabeth Moss), was renamed Offred, a patronym made with the preposition "of" and the first name of her Commander, Fred Waterford (Joseph Fiennes). The other Handmaids are given similar names: Ofglen/Emily (Alexis Bledel), Ofwarren/Janine (Madeline Brewer), and so forth. Dispossessed of their real names and identities, the Handmaids belong to their respective masters who henceforth command their lives. While the Wives and the Marthas are also subjected to men's will, they are not as commodified as the Handmaids who become mere tools of reproduction and a "collective resource"[7] for society. As J. Brooks Bouson underlines, Gilead "robs women of the individual identities and transforms them into replaceable objects in the phallocentric economy."[8]

The infantilization of Handmaids is exemplified by the management of their behavior and limited circulation and their supervision by the Aunts, surrogate members of their new oppressive family. For instance, Offred is very often locked in her room by the Waterfords when she does not obey, or she is given rewards for her good behavior, for example, being lent a prohibited magazine by Fred or a music box by Serena Joy, reminiscent of those kept in a child's room. Offred comments on the irony of recompensing her with the music box: "A perfect gift. A girl trapped in a box. She only dances when someone opens the lid, when someone else winds her up."[9] In the TV series, the couple is rather young, about the same age as Offred, but they are older in the novel and the father-like Commander shares with her a kind of incestuous relationship.[10]

If *The Handmaid's Tale* portrays a society where infertility has made children a source of power and glory, *Metropolis* underlines the discrepancy between the children of the well-off and those of the workers whose lives are considered less precious. In *The Handmaid's Tale*, the very structure of Gilead is based on the necessity to procreate, and the sexual exploitation of the Handmaids is justified by the need to ensure the survival of human species. Actually, children are not only synonymous with life but also with influence, as a viable newborn in the family of a Commander means favorable attention and access to a higher status. The birth of a healthy baby, a so-called "Keeper," will provide them with opportunities for upward mobility which are probably more important than the promise of a new life.[11]

Children appear as instruments in the conquest of political power but can also be seen as a form of protection for the Wives in case of scandal, like the debacle of Commander Putnam after his Handmaid tries to kill herself and her child by jumping off a bridge.[12] In *Metropolis*, the young children of the workers are presented as sacrificial lambs whose lives are valued neither by their parents nor by the capitalist system. Because they are disconnected from the life on the production chain and the profitability process, children stand at the margins of *Metropolis* and of the concerns of adults. Under the wing of Maria, their surrogate mother, they discover life outside the depths of the Lower City when they enter the Eternal Gardens in the Upper City and become aware of the existence of another type of childhood embodied by Freder, the golden child. The young man acknowledges them as his brothers and sisters and saves them along with Maria when the underground city is flooded after the heart machine breaks. Abandoned by their parents who have gathered as a reckless mob, the poor children would have been casualties of the war against the machines without Maria and Freder's kindness and brav-ery when the Lower City collapses. As Gabriela Stoicea explains, "The prole-tarians' thirst for revenge trumps their concerns for their own children,"[13] and they never return to save their little ones, the film thus offering a demonized vision of parenthood. In both the Weimar film and the contemporary Hulu TV series, children are assessed according to their utility, and familial alienation is a key component of the autocratic societies portrayed.

THE MADONNA-WHORE DICHOTOMY IN DYSTOPIAS

The Handmaid's Tale and *Metropolis* also play with the Madonna-Whore dichotomy and examine the issue of the duality of female sexuality and the tensions between procreation and pleasure. The fact that women can be lovers and mothers is negated as they seem forced to strictly choose between these two irreconcilable roles. In *Metropolis*, the inventor Rotwang (Rudolf Klein-Rogge) reminds Fredersen that Hel, the woman they both loved, played differ-ent parts, being a mistress for the scientist and a breeding wife for the master of the city: "The woman is mine, Joh Fredersen! The son of Hel was yours!"

The character of Maria and her evil cyborg double illustrate the desexual-ized/sexualized dichotomy regarding female identity in the film. While the real Maria appears as a saintlike figure preaching for love and understanding among men in the secret chapel of the catacombs, the robot Maria created by Rotwang's twisted mind is a sensual temptress. If Maria is earnest, the robot manipulates rich sons with her erotic dance as well as the workers with her alluring contortions and suggestive remarks: "Who lubricates the joints with their own blood? Who feeds the machines with their own flesh?" Josaphat (Theodor Loss), Freder's companion, underlines the confusion about Maria's double personality: "This woman at whose feet all sins are heaped is also named Maria . . . the same woman those in the depths look up as a saint." The saint/whore division is also present in *The Handmaid's Tale* when Of-fred is transformed by the Commander. She is requested to abandon the red Handmaid's garments of humility and dresses up as a call-girl to accompany him to a brothel, controlled by and accessible only to the Gilead elite. She has been asked before by Waterford to step out of her role of obedient servant when he touched her thigh during the Ceremony or, when one evening in his office, he asked her: "Kiss me like you mean it."

The scene of Offred's transformation into an erotic woman before going to the whorehouse stages Waterford as the conductor and the spectator of the makeover. Admiring how she changes, he remains by her side and holds the mirror for her when she puts on the makeup he has provided. He then hands

Offred a silvery sequin short dress. Once she is ready, he looks at her and says "You look . . . stunning." He adds "Just one thing" and undoes her hair to let it loose on her shoulders. At Waterford's request, she puts on the mask of womanliness as he fantasizes it.[14] Whereas her body and her hair have been constantly covered by her long red dress and her bonnet, Offred is suddenly exposed. She is also asked to wear Serena Waterford's (Yvonne Strahovski) green hood and pretend she is the Wife to make it through the paramilitary checkpoints on the road. The combination of the glittering dress and the hood illustrates how the Commander wants Offred to perform both as a woman of ill-repute and a respectable figure. However, we may wonder if the Hand-maid's red outfit is not already a way of pointing out her status as a potentially fallen woman: the red dress may symbolize the fertility and the menstrual blood, but it also echoes the biblical scarlet woman, the Whore of Babylon.

Normally the Handmaids are not supposed to be associated with sexual pleasure because their role should be limited to the biological act of concep-tion, pregnancy, and childbirth on behalf of the sterile Commanders' Wives and they are similar to incubators with no feelings. The Sons of Jacob who rule Gilead have based the new system on the story of the barren Rachel who offers her servant to bear the children of Jacob, and the Commanders rob the Handmaids from their humanity, turning them into "two-legged wombs."[15] The sanctified copulation ceremony gathers all the servants of the house who are forced to pray with their masters before the Handmaid has to lie between the legs of the wife in her bedroom; she entraps the wrists of her servant as the husband negligently penetrates his Handmaid.

The twisted rituals of the ceremony emphasize the mechanization of the sexual act and the lack of consideration and love in the intercourse. The ceremony is a rape under the guise of a religious mythology and enables the commanding class to enslave those under their power. Because the reproduc-tion is deprived of love in Gilead and Handmaids are treated as appliances, maternity is perverted and becomes meaningless or disruptive. The mother-child bonds are broken as infants are stolen from their real mothers. In sea-son 1, episode 9, Janine has to hand over her newborn baby to the Putnams, Naomi (Ever Carradine) and Warren Putnam (Stephen Kunken), before being removed to another family in need of a child, but she loses her mind and tries to commit suicide. As opposed to the codified domineering intercourses of the ceremony, the physical relation between Offred and the chauffeur Nick (Max Minghella) is based on reciprocity, more equality, and even tenderness, even if it was initiated by Serena Joy who feared her husband might not get the Handmaid pregnant. The reintroduction of pleasurable and affectionate sexuality is a form of empowerment and resistance both for Nick and Offred, who challenge the rules of the regime with their clandestine love-making.

In *Metropolis*, sterility is related to technology and the way automated machines exhaust human laborers and turn them into zombified crowds of male workers. They experience a life of suffering and find no solace in their interactions with their wives. On the contrary, the capitalist leaders and their sons are offered sexual freedom in the company of the prostitutes of the Eternal Gardens. Two forms of sexuality are linked with these social groups: "the proletariat is confined by a reproduction-oriented sexuality" while the upper class is offered a pleasure-oriented sexuality.[16] *Metropolis* separates reproductive and nonreproductive sexuality but denigrates the female characters who use their bodies outside the purposes of procreation.

The virginal real Maria is praised as an idealized figure of motherhood who nurtures the abandoned children of the workers, whereas the racy cyborg Maria and the prostitutes of the Eternal Gardens are disparaged for representing the freedom of the female body. Freder longs for the chaste woman, rejects easy women, and is not fooled by Maria's mechanical double when he shouts in the underground chapel "You are not Maria!" as she is giving an inflammatory speech to trigger the workers' wrath. Revealed to the lustful eyes of the rich sons during an erotic performance, the cyborg is indeed "the incarnation of 'pure' female sexuality cleansed of all maternal feelings"[17] and cannot be mistaken with the motherly aspirations of the real Maria. The film's message is conservative as it castigates the women who give way to their carnal appetites and the traitorous fake Maria is overthrown by the workers who decide to burn her. The cyborg, even if driven by vile instincts, has accelerated the rebellion of the workers against the exploitative capitalists, but she ends up condemned as a witch, both by the proletarian mob and the wealthy.

If the fake Maria is eventually held responsible for the evils of *Metropolis* and destroyed, the other women of easy virtue are just discarded because they cannot compare with the superior canon of maternity personified by the real Maria. In *The Handmaid's Tale*, prostitutes are of a different kind. Locked in the Jezebel's Club, the whore population is made of women who have refused the rules of Gilead but try to escape a slow death in the Colonies. They are still degraded and treated as sexual objects by the patrons of the brothel, but they don't have to engage in the hypocritical puritan folklore imposed by the regime. Even if they are scared and disheartened, the prostitutes are nevertheless granted a certain amount of freedom because they can interact more freely with their female counterparts. The Jezebels are considered marked women who need to be hidden and kept away from the "good women" of Gilead, but they don't suffer from the same isolation and division. Their closeness is illustrated by the scene presenting their improvised dormitory where Offred and her long-lost friend Moira can rekindle their friendship and speak openly.

As weird as it sounds, the whorehouse presented in series 1, episode 8 is, however, a forthright place where men don't pretend to be respectable and where language is less duplicitous. Strangely, there is more hope for enslaved women in this secret brothel than in the sanitized suburbia where the commanding families dwell, because they are able to live somehow as a community. The bordello is less of a prison than the houses where the Handmaids are under the watch of their masters but also the Eyes of the Regime. The Jezebels can be seen as hookers with hearts of gold helping the heroine in her quest for freedom rather than dangerous temptresses, as the club is also a hub of the Mayday resistance group with the character of Rachel who is supposed to work at the bar and circulate messages for the rebels.

After her visit to the Club, Offred is contacted by the rebellion while she runs an errand at the butcher's and is given a package of letters, written by women to testify of their experiences as suffering Handmaids. In *Metropolis*, the realm of the courtesans in the Eternal Gardens is also transformed into a place of hope. Once the home of frivolous pleasures, the Gardens becomes a safe haven for the abandoned children after Maria and Freder have saved them. Following Maria's initial lead when she took the children to the Gardens, Freder abolishes the vertical separation between the rich Upper City and the underground tenements by opening the golden gates for the poor infants. He endorses his role as the compassionate mediator between the different parts of the same body and acknowledges the brotherhood of mankind.

Fritz Lang's film and the Hulu television series both portray a not-so-fictional society divided between the haves and the have-nots, a minority of powerful exploiters (the rich capitalists or the Commanders) and a large majority of wretched exploited (the workers and the women). If *Metropolis* perpetuates a male-oriented and rather conservative vision, especially with the final reconciliation between the proletariat and the agents of capitalism, *The Handmaid's Tale* adopts a female point of view to debunk the inconsistencies of patriarchal traditions and the subversion of religious principles. These works underline the fragmentation of the social body through intensified gender and class polarization[18] and question the crisis of human progress in general.

Despite reliance on technology and modernity, *Metropolis* and more specifically *The Handmaid's Tale* are stories of regress in which the present and the future are grasping for the past. When Atwood's novel came out in 1986, people interpreted it as a fictional realization of the right-wing backlash against the second wave of feminism and women's rights;[19] in 2017 and 2018 the TV series resonates with President Donald Trump's agenda to restore a retrograde American greatness based on intolerance and isolationism. But the series should not be limited to assessing current American politics, as it carries a more global message on "how women's bodies have been—and are now, and can be again—weaponized against them,"[20] as journalist Inkoo Kang stated.

NOTES

1. "Emma Watson Interviews Margaret Atwood about *The Handmaid's Tale,*" *Entertainment Weekly*, July 21, 2017, http://ew.com/books/2017/07/14/emma-watson-interviews-margaret-atwood-handmaids-tale/.

2. *The Handmaid's Tale*: Margaret Atwood and showrunner Bruce Miller (full panel). BookCon 2017, June 2017.

3. "Emma Watson interviews Margaret Atwood," *Entertainment Weekly*.

4. The Econowives are low-ranking married women—not much seen in the TV series.

5. Alice Elaine Adams, *Reproducing the Womb: Images of Childbirth in Science, Feminist Theory, and Literature* (Cornell University Press, 1994), 106.

6. *The Handmaid's Tale*, "Late," Season 1, Episode 3, directed by Reed Morano, written by Bruce Miller, Hulu, April 26, 2017.

7. Adams, *Reproducing the Womb*, 106.

8. J. Brooks Bouson, *Brutal Choreographies: Oppositional Strategies and Narrative Design in the Novels of Margaret Atwood* (University Press of Massachusetts, 1993), 136.

9. *The Handmaid's Tale*, "The Bridge," Season 1, Episode 9, directed by Kate Dennis, written by Eric Tuchman, Hulu, June 7, 2017.

10. Kristi Myers, "We Come Apart: Mother-Child Relationships in Margaret Atwood's Dystopias," *Iowa State University*, 23.

11. Myers, "We Come Apart," 18.

12. *The Handmaid's Tale*, "The Bridge," directed by Kate Dennis.

13. Gabriela Stoicea, "Re-Producing the Class and Gender Divide: Fritz Lang's Metropolis," *Women in German Yearbook* 22 (2006): 37.

14. See Joan Rivière, *Womanliness as masquerade*, 1927.

15. Atwood, *The Handmaid's Tale*, 128.

16. Stoicea, "Re-Producing the Class and Gender Divide," 31.

17. Stoicea, "Re-Producing the Class and Gender Divide," 35.

18. Adams, *Reproducing the Womb*, 104.

19. Shirley Neuman, "'Just a Backlash': Margaret Atwood, Feminism, and *The Handmaid's Tale*," *University of Toronto Quarterly*, Vol. 75 No. 3, 2006, 858.

20. Inkoo Kang, "*The Handmaid's Tale*: Motherhood or Death," MTV, April 27, 2017, http://www.mtv.com/news/3007036/the-handmaids-tale-motherhood-or-death/.

WORKS CITED

Adams, Alice Elaine. *Reproducing the Womb: Images of Childbirth in Science, Feminist Theory, and Literature*. Cornell University Press, 1994.

Atwood, Margaret. "*The Handmaid's Tale* and *Oryx and Crake* In Context." *PMLA Vol. 119, No. 3, Special Topic: Science Fiction and Literary Studies: The Next Millennium* (2004), 513–17.

Bouson, J. Brooks. *Brutal Choreographies: Oppositional Strategies and Narrative Design in the Novels of Margaret Atwood*. University Press of Massachusetts, 1993.

"Emma Watson Interviews Margaret Atwood about *The Handmaid's Tale*." *Entertainment Weekly*, July 21, 2017. http://ew.com/books/2017/07/14/emma-watson -interviews-margaret-atwood-handmaids-tale/.

Huyssen, Andreas. "The Vamp and the Machine: Technology and Sexuality in Fritz Lang's *Metropolis*." *New German Critique, No. 24/25, Special Double Issue on New German Cinema* (Autumn, 1981–Winter, 1982), 221–37.

Kang, Inkoo. "*The Handmaid's Tale*: Motherhood or Death." MTV, April 27, 2017. www.mtv.com/news/3007036/the-handmaids-tale-motherhood-or-death.

Myers, Kristi. "We Come Apart: Mother-Child Relationships in Margaret Atwood's Dystopias." *Graduate Theses and Dissertations* (2011). http://lib.dr.iastate.edu /etd/12006.

Neuman, Shirley. "'Just a Backlash': Margaret Atwood, Feminism, and *The Handmaid's Tale*." *University of Toronto Quarterly* 75, no. 3 (2006): 857–68. *Project MUSE*. doi:10.1353/utq.2006.0260

Riviere, Joan. (1929). Womanliness as a masquerade. *The International Journal of Psychoanalysis*, 10, 303–13.

Stoicea, Gabriela. "Re-Producing the Class and Gender Divide: Fritz Lang's *Metropolis*," *Women in German Yearbook*, 22 (2006): 21–42.

The Handmaid's Tale: Margaret Atwood and showrunner Bruce Miller (full panel) | BookCon 2017, YouTube, June 2017. www.youtube.com/watch?v=tFqJ8wqUpwk.

FILM AND TELEVISION

Metropolis. Directed by Fritz Lang. Ufa, 1927.

The Handmaid's Tale. "Late." Season 1, Episode 3. Directed by Reed Morano. Written by Bruce Miller. Hulu, April 26, 2017.

The Handmaid's Tale. "The Bridge." Season 1, Episode 9. Directed by Kate Dennis. Written by Eric Tuchman. Hulu, June 7, 2017.

Chapter Twenty-Three

"Topia" Extended

"Historical" Judgment of The Handmaid's Tale

Cecilia Gigliotti

Margaret Atwood's *The Handmaid's Tale* does not end where it appears to. Unanticipated but crucial, the appendix or honorary forty-fifth chapter, entitled "Historical Notes on *The Handmaid's Tale*," takes the form of a fictional lecture presented by a fictional professor at a fictional "Symposium on Gileadean Studies" on June 25, 2195. Having borne us through to the conclusion of the story proper, Atwood further capsizes readers' expectations by extending the narrative into a future period in which the Republic of Gilead has fallen and is subject to scrutiny, and from which we may gather clues as to what became of our narrator, Offred, of her allies, and of her enemies. Once we absorb the dehumanizing effects of Atwood's Gilead, one hallmark of which is the absence of a women's lexicon, we are then given to question what meaning literature and literary criticism hold for us. The institution of teaching, a form of literary criticism based on the transfer of knowledge from one generation to another, also is highlighted and has its integrity questioned. All this is done in a context which both takes aim at the foibles of academia and exalts its retrospective practices as potentially preventative measures.

That Atwood would frame her epilogue in such a parodically stuffy context likely strikes readers as odd at first, at least readers familiar with the author's distinctly nonacademic professional history. We might better understand her choice by examining the North American literary "canon" as defined by academic standard, a majority of which portrays women's lives and minds through a cisgender, heterosexual male lens. Just as countless real-world academic societies host conferences challenging these traditional, narrow-minded notions in favor of more inclusive perspectives (some groups going so far as to entertain ideas of the world we know as "postracial" or "post-gender"), so too does Atwood model her post-Gileadean convention in a tone of cool reserve, reflecting back on a society which fell and yielded to more "enlightened" times. The novel represents the entrenched inequality of the "past," while the Symposium is the removed "present" which feels qualified to judge its predecessors with impartiality. Readers observe how the world within the novel curiously combines European sensibilities (heightened female modesty, to the point that it is nigh-on impossible for the Handmaids to share any direct gaze) and so-called American values (nightly household Bible readings, uniform familial ties, special emphasis on child-bearing and -rearing). The naming pattern of Handmaids resembles that of Russian patronymics and the genealogical lines of Romance-language-speaking cultures; "Offred," as Atwood notes, has the added advantage of invoking the term "offered" alongside the idea of ritual sacrifice. Old World traditions echo in the flagrant persecution of any and all dissenting religious sects, while the Aunts' famous fixation on "freedoms"—freedom *to* versus freedom *from*—root us firmly in the New World.

But Atwood takes a step further from the New World. She designs this Symposium to give her audience twofold satisfaction: one, that the tyrannical Gilead did indeed reach a definitive end; two, that its architects and supporters now, many years on, face a reckoning, a Nuremberg of sorts.[1] The Symposium hosts delegations from hallmark institutions like Cambridge, as well as from entirely foreign-sounding universities, signifying the international reconfigurations and tessellations which have replaced Gilead, and suggesting that some bastions of education will outlast them all. In fact, that Cambridge's Professor James Darcy Pieixoto gives the keynote address is a mark of longevity; he is accorded a place of honor for representing a university which has seen the Dark Ages, various colonial endeavors, the rise and fall of modern America, the violent extremist revolution which resulted in Gilead, and the gradual global slide into the great (but nevertheless scholarly minded) unknown. Readers are invited to consider the way societies revere educational institutions because, quite frankly, they symbolize civilization at its core; the idea persists that humanity can discipline and better itself through educational structures.

Her own work having been the subject of intense academic conversation throughout her career, Atwood is uniquely equipped to skewer its minutiae. Pieixoto and Professor Maryann Crescent Moon use industry jargon and familiar references to place us in the realm of academic convention, a peculiar warning to instructors who cut their professional teeth on such language and then set out to teach *The Handmaid's Tale*. They speak with blended curiosity, uncertainty, and self-righteousness which resonates with and discomfits anyone who has ever dabbled in the academic setting. Pieixoto explains that, among the other artifacts he and his research partner unearthed in their quest to piece together Offred's story in manuscript form, a tape entitled "'Twisted

Sisters at Carnegie Hall' is one of which [he is] particularly fond."[2] The purportedly endearing pop culture allusions accentuate the scholars' extensive research and heighten the audience's response. Atwood's transcript even includes parenthesized "stage directions," including breaks for laughter and applause; the Symposium's attendees are so steeped in their own work as to be "in" on Pieixoto's jokes and jibes. The reader gets an impression not only of the seriousness of the scholarly endeavor but of the insular community which parallels academia today. Specialties tend to compartmentalize both faculties and students into units, quasi-military details armed with inside language and humor, designed to perpetuate the lingo through future generations of academics. Although never a professor herself, Atwood has enough experience with and knowledge of the field to employ this recognizable motif to harrowing effect.

One distinguishing feature of literary academia, and the criticism on which it prides itself, is the absence of bias. Researchers take pains to examine a piece of writing—a creature born from the emotions of the writer and judged on its ability to empathetically portray the emotions of characters—from a stoic standpoint and to separate their own feelings about the work from its objective merits or faults. Atwood crowns her story with an historical dimension in which scholars examine a hardly remote past with no small amount of this stoicism. Professor Pieixoto and his Symposium fellows appear to treat the Republic of Gilead as today's scholars treat the Third Reich, commenting with impressive emotional distance on its shocking standards and social structures, attempting to discern the true identity of Offred's "Fred" by comparing the men whose dictatorial politics could have elevated them to the indicated rank. The Society for U.S. Intellectual History (SUSIH) reveals the musings of one writer on the unidentified "Fred's" raised consciousness:

> "Better never means better for everyone. . . . It always means worse for some." What caught my eye here is that although this is spoken from the vantage point of a powerful man in a patriarchal, anti-feminist society . . . his character never denies the nature of what he helped create—he owns it, and states as necessary the suffering of others. . . . But we cannot at all say the same for those still inclined to think on the revolution as radical, whether that may be a professional historian or just someone with a passing interest in politics who likes to quote Jefferson.[3]

Even so, not all items are discussed with the anticipated reverence and solemnity. The aforementioned "inside humor" reaches one judgmental peak as Pieixoto mentions the "'bone' of contention"[4] between the Handmaids and their Commanders, a risky bit of levity which demands the cushion of considerable hindsight. Clearly this community feels at liberty to joke at the expense of scores of oppressed Gileadeans who did not enjoy Offred's "fortune"; the community also feels morally superior enough to condemn this supposedly savage period of Western history, enough to claim that it would never have been complicit in the atrocity—though this is the common claim of retrospect. As the writer notes:

> There's much recognizable here to the historian, from the problem of dealing with an old medium . . . to the challenge of identifying the author. . . . "If I may be permitted an editorial aside," the professor begins, "allow me to say that in my opinion we must be cautious about passing moral judgment upon the Gileadeans. . . . Our job is not to censure but to understand." (*Applause*.)[5]

Despite academia's best efforts, some censure is usually inevitable—this is the nature of the backward glance.

Yet the mood of this Assembly is one of having reached a high enough plane from which to look down on darker times. Readers may deduce that by 2195 there is no "outside world" boundary to be reached in order to relay one's story, nor is the exchange of intelligence so severely limited. Pieixoto, in fact, expresses a determination on behalf of his research team to recover and assemble as much of Offred's case as they can, an effort to compensate for lost time and for Offred's own gradually waning hunger for knowledge (for example, he demonstrates an interest in somehow pinpointing the kind of illicit magazines the Commander possessed, which Offred grew to despise as she grew to despise the Commander himself). This society appears to have risen from the ashes of Gilead and resolved to lead the way into a fairer future; yet, we cannot help wondering what kind of society it must be, whether skewed more dystopian or utopian, to pick itself up and forge ahead.

Typical of an academic convention of its ilk, Professor Pieixoto's address ends with a call for questions. Upon the release of Hulu's hugely successful two television series adapted from the novel in 2017 and 2018, Atwood wrote text for, and participated in the recording of, a podcast providing a glimpse into some of those questions. Rebecca Mead, who covered the "grimly playful project" for *The New Yorker*, acknowledges that "several [questions] give [Atwood] an opportunity for contemporary allusion. . . . Atwood's professor makes some observations about the repressive habits of authoritarian governments: shooting or otherwise silencing members of the resistance, shuttering news organizations, and the like."[6] There are references to a "top-heavy" economic structure, "with too much wealth being concentrated among too few," and a parallel between the Aunts' distinctions of freedom and the enduring, divisive debate between "what we think of as 'liberty' [and] what we think of as 'safety.'"[7]

This addendum to an already topical work drives home the often prophetic nature of academic work: scholars and other critics of cultural history are sometimes afforded rare opportunities to predict events based on the trends they trace. In assisting to update her novel for the screen, Atwood also felt compelled to update the academic conversation, stressing the need for us not only to consume media but to engage in active and discerning analysis of media—whether it be current content or artifacts discovered in a metal footlocker.

The interplay of primary and secondary sources in this fictional future evaluation of Offred's tale continues to be of immense interest, not least to me in my age of postgraduate study, which emphasizes the virtues of research and effective instruction. Certainly it invites rumination on the difficulties of teaching literature, for what is literature but a preserved record of the cultural and sociopolitical structures of its day? With patent creativity and an element of surprise, Atwood gives us a means to examine our own critical and pedagogical methods by imagining the response of a fictionalized but possible future congregation. Perhaps these answers to *The Handmaid's Tale* will encourage us to cultivate our own with new thoughtfulness and understanding.

NOTES

1. The Nuremberg Trials (November 20, 1945–October 1, 1946) sought to bring the primary engineers of the Holocaust and the Nazi Party to justice.

2. Margaret Atwood, *The Handmaid's Tale* (Boston: Houghton Mifflin Company, 1986), 302.

3. Atwood, *The Handmaid's Tale*, 302.

4. Atwood, *The Handmaid's Tale*, 302.

5. Atwood, *The Handmaid's Tale*, 305.

6. Rebecca Mead. "Margaret Atwood's Grimly Relevant Additions to *The Handmaid's Tale* Audiobook," *The New Yorker*, April 13, 2017.

7. Mead, "Margaret Atwood's Grimly Relevant Additions."

WORKS CITED

Atwood, Margaret. *The Handmaid's Tale*. Boston: Houghton Mifflin Company, 1986.

Marie, Robin. "On the 'Historical Notes' of *The Handmaid's Tale*." *The Society for U.S. Intellectual History*, June 1, 2017.

Mead, Rebecca. "Margaret Atwood's Grimly Relevant Additions to *The Handmaid's Tale* Audiobook." *The New Yorker*, April 13, 2017.

Index

About the Editors

Dr. Karen A. Ritzenhoff is a professor in the Department of Communication at Central Connecticut State University (USA). She is affiliated with the Women, Gender, and Sexuality Studies (WGSS) Program and cinema studies. In 2015, she coedited *The Apocalypse in Film* with Angela Krewani (Germany); *Selling Sex on Screen: From Weimar Cinema to Zombie Porn* with Catriona McAvoy (UK); and *Humor, Entertainment, and Popular Culture during World War I* with Clémentine Tholas (France). Ritzenhoff is also coeditor of *Heroism and Gender in War Films* (2014) with Jakub Kazecki; *Border Visions: Diaspora and Identity in Film* (2013) with Jakub Kazecki and Cynthia J. Miller; *Screening the Dark Side of Love: From Euro-Horror to American Cinema* (2012) with Karen Randell.

Dr. Janis L. Goldie is an associate professor and chair of the Communication Studies Department at Huntington University, a federated partner of Laurentian University in Sudbury, ON, Canada. Her research focuses on the Canadian war film genre and the constructions of the Canadian military in media culture products such as film, video games, graphic novels, and television advertisements. Previously, Goldie has published on war and memory, privacy and the Internet, and research ethics. She also is currently coediting a volume on *New Perspectives on the War Film* with Clémentine Tholas and Karen A. Ritzenhoff (2019).

About the Contributors

Christina Barmon is an assistant professor of sociology and the cochair of the Gerontology Minor Program at Central Connecticut State University. Her research focuses on sexuality and aging with an emphasis on the social construction of sex, health, and aging. Her areas of expertise include medical sociology, social gerontology, feminist gerontology, and sex and gender studies.

Michelle A. Cubellis is an assistant professor in the Department of Criminology and Criminal Justice at Central Connecticut State University. She received her PhD in criminal justice from John Jay College. Her research focuses on institutional responses to deviance, sexual victimization and offending, child sexual abuse, macrolevel responses to violence and victimization, and domestic violence.

Sarah Dodd has devoted her professional life to ending sexual violence on college campuses. She has spent the last ten years working in higher education as an advocate for survivors as well as developing and facilitating innovative and effective prevention initiatives. During this time, Sarah has worked with hundreds of survivors and facilitated programs for thousands of college students. She is currently pursuing a PhD in social work at the University of Connecticut. Sarah lives, works, teaches, and writes in Hartford, Connecticut.

Susan Gilmore is an associate professor of English at Central Connecticut State University. She received her PhD and MFA in poetry from Cornell University. She has published articles on the poetry and plays of Mina Loy, Sophie Treadwell, and Edna St. Vincent Millay; on Margaret Fuller's Native American encounters in *Summer on the Lakes*; and on Gwendolyn Brooks's verse journalism. Her poems and essays have appeared in the *Connecticut*

Review and *Drunken Boat*, and in *Touches of Venus: An Anthology of Poems about Ava Gardner,* edited by Gilbert L. Gigliotti (2010). She is the editor of a special cluster on "Riot" for *Modern Language Studies* (February 2019) and is currently expanding this project into the critical anthology *"Language of the Unheard": Riot on the American Cultural Stage.*

Cecilia Gigliotti holds a BA in creative writing from Susquehanna University. Now a candidate for the MA in English Literature at Central Connecticut State University, she is preparing for a thesis on Lewis Carroll by conducting research at various British institutions. Her conference credits include a sociopolitical analysis of the musical *Hamilton* at NeMLA in Pittsburgh and the National Association for African American Studies in Dallas, as well as a cultural study of the poet Dylan Thomas at the International Journal of Arts & Sciences in London.

Ellen Grabiner is an associate professor and chair of the Communications Department in the Gwen Ifill College of Media, Arts, and Humanities at Simmons College in Boston. She is a dissertation director for the Institute of Doctoral Studies in the Visual Arts. A painter, writer, and author of *I See You: The Shifting Paradigm of James Cameron's* Avatar, Grabiner lives in Cambridge, Massachusetts, with her eleven-year-old pit bull.

Jessica Greenebaum is a professor of sociology at Central Connecticut State University and member and former cochair of the Women, Gender, Sexuality Studies (WGSS) program. She teaches courses on the Sociology of Gender, Qualitative Methods, Animals & Society, and the Culture and Politics of Food.

Rati Kumar is an associate professor in the Department of Communication at Central Connecticut State University. She teaches courses on public relations, business and professional communication, public health, health communication, and health campaigns. Kumar is also directing the graduate program in Strategic Communication. After starting her education at Nagpur University in India, she completed her master's degree at the University of Florida in Gainesville and her PhD at Purdue University.

Kristine Larsen is professor of astronomy at Central Connecticut State University, where she has taught in interdisciplinary programs such as the Honors Program and Women, Gender, and Sexuality Program (WGSS). Her teaching and research focus on issues of science and society, the history of women in science, and science and popular culture. She is the author of *Stephen*

Hawking: A Biography, *Cosmology 101*, and *The Women Who Popularized Geology in the 19th Century*, and coeditor of *The Mythological Dimensions of Doctor Who* and *The Mythological Dimensions of Neil Gaiman*.

Charisse Levchak is an assistant professor of sociology at Central Connecticut State University. She is an interdisciplinary scholar with a PhD in sociology. She also has a licensed master of social work with a focus on integrated social work, cultural competence, and diversity. Her research focuses on race-based microaggressions and macroaggressions as seen in her new book *Microaggressions and Modern Racism: Endurance and Evolution* (2018). She primarily teaches social justice–related courses such as Oppression & Liberation and Social Movements & Social Action.

Kelly Marino is a visiting assistant professor of history at Central Connecticut State University and also teaches in the Women, Gender, and Sexuality Studies (WGSS) Program. She earned her PhD in history from the State University of New York at Binghamton in 2016 and her MA from the University of Massachusetts, Amherst in 2010. Her research focuses on American Women's History and the History of Sexuality. She currently holds a Connecticut Teacher's Certification in History and Social Studies for grades 7 to 12.

Jacqueline Maxwell is an English teacher at Wellesley High School in Massachusetts, where she teaches introductory English, American Literature, and a senior elective, "Beyond the Binary: Gender and Sexuality in Literature." Maxwell received her BA in English from Boston University and her MEd in Secondary Education from Boston College. She is currently a Master's Candidate in the Gender and Cultural Studies Program at Simmons University in Boston.

Kate McGrath earned her PhD in medieval history from Emory University in 2007. She is a full professor of history at Central Connecticut State University. Her principal research and teaching focuses on the history of emotions and gender in Anglo-Norman society. She is also active in the Women, Gender, and Sexuality Studies (WGSS) Program and Social Studies Education program.

Aven McMaster is an assistant professor of ancient studies at Thorneloe University at Laurentian, Canada, with a PhD in classics from the University of Toronto. Her main area of study is Latin poetry, with an emphasis on issues of gender, identity, gift exchange and obligation, and the relationships between poets and patrons. She also works on the reception of the ancient world, and political and cultural appropriation of Classical themes in contemporary society. As well, Aven is cohost of a podcast about the ancient and medieval world, and works on educational videos about language and history.

Beth Merenstein is a professor of sociology at Central Connecticut State University. She teaches courses and conducts research in the areas of Poverty and Homelessness, Race and Ethnic Relations, Community Engagement and Qualitative Methods.

Heather Munro Prescott is professor of history at Central Connecticut State University. She received her PhD in science and technology studies from Cornell University. She specializes in the history of women and health in the United States. She is the author of numerous books and articles, including *The Morning After: A History of Emergency Contraception in the United States* (2011).

Paul Moffett is an instructor of English at Memorial University of Newfoundland. He holds a PhD in English Literature from Memorial University, and his primary research focus is on intersections of the sacred and the secular in late medieval Arthurian literature. He maintains an enthusiastic secondary research interest in popular culture, especially comics and television, as well as an interest in critical adaptation theory. He is currently working on a short project on racialized others in *Sir Gawain and the Green Knight* and its analogues, and on a teaching project focused on monsters, from the medieval *Bisclavret* to modern zombies.

Eileen Rositzka is a postdoctoral researcher at the Cinepoetics Center for Advanced Film Studies (Freie Universität Berlin, Germany). She holds a PhD in film studies from the University of St. Andrews, Scotland, where she wrote her dissertation on the "cinematic corpography" of the Hollywood war film—an analysis of the genre's specific modes of staging spatial perception. Further publications include book chapters and articles on film genre, art history, and the representation of women in James Bond films. Having worked as a research associate and lecturer at Freie Universität Berlin, she is now working on a research project which aims at assembling and further developing approaches to cartography, media, and embodiment.

Theodora Ruhs is an assistant professor in the Department of Journalism at Central Connecticut State University. She received her doctorate from the University of Maine in communication and a master's degree in media ecology from New York University. Her teaching interests include journalistic ideology, standards, and practices. She currently teaches multiple journalism courses, including multimedia and editing.

Sheila Siragusa teaches Acting, Directing and First Folio Shakespeare in Performance and is a professional stage director based in the Pioneer Valley in Massachusetts. She has served on the faculty at NYU's Stella Adler Conservatory, State University of New York in Oneonta, Central Connecticut State University, the University of Massachusetts in Amherst, and Smith College.

Katherine Sugg is an associate professor of English and Latino and Puerto Rican Studies at Central Connecticut State University. She specializes in narrative and cultural studies of the Americas, including a focus on narrative theory, gender and race studies, performance and media, and comparative cultural analysis. Recent publications include *Gender and Allegory in Transamerican Fiction and Performance* (2008) and "*The Walking Dead*: Late Liberalism and Masculine Subjection in Apocalypse Fictions" (2015). Her manuscript, *Masculinity and Apocalypse in Popular Culture: Allegories of Crisis* is forthcoming in 2019.

Clémentine Tholas is an associate professor of American history in the English and applied foreign languages department at the Paris III-Sorbonne Nouvelle University, and holds a PhD in American studies. Her research interests focus on early motion pictures in the United States, namely on WWI cinematic propaganda and the role of silent films as tools of progressivism. Clémentine Tholas published *Le Cinéma américain et ses premiers récits filmiques* (2014) and coedited with Karen A. Ritzenhoff a collective volume entitled *Humor, Entertainment, and Popular Culture during World War I* (2015).

Dennis Tredy is an associate professor of American literature at the Université de Paris III—Sorbonne Nouvelle. He is also cofounder of the ESJS (*European Society of Jamesian Studies*) and has published three volumes on Henry James: *Henry James's Europe: Heritage and Transfer* (2011), *Henry James and the Poetics of Duplicity* (2013), and *Reading Henry James in the 21st Century* (due out in 2019). In addition to his publications on James and on other American novelists, Tredy has published studies of film and television adaptations of the works of Henry James, Edgar Allan Poe, and Vladimir Nabokov, among others. His recent work on film and television has centered on adaptation of gothic literature and of radio programs for television, on the early days of television broadcasting and Network programming, and on media representations of American culture, diversity, and counterculture in the 1950s, 1960s and 1970s.